THE SACRED BOOKS OF THE EAST

Translated by

VARIOUS ORIENTAL SCHOLARS

Edited by

F. MAX MÜLLER

Vol. 45

SACRED BOOKS OF THE EAST

(50 VOLUMES)

Series Editor : *F. Max-Müller*

ISBN: 978-81-208-0101-1 (Set) Rs. 15000 (Each Vol. Rs. 350)

These volumes of the Sacred Books of the East series include translations of all the most important works of the seven non-Christian religions that have exercised a profound influence on the civilisations of the continent of Asia. The Vedic Brahmanic system claims 21 volumes, Buddhism 10, and Jainism 2; 8 volumes comprise Sacred Books of the Parsis; 2 volumes represent Islam; and 6 the two main indigenous systems of China. Translated by twenty leading authorities in their respective fields, the volumes have been edited by the late F. Max Müller. The inception, publication and the compilation of these books cover almost 34 years.

I. BUDDHISM

Vol. 49: Buddhist Mahayana Texts (2 Parts)
Vol. 11: Buddhist Suttas
Vol. 10: The Dhammapada and Sutta Nipata
Vols. 35 & 36: The Questions of King Milinda (2 Parts)
Vol. 21: The Saddharma Pundarika or the Lotus of the True Law
Vols. 13, 17 & 20: Vinaya Texts (3 Parts)

II. CHINESE

Vol. 19: The Fo-Sho-Hing-Tsan-King
Vols. 3, 16, 27, 28, 39 & 40: The Sacred Books of China (6 Parts)

III. A GENERAL INDEX

Vol. 50: A General Index to the Names and Subject-matter of the Sacred Books of the East

IV. ISLAM

Vols. 6 & 9: The Qur'an (2 Parts)

V. JAINISM

Vols. 22 & 45: The Jaina Sutras (2 Parts)

VI. PARSIS

Vols. 5, 18, 24, 37 & 47: Pahlavi Texts (5 Parts)
Vols. 4, 23 & 31: The Zend-Avesta (3 Parts)

VII. VEDIC-BRAHMANIC SYSTEM

Vol. 8: The Bhagavadgita with the Sanatsujatiya and the Anugita
Vols. 29 & 30: The Grihya-Sutras: Rules of Vedic Domestic Ceremonies (2 Parts)
Vol. 42: Hymns of the Atharva Veda together with Extracts from the Ritual Books and the Commentaries
Vol. 7: The Institutes of Vishnu
Vol. 25: The Laws of Manu
Vol. 33: The Minor Law Books
Vols. 2 & 14: The Sacred Laws of the Aryas as Taught in the Schools of Apastamba, Gautama, Vasishtha and Baudhayana (2 Parts)
Vols. 12, 26, 41, 43 & 44: The Satapatha Brahmana According to the Text of the Madhyandina School (5 Parts)
Vols. 1 & 15: The Upanishads (2 Parts)
Vols. 34 & 38: The Vedanta Sutras (2 Parts)
Vol. 48: The Vedanta-Sutras (with the commentary by Ramanuja)
Vols. 32 & 46: Vedic Hymns (2 Parts)

*G*AINA SÛTRAS

(JAINA SŪTRAS)

Translated from Prakrit by

HERMANN JACOBI

PART II

THE UTTARÂDHYAYANA SÛTRA

THE SÛTRAKA*RI*TÂṄGA SÛTRA

MOTILAL BANARSIDASS PUBLISHERS
PRIVATE LIMITED • DELHI

Eight Edition
Reprint: Delhi, ***2010***
First Published by Oxford Univesity Press, 1895

ISBN: 978-81-208-0146-2

MOTILAL BANARSIDASS
41 U.A. Bungalow Road, Jawahar Nagar, Delhi 110 007
8 Mahalaxmi Chamber, 22 Bhulabhai Desai Road, Mumbai 400 026
203 Royapettah High Road, Mylapore, Chennai 600 004
236, 9th Main III Block, Jayanagar, Bangalore 560 011
Sanas Plaza, 1302 Baji Rao Road, Pune 411 002
8 Camac Street, Kolkata 700 017
Ashok Rajpath, Patna 800 004
Chowk, Varanasi 221 001

UNESCO COLECTION OF REPRESENTATIVE WORKS— Indian Series
This book has been accepted in the Indian Translation Series of the UNESCO Collection of Representative Works, jointly sponsored by the United Nations Educational Scientific and Cultural Organization (UNESCO) and the Government of India

PRINTED IN INDIA

BY JAINENDRA PRAKASH JAIN AT SHRI JAINENDRA PRESS,
A-45 NARAINA, PHASE-I, NEW DELHI 110 028
AND PUBLISHED BY NARENDRA PRAKASH JAIN FOR
MOTILAL BANARSIDASS PUBLISHERS PRIVATE LIMITED,
BUNGALOW ROAD, DELHI 110 007

Rashtrapati Bhavan,
New Delhi-4
June 10, 1962

I am very glad to know that the Sacred Books of the East published years ago by the Clarendon Press, Oxford, which have been out-of-print for a number of years, will now be available to all students of religion and philosophy. The enterprise of the publishers is commendable and I hope the books will be widely read.

S. Radhakrishnan

PREFATORY NOTE TO THE NEW EDITION

Since 1948 the United Nations Educational, Scientific and Cultural Organization (UNESCO), upon the recommendation of the General Assembly of the United Nations, has been concerned with facilitating the translation of the works most representative of the culture of certain of its Member States, and, in particular, those of Asia.

One of the major difficulties confronting this programme is the lack of translators having both the qualifications and the time to undertake translations of the many outstanding books meriting publication. To help overcome this difficulty in part, UNESCO's advisers in this field (a panel of experts convened every other year by the International Council for Philosophy and Humanisitic Studies), have recommended that many worthwhile translations published during the 19th century, and now impossible to find except in a limited number of libraries, should be brought back into print in low-priced editions, for the use of students and of the general public. The experts also pointed out that in certain cases, even though there might be in existence more recent and more accurate translations endowed with a more modern apparatus of scholarship, a number of pioneer works of the greatest value and interest to students of Eastern religions also merited republication.

This point of view was warmly endorsed by the Indian National Academy of Letters (Sahitya Akademi), and the Indian National Commission for UNESCO.

It is in the spirit of these recommendations that this work from the famous series "Sacred Books of the East" is now once again being made available to the general public as part of the UNESCO Collection of Representative Works.

PUBLISHER'S NOTE

First, the man distinguished between eternal and perishable. Later he discovered within himself the germ of the Eternal. This discovery was an epoch in the history of the human mind and the *East was the first to discover it.*

To watch in the Sacred Books of the East the dawn of this religious consciousness of man, must always remain one of the most inspiring and hallowing sights in the whole history of the world. In order to have a solid foundation for a comparative study of the Religions of the East, we must have before all things, complete and thoroughly faithful translation of their Sacred Books in which some of the ancient sayings were preserved because they were so true and so striking that they could not be forgotten. They contained eternal truths, expressed for the first time in human language.

With profoundest reverence for Dr. S. Radhakrishnan, President of India, who inspired us for the task; our deep sense of gratitude for Dr. C. D. Deshmukh & Dr. D. S. Kothari, for encouraging assistance; esteemed appreciation of UNESCO for the warm endorsement of the cause; and finally with indebtedness to Dr. H. Rau, Director, Max Müller Bhawan, New Delhi, in procuring us the texts of the Series for reprint, we humbly conclude.

CONTENTS.

SÛTRAK*RI*TÂṄGA.

FIRST BOOK.

SECOND BOOK.

INTRODUCTION

Ten years have elapsed since the first part of my translation of *G*aina Sûtras appeared. During that decennium many and very important additions to our knowledge of *G*ainism and its history have been made by a small number of excellent scholars. The text of the canonical books, together with good commentaries in Sanskrit and Guzeratî, has been made accessible in fair editions published by native scholars in India. Critical editions of two of them have been published by Professors Leumann [1] and Hoernle [2]; and the latter scholar has added a careful translation and ample illustrations to his edition of the text. A general survey of the whole *G*aina literature has been given by Professor Weber in his catalogue of the Berlin Manuscripts [3] and in his learned treatise [4] on the sacred literature of the *G*ainas. The development of *G*aina learning and science has been studied by Professor Leumann, and some *G*aina legends and their relations to those of the Brahmans and Buddhists have been investigated by the same scholar [5]. An important document for our knowledge of the old history of the *S*vêtâmbara sect has been edited

[1] Das Aupapâtika Sûtra, in the Abhandlungen für die Kunde des Morgenlandes, vol. viii; and Da*s*avaikâlika Sûtra und Niryukti, in the Journal of the German Oriental Society, vol. xlvi.

[2] The Uvâsaga Dasâo: (in the Bibliotheca Indica), vol. i. Text and Commentary, Calcutta, 1890; vol. ii. Translation, 1888.

[3] Berlin, 1888 and 1892.

[4] In the Indische Studien, vol. xvi, p. 211 ff., and xvii, p. 1 ff.; translated in the Indian Antiquary and edited separately, Bombay, 1893.

[5] In the Actes du VI Congrès International des Orientalistes, section Arienne, p. 469 ff., in the 5th and 6th vols. of the Wiener Zeitschrift für die Kunde des Morgenlandes, and in the 48th vol. of the Journal of the German Oriental Society.

by myself[1], and the history of some of their Ga*kkh*as has been made known from their lists of teachers by Hoernle and Klatt. The last-named scholar, whom we have all but lost by this time, has prepared a biographical dictionary of all *G*aina writers and historical persons, and he has issued specimens of this great Onomasticon, while Hofrat Bühler has written a detailed biography of the famous encyclopaedist Hêma*k*andra[2]. The same scholar has deciphered the ancient inscriptions, and discussed the sculptures excavated by Dr. Führer at Mathurâ[3], and the important inscriptions at *S*rava*n*a Be*l*go*l*a have been edited by Mr. Lewis Rice[4]; M. A. Barth has reviewed our knowledge of *G*ainism[5], and likewise Bühler in a short paper[6]. Lastly Bhandarkar has given a most valuable sketch of the whole of *G*ainism[7]. All these additions to our knowledge of *G*ainism (and I have but mentioned the most remarkable ones) have shed so much clear light on the whole subject that little room is left now for mere guesswork, and the true historical and philological method can be applied to all its parts. Still some of the principal problems require elucidation, while the proffered solution of others is not accepted by all scholars. I, therefore, gladly avail myself of this opportunity to discuss some of the disputed points, for the settling of which the works translated in this volume offer valuable materials.

It is now admitted by all that Nâtaputta (*Gñ*ât*ri*putra), who is commonly called Mahâvîra or Vardhamâna, was a contemporary of Buddha; and that the Niga*nth*as[8]

[1] The Pari*s*ish*t*aparvan by Hêma*k*andra, Bibliotheca Indica.

[2] Denkschriften der philos.-histor. Classe der kaiserl. Akademie der Wissenschaften, vol. xxxvii, p. 171 ff.

[3] Wiener Zeitschrift für die Kunde des Morgenlandes, vols. ii and iii. Epigraphia Indica, vols. i and ii.

[4] Bangalore, 1889.

[5] The Religions of India. Bulletin des Religions de l'Inde, 1889–94.

[6] Über die indische Secte der Jaina. Wien, 1887.

[7] Report for 1883–84.

[8] Niga*nth*a is apparently the original form of the word, since it is thus spelled in the A*s*ôka inscription, in Pâli, and occasionally by the *G*ainas, though the phonetic laws of all three idioms would have given preference to the form niggantha, the more frequent spelling in *G*aina works.

(Nirgranthas), now better known under the name of *G*ainas or Ârhatas, already existed as an important sect at the time when the Buddhist church was being founded. But it is still open to doubt whether the religion of the early Nirgranthas was essentially the same as that taught in the canonical and other books of the present *G*ainas, or underwent a great change up to the time of the composition of the Siddhânta. In order to come nearer the solution of this question, it may be desirable to collect from the published Buddhist works, as the oldest witnesses we can summon, all available information about the Niga*nth*as, their doctrines and religious practices.

In the Aṅguttara Nikâya, III, 74, a learned prince of the Li*kkh*avis of Vai*s*âlî, Abhaya [1], gives the following account of some Niga*nth*a doctrines: 'The Niga*nth*a Nâtaputta, sir, who knows and sees all things, who claims perfect knowledge and faith (in the following terms): "walking and standing, sleeping or waking, I am always possessed of perfect knowledge and faith;" teaches the annihilation by austerities of the old Karman, and the prevention by inactivity of new Karman. When Karman ceases, misery ceases; when misery ceases, perception ceases; when perception ceases, every misery will come to an end. In this way a man is saved by pure annihilation of sin (ni*gg*arâ) which is really effective.'

The *G*aina counterpart to these tenets can be collected from the Uttarâdhyayana XXIX. 'By austerities he cuts off Karman,' § 27. 'By renouncing activity he obtains inactivity; by ceasing to act he acquires no new Karman, and destroys the Karman he had acquired before,' § 37. The last stages in this process are fully described in §§ 71,

[1] There are apparently two persons of this name. The other Abhaya, a son of king *S*rê*n*ika, was a patron of the *G*ainas, and is frequently mentioned in their legends and in the canonical books. In the Ma*gg*h*ima Nikâya 58 Abhayakumâra Sutta) it is related that the Niga*nth*a Nâtaputta made him engage in a disputation with Buddha. The question was so adroitly framed that whether the answer was Yes or No, it involved Buddha in self-contradiction. But the plan did not succeed, and Abhaya was converted by Buddha. There is nothing in this account to elucidate the doctrines of Nâtaputta.

72. And again, in XXXII, v. 7, we read: 'Karman is the root of birth and death, and birth and death they call misery.' The nearly identical verses 34, 47, 60, 73, 86, 99 may be thus condensed: 'But a man who is indifferent to the object of the senses, and to the feelings of the mind [this comes nearest to the Buddhist vêdanâ, perception], is free from sorrows; though still in the Sa*m*sâra, he is not afflicted by that long succession of pains just as the leaf of the Lotus (is not moistened) by water.'

The above assertion that Nâtaputta claimed the possession of perfect knowledge and faith, requires no further proof; for it is one of the fundamental dogmas of the *G*ainas.

Another piece of information about Niga*nth*a doctrines may be gathered from the Mahâvagga VI, 31 (S. B. E., vol. xvii, p. 108 ff.) There a story is told of Sîha [1], the general of the Li*kkh*avis, who was a lay disciple of Nâtaputta. He wanted to pay the Buddha a visit, but Nâtaputta tried to dissuade him from it, because the Niga*nth*as held the Kriyâvâda, while the Buddha taught the Akriyâvâda. Sîha, however, setting his master's prohibition at nought, went to the Buddha on his own account, and was, of course, converted by him. Now the statement that the Niga*nth*as embraced the Kriyâvâda is borne out by our texts; for in the Sûtrak*ri*tâṅga I, 12, 21, below, p. 319, it is said that a perfect ascetic 'is entitled to expound the Kriyâvâda;' and this doctrine is thus expressed in the Â*k*ârâṅga Sûtra I, 1, 1, 4 (part i, p. 2): 'He believes in soul, believes in the world, believes in reward, believes in action (believed to be our own doing in such judgments as these): "I did it;" "I shall cause another to do it;" "I shall allow another to do it."'

Another lay disciple of Mahâvîra, converted by the Buddha, was Upâli. As narrated in the Ma*ggh*ima Nikâya 56, he ventured upon a dispute with him whether the sins of the mind are heaviest, as the Buddha teaches, or the

[1] The name Sîha occurs in the Bhagavatî (Calcutta edition, p. 1267, see Hoernle, Uvâsaga Dasâo Appendix, p. 10) as that of a disciple of Mahâvîra; but as he was a monk, he cannot be identified with his namesake in the Mahâvagga.

sins of the body, as the Niga*nth*a Nâtaputta contends. In the beginning of the discourse Upâli states that his master uses the term da*nd*a, punishment, for what is commonly called kamma, deed, act. This is true, though not quite to the letter; for the word kamma occurs also in the *G*aina Sûtras in that sense. The term da*nd*a, however, is at least as frequently used. Thus, in the Sûtrak*ri*tâṅga II, 2, p. 357 ff., the thirteen kinds of 'committing sins' are treated of, and in the first five cases the word which I have translated 'committing sins' is in the original da*nd*a-samâdâ*n*e, and in the remaining cases kiriyâ*th*â*n*e, i.e. kriyâsthâna.

The Niga*nth*a Upâli goes on to explain that there are three da*nd*as, the da*nd*a of body, that of speech, and that of mind. This agrees with the *G*aina doctrine expressed in nearly the same words in the Sthânâṅga Sûtra, 3rd uddê*s*aka (see Indian Antiquary, IX, p. 159).

The second statement of Upâli, that the Niga*nth*as consider sins of the body more important than sins of the mind, is in perfect harmony with *G*aina views. For in the Sûtrak*ri*tâṅga II, 4, p. 398 ff., the question is discussed whether sins may be committed unconsciously, and it is boldly answered in the affirmative (compare note 6, p. 399); and in the Sixth Lecture of the same book (p. 414) the Buddhists are severely ridiculed for maintaining that it depends on the intention of the man whether a deed of his be a sin or not.

In the Aṅguttara Nikâya III, 70, 3, some practices of Niga*nth*a laymen are discussed. I translate the passage thus: 'O Visâkhâ, there is a class of Sama*n*as who are called Niga*nth*as. They exhort a Sâvaka thus: "Well, sir, you must desist from doing injury to beings in the East beyond a yô*g*ana from here, or to those in the West, North, South, always beyond a yô*g*ana from here." In this way they enjoin tenderness by making him spare some living beings; in this way they enjoin cruelty by making him not spare other living beings.' It is not difficult to recognise under these words the Digvirati vow of the *G*ainas, which consists in laying down the limits beyond which one shall not travel nor do business in the different directions. A man who keeps this vow cannot, of course, do any harm to beings beyond the limits within which he is obliged to keep. This is so distorted by the hostile sect as to lay the rule under discussion open to blame. We cannot expect one sect to give a fair and honest exposition of the tenets of their opponents; it is but natural that they should put them in such a form as to make the objections to be raised against them all the better applicable. The *G*ainas were not a whit better in this respect than the Bauddhas, and they have retorted upon them in the same way; witness their misrepresentation of the Buddhist idea that a deed becomes a sin only through the sinful intention of the doer, in a passage in the present volume, p. 414, v. 26 ff., where the sound principle of the Buddhists is ridiculed by applying it to a fictitious and almost absurd case.

The passage in the Aṅguttara Nikâya, which we have just discussed, goes on as follows: 'On the Upôsatha day they exhort a Sâvaka thus: "Well, sir, take off all your clothes and declare: I belong to nobody, and nobody belongs to me." Now his parents know him to be their son, and he knows them to be his parents. His son or wife know him to be their father or husband, and he knows them to be his son or wife. His slaves and servants know him to be their master, and he knows them to be his slaves and servants. Therefore (the Niga*nth*as) make him use lying speech at the time when he makes the above declarations. On this account I charge him with lying speech. After the lapse of that night he enjoys pleasures (by means of things) that were not freely given. On this account I charge him with taking of what is not freely given.'

According to this statement, the duties of a Niga*nth*a layman became, during the Upôsatha days, equal to those of a monk; it was on common days only that the difference between layman and monk was realised. This description, however, does not quite agree with the Pôsaha rules of the *G*ainas. Bhandarkar gives the following definition of Pôsaha according to the Tattvârthasâradîpikâ, which agrees with what we know about it from other sources: 'Pôsaha, i.e. to observe a fast or eat once only or one dish only on the two holy days (the eighth and the fourteenth of each fortnight), after having given up bathing, unguents, ornaments, company of women, odours, incense, lights, &c., and assumed renunciation as an ornament.' Though the Pôsaha observances of the present *G*ainas are apparently more severe than those of the Buddhists, still they fall short of the above description of the Niga*nth*a rules; for a *G*aina layman does not, to my knowledge, take off his clothes during the Pôsaha days, though he discards all ornaments and every kind of luxury; nor must he pronounce any formula of renunciation similar to that which the monks utter on entering the order. Therefore, unless the Buddhist account contains some mistake or a gross misstatement, it would appear that the *G*ainas have abated somewhat in their rigidity with regard to the duties of laymen.

Buddhaghôsa, in his commentary on the Brahma*g*âla Sutta, Dîgha Nikâya I, 2, 38[1], mentions the Niga*nth*as as holding the opinion, discussed in the text, that the soul has no colour, in contradistinction to the Â*g*îvikas, who divide mankind into six classes according to the colour of the Âtman; both Niga*nth*as and Â*g*îvikas, however, agree in maintaining that the soul continues to exist after death and is free from ailments (arôgô). Whatever may be the exact meaning of the last expression, it is clear that the above description squares with the opinions of the *G*ainas about the nature of the soul, as described below, p. 172 f.

In another passage (l.c. p. 168) Buddhaghôsa says that Niga*nth*a Nâtaputta considers cold water to be possessed of life (so kira sîtôdakê sattasa*ññ*î hôti), for which reason he does not use it. This doctrine of the *G*ainas is so generally known that I need not bring forward any quotation from the Sûtras in support of its genuineness.

This is nearly all the information on the doctrines of the

[1] Sumangala Vilâsinî, p. 119 of the Pali Text Society edition.

ancient Niga*nth*as which I have been able to gather from the Pâli texts. Though it is less than we desire, its value is not to be underrated. For with one exception all the doctrines and usages of the ancient Niga*nth*as mentioned agree with those of the present *G*ainas, and they comprise some of the fundamental ideas of *G*ainism. It is therefore not probable that the doctrines of the *G*ainas have undergone a great change in the interval between the quoted Buddhist records and the composition of the *G*aina canon.

I have purposely deferred the discussion of the classical passage on the doctrines of Niga*nth*a Nâtaputta, because it leads us to a new line of inquiry. The passage in question occurs in the Sâma*ññ*aphala Sutta of the Dîgha Nikâya[1]. I translate it in accordance with Buddhaghôsa's comment in the Sumaṅgala Vilâsinî. 'Here, great king, a Niga*nth*a is protected by restraint in four directions (*k*âtuyâmasa*m*varasa*m*vutô). How, great king, is a Niga*nth*a protected by restraint in four directions? Here, great king, a Niga*nth*a abstains from all (cold) water, he abstains from all bad deeds, by abstinence from all bad deeds he is free from sins, he realises abstinence from all bad deeds. In this way, great king, a Niga*nth*a is protected by restraint in four directions. And, great king, because he is thus protected, the Niga*nth*a Nâtaputta's soul is exalted, is restrained, is well settled[2].'—This is, certainly, not an accurate nor an exhaustive description of the *G*aina creed, though it contains nothing alien from it, and successfully imitates the language of the *G*aina Sûtras. As I have already explained elsewhere[3], I think the term *k*âtuyâmasa*m*varasa*m*vutô has been misunderstood not only by the commentator, but also by the author of the text. For

---

[1] Page 57 of the edition in the Pali Text Society.

[2] The translations of Gogerly and of Burnouf in Grimblot, Sept Suttas Pâlis, were made without the help of a commentary, and may, therefore, be passed by. It is, however, open to doubt whether Buddhaghôsa has drawn his information from genuine tradition, or had to rely on conjectures of his own.

[3] See my paper, 'On Mahâvîra and his Predecessors,' in the Indian Antiquary, IX, 158 ff., where some of the above problems have been treated.

the Pâli *k*âtuyâma is equivalent to the Prâk*ri*t *k*âtug*g*âma, a well-known *G*aina term which denotes the four vows of Pâr*s*va in contradistinction to the five vows (pa*ñk*a mahavvaya) of Mahâvîra. Here, then, the Buddhists, I suppose, have made a mistake in ascribing to Nâtaputta Mahâvîra a doctrine which properly belonged to his predecessor Pâr*s*va. This is a significant mistake; for the Buddhists could not have used the above term as descriptive of the Niga*nth*a creed unless they had heard it from followers of Pâr*s*va, and they would not have used it if the reforms of Mahâvîra had already been generally adopted by the Niga*nth*as at the time of the Buddha. I, therefore, look on this blunder of the Buddhists as a proof for the correctness of the *G*aina tradition, that followers of Pâr*s*va actually existed at the time of Mahâvîra.

Before following up this line of inquiry, I have to call attention to another significant blunder of the Buddhists: they call Nâtaputta an Aggivêsana, i.e. Agnivai*s*yâyana; according to the *G*ainas, however, he was a Kâ*s*yapa, and we may credit them in such particulars about their own Tîrthakara. But Sudharman, his chief disciple, who in the Sûtras is made the expounder of his creed, was an Agnivai*s*yâyana, and as he played a prominent part in the propagation of the *G*aina religion, the disciple may often have been confounded by outsiders with the master, so that the Gôtra of the former was erroneously assigned to the latter. Thus by a double blunder the Buddhists attest the existence of Mahâvîra's predecessor Pâr*s*va and of his chief disciple Sudharman.

That Pâr*s*va was a historical person, is now admitted by all as very probable; indeed, his followers, especially Kê*s*i[1], who seems to have been the leader of the sect at the time of Mahâvîra, are frequently mentioned in *G*aina Sûtras in such a matter-of-fact way, as to give us no reason for doubting the authenticity of those records. The legend in

[1] In the Râ*g*apra*s*nî Pâr*s*va has a discussion with king Paêsi and converts him, see Actes du VI Congrès International des Orientalistes, vol. iii, p. 490 ff.

the Uttarâdhyayana, Lecture XXIII, how the union of the old and the new church was effected, is of much interest in this respect. Kêsi and Gautama, the representatives and leaders of the two branches of the Gaina church, both at the head of their pupils, meet in a park near Srâvastî; the differences in their creed concerning the number of great vows, and the use or disuse of clothes are explained away without further discussion, and full harmony with regard to the fundamental ethical ideas is satisfactorily established by the readiness with which allegorical expressions of the one speaker are understood and explained by the other. There seems to have been some estrangement, but no hostility between the two branches of the church; and though the members of the older branch invariably are made to adopt the Law of Mahâvîra, 'which enjoins five vows,' it may be imagined that they continued in some of their old practices, especially with regard to the use of clothes, which Mahâvîra had abandoned. On this assumption we can account for the division of the church in Svêtâmbaras and Digambaras, about the origin of which both sects have contradictory legends[1]. There was apparently no sudden rupture; but an original diversity (such as e.g. subsists now between the several Gakkhas of the Svêtâmbaras) ripened into division, and in the end brought about the great schism.

The records in the Buddhist Canon are not repugnant to our views about the existence of the Niganthas before Nâtaputta; for the Niganthas must have been an important sect at the time when Buddhism took its rise. This may be inferred from the fact that they are so frequently mentioned in the Pitakas as opponents or converts of Buddha and his disciples; and as it is nowhere said or even merely implied that the Niganthas were a newly-founded sect, we may conclude that they had already existed a considerable time before the advent of the Buddha. This conclusion is supported by another fact. Makkhali Gôsâla, a contemporary

---

1 See my paper on the origin of the Svêtâmbara and Digambara sects in the Journal of the German Oriental Society, vol. xxxviii, p. 1 ff.

of Buddha and Mahâvîra, divided mankind into six classes [1]. Of these, according to Buddhaghôsa [2], the third class contains the Niga*nth*as. Gôsâla probably would not have ranked them as a separate, i. e. fundamental subdivision of mankind, if they had only recently come into existence. He must have looked upon them as a very important, and at the same time, an old sect, in the same way in which, in my opinion, the early Buddhists looked upon them. As a last argument in favour of my theory I may mention that in the Ma*ggh*ima Nikâya 35, a disputation between the Buddha and Sa*kk*aka, the son of a Niga*nth*a, is narrated. Sa*kk*aka is not a Niga*nth*a himself, as he boasts of having vanquished Nâtaputta in disputation [3], and, moreover, the tenets he defends are not those of the *G*ainas. Now when a famous controversialist, whose father was a Niga*nth*a, was a contemporary of the Buddha, the Niga*nth*as can scarcely have been a sect founded during Buddha's life.

Let us now confront the records of the *G*ainas about the philosophical doctrines of heretics, which they had to combat, with such as the Buddhists describe. In the Sûtrak*ri*tâṅga II, 1, 15 (p. 339 f.) and 21 f. (p. 343) two materialistic theories which have much in common are spoken of. The first passage treats of the opinion of those who contend that the body and the soul are one and the same thing; the second passage is concerned with the doctrine that the five elements are eternal and constitute everything. The adherents of either philosophy maintain that it is no sin to kill living beings. Similar opinions are, in the Sâma*ññ*aphala Sutta, ascribed to Pûra*n*a Kassapa and A*g*ita Kêsakambalî. The former denies that there is such a thing as sin or merit. A*g*ita Kêsakambalî holds that nothing real

[1] Sâma*ññ*aphala Sutta, Dîgha Nikâya II, 20.

[2] Sumaṅgala Vilâsinî, p. 162. Buddhaghôsa expressly states that Gôsâla reckoned the Niga*nth*as lower than his own lay disciples, who form the fourth class.—As Buddhaghôsa does not take umbrage at Gôsâla's reckoning the Bhikkhus still lower, it is clear that he did not identify the Bhikkhus with the Buddhist monks.

[3] See p. 250 of the Pali Text Society edition.

corresponds to the current transcendental ideas. He moreover maintains: 'Man (purisô) consists of the four elements; when he dies, earth returns to earth, water to water, fire to fire, wind to wind, and the organs of sense merge into air (or space)[1]. Four bearers with the hearse carry the corpse to the place of cremation (or, while it is burned) they make lamentations; the dove-coloured bones remain, the offerings are reduced to ashes.' The last passage recurs with few alterations in the Sûtrak*ri*tâṅga, p. 340: 'Other men carry the corpse away to burn it. When it has been consumed by fire, only dove-coloured bones remain, and the four bearers return with the hearse to their village[2].'

In connection with the second materialistic system (p. 343, § 22, and p. 237 f., vv. 15, 16) a variety of it is mentioned, which adds the permanent Âtman or soul as a sixth to the five permanent elements. This seems to have been a primitive or a popular form of the philosophy which we now know under the name of Vai*s*êshika. To this school of philosophy we must perhaps assign Pakudha Ka*kk*âyana of Buddhist record. He maintained[3] that there are seven eternal, unchangeable, mutually independent things: the four elements, pleasure, pain, and the soul. As they have no influence upon one another, it is impossible to do any real harm to anybody. I confess that to maintain the eternal existence of pleasure and pain (sukha and dukkha) and to deny their influence on the soul, seems to me absurd; but the Buddhists have perhaps misstated the original tenets. At any rate, the views of Pakudha Ka*kk*âyana

---

[1] Âkâ*s*a; it is not reckoned as a fifth element in the Buddhist account, but it is so in that of the *G*ainas, see below, p. 343, and p. 237, verse 15. This is a verbal, rather than a material difference.

[2] I put here the original texts side by side so that their likeness may be more obvious:

âsandipa*ñk*amâ purisâ mata*m* âdâya ga*kkh*anti yâva â*l*âhanâ padâni pa*ññ*âpenti, kâpôtakâni a*tth*îni bhavanti, bhassantâ*hutiyô.

âdaha*n*âe parêhi ni*gg*ai, aga*n*ig*gh*âmitê sarîre kavôtava*nn*âim a*tth*î*n*i âsandîpa*ñk*amâ purisâ gâma*m* pa*kk*âga*kkh*anti.

[3] Loc. cit., p. 56.

come under the denomination of Akriyâvâda; and in this they differ from the Vaisêshika proper, which is a Kriyâvâda system. As these two terms are frequently used both by Buddhists and *G*ainas, it will not be amiss to define them more accurately. Kriyâvâda is the doctrine which teaches that the soul acts or is affected by acts. Under this head comes *G*ainism, and of Brahmanical philosophies Vai*s*êshika and Nyâya (which, however, are not expressly quoted in the canonical books of either Buddhists or *G*ainas), and apparently a great many systems of which the names have not been preserved, but the existence of which is implied in our texts. Akriyâvâda is the doctrine which teaches either that a soul does not exist, or that it does not act or is not affected by acts. Under this subdivision fall the different schools of materialists; of Brahmanical philosophies the Vêdânta, Sâṅkhya, and Yôga; and the Buddhists. Of the latter the doctrines of the Ksha*n*ikavâdins and the *S*ûnyavâdins are alluded to in Sûtrak*ri*tâṅga I, 14, verses 4 and 7. It may be mentioned here that the Vêdântists or their opinions are frequently mentioned in the Siddhânta; in the Sûtrak*ri*tâṅga the Vêdânta is the third heresy described in the First Lecture of the Second Book, p. 344; it is also adverted to in the Sixth Lecture, p. 417. But as no professor of it was among the six heretical teachers (titthiya) of the Buddhists, we may pass them over here [1].

The fourth heresy discussed in the First Lecture of the Second Book of the Sûtrak*ri*tâṅga [2] is Fatalism. In the Sâma*ññ*aphala Sutta this system is expounded by Makkhali Gôsâla in the following words [3]: 'Great king, there is no cause, nor any previously existing principle productive of the pollution of sentient beings; their defilement is uncaused and unproduced by anything previously existing. There is no cause nor any previously existing principle

[1] It is worthy of remark that the Vêdântists play no conspicuous part, if any, among Buddha's opponents. As they were, however, the foremost of Brahmanical philosophers, we must conclude that Brahmans of learning held aloof from the classes of society to which the new religion appealed.

[2] Page 345 f., see also p. 239.

[3] Grimblot, Sept Suttas Pâlis, p. 170.

productive of the purity of sentient beings: their purity is uncaused and unproduced by anything previously existing. For their production there is nothing that results from the conduct of the individuals, nothing from the actions of others, nothing from human effort: they result neither from power nor effort, neither from manly fortitude nor manly energy. Every sentient being, every insect, every living thing, whether animal or vegetable[1], is destitute of intrinsic force, power, or energy, but, being held by the necessity of its nature, experiences happiness or misery in the six forms of existence, &c.' The explanation of these doctrines in the Sûtrak*ri*tâṅga (l. c.), though less wordy, comes to the same; it does not, however, expressly ascribe them to Gôsâla, the son of Makkhali.

The *G*ainas enumerate four principal schools of philosophy[2]: Kriyâvâda, Akriyâvâda, A*gñ*ânavâda, and Vainayikavâda. The views of the A*gñ*ânikas, or Agnostics, are not clearly stated in the texts, and the explanation of the commentators of all these philosophies which I have given in note 2, p. 83, is vague and misleading. But from Buddhist writings we may form a pretty correct idea of what Agnosticism was like. It is, according to the Sâma*ññ*aphala Sutta, the doctrine of Sa*ñg*aya Bêla*tth*iputta, and is there stated in the following way[3]: 'If you inquire of me whether there be a future state of being, I answer: If I experience a future state of existence, I will then explain the nature of that state. If they inquire, Is it after this manner? that is

[1] In the original: sabbê sattâ, sabbê pâ*n*â, sabbê bhûtâ, sabbê *g*îvâ. The same enumeration frequently occurs in *G*aina Sûtras, and has, in my translation, been abbreviated in 'all classes of living beings.' Buddhaghôsa's explanation has been thus rendered by Hoernle, Uvâsaga Dasâo, Appendix II, p. 16: 'In the term *all beings* (sabbê sattâ) he comprises camels, oxen, asses, and other animals without exception. The term *all sensive beings* (sabbê pâ*n*â) he uses to denote those with one sense, those with two senses, and so forth. The term *all generated beings* (sabbê bhûtâ) he uses with reference to those that are generated or produced from an egg or from the womb. The term *all living beings* (sabbê *g*îvâ) he uses with reference to rice, barley, wheat, and so forth; in these he conceives that there is life, because it is their nature to grow.'

[2] See pp. 83, 291, 316, 385.

[3] Grimblot, l. c., p. 174.

not my concern. Is it after that fashion? that is not my concern. Is it different from these? that is not my concern. Is it not? that is not my concern. No, is it not? It is no concern of mine.' In the same way he e. g. refuses a definite answer to the questions whether the Tathâgata is after death, or is not; is and is not at the same time, is not nor is not at the same time. It is evident that the Agnostics examined all modes of expression of the existence or non-existence of a thing, and if it were anything transcendental or beyond human experience, they negatived all those modes of expression.

The records of the Buddhists and *G*ainas about the philosophical ideas current at the time of the Buddha and Mahâvîra, meagre though they be, are of the greatest importance to the historian of that epoch. For they show us the ground on which, and the materials with which, a religious reformer had to build his system. The similarity between some of those 'heretical' doctrines on the one side, and *G*aina or Buddhist ideas on the other, is very suggestive, and favours the assumption that the Buddha, as well as Mahâvîra, owed some of his conceptions to these very heretics, and formulated others under the influence of the controversies which were continually going on with them. Thus, I think, that in opposition to the Agnosticism of Sa*ñg*aya, Mahâvîra has established the Syâdvâda. For as the A*gñ*ânavâda declares that of a thing beyond our experience the existence, or non-existence or simultaneous existence and non-existence, can neither be affirmed nor denied, so in a similar way, but one leading to contrary results, the Syâdvâda declares that 'you can affirm the existence of a thing from one point of view (syâd asti), deny it from another (syâd nâsti); and affirm both existence and non-existence with reference to it at different times (syâd asti nâsti). If you should think of affirming existence and non-existence at the same time from the same point of view, you must say that the thing cannot be spoken of (syâd avaktavya*h*). Similarly, under certain circumstances, the affirmation of existence is not possible (syâd asti avaktavya*h*); of non-existence (syân nâsti avaktavya*h*); and also of both (syâd asti nâsti avaktavya*h*)[1].'

This is the famous Saptabhaṅgînaya of the *G*ainas. Would any philosopher have enunciated such truisms, unless they served to silence some dangerous opponents? The subtle discussions of the Agnostics had probably bewildered and misled many of their contemporaries. Consequently the Syâdvâda must have appeared to them as a happy way leading out of the maze of the A*gñ*ânavâda. It was the weapon with which the Agnostics assailed the enemy, turned against themselves. Who knows how many of their followers went over to Mahâvîra's creed convinced by the truth of the Saptabhaṅgînaya!

We can trace, I imagine, the influence of Agnosticism also in the doctrine of the Buddha about the Nirvâ*n*a, as it is stated in Pâli books. Professor Oldenberg was the first to draw attention to the decisive passages which prove beyond the possibility of doubt that the Buddha declined answering the question whether the Tathâgata (i.e. the liberated soul, or rather principle of individuality) is after death or not. If the public of his time had not been accustomed to be told that some things, and those of the greatest interest, were beyond the ken of the human mind, and had not acquiesced in such answers, it certainly would not have lent a willing ear to a religious reformer who declined to speak out on what in Brahmanical philosophy is considered the end and goal of all speculations. As it is, Agnosticism seems to have prepared the way for the Buddhist doctrine of the Nirvâ*n*a[2]. It is worthy of note

[1] Bhandarkar, Report for 1883-4, p. 95 f.

[2] The reticence of Buddha on the nature of the Nirvâ*n*a may have been wise at his time; but it was fraught with very important results for the development of the church. For his followers, having to hold their own against such split-hair dialecticians as the Brahmanical philosophers, were almost driven to enunciate more explicit ideas about the great problem which the founder of the church had left unsolved. The tendency to supply the crowning stone to an edifice which appeared to have been left unfinished by the hand of the master, led to the division of the community into numerous

that in a dialogue between king Pasênadi and the nun Khêmâ, told in the Sa*m*yutta Nikâya, and translated by Oldenberg, the king puts his questions about the existence or non-existence of the Tathâgata after death in the same formulas which Sa*ñg*aya is made to use in the passage translated above from the Sâma*ññ*aphala Sutta.

In support of my assumption that the Buddha was influenced by contemporary Agnosticism, I may adduce a tradition incorporated in the Mahâvagga I, 23 and 24. There we are told that the most distinguished pair of his disciples, Sâriputta and Moggalâna, had, previously to their conversion, been adherents of Sa*ñg*aya, and had brought over to Buddha 250 disciples of their former teacher. This happened not long after Buddha's reaching Bôdhi, i.e. at the very beginning of the new sect, when its founder must have been willing, in order to win pupils, to treat prevalent opinions with all due consideration.

The greatest influence on the development of Mahâvîra's doctrines must, I believe, be ascribed to Gôsâla, the son of Makkhali. A history of his life, contained in the Bhagavatî XV, 1, has been briefly translated by Hoernle in the Appendix to his translation of the Uvâsaga Dasâo. It is there recorded that Gôsâla lived six years together with Mahâvîra as his disciple, practising asceticism, but afterwards separated from him, started a Law of his own, and set up as a *G*ina, the leader of the Â*g*îvikas. The Buddhist records, however, speak of him as the successor of Nanda Va*kkh*a and Kisa Sa*m*ki*kk*a, and of his sect, the a*k*êlaka paribbâ*g*akas, as a long-established order of monks. We have no reason to doubt the statement of the *G*ainas, that Mahâvîra and Gôsâla for some time practised austerities together; but the relation between them probably was different from what the *G*ainas would have us believe. I suppose, and shall now bring forward some arguments in favour of my opinion, that Mahâvîra and Gôsâla asso-

sects soon after the Nirvâ*n*a of Buddha. We need not wonder therefore that in Ceylon, which is at such a distance from the centre of Brahmanical learning, Buddhists could retain the doctrine of the Nirvâ*n*a in its original form.

ciated with the intention of combining their sects and fusing them into one. The fact that these two teachers lived together for a long period, presupposes, it would appear, some similarity between their opinions. I have already pointed out above, in the note on p. xxvi, that the expression sabbê sattâ sabbê pâ*n*â sabbê bhûtâ sabbê *g*îvâ is common to both Gôsâla and the *G*ainas, and from the commentary we learn that the division of animals into êkêndriyas, dvîndriyas, &c., which is so common in *G*aina texts, was also used by Gôsâla. The curious and almost paradoxical *G*aina doctrine of the six Lê*s*yâs closely resembles, as Professor Leumann was the first to perceive, Gôsâla's division of mankind into six classes; but in this particular I am inclined to believe that the *G*ainas borrowed the idea from the Â*g*îvikas and altered it so as to bring it into harmony with the rest of their own doctrines. With regard to the rules of conduct the collective evidence obtainable is such as to amount nearly to proof that Mahâvîra borrowed the more rigid rules from Gôsâla. For as stated in the Uttarâdhyayana XXIII, 13, p. 121, the Law of Pâr*s*va allowed monks to wear an under and upper garment, but the Law of Vardhamâna forbade clothes. A term[1] for naked friar, frequently met with in the *G*aina Sûtras, is a*k*êlaka, literally 'unclothed.' Now the Buddhists distinguish between A*k*êlakas and Niga*nth*as; e.g. in Buddhaghôsa's commentary on the Dhammapadam[2] it is said of some Bhikkhus that they gave the preference to the Niga*nth*as before the A*k*êlakas, because the latter are stark naked (sabbasô apa*t*i*kkh*annâ), while the Niga*nth*as use some sort of cover[3] 'for the sake of decency,' as was wrongly assumed by those Bhikkhus. The Buddhists de-

[1] Another term is *G*inakalpika which may be rendered: adopting the standard of the *G*inas. The *S*vêtâmbaras say that the *G*inakalpa was early replaced by the Sthavirakalpa, which allows the use of clothes.

[2] Fausböll's edition, p. 398.

[3] The words sêsakam purimasamappitâ va pa*t*i*kkh*âdenti are not quite clear, but the contrast leaves no doubt about what is meant. Sêsaka is, I believe, the Pâli for *s*i*s*naka. If this is right, the above words may be translated: 'they cover the pudenda wearing (a cloth) about the forepart (of their body).'

note by A*k*êlaka the followers of Makkhali Gôsâla and his two predecessors Kisa Sa*m*ki*kk*a and Nanda Va*kkh*a, and have preserved an account of their religious practices in the Ma*ggh*ima Nikâya 36. There Sa*kk*aka, the son of a Niga*nth*a, whom we are already acquainted with, explains the meaning of kâyabhâvanâ, bodily purity, by referring to the conduct of the A*k*êlakas. Some details of Sa*kk*aka's account are unintelligible in the absence of a commentary, but many are quite clear, and bear a close resemblance to well-known *G*aina usages. Thus the A*k*êlakas, like the *G*aina monks, may not accept an invitation for dinner; they are forbidden food that is abhiha*t*a or uddissaka*t*a, which terms are, in all likelihood, identical with adhyâh*ri*ta and auddê*s*ika of the *G*ainas (see p. 132, note); they are not allowed to eat meat or to drink liquor. 'Some beg only in one house and accept but one morsel of food, some in more up to seven; some live upon one donation of food, some on more up to seven.' Similar to these are some practices of *G*aina monks described in the Kalpa Sûtra, 'Rules for Yatis,' § 26, part i, p. 300, and below, p. 176 f., verses 15 and 19. The following practice of the A*k*êlakas is identically the same as that observed by the *G*ainas: 'some eat but one meal every day, or every second day[1], &c., up to every half month.' All the rules of the A*k*êlakas are either identical with those of the *G*ainas or extremely like them, and dictated, so to say, by the same spirit. And still Sa*kk*aka does not quote the Niga*nth*as as a standard of 'bodily purity,' though he was the son of a Niga*nth*a, and therefore must have known their religious practices. This curious fact may most easily be accounted for by our assuming that the original Niga*nth*as, of whom the Buddhist records usually speak, were not the section of the church, which submitted to the more rigid rules of Mahâvîra, but those followers of Pâr*s*va, who,

[1] These fasts are called by the *G*ainas *k*autthabhatta, *khatth*abhatta, &c. (see e. g. Aupapâtika Sûtra, ed. Leumann, § 30 I A); and monks observing them, *k*autthabhattiya, *khatth*abhattiya, &c. (see e. g. Kalpa Sûtra, 'Rules for Yatis,' § 21 ff.)

without forming a hostile party, yet continued, I imagine, to retain within the united church some particular usages of the old one[1]. As those rigid rules formed no part of the ancient creed, and Mahâvîra, therefore, must have introduced them, it is probable that he borrowed them from the A*k*êlakas or Â*g*îvikas, the followers of Gôsâla, with whom he is said to have lived in close companionship for six years practising austerities. We may regard Mahâvîra's adoption of some religious ideas and practices of the Â*g*îvikas as concessions made to them in order to win over Gôsâla and his disciples. This plan seems to have succeeded for some time; but at last the allied teachers quarrelled, it may be supposed, on the question who was to be the leader of the united sects. Mahâvîra's position apparently was strengthened by his temporary association with Gôsâla, but the latter seems to have lost by it, if we are to believe the account of the *G*ainas, and his tragic end must have been a severe blow to the prospects of his sect.

Mahâvîra probably borrowed much more from other sects than we shall ever be able to prove. It must have been easy to add new doctrines to the *G*aina creed, as it scarcely forms a system in the true sense of the word. Each sect, or fraction of a sect, which was united with the *G*aina church by the successful policy of Mahâvîra[2], may have brought with it some of its favourite speculations, and most probably its favourite saints too, who were recognised as *K*akravartins or Tîrthakaras. This is, of course, a mere conjecture of mine; but it would account for the strange hagiology of the *G*ainas, and in the absence of any trace of direct evidence we are driven to rely upon guesses, and those deserve the preference which are the most

[1] As I have said above and in note 2, p. 119, this difference has probably given rise to the division of the church into *S*vêtâmbaras and Digambaras. But these two branches have not directly grown out of the party of Pâr*s*va and that of Mahâvîra; for both recognise Mahâvîra as a Tîrthakara.

[2] Mahâvîra must have been a great man in his way, and an eminent leader among his contemporaries; he owed the position of a Tîrthakara probably not so much to the sanctity of his life, as to his success in propagating his creed.

plausible. For the rest, however, of the hypotheses which I have tried to establish in the preceding pages, I claim a higher degree of probability. For on the one hand I do no violence to the tradition of the *G*ainas, which in the absence of documents deserves most careful attention, and on the other, I assume but what under the given circumstances would have been most likely to happen. The cardinal feature in my construction of the early history of the *G*aina church consists in my turning to account the alleged existence of followers of Pâr*s*va in the time of Mahâvîra, a tradition which seems to be almost unanimously accepted by modern scholars.

If *G*ainism dates from an early period, and is older than Buddha and Mahâvîra, we may expect to find marks of its antiquity in the character of *G*aina philosophy. Such a mark is the animistic belief that nearly everything is possessed of a soul; not only have plants their own souls, but particles of earth, cold water, fire, and wind also. Now ethnology teaches us that the animistic theory forms the basis of many beliefs that have been called the philosophy of savages; that it is more and more relinquished or changed into purer anthropomorphism as civilisation advances. If, therefore, *G*aina ethics are for their greater part based on primitive animism, it must have extensively existed in large classes of Indian society when *G*ainism was first originated. This must have happened at a very early time, when higher forms of religious beliefs and cults had not yet, more generally, taken hold of the Indian mind.

Another mark of antiquity *G*ainism has in common with the oldest Brahmanical philosophies, Vêdânta and Sâṅkhya. For at this early epoch in the development of metaphysics, the Category of Quality is not yet clearly and distinctly conceived, but it is just evolving, as it were, out of the Category of Substance: things which we recognise as qualities are constantly mistaken for and mixed up with substances. Thus in the Vêdânta the highest Brahman is not possessed of pure existence, intellect, and joy as qualities of his nature, but Brahman is existence, intellect, and joy itself. In the Sâṅkhya the nature of purusha or soul is similarly defined as being intelligence or light; and the three gunas are described as goodness, energy, and delusion, or light, colour, and darkness; yet these gunas are not qualities in our sense of the word, but, as Professor Garbe adequately calls them, constituents of primitive matter. It is quite in accordance with this way of thinking that the ancient Gaina texts usually speak only of substances, dravyas, and their development or modifications, paryâyas; and when they mention gunas, qualities, besides, which however is done but rarely in the Sûtras and regularly in comparatively modern books only, this seems to be a later innovation due to the influence which the philosophy and terminology of Nyâya-Vaisêshika gradually gained over the scientific thoughts of the Hindus. For at the side of paryâya, development or modification, there seems to be no room for an independent category 'quality,' since paryâya is the state in which a thing, dravya, is at any moment of its existence, and this must, therefore, include qualities, as seems to be actually the view embodied in the oldest text. Another instance of the Gainas applying the category 'substance' to things which are beyond its sphere, and come rather under that of 'quality,' is seen in their treating merit and demerit, dharma and adharma, as kinds of substances with which the soul comes into contact [1]; for they are regarded as coextensive with the world, not unlike space, which even the Vaisêshikas count as a substance. If the categories of substance and quality had already been clearly distinguished from one another, and had been recognised as correlative terms, as they are in Vaisêshika philosophy (which defines substance as the substratum of qualities, and quality as that which is inherent in substance), Gainism would almost certainly not have adopted such confused ideas as those just expounded.

---

[1] That this was the primitive conception of the Vedic Hindus has been noted by Oldenberg, Die Religion des Veda, p. 317 f.

From the preceding remarks it will be evident that I do not agree with Bhandarkar [1], who claims a late origin for *G*ainism, because, on some points, it entertains the same views as the Vai*s*êshika. The Vai*s*êshika philosophy may be briefly described as a philosophical treatment and systematical arrangement of those general concepts and ideas which were incorporated in the language, and formed therefore the mental property common to all who spoke or knew Sanskrit. The first attempts to arrive at such a natural philosophy may have been made at an early epoch; but the perfection of the system, as taught in the aphorisms of Ka*n*âda, could not be reached till after many centuries of patient mental labour and continuous philosophical discussion. In the interval between the origin and the final establishment of the system those borrowings may have taken place of which, rightly or wrongly, the *G*ainas may be accused. I must, however, remark that Bhandarkar believes the *G*ainas to hold, on the points presently to be discussed, a view 'which is of the nature of a compromise between the Sâṅkhyas and the Vêdântins on the one hand and the Vai*s*êshika on the other.' But for our discussion it makes no difference whether direct borrowing or a compromise between two conflicting views be assumed. The points in question are the following: (1) both *G*ainism and Vai*s*êshika embrace the Kriyâvâda, i. e. they maintain that the soul is directly affected by actions, passions, &c.; (2) both advocate the doctrine of asatkârya, i. e. that the product is different from its material cause, while the Vêdânta and Sâṅkhya hold that they are the same (satkârya); (3) that they distinguish qualities from their substratum (dravya). The latter item has been discussed above; we have to deal, therefore, with the first two only. It will be seen that the opinions under (1) and (2) are the common-sense views; for that we are directly affected by passions, and that the product is different from its cause, e.g. the tree from the seed, will always and everywhere be the primâ faciê con-

[1] See his Report for 1883–84, p. 101 f.

clusion of an unbiassed mind, or rather will appear as the simple statement of what common experience teaches. Such opinions cannot be regarded as characteristic marks of a certain philosophy, and their occurrence in another system need not be explained by the assumption of borrowing. The case would be different if a paradoxical opinion were found in two different schools; for a paradoxical opinion is most likely the product of but one school, and, when once established, it may be adopted by another. But such opinions of the Vaisêshika, as are the result of a peculiar train of reasoning, e.g. that space (dis) and air (âkâsa) are two separate substances, do not recur in Gainism. For in it, as well as in the older Brahmanical systems, Vêdânta and Sâṅkhya, space and air are not yet distinguished from one another, but âkâsa is made to serve for both.

Some other instances of difference in fundamental doctrines between Vaisêshikas and Gainas are, that according to the former the souls are infinite and all-pervading, while to the latter they are of limited dimensions, and that the Vaisêshikas make dharma and adharma qualities of the soul, while, as has been said above, the Gainas look on them as a sort of substances. In one point, however, there is some resemblance between a paradoxical Vaisêshika opinion and a distinct Gaina doctrine. According to the Vaisêshika there are four kinds of bodies: bodies of earth, as those of men, animals, &c.; bodies of water in the world of Varuna; bodies of fire in the world of Agni; and bodies of wind in the world of Vâyu. This curious opinion has its counterpart in Gainism; for the Gainas, too, assume Earth-bodies, Water-bodies, Fire-bodies, and Wind-bodies. However, these elementary bodies are the elements or the most minute particles of them, inhabited by particular souls. This hylozoistic doctrine is, as I have said above, the outcome of primitive animism, while the Vaisêshika opinion, though probably derived from the same current of thought, is an adaptation of it to popular mythology. I make no doubt that the Gaina opinion is much more primitive and belongs to an older stage in the development of philosophical thought than the Vai*s*êshika assumption of four kinds of bodies.

Though I am of opinion that between Vai*s*êshika and *G*ainism no such connection existed as could be proved by borrowings of the one system from the other, still I am ready to admit that they are related to each other by a kind of affinity of ideas. For the fundamental ideas of the Vêdântins and Sâṅkhyas go directly counter to those of the *G*ainas, and the latter could not adopt them without breaking with their religion. But they could go a part of their way together with the Vai*s*êshika, and still retain their religious persuasion. We need, therefore, not wonder that among the writers on the Nyâya-Vai*s*êshika some names of *G*ainas occur. The *G*ainas themselves go still farther, and maintain that the Vai*s*êshika philosophy was established by a schismatical teacher of theirs, *Kh*aluya Rôhagutta of the Kau*s*ika Gôtra, with whom originated the sixth schism of the *G*ainas, the Trairâ*s*ika-matam, in 544 A.V.[1] (18 A.D.) The details of this system given in the Âva*s*yaka, vv. 77–83, are apparently reproduced from Ka*n*âda's Vai*s*êshika Dar*s*ana; for they consist in the enumeration of the six (not seven) categories with their subdivisions, among which that of qualities contains but seventeen items (not twenty-four), and those identical with Vai*s*êshika Dar*s*ana I, 1, 6.

I believe that in this case, as in many others, the *G*ainas claim more honour than is their due in connecting every Indian celebrity with the history of their creed. My reason for doubting the correctness of the above *G*aina legend is the following. The Vai*s*êshika philosophy is reckoned as one of the orthodox Brahmanical philosophies, and it has chiefly, though not exclusively, been cultivated by orthodox Hindus. We have, therefore, no reason for doubting that they have misstated the name and Gôtra of the author of the Sûtras, viz. Ka*n*âda of the Kâ*s*yapa Gôtra. No trace

[1] See Indische Studien, vol. xvii, p. 116 ff.

has been found in Brahmanical literature that the name of the real author of the Vaiseshika was Rôhagupta, and his Gôtra the Kausika Gôtra ; nor can Rôhagupta and Kanâda be taken as different names of the same person, because their Gôtras also differ. Kânâda, follower of Kanâda, means etymologically crow-eater, owl ; hence his system has been nicknamed Aulûkya Darsana, owl-philosophy[1]. In Rôhagupta's second name, *Kh*uluya, which stands for Shadulûka[2], allusion is made to the 'owl,' probably to the Kânâdas ; but the *G*ainas refer ulûka to the Gôtra of the Rôhagupta, viz. Kausika[3], which word also means owl. As the unanimous tradition of the Brahmans deserves the preference before that of the *G*ainas, we can most easily account for the latter by assuming that Rôhagupta did not invent, but only adopted the Vaiseshika philosophy to support his schismatical views.

About the two works translated in this volume, the Uttarâdhyayana and Sûtrakritâṅga, I have little to add to the remarks of Professor Weber in the Indische Studien, vol. xvi, p. 259 ff., and vol. xvii, p. 43 ff. The Sûtrakritâṅga is probably the older of the two, as it is the second Aṅga, and the Aṅgas obtain the foremost rank among the canonical books of the *G*ainas, while the Uttarâdhyayana, the first Mûlasûtra, belongs to the last section of the Siddhânta. According to the summary in the fourth Aṅga the object of the Sûtrakritâṅga is to fortify young monks against the heretical opinions of alien teachers, to confirm them in the right faith, and to lead them to the highest good. This description is correct on the whole, but not exhaustive, as will be seen by going over our table of contents. The work opens with the refutation of heretical doctrines, and the same object is again treated at greater length in the

[1] See my edition of the Kalpa Sûtra, p. 119.

[2] Literally Six-owl. The number six refers to the six categories of the Vaiseshika.

[3] Part i, p. 290. But in the legend translated by Professor Leumann, l. c., p. 121, his Gôtra is called *Kh*aûlû.

First Lecture of the Second Book. It is followed in the First Book by Lectures on a holy life in general, on the difficulties a monk has to overcome, especially the temptations thrown in his way, the punishment of the unholy, and the praise of Mahâvîra as the standard of righteousness. Then come some Lectures on cognate subjects. The Second Book, which is almost entirely in prose, treats of similar subjects, but without any apparent connection of its parts. It may therefore be considered as supplementary, and as a later addition to the First Book. The latter was apparently intended as a guide for young monks[1]. Its form, too, seems adapted to this purpose; for it lays some claim to poetical art in the variety of the metres employed, and in the artificial character of some verses. It may, therefore, be considered as the composition of one author, while the Second Book is a collection of tracts which treat on the subjects discussed in the first.

The Uttarâdhyayana resembles the Sûtrak*ri*tâṅga with regard to its object and part of the subjects treated; but it is of greater extent than the original part of the Sûtrak*ri*tâṅga, and the plan of the work is carried out with more skill. Its intention is to instruct a young monk in his principal duties, to commend an ascetic life by precepts and examples, to warn him against the dangers in his spiritual career, and to give some theoretical information. The heretical doctrines are only occasionally alluded to, not fully discussed; apparently the dangers expected from that quarter grew less in the same measure as time advanced and the institutions of the sect were more firmly established. Of more importance to a young monk seems to have been an accurate knowledge of animate and inanimate things, as a rather long treatise on this subject has been added at the end of the book.—Though there is an apparent plan in the selection and arrangement of the single Lectures, still it is open to doubt whether they were all composed by one

[1] According to an old tradition (see Indische Studien, vol. xvi, p. 223) the Sûtrak*ri*tâṅga is studied in the fourth year after the ordination of a monk.

author, or only selected from the traditional literature, written or oral, which among the *G*ainas, as everywhere else, must have preceded the formation of a canon. I am inclined to adopt the latter alternative, because there is a greater variety of treatment and style in the different parts than seems compatible with the supposition of one author, and because a similar origin must be assumed for many works of the present canon.

At what time the works under discussion were composed or brought into their present shape is a problem which cannot be satisfactorily solved. As, however, the reader of the present volume will naturally expect the translator to give expression to his personal conviction on this point, I give my opinion with all reserve, viz. that most parts, tracts, or treatises of which the canonical books consist, are old; that the redaction of the Aṅgas took place at an early period (tradition places it under Bhadrabâhu); that the other works of the Siddhânta were collected in course of time, probably in the first centuries before our era, and that additions or alterations may have been made in the canonical works till the time of their first edition under Devardhiga*n*in (980 A.V. = 454 A.D.)

I have based my translation of the Uttarâdhyayana and Sûtrak*ri*tâṅga on the text adopted by the oldest commentators I could consult. This text differs little from that of the MSS. and the printed editions. I had prepared a text of my own from some MSS. at my disposal, and this has served to check the printed text.

The Calcutta edition of the Uttarâdhyayana (Sa*m*vat 1936 = 1879 A.D.) contains, besides a Guzeratî gloss, the Sûtradîpikâ of Lakshmîvallabha, pupil of Lakshmîkîrtiga*n*in of the Kharatara Ga*kkh*a. Older than this commentary is the *T*îkâ of Dêvêndra, which I have made my principal guide. It was composed in Sa*m*vat 1179 or 1123 A.D., and is confessedly an abstract from *S*ântyâ*k*ârya's V*ri*tti, which I have not used. But I have had at my disposal an illuminated old MS. of the Ava*k*ûri, belonging to the

Strassburg University Library. This work is apparently an abstract from the V*ri*tti of *S*ântyâ*k*ârya, as in a great many passages it almost verbally agrees with Dêvêndra's work.

The Bombay edition of the Sûtrak*ri*tâṅga (Sa*m*vat 1936 or 1880 A. D.) contains three commentaries: (1) *S*îlâṅka's *T*îkâ, in which is incorporated Bhadrabâhu's Niryukti. This is the oldest commentary extant; but it was not without predecessors, as *S*îlâṅka occasionally alludes to old commentators. *S*îlâṅka lived in the second half of the ninth century A. D., as he is said to have finished his commentary on the Â*k*ârâṅga Sûtra in the *S*aka year 798 or 876 A. D. (2) The Dîpika, an abstract from the last by Harshakula, which was composed in Sa*m*vat 1583 or 1517 A. D. I have also used a MS. of the Dîpika in my possession. (3) Pâ*s*a*k*andra's Bâlâvabôdha, a Guzeratî gloss.—My principal guide was, of course, *S*îlâṅka; when he and Harshakula agree, I refer to them in my notes as the 'commentators;' I name *S*îlâṅka when his remark in question has been omitted by Harshakula, and I quote the latter when he gives some original matter of interest. I may add that one of my MSS. is covered with marginal and interlinear glosses which have now and then given me some help in ascertaining the meaning of the text.

H. JACOBI.

BONN:
November, 1894.

ADDITIONAL NOTE.

I may here add a remark on the Parable of the Three Merchants, see p. 29 f., which agrees with Matthew xxv. 14 and Luke xix. 11. It seems, however, to have had a still greater resemblance to the version of the parable in The Gospel according to the Hebrews, as will appear from the following passage from Eusebius' Theophania (ed. Migne's Patrologia Graeca, iv. 155), translated by Nicholson, The Gospel according to the Hebrews (London, 1879): 'The Gospel, which comes to us in Hebrew characters, has directed the threat not against the hider, but against the abandoned liver. For it has included three servants, one which devoured the substance with harlots and flute-women, one which multiplied, and one which hid the talent: one was accepted, one only blamed, and one shut up in prison.' I owe this quotation to my colleague Arnold Meyer.

Taking into consideration (1) that the *G*aina version contains only the essential elements of the parable, which in the Gospels are developed into a full story; and (2) that it is expressly stated in the Uttarâdhyayana VII, 15 that 'this parable is taken from common life,' I think it probable that the Parable of the Three Merchants was invented in India, and not in Palestine.

H. J.

UTTARÂDHYAYANA.

FIRST LECTURE.

ON DISCIPLINE.

I shall explain in due order the discipline of a houseless monk, who has got rid of all worldly ties. Listen to me. (1)

A monk who, on receiving an order[1] from his superior[2], walks up to him, watching his nods and motions, is called well-behaved. (2)

But a monk who, on receiving an order from his superior, does not walk up to him, being insubordinate and inattentive, is called ill-behaved. (3)

As a bitch with sore ears is driven away every-

---

[1] Â*n*â-niddêsa-karê. Â*g\~n*â is the order itself; nirdê*s*a, the assent to it.

[2] The original has the plural instead of the singular. It takes great liberties in this respect, and the commentators constantly call to help a va*k*anavyatyaya or liṅgavyatyaya, exchange of number or gender, as the case may be. It is impossible in the translation to follow the original in this respect, and useless to note all such grammatical blunders. The conclusion we may draw from them is that in the spoken language many grammatical forms which in the literary language continued to be used, were on the point of dying out or had already actually become obsolete. I am almost sure that the vernacular of the time when the Sûtras were composed began to drop the distinction between the singular and plural in the verb. It was, however, artificially revived in the literary Mâhârâsh*t*rî of later days.

where, thus a bad, insubordinate, and talkative (pupil) is turned out. (4)

As a pig leaves a trough filled with grain to feed on faeces, so a brute (of a man) turns away from virtue, and takes to evil ways. (5)

Hearing a man thus compared to a dog and a pig, he who desires his own welfare, should adhere to good conduct. (6)

Therefore be eager for discipline, that you may acquire righteousness; a son of the wise[1], who desires liberation[2], will not be turned away from anywhere. (7)

One should always be meek, and not be talkative in the presence of the wise; one should acquire valuable knowledge, and avoid what is worthless. (8)

When reprimanded a wise man should not be angry, but he should be of a forbearing mood; he should not associate, laugh, and play with mean men. (9)

He should do nothing mean[3], nor talk much; but after having learned his lesson, he should meditate by himself. (10)

---

[1] Buddhaputta. Buddha is here and in the sequel explained by â*k*ârya, teacher. The word is in the crude form, not in the inflected form, as the nominative would not suit the metre. Liberties of this kind are frequently met with in our text.

[2] Niôga*tth*î = niyôgarthin. It is always explained and usually means môkshârthin. But here and in verse 20 niyôga has perhaps its common meaning: appointment, order. In that case we must translate: he who waits for an order.

[3] *K*a*nd*âliya, literally, he should not demean himself like a *K*â*nd*âla. The commentators, however, divide the word in *k*a*nd*a, violent, hot, and alîka, untrue, false. This explanation is too artificial to be accepted, though the meaning comes to the same thing.

If he by chance does anything mean, he should never deny it, but if he has done it, he should say: 'I have done it;' if he has not done it, 'I have not done it.' (11)

He should not, in every case, wait for the express command (of the teacher) like an unbroken horse for the whip (of the rider), but like a broken horse which sees the whip (of the rider) he should commit no evil act. (12)

Disobedient, rough speaking, ill-behaved pupils will exasperate even a gentle teacher; but those will soon win even a hot-tempered teacher who humour him and are polite. (13)

He should not speak unasked, and asked he should not tell a lie; he should not give way to his anger, and bear with indifference pleasant and unpleasant occurrences. (14)

Subdue your Self, for the Self is difficult to subdue; if your Self is subdued, you will be happy in this world and in the next. (15)

Better it is that I should subdue my Self by self-control and penance, than be subdued by others with fetters and corporal punishment. (16)

He should never do anything disagreeable to the wise[1], neither in words nor deeds, neither openly nor secretly. (17)

He should not (sit) by the side of the teacher, nor before him, nor behind him; he should not touch (the teacher's) thigh with his own, nor answer his call from the couch. (18)

A well-behaved monk should not sit on his hams[2],

[1] Buddhâ*nam*, i. e. the superiors.

[2] Palhatthiyâ = paryastikâ: so that his clothes cover his knees and shanks.

nor cross his arms[1], nor stretch out his legs, nor stand (too) close to his teacher. (19)

If spoken to by the superior, he should never remain silent, but should consider it as a favour; asking for his command[2], he should always politely approach his teacher. (20)

If the teacher speaks little or much, he should never grow impatient; but an intelligent pupil should rise from his seat and answer (the teacher's) call modestly and attentively. (21)

He should never ask a question when sitting on his stool or his bed, but rising from his seat[3] and coming near, he should ask him with folded hands. (22)

When a pupil who observes the above rules of conduct, questions the teacher about the sacred text, its meaning, or both, he should deliver it according to tradition. (23)

A monk should avoid untruth, nor should he speak positively (about future things, his plans, &c.); he should avoid sinful speech, and always keep free from deceit. (24)

He should not tell anything sinful or meaningless[4]

---

[1] Pakshapi*nd*a.

[2] Niyâga*tth*î or niôga*tth*î. The commentator explains it, as in verse 7, by 'desiring liberation.'

[3] Ukku*d*uô. The commentator explains it by muktâsana*h*, kâra*n*ata*h* pâdapu*ñkh*anâdigata*h*.

[4] In illustration of this the commentator (Dêvêndra) quotes the following verse: êsha bandhyâsutô yâti khapushpak*ri*ta*s*êkhara*h* | m*ri*gat*ri*sh*n*âmbhasi snâta*h* *s*a*s*as*ri*ṅgadhanurdhara*h* || There goes the son of a barren woman, bearing a chaplet of sky-flowers, having bathed in the water of a fata morgana, and carrying a bow made of a hare's horn.

or hurtful, neither for his own sake nor for anybody else's, nor without such a motive. (25).

In barbers' shops[1] or houses, on the ground separating two houses, or on the highway a single monk should not stand with a single woman, nor should he converse with her. (26)

Any instruction the wise ones[2] may give me in a kind or a rough way, I shall devotedly accept, thinking that it is for my benefit. (27)

(The teacher's) instruction, his manner of giving it, and his blaming evil acts are considered blissful by the intelligent, but hateful by the bad monk. (28)

Wise, fearless monks consider even a rough instruction as a benefit, but the fools hate it, though it produces patience and purity of mind. (29)

He should occupy a low, firm seat, which does not rock; seldom rising and never without a cause, he should sit motionless. (30)

At the right time a monk should sally forth, and he should return at the right time; avoiding to do anything out of time, he should do what is appropriate for each period of the day. (31)

A monk should not approach (dining people) sitting in a row, but should collect alms that are freely given; having begged according to the sanctioned rules, he should eat a moderate portion at the proper time. (32)

A monk should wait (for his alms) alone, not too far from other monks, nor too near them, but so that he is not seen by another party; another monk should not pass him to get the start of him. (33)

---

[1] Samara, explained by the commentator barbers' shop or smithy, with the addition that it includes all places of low people.

[2] Buddhâ*h*.

Neither boldly erect nor humbly bowing down, standing neither too close by nor too far off, a monk should accept permitted[1] food that was prepared for somebody else[2]. (34)

In a place that is covered above and sheltered on all sides, where there are no living beings nor seeds, a monk should eat in company, restrained and undressed. (35)

A monk should avoid as unallowed such food as is well dressed, or well cooked, or well cut, or such in which is much seasoning, or which is very rich, or very much flavoured, or much sweetened[3]. (36)

(The teacher) takes delight in instructing a clever (pupil), just as the rider (in managing) a well-broken horse; but he tires to instruct a foolish (pupil), just as the rider (tires to manage) an unbroken horse. (37)

(A bad pupil thinks:) 'I get but knocks and boxes on the ear, hard words and blows;' and he believes a teacher who instructs him well, to be a malevolent man. (38)

A good pupil has the best opinion (of his teacher), thinking that he treats him like his son or brother or a near relation[4]; but a malevolent pupil imagines himself treated like a slave. (39)

He should not provoke his teacher's anger, nor

---

[1] Phâsuya, translated prâsuka, and explained: free from living beings.

[2] Parakada, prepared for the householder or some other person, but not for the monk himself.

[3] The translation of the terms in this verse is rather conjectural, notwithstanding the explanations in the commentary.

[4] I translate according to the interpretation of the commentator, which is probably right; but the text sets all rules of grammar at defiance.

should he himself grow angry; he should not offend the teacher nor irritate him by proclaiming his faults[1]. (40)

Perceiving the teacher's anger one should pacify him by kindness, appease him with folded hands, and promise not to do wrong again. (41)

He who adopts the conduct which the wise ones[2] have attained by their virtues and always practised, will not incur blame. (42)

Guessing the teacher's thoughts and the purport of his words, one should express one's assent, and execute (what he desires to be done). (43)

An excellent pupil needs no express directions, or he is (at least) quickly directed; he always carries out his duties as he is told. (44)

An intelligent man who has learned (the sacred texts) takes his duties upon himself[3], and he becomes renowned in the world; as the earth is the dwelling of all beings, so he will be a dwelling of all duties. (45)

When the worthy teachers, who are thoroughly enlightened and from early times well versed in conduct[4], are satisfied (with a pupil), they will make over to him their extensive and weighty[5] knowledge of the sacred texts. (46)

His knowledge will be honoured, his doubts will be removed, he will gladden the heart of his teacher

---

[1] Literally, search for the goad.

[2] Buddha.

[3] Namati, literally, bows down.

[4] Puvvasa*m*thuya = pûrvasa*m*stuta. Besides the meaning rendered in my translation the commentator proposes another: already famous.

[5] A*tth*iya = arthika, having an object or purpose, viz. môksha; it is therefore frequently rendered: leading to liberation.

by his good acts; kept in safety by the performance of austerities and by meditation, being as it were a great light, he will keep the five vows. (47)

Honoured by gods, Gandharvas, and men, he will, on leaving this body which consists of dirt and impurities, become either an eternal Siddha[1], or a god of great power and small imperfections. (48)

Thus I say[2].

SECOND LECTURE.

ON TROUBLES[3].

O long-lived (*G*ambûsvâmin)! I (Sudharman) have heard the following Discourse[4] from the Venerable (Mahâvîra):

Here[5], forsooth, the Venerable Ascetic Mahâvîra of the Kâ*s*yapa Gôtra has declared twenty-two troubles which a monk must learn and know, bear and conquer, in order not to be vanquished by them when he lives the life of a wandering mendicant.

---

[1] I. e. a liberated or perfected soul.

[2] Ti bêmi = iti bravîmi. These words serve to mark the end of every chapter in all canonical books; compare the Latin dixi.

[3] Parîsaha, that which may cause trouble to an ascetic, and which must be cheerfully borne.

[4] The commentator (Dêvêndra) says that when Mahâvîra spoke, he was understood by all creatures, whatever was their language. He quotes the following verse: dêvâ dêvî*m* narâ nârî*m* *s*abarâ*s* *k*âpi *s*âbarî*m* | tirya*ñk*o pi *k*a taira*sk*î*m* mênirê bhagavadgira*m* || The gods, men, *S*abaras, and animals took the language of the Lord for their own. Cf. Acts ii. 11.

[5] I. e. in our creed or religion. This is generally the meaning of the word iha, here, opening a sentence.

These, then, are the twenty-two troubles declared by the Venerable Ascetic Mahâvîra, which a monk must learn and know, bear and conquer, in order not to be vanquished by them when he lives the life of a wandering mendicant:

1. digañkhâ (*g*ugupsâ)-parîsahâ, hunger;
2. pivâsâ (pipâsâ)-p., thirst;
3. sîya (*s*îta)-p., cold;
4. usi*n*a (ush*n*a)-p., heat;
5. da*m*samasaya (da*ms*ama*s*aka)-p., gad-flies, and gnats[1];
6. a*k*êla-p., nakedness[2];
7. arati-p., to be discontented with the objects of control.
8. itthî (strî)-p., women;
9. *k*ariyâ (*k*aryâ)-p., erratic life;
10. nisîhiyâ (naishêdhikî)-p., place for study;
11. se*gg*â (*s*ayyâ)-p., lodging;
12. akkôsa (âkrô*s*a)-p., abuse;
13. vaha (vadha)-p., corporal punishment;
14. *g*âya*n*â (yâ*k*anâ)-p., to ask for something;
15. alâbha-p., to be refused;
16. rôga-p., illness;
17. ta*n*a-phâsa (t*rin*aspar*s*a), pricking of grass;
18. *g*alla-p., dirt;
19. sakkârapurakkâra (satkârapura*h*kâra)-p., kind and respectful treatment;
20. pannâ (pra*gñ*â)-p., understanding;
21. annâ*n*a (a*gñ*âna)-p., ignorance;
22. sammatta (samyaktva)-p., righteousness.

---

[1] This is to include all biting or stinging insects, as lice, &c.

[2] This is binding on the *G*inakalpikas only, not on common monks.

[1]The enumeration of the troubles has been delivered by the Kâ*s*yapa[2], I shall explain them to you in due order. Listen to me. (1)

1. Though his body be weakened by hunger, a monk who is strong (in self-control) and does penance, should not cut or cause another to cut (anything to be eaten), nor cook it or cause another to cook it. (2)

Though emaciated like the joint of a crow's (leg) and covered with a network of veins, he should know the permitted measure of food and drink, and wander about with a cheerful mind. (3)

2. Though overcome by thirst, he should drink no cold water, restrained by shame and aversion (from forbidden things); he should try to get distilled[3] water. (4)

Wandering about on deserted ways, in pain, thirsty, with dry throat, and distressed, he should bear this trouble (of thirst). (5)

3. If a restrained, austere ascetic occasionally suffers from cold on his wanderings, he should not walk beyond the (prescribed) time, remembering the teaching of the *G*ina. (6)

'I have no shelter and nothing to cover my skin, therefore I shall make a fire to warm myself;' such a thought should not be entertained by a monk. (7)

---

[1] The preceding part of this lecture is in prose, the rest is in *s*lôka. The numbers placed before the verses refer to the above enumeration of the troubles. It will be seen that two stanzas are allotted to each of them.

[2] I.e. Mahâvîra, who belonged to the Gôtra of Kâ*s*yapa.

[3] Viga*d*a = vik*ri*ta. It means water which by boiling or some other process has become so changed that it may be regarded as lifeless.

4. If he suffers from the heat of hot things, or from the heat of his body, or from the heat of summer, he should not lament the loss of comfort. (8)

A wise man, suffering from heat, should not long for a bath, or pour water over his body, or fan himself. (9)

5. Suffering from insects a great sage remains undisturbed. As an elephant at the head of the battle kills the enemy, so does a hero (in self-control conquer the internal foe). (10)

He should not scare away (insects), nor keep them off, nor be in the least provoked to passion by them. Tolerate living beings, do not kill them, though they eat your flesh and blood. (11)

6. 'My clothes being torn, I shall (soon) go naked,' or 'I shall get a new suit;' such thoughts should not be entertained by a monk. (12)

At one time he will have no clothes, at another he will have some; knowing this to be a salutary rule, a wise (monk) should not complain about it. (13)

7. A houseless and poor monk who wanders from village to village may become tired of ascetic life: he should bear this trouble. (14)

A sage should turn away from this discontent; he should wander about free from sins, guarded in himself, a tabernacle (as it were) of the Law, doing no actions, and perfectly passionless. (15)

8. In this world men have a natural liking for women; he who knows (and renounces) them, will easily perform his duties as a *S*rama*n*a. (16)

A wise man who knows that women are a slough, as it were, will get no harm from them, but will wander about searching for the Self. (17)

9. Alone, living on allowed food[1], he should wander about, bearing all troubles, in a village or a town or a market-place or a capital. (18)

Different (from other men) a monk should wander about, he should acquire no property; but not being attached to householders, he should live without a fixed residence. (19)

10. In a burial-place, or a deserted house, or below a tree he should sit down, alone, without moving, and he should not drive away any one. (20)

Sitting there he should brave all dangers; when seized with fear, he should not rise and go to some other place. (21)

11. A monk who does penance and is strong (in self-control), will not be affected beyond measure by good or bad lodgings, but an evil-minded monk will. (22)

Having obtained a good or bad lodging in an empty house[2], he should stay there thinking: 'What does it matter for one night?' (23)

12. If a layman abuses a monk, he should not grow angry against him; because he would be like a child[3], a monk should not grow angry. (24)

If a monk hears bad words, cruel and rankling ones, he should silently overlook them, and not take them to heart. (25)

13. A monk should not be angry if beaten, nor should he therefore entertain sinful thoughts; knowing patience to be the highest good, a monk should meditate on the Law. (26)

---

[1] Lâ*dh*a; see also note on XVII, 2.

[2] I.e. in which there are no women.

[3] Or like an ignorant man, bâla.

If somebody strikes a restrained, resigned *S*rama*n*a somewhere, he should think: 'I have not lost my life.' (27)

14. It will always cause difficulties to a houseless monk to get everything by begging, and nothing without begging. (28)

The hand (of the giver) is not always kindly stretched out to a monk when he is on his begging tour; but he should not think that it would be better to live as a householder. (29)

15. He should beg food from the householder when his dinner is ready; a wise man should not care whether he gets alms or not. (30)

'I get nothing to-day, perhaps I shall get something to-morrow;' a monk who thinks thus, will not be grieved by his want of success. (31)

16. If any misfortune[1] happens and he suffers pain, he should cheerfully steady his mind, and bear the ills that attack him. (32)

He should not long for medical treatment, but he should continue to search for the welfare of his soul; thus he will be a true *S*rama*n*a by neither acting himself nor causing others to act. (33)

17. When a naked, rough, restrained ascetic lies on the grass, his body will be hurt. (34)

In the sun his pain will grow insupportable; still a monk, though hurt by the grass, will not use clothes[2]. (35)

18. When by the heat of summer his body sweats and is covered with dirt and dust, a wise monk should not lament his loss of comfort. (36)

---

[1] Viz. if he falls sick.

[2] Tantu*g*a, what is manufactured from threads.

He should bear (all this), waiting for the destruction of his Karman[1], (and practising) the noble, excellent Law; he should carry the filth on his body till he expires. (37)

19. It may be that a gentleman salutes a monk, or rises from his seat on his approach, or invites him (to accept alms in his house): a monk should evince no predilection for men of this sort, who show him such marks of respect. (38)

Not resentful, having few wants, begging from strangers, and not being dainty, a wise man should not long for pleasant things, nor be sorry afterwards (for not having got them). (39)

20. 'Forsooth, in bygone times I have done actions productive of ignorance, for I do not remember them when asked by anybody anywhere[2].' (40)

'Afterwards, however, actions productive of ignorance take effect.' Therefore comfort yourself, knowing the consequences of actions. (41)

21. 'It was of no use to turn away from the lust of the senses and to live restrainedly. for I do not properly recognise good and bad things.' (42)

'Though in practising austerities and religious observances I live according to strict rules, still the hindrances to knowledge will not go off.' (43)

22. A monk should not think: 'There is, indeed, no life to come, nor an exalted state to be acquired by penances; in short, I have been deceived.' (44)

A monk should not think: 'Those lied who said that there were, are, and will be *G*inas.' (45)

---

[1] Nir*g*arâ.

[2] The commentators refer the word 'anywhere' to the place or object of the former actions.

All these troubles have been declared by the Kâsyapa. A monk should not be vanquished by them, when attacked by any anywhere.

Thus I say.

THIRD LECTURE.

THE FOUR REQUISITES.

Four things of paramount value are difficult to obtain here by a living being: human birth, instruction in the Law, belief in it, and energy in self-control. (1)

I. The universe is peopled by manifold creatures, who are, in this Samsâra, born in different families and castes for having done various actions. (2)

Sometimes they go to the world of the gods, sometimes to the hells, sometimes they become Asuras in accordance with their actions. (3)

Sometimes they become Kshattriyas, or *Kand*âlas and Bukkasas, or worms and moths, or (insects called) Kunthu[1] and ants. (4)

Thus living beings of sinful actions, who are born again and again in ever-recurring births, are not disgusted with the Samsâra, but they are like warriors (never tired of the battle of life). (5)

Living beings bewildered through the influence of their actions, distressed and suffering pains, undergo misery in non-human births. (6)

But by the cessation of Karman, perchance, living

---

[1] About the Kunthu see below, Thirty-sixth Lecture, v. 138 and note.

beings will reach in due time a pure state and be born as men. (7)

II. And though they be born with a human body, it will be difficult for them to hear the Law, having heard which they will do penances, combat their passions and abstain from killing living beings. (8)

III. And though, by chance, they may hear the Law, it will be difficult for them to believe in it; many who are shown the right way, stray from it. (9)

IV. And though they have heard the Law and believe in it, it is difficult for them to fulfill it strenuously; many who approve of the religion, do not adopt it. (10)

Having been born as a man, having heard the Law, believing in it, and fulfilling it strenuously, an ascetic should restrain himself and shake off sinfulness. (11)

The pious obtain purity, and the pure stand firmly in the Law: (the soul afterwards) reaches the highest Nirvâ*n*a, being like unto a fire fed with ghee. (12)

Leave off the causes of sin, acquire fame through patience! (A man who acts up to this) will rise to the upper regions after having left this body of clay. (13)

The Yakshas who are gifted with various virtues, (live in the heavenly regions, situated) one above the other, shining forth like the great luminaries, and hoping never to descend thence. (14)

Intent on enjoying divine pleasures and changing their form at will, they live in the upper Kalpa heavens many centuries of former[1] years. (15)

---

[1] One 'former' (pûrva) year consists of 7,560 millions of common years. The idea that years were longer when the world was still young, is apparently suggested by the experience which everybody will have made, that a year seemed to us an enormously long time when we were young, and the same space of time

The Yakshas, having remained there according to their merit, descend thence at the expiration of their life and are born as men.

Men are of ten kinds. (16)

Fields and houses, gold, cattle, slaves and servants: where these four goods, the causes of pleasure, are present, in such families he is born[1]. (17)

He will have friends and relations, be of good family, of fine complexion, healthy, wise, noble, famous, and powerful. (18)

After having enjoyed, at their proper time, the unrivalled pleasures of human life, he will obtain true knowledge by his pure religious merit acquired in a former life. (19)

---

appears to us shorter and shorter as we advance in life. A similar analogy with our life has probably caused the belief in the four ages of the world, shared by the Hindus and the ancients. For does not childhood to most of us appear the happiest period of our life, and youth better still than the time of full-grown manhood? As in retrospect our life appears to us, so primitive man imagines the life of the world to have been: the first age was the best and the longest, and the following ages grew worse and worse, and became shorter at the same time. This primitive conceit was by the ancients combined with the conceit of the year, so that the four ages were compared with the four seasons of the year. Something similar seems to have happened in India, where, however, there are three or six seasons. For the *G*ainas seem to have originally divided one Eon into six minor periods. Now the year was frequently compared to a wheel, and this second metaphor was worked out by the *G*ainas. They named the six minor periods aras, literally spokes of a wheel, and divided the whole Eon into one descending part (of the wheel), avasarpi*n*î, and one rising part, utsarpi*n*î. These Avasarpi*n*îs and Utsarpi*n*îs are probably a later improvement, and the Eon originally contained but six Aras. But if there were indeed twelve Aras from the beginning, they must have been suggested by the twelve months of the year.

[1] This is the first of the ten kinds of men mentioned above; the remaining nine are enumerated in the following verse.

Perceiving that the four requisites are difficult to obtain, he will apply himself to self-control, and when by penances he has shaken off the remnant of Karman, he will become an eternal Siddha. (20)

Thus I say.

FOURTH LECTURE.

IMPURITY.

You cannot prolong your life[1], therefore be not careless; you are past help when old age approaches. Consider this: what (protection) will careless people get, who kill living beings and do not exert themselves? (1)

Men who adhering to wrong principles acquire wealth by evil deeds, will lose it, falling into the snares (of their passions) and being held captive by their hatred. (2)

As the burglar[2] caught in the breach of the wall perishes by the work the sinner himself had executed, thus people in this life and the next cannot escape the effect of their own actions. (3)

If a man living in the Sa*m*sâra does an action for the sake of somebody else, or one by which he him-

---

[1] A similar expression is used in Sûtrak*ri*tâṅga I, 2, 2, 21.

[2] Dêvêndra relates two stories of burglars, one of which is supposed to be hinted at in the text. It comes to this. A burglar is caught, in the breach he had excavated, by the owner of the house, who takes hold of his feet protruding from the breach. But the burglar's companion tries to drag him out from the other side of the wall. In this position he is smashed by the upper part of the wall coming down.

self also profits, then, at the time of reaping the fruit of his actions, his relations will not act as true relations (i.e. will not come to his help). (4)

Wealth will not protect a careless man in this world and the next. Though he had seen the right way, he does not see it, even as one in the dark whose lamp has suddenly been put out. (5)

Though others sleep, be thou awake! Like a wise man, trust nobody, but be always on the alert; for dangerous is the time and weak the body. Be always watchful like a Bhâru*nd*a[1] bird! (6)

A monk should step carefully in his walk (i.e. in his life), supposing everything to be a snare for him. First he must bestow care on his life till he wins the stake (viz. enlightenment), and afterwards he should despise it, annihilating his sins. (7)

By conquering his will, (a monk) reaches liberation, as a well-broken horse which is clad in harness (goes to battle). Be watchful in your young years; for thereby a monk quickly obtains liberation. (8)

'If he does not get (victory over his will) early, he will get it afterwards;' such reasoning[2] presupposes the eternity of human life. But such a man despairs when his life draws to its close, and the dissolution of his body approaches. (9)

One cannot quickly arrive at discernment; therefore one should exert one's self, abstain from pleasures, understand the world, be impartial like

---

[1] Each of these birds has two necks and three legs.

[2] Upamâ. Literally translated: 'this is the comparison of those who contend that life is eternal.' The commentator gives a forced interpretation of the first part of the verse to bring about a comparison. But the meaning 'comparison' will not suit the context, the word must here mean: conclusion, reasoning.

a sage, and guard one's self: (thus) never be careless. (10)

A *S*rama*n*a who again and again suppresses the effects of delusion, and controls himself, will be affected in a rough way by external things; but a monk should not hate them in his mind. (11)

External things weaken the intellect and allure many; therefore keep them out of your mind. Keep off delusion, remove pride, do not practise deceit, leave off greed. (12)

Heretics who are impure and vain, are always subject to love and hate, and are wholly under the influence (of their passions). Despising them as unholy men, desire virtues till the end of your life. (13)

Thus I say.

FIFTH LECTURE.

DEATH AGAINST ONE'S WILL.

In this ocean (of life) with its currents (viz. births) difficult to cross, one man has reached the opposite shore; one wise man has given an answer to the following question. (1)

These two ways of life ending with death have been declared: death with one's will, and death against one's will. (2)

Death against one's will is that of ignorant men, and it happens (to the same individual) many times. Death with one's will is that of wise men, and at best[1] it happens but once. (3)

[1] Viz. in the case of a Kêvalin. Other sages die this death seven or eight times before reaching mukti.

Mahâvîra has (thus) described the first kind in which an ignorant man, being attached to pleasures, does very cruel actions. (4)

A man attached to pleasures and amusements will be caught in the trap (of deceit). (He thinks): 'I never saw the next world, but I have seen with my own eyes the pleasures of this life.' (5)

'The pleasures of this life are (as it were) in your hand, but the future ones are uncertain[1]. Who knows whether there is a next world or not?' (6)

The fool boasts: 'I shall have the company of (most) men[2].' But by his love of pleasures and amusements he will come to grief. (7)

Then he begins to act cruelly against movable and immovable beings, and he kills living beings with a purpose or without. (8)

An ignorant man kills, lies, deceives, calumniates, dissembles, drinks liquor, and eats meat, thinking that this is the right thing to do. (9)

Overbearing in acts and words, desirous for wealth and women, he accumulates sins in two ways[3], just as a young snake gathers dust (both on and in its body). (10)

Then he suffers ill and is attacked by disease; and he is in dread of the next world when he reflects on his deeds. (11)

I have heard of the places in hell, and of the destination of the sinner, where the fools who do cruel deeds will suffer violently. (12)

---

[1] Kâlikâ, doubtful as regards the time when they will be enjoyed.

[2] I. e. I shall do as people generally do, viz. enjoy pleasures.

[3] Viz. By his acts and thoughts.

Then going to the place where he is to be born again according to his deeds, he feels remorse, as I have heard (from my teacher). (13)

As a charioteer, who against his better judgment leaves the smooth highway and gets on a rugged road, repents when the axle breaks; so the fool, who transgresses the Law and embraces unrighteousness, repents in the hour of death, like (the charioteer) over the broken axle. (14, 15)

Then when death comes at last, the fool trembles in fear; he dies the 'death against one's will,' (having lost his chance) like a gambler vanquished by Kali. (16)

Thus has been explained the fools' 'death against one's will;' now hear from me the wise men's 'death with one's will!' (17)

Full of peace and without injury to any one is, as I have heard (from my teachers), the death of the virtuous who control themselves and subdue their senses[1]. (18)

(Such a death) does not fall to the lot of every monk, nor of every householder; for the morality of householders is of various character, and that of monks is not always good throughout. (19)

Some householders are superior to some monks in self-control; but the saints are superior to all householders in self-control. (20)

Bark and skin (of a goat), nakedness, twisted

---

[1] Sa*m*gayâ*n*a*m* vusîmao = sa*m*yatânâ*m* va*s*yavatâ*m*. Vusîmao is gen. sing., it is here used in juxtaposition with a word in gen. plur. Such an irregularity would of course be impossible in classical Prâk*ri*t, but the authors of metrical *G*aina Sûtras take such liberties with grammar that we must put up with any faulty expression, though it would be easy to correct it by a conjecture.

hair, baldness—these (outward tokens) will not save a sinful ascetic. (21)

A sinner, though he be a mendicant (friar), will not escape hell; but a pious man, whether monk or householder, ascends to heaven. (22)

A faithful man should practise[1] the rules of conduct for householders; he should never neglect the Pôsaha fast[2] in both fortnights, not even for a single night. (23)

When under such discipline he lives piously even as a householder, he will, on quitting flesh and bones[3], share the world of the Yakshas. (24)

Now a restrained monk will become one of the two: either one free from all misery or a god of great power. (25)

To the highest regions, in due order, to those where there is no delusion, and to those which are full of light, where the glorious (gods dwell)—who have long life, great power, great lustre, who can change their shape at will, who are beautiful as on their first day, and have the brilliancy of many suns—to such places go those who are trained in self-control and penance, monks or householders, who have obtained liberation by absence of passion. (26–28)

Having heard (this) from the venerable men who control themselves and subdue their senses, the virtuous and the learned do not tremble in the hour of death. (29)

---

[1] Kâê*n*a phâsaê=kâyêna sp*ri*s*ê*t, literally, touch with his body.

[2] The Pôsaha of the *G*ainas corresponds to the Upôsatha of the Buddhists. Hoernle in note 87 of his translation of the Uvâsaga Dasâo (Bibliotheca Indica) says of the Pôsaha: it is distinguished by the four abstinences (uvavâsa) from food (âhâra), bodily attentions (*s*arîrasatkâra), sexual intercourse (abrahma) and daily work (vyâpâra).

[3] Literally, skin and joints.

A wise man having weighed (both kinds of death) and chosen the better one (taught in) the Law of Compassion, will become calm through patience, with an undisturbed mind (at the time of death). (30)

When the right time (to prepare for death) has arrived, a faithful (monk) should in the presence (of his teacher) suppress all emotions (of fear or joy) and wait for the dissolution of his body. (31)

When the time for quitting the body has come, a sage dies the 'death with one's will,' according to one of the three methods[1]. (32)

Thus I say.

SIXTH LECTURE.

THE FALSE ASCETIC[2].

All men who are ignorant of the Truth are subject to pain; in the endless Sa*m*sâra they suffer in many ways. (1)

Therefore a wise man, who considers well the ways that lead to bondage[3] and birth, should

---

[1] These three methods are (1) bhaktapratyâkhyâna, (2) iṅgitamara*n*a, (3) pâdapôpagamana. They are fully described in the Â*k*ârâṅga Sûtra I, 7, 8, 7 ff., see part i, p. 75 f.

[2] Khu*dd*âganiya*nth*igg*am* = Kshullakanirgranthîyam. Kshullaka originally means 'small, young,' but I do not see that the contents of this lecture support this translation, though the commentators would seem to favour it.

[3] Dêvêndra here quotes the following Sanskrit verse: Kalatraniga*dam* dattvâ na sa*m*tush*t*a*h* pra*g*âpati*h* । bhûyô*py apatyarûpê*n*a dadâti gala*sri*ṅkhalam. The creator was not satisfied when he had given (to man) the wife as a fetter, he added a chain round his neck in the form of children.

himself search for the truth, and be kind towards all creatures. (2)

'Mother, father, daughter-in-law, brother, wife, and sons will not be able to help me, when I suffer for my own deeds [1].' (3)

This truth should be taken to heart [2] by a man of pure faith; he should (therefore) cut off greed and love, and not hanker after his former connections. (4)

Cows and horses, jewels and earrings, cattle, slaves and servants: all these (possessions) you must give up in order to obtain the power of changing your form at will. (5) [3]

Everything that happens to somebody, affects him personally; therefore, knowing the creatures' love of their own self, do not deprive them of their life, but cease from endangering and combating them. (6)

Seeing that to accept (presents) leads to hell, one should not accept even a blade of grass; only to preserve one's life [4] one should eat the food that is put in one's own alms-bowl. (7)

Here some are of opinion that they will be delivered from all misery by merely attending the teacher [5], without abstaining from sins. (8)

---

[1] This verse recurs in Sûtrak*ri*tâṅga I, 9, 5.

[2] Sapêhâê pâsê = svaprêkshayâ pa*s*yêt, he should look at it with his mind or reflectively. However sapêhâê is usually the absolute participle samprêkshya. The meaning is the same in both cases.

[3] Some MSS. insert here the following verse: 'Movables and immovables, corn, and furniture can not deliver a man from pain, who is suffering for his deeds.'

[4] This is according to the commentators the meaning of the word dôgu*ññkh*î = *g*ugupsin.

[5] Âyariya*m* vidittâ*n*a*m*. The commentator makes this out

Acknowledging the truth about bondage and liberation, but talking only, not acting (in accordance with these tenets), they seek comfort for themselves in mighty words. (9)

Clever talking will not work salvation; how should philosophical instruction do it? Fools, though sinking lower and lower through their sins, believe themselves to be wise men. (10)

They are (going) a long way in the endless Sa*m*sâra; therefore looking out carefully one should wander about carefully[1]. (11)

Choosing what is beyond and above (this world, viz. liberation), one should never desire (worldly objects), but sustain one's body only to be able to annihilate one's Karman. (12)

Those will reap pains who, in thoughts, words, or acts, are attached to their body, to colours, and to forms. (13)

Recognising the cause of Karman, one should wander about waiting for one's death; (knowing) the permitted quantity of food and drink, one should eat (such food as has been) prepared (by the householders for their own consumption). (14)

An ascetic should not lay by any store, not even so little as the grease (sticking to his alms-bowl); but as a bird with its plumage[2], so he with his alms-bowl should wander about without desires. (15)

---

to mean: by learning only what right conduct (â*k*ârikam) is, without living up to it. But it is obvious that the author intends a censure upon the *Gñ*ânamârga.

[1] As usual this phrase means: one should conduct one's self so as to commit no sin.

[2] There is a pun in the original on the word patta, which means plumes (patra) and alms-bowl (pâtra).

Receiving alms in a manner to avoid faults [1], and controlling one's self, one should wander about in a village (&c.) without a fixed residence; careful among the careless one should beg one's food. (16)

Thus has spoken the Arhat *Gñâtri*putra, the venerable native of Vai*s*âlî [2], who possesses the highest knowledge and who possesses the highest faith, who possesses (at the same time) the highest knowledge and the highest faith. (17)

Thus I say.

SEVENTH LECTURE.

THE PARABLE OF THE RAM, ETC.

As somebody, to provide for (the arrival of) a guest, brings up a young ram, gives it rice and gram [3], and brings it up in his yard; (1)

Then when it is grown up and big, fat and of a large belly, fattened and of a plump body, it is ready for the guest. (2)

As long as no guest comes, the poor (animal) lives; but as soon as a guest arrives, its head is cut off, and it is eaten. (3)

As this ram is well treated for the sake of

---

[1] This is the êsha*n*âsamiti. On the samitis see below, Twelfth Lecture, 2.

[2] Vêsaliê = Vai*s*âlika. See my remarks on this statement in part i, introduction, p. xi, and Hoernle's notes in his translation of the Uvâsaga Dasâo, p. 3 ff.

[3] Yavasa, explained by mudgamâshâdi. Mutton of gram-fed sheep is greatly appreciated in India.

a guest, even so an ignorant, great sinner longs (as it were) for life in hell. (4)

An ignorant man kills, tells lies, robs on the highway, steals foreign goods, deceives, (always thinking of some one) whom he could plunder, the villain. (5)

He is desirous of women and pleasures, he enters on undertakings and business, drinks liquor, eats meat, becomes strong, a subduer of foes. (6)

He eats crisp goats' meat, his belly grows, and his veins swell with blood—but he gains nothing but life in hell, just as the ram is only fed to be killed for the sake of a guest. (7)

After having enjoyed pleasant seats, beds, carriages, riches, and pleasures, after having squandered his wealth which he had so much trouble in gaining, and after having committed many sins, he will, under the burden of his Karman, and believing only in the visible world, be grieved in the hour of death like the ram [1] at the arrival of a guest. (8, 9)

Then the sinner who has been killing living beings, at the end of his life falls from his state [2], and against his will he goes to the world of the Asuras, to the dark place. (10)

As a man for the sake of one Kâkinî [3] (risks and) loses a thousand (Kârshâpa*n*as), or as the king lost his kingdom (and life) by eating a mango-fruit which he was strictly forbidden (by his physician) [4]: (11)

---

[1] Aya = a*g*a, literally goat.

[2] *K*uya = kyuta is said of one who is born after his death in a lower sphere than that in which he lived before.

[3] According to the commentators the eightieth part of a rupee.

[4] The commentators relate 'old stories' to explain allusions in the text; they will, however, be intelligible without further comment, though I do not contend that those stories were not really old and known to the author of the Sûtra.

Even so are human pleasures compared with the pleasures of the gods: divine life and pleasures surpass (the former) a thousand times and more. (12)

Those endowed with excellent knowledge live many nayutas[1] of years; so great a loss suffer the fools in a life of less than a hundred years! (13)

Three merchants set out on their travels, each with his capital; one of them gained there much, the second returned with his capital, and the third merchant came home after having lost his capital. This parable[2] is taken from common life; learn (to apply it) to the Law. (14, 15)

The capital is human life, the gain is heaven; through the loss of that capital man must be born as a denizen of hell or a brute animal. (16)

These are the two courses open to the sinner; they consist in misery, as corporal punishment, &c.; for the slave to his lusts[3] has forfeited human life and divine life. (17)

Having once forfeited them, he will have to endure these two states of misery; it will be

---

[1] A nayuta or niyuta is equal to

49,786,136,000,000,000,000,000,000,000,000.

It is derived in the following way:

1 pûrvâṅga = 8,400,000
1 pûrva = 8,400,000 pûrvâṅgas.
1 nayutâṅga = 8,400,000 pûrvas.
1 nayuta = 8,400,000 nayutâṅgas.

[2] This parable closely corresponds to Matth. xxv. 14, Luke xix. 11. I need not here discuss the problems raised by this coincidence since they will, as I hear, be fully treated by Herr Hüttemann, a pupil of Professor Leumann of Strassburg.

[3] Lôlayâsa*dh*ê = lôlatâ*sath*a. The commentator takes lôlatâ for lôla and makes the word a karmadhâraya. I think that the word *sath*a which originally means 'one who deceives others' is used here in the sense 'one who deceives himself.'

difficult for him to attain an upward course[1] for a long time to come. (18)

Considering what is at stake, one should weigh (the chances of) the sinner and of the virtuous man (in one's mind).

He who brings back his capital, is (to be compared to) one who is born again as a man. (19)

Those men who through the exercise of various virtues[2] become pious householders, will be born again as men; for all beings will reap the fruit of their actions. (20)

But he who increases his capital, is (to be compared to) one who practises eminent virtues; the virtuous, excellent man cheerfully attains the state of gods[3]. (21)

When one thus knows that a (virtuous) monk or householder will be gladdened (by his gain), how, then, should a man, whilst he is losing (his chance), not be conscious of his losing it? (22)

As a drop of water at the top of a blade of Kusa-grass dwindles down to naught when compared with the ocean, so do human pleasures when compared with divine pleasures. (23)

The pleasures in this very limited life of men are like (the water at) the top of a blade of Kusa-grass; for the sake of what will a man not care to gain and

---

[1] I. e. birth as a man or a god.

[2] Sikshâ. The commentator quotes the following passage in Prâkrit: Souls gain human birth through four causes: (1) a kind disposition (prakritibhadratâ), (2) love of discipline (prakritivinîtatâ), (3) compassion (sânukrosanatâ), and (4) want of envy (amatsaritâ).

[3] For a higher rank than that of a god, e. g. that of a Kêvalin, cannot, in the present state of the world, be attained.

to keep (so precious a good which he risks to lose)? (24)

He who has not renounced pleasure, will miss his aim (i.e. the true end of his soul); for though he has been taught the right way, he will go astray again and again. (25)

But he who has renounced pleasure, will not miss his aim; (he will think): I have learned that, by getting rid of this vile body, I shall become a god. (26)

He will be born among men where there is wealth, beauty, glory, fame, long life, and eminent happiness. (27)

See the folly of the sinner who practises unrighteousness: turning away from the Law, the great sinner will be born in hell. (28)

See the wisdom of the wise man who follows the true Law: turning away from unrighteousness, the virtuous man will be born as a god. (29)

A wise man weighs in his mind the state of the sinner and that of the virtuous man; quitting the state of the sinner, a sage realises that of the virtuous. (30)

Thus I say.

EIGHTH LECTURE.

KAPILA'S VERSES[1].

By what acts can I escape a sorrowful lot in this unstable ineternal Sa*m*sâra, which is full of misery? (1)

---

[1] This lecture is ascribed to Kapila. According to an old story, told in the commentary, he was the son of Kâ*s*yapa, a Brahman

Quitting your former connections place your affection on nothing; a monk who loves not even those who love him, will be freed from sin and hatred. (2)

Then the best of sages, who is exempt from

---

of Kau*s*âmbî, and his wife Ya*s*â. When Kâ*s*yapa died, his place was given to another man. His wife then sent her boy to *S*râvastî to study under Indradatta, a friend of his father's. That man was willing to instruct the boy, and procured him board and lodging in a rich merchant's house. Kapila, however, soon fell in love with the servant-girl who was appointed to his service. Once, at a festival kept by her caste, the girl in tears told him that she could not take part in the festivity as she had no money to buy ornaments. To get some she asked him to go to Dhana, a merchant, who used to give two pieces of gold to the man who saluted him first in the morning. Accordingly Kapila set out in the night, but was taken up by the police and brought before the king, Prasêna*g*it. The student made a clear breast before the king, who was so pleased with him that he promised to give him whatever he should ask. Kapila went in the garden to consider what he should ask; and the more he thought about it, the more he raised the sum which he believed he wanted, till it came to be ten thousand millions. But then, all of a sudden, the light came upon him; he began to repent of the sinful life he had led up to that time, and tearing out his hair he became a Svaya*m*sa*m*buddha. Returning to the king, he pronounced verse 17: The more you get, &c., and giving him the Dharmalâbha, he went his way. He practised austerities and acquired superior knowledge, by dint of which he came to know that in a wood, eighteen leagues from Râ*g*ag*ri*ha, lived a gang of five hundred robbers, under a chief Balabhadra. These men, he knew, would become converts to the right faith; accordingly he went to the wood where they lived. He was made prisoner, and brought before the leader of the robbers. To have some fun out of him they ordered him to dance, and on his objecting that there was none to play up, they all clapped their hands to beat the time. He then sang the first stanza of this lecture, by which some robbers were converted, and he continued to sing, repeating this stanza after each following verse (as dhruva), till at last all the robbers were converted.

delusion and possesses perfect knowledge and faith, speaks for the benefit and eternal welfare, and for the final liberation of all beings. (3)

All fetters (of the soul), and all hatred, everything of this kind, should a monk cast aside; he should not be attached to any pleasures, examining them well and taking care of himself. (4)

A stupid, ignorant sinner who never fixes his thoughts on the soul's benefit and eternal welfare, but sinks down through hatred and the temptation of lust, will be ensnared as a fly is caught on glue. (5)

It is difficult to cast aside the pleasures of life, weak men will not easily give them up; but there are pious ascetics (sâdhu) who get over the impassable (Sa*m*sâra) as merchants cross the sea. (6)

Some there are who call themselves *S*rama*n*as, though they are like the beasts ignorant of (the prohibition of) killing living beings; the stupid sinners go to hell through their superstitious beliefs[1]. (7)

One should not permit (or consent to) the killing of living beings; then he will perhaps be delivered from all misery; thus have spoken the preceptors who have proclaimed the Law of ascetics. (8)

A careful man who does not injure living beings, is called 'circumspect' (samita). The sinful Karman will quit him as water quits raised ground. (9)

In thoughts, words, and acts he should do

[1] The commentator quotes the following words: brahma*n*ê brâhma*n*am âlabhêta, indrâya kshattram, marudbhyô vai*s*ya*m*, tapasê *s*ûdram, and explains them: he who kills a Brâhma*n*a will acquire Brahma knowledge.

nothing injurious to beings who people the world, whether they move or not. (10)

He should know what alms may be accepted, and should strictly keep these rules; a monk should beg food only for the sustenance of life, and should not be dainty. (11)

He should eat what tastes badly, cold food, old beans, Vakkasa Pulâga, and for the sustenance of his life he should eat Manghu (ground badara). (12)

Those who interpret the marks of the body, and dreams, and who know the foreboding changes in the body (aṅgavidyâ)[1], are not to be called *S*rama*n*as; thus the preceptors have declared. (13)

Those who do not take their life under discipline, who cease from meditation and ascetic practices[2], and who are desirous of pleasures, amusements, and good fare, will be born again as Asuras. (14)

And when they rise (in another birth) from the world of the Asuras, they err about, for a long time, in the Sa*m*sâra; those whose souls are sullied by many sins, will hardly ever attain Bôdhi. (15)

And if somebody should give the whole earth to one man, he would not have enough; so difficult is it to satisfy anybody. (16)

The more you get, the more you want; your desires increase with your means. Though two mâshas would do to supply your want, still you would scarcely think ten millions sufficient. (17)

---

[1] See the note on verse 17 of the Fifteenth Lecture.

[2] Samâdhiyôgâ*h*. Samâdhi is concentration of the mind, and the yôgâs are, in this connection, the operations (vyâpâra) of mind, speech, and body conducive to it.

Do not desire (women), those female demons[1], on whose breasts grow two lumps of flesh, who continually change their mind, who entice men, and then make a sport of them as of slaves. (18)

A houseless (monk) should not desire women, he should turn away from females; learning thoroughly the Law, a monk should strictly keep its rules. (19)

This Law has been taught by Kapila of pure knowledge; those who follow it, will be saved and will gain both worlds. (20)

Thus I say.

NINTH LECTURE.

THE PRAVRAGYÂ OF KING NAMI[2].

After (Nami) had descended from the world of the gods, and had been born as a man, he put an end to the influence of delusion, and remembered his former birth. (1)

Remembering his former birth, king Nami

[1] Râkshasîs in the original.

[2] The Life of king Nami and his Bôdhi is told in the commentary. The Prâk*ri*t text of this romance is printed in my 'Ausgewählte Erzählungen in Mâhârâsh*t*rî,' Leipzig, 1886, p. 41 ff. Nami is one of the four simultaneous Pratyêkabuddhas, i.e. one of those saints who reach the highest stage of knowledge by an effort of their own, not through regular instruction and religious discipline. The Pratyêkabuddhas or Svaya*m*sa*m*buddhas (Sahasambuddha in Prâk*ri*t) do not, however, propagate the true Law, as the Tîrthakaras do. As the legend of Nami is not materially connected with our text, I need not give an abstract of it here.

became a Svaya*m*sa*m*buddha in the true Law, and placing his son on the throne he retired from the world. (2)

After having enjoyed, in the company of the beautiful ladies of his seraglio, excellent pleasures which match those of the heavens, king Nami became enlightened and gave up his pleasures. (3)

Having given up the town and country of Mithilâ, his army, seraglio, and all his retinue, the venerable man retired from the world and resorted to a lonely place. (4)

When the royal Seer Nami retired from the world, at the occasion of his Pravra*g*yâ there was an uproar in Mithilâ. (5)

To the royal Seer who had reached the excellent stage of Pravra*g*yâ, *S*akra in the guise of a Brâhma*n*a addressed the following words: (6)

'Why is now Mithilâ[1] full of uproar? Dreadful noises are heard from palaces and houses.' (7)

On hearing this, the royal Seer Nami, pursuing his reasons and arguments, answered the king of the gods thus: (8)

'In Mithilâ is the sacred[2] tree Manôrama, full of leaves, flowers, and fruits, which sheds a cool shadow; this tree is always a favourite resort of many (birds). (9)

---

[1] The text has Mahilâê, which is against the metre. The locative makes the construction needlessly involved.

[2] *K*êiê, *k*aitya. The commentator interprets it as meaning udyâna, park; but to make good his interpretation he takes va*kkh*ê for an instrumental plural instead of a nominative singular. The context itself seems to militate against this interpretation; for it is natural to say of a tree that it has many leaves, but it is rather strained to say the same of a park.

'Now, as this sacred tree Manôrama is shaken by the storm, the birds, suffering, destitute of refuge, and miserable, scream aloud.' (10)

On hearing this, the king of gods, pursuing his reasons and arguments, answered the royal Seer Nami thus: (11)

"This is fire and storm, your palace is on fire! Reverend sir, why do you not look after your seraglio?" (12)

Nami answered (see verse 8): (13)

'Happy are we, happy live we who call nothing our own; when Mithilâ is on fire, nothing is burned that belongs to me. (14)

'To a monk who has left his sons and wives, and who has ceased to act, nothing pleasant can occur, nor anything unpleasant. (15)

'There is much happiness for the sage, for the houseless monk, who is free from all ties, and knows himself to be single and unconnected (with the rest of the world).' (16)

Indra answered (see verse 11): (17)

"Erect a wall, gates, and battlements; dig a moat; construct *s*ataghnîs[1]: then you will be[2] a Kshattriya." (18)

Nami answered (see verse 8): (19)

'Making Faith his fortress, Penance and Self-control the bolt (of its gate), Patience its strong wall, so that guarded in three ways[3] it is impregnable; making Zeal his bow, its string Carefulness in walking (iriyâ), and its top (where the string is

[1] An instrument for defending a town.

[2] Ga*kkh*asi. The commentator explains this as an imperative, but there is no necessity for it.

[3] Tigutta, this is a pun on the three guptis.

fastened) Content, he should bend (this bow) with Truth, piercing with the arrow, Penance, (the foe's) mail, Karman—(in this way) a sage will be the victor in battle and get rid of the Sa*m*sâra.' (20–22)

Indra answered (see verse 11): (23)

"Build palaces, excellent houses[1], and turrets; thus you will be a Kshattriya." (24)

Nami answered (see verse 8): (25)

'He who builds his house on the road, will certainly get into trouble; wherever he wants to go, there he may take up his lodgings.' (26)

Indra answered (see verse 11): (27)

"Punishing thieves and robbers, cut-purses and burglars, you should establish public safety; thus you will be a Kshattriya." (28)

Nami answered (see verse 8): (29)

'Men frequently apply punishment wrongly: the innocent are put in prison, and the perpetrator of the crime is set at liberty.' (30)

Indra answered (see verse 11): (31)

"O king, bring into subjection all princes who do not acknowledge you; thus you will be a true Kshattriya." (32)

Nami answered (see verse 8): (33)

'Though a man should conquer thousands and thousands of valiant (foes), greater will be his victory if he conquers nobody but himself. (34)

'Fight with your Self; why fight with external foes? He who conquers himself through himself, will obtain happiness. (35)

'The five senses, anger, pride, delusion, and greed

---

[1] Vardhamânagr*i*ha; the houses which are so called, belong to the best kind, see Varâha Mihira, B*ri*hat Sa*m*hitâ 53, 36.

—difficult to conquer is one's self; but when that is conquered, everything is conquered[1].' (36)

Indra answered (see verse 11): (37)

"Offer great sacrifices, feed *S*rama*n*as and Brâhma*n*as, give alms, enjoy yourself, and offer sacrifices: thus you will be a true Kshattriya." (38)

Nami answered: (39)

'Though a man should give, every month, thousands and thousands of cows, better will be he who controls himself, though he give no alms.' (40)

Indra answered: (41)

"You have left the dreadful â*s*rama (that of the householder)[2] and are wanting to enter another; (remain what you were), O king, and be content with observing the Pôsaha-days." (42)

Nami answered: (43)

'If an ignorant man should eat but a blade of Ku*s*a-grass every month, (the merit of his penance) will not equal the sixteenth part of his who possesses the Law as it has been taught.' (44)

Indra answered: (45)

"Multiply your gold and silver, your jewels and

---

[1] The first line of this verse is in the Âryâ-metre, the second in Anush*t*ubh; the whole will not construe, but the meaning is clear. There are numerous instances in which the metre changes in the same stanza from Âryâ to Anush*t*ubh, and vice versa, so frequent they are that we are forced to admit the fact that the authors of these metrical texts did not shrink from taking such liberties.

[2] Ghôrâsama. A *G*aina author cannot forbear to name things from his religious point of looking at them. Thus only can it be explained that here Indra is made to apply to the â*s*rama of the householder an attribute which not he but his opponent could have used. Our verse is, however, probably only a later addition, as it has not the burden of the verses put into the mouth of Indra.

pearls, your copper, fine robes, and carriages, and your treasury; then you will be a true Kshattriya." (46)

Nami answered: (47)

'If there were numberless mountains of gold and silver, as big as Kailâsa, they would not satisfy a greedy man; for his avidity is boundless like space. (48)

'Knowing that the earth with its crops of rice and barley, with its gold and cattle, that all this put together will not satisfy one single man, one should practise austerities.' (49)

Indra answered: (50)

"A miracle! O king, you give up those wonderful pleasures, in search of imaginary objects; your very hope will cause your ruin." (51)

Nami answered: (52)

'Pleasures are the thorn that rankles, pleasures are poison, pleasures are like a venomous snake; he who is desirous of pleasures will not get them, and will come to a bad end at last. (53)

'He will sink through anger; he will go down through pride; delusion will block up his path; through greed he will incur dangers in both worlds.' (54)

Throwing off the guise of a Brâhma*n*a, and making visible his true form, *S*akra saluted him respectfully and praised him with these sweet words: (55)

"Bravo! you have conquered anger; bravo! you have vanquished pride; bravo! you have banished delusion; bravo! you have subdued greed. (56)

"Bravo for your simplicity, O saint! bravo for your humility, O saint! bravo for your perfect patience! bravo for your perfect liberation! (57)

"Here (on earth) you are the highest man, Reverend sir, and hereafter you will be the highest; exempt from all blemishes you will reach Perfection, a higher state than which there is none in this world." (58)

Thus praising the royal Seer, *S*akra in perfect faith kept his right side towards him and paid reverence to him, again and again. (59)

After having adored the best sage's feet marked by the *K*akra and the Ankus*a*[1], he flew up through the air, with his crown and his earrings prettily trembling. (60)

Nami humbled himself; enjoined by *S*akra in person, the king of Vidêha left the house, and took upon him *S*rama*n*ahood. (61)

Thus act the enlightened, the wise, the clever ones; they turn away from pleasures, as did Nami, the royal Seer. (62)

Thus I say.

TENTH LECTURE[2].

THE LEAF OF THE TREE.

As the fallow leaf of the tree falls to the ground, when its days are gone, even so the life of men (will

---

[1] The wheel and the hook.

[2] This is a sermon delivered by Mahâvîra to his disciple Indrabhûti, who belonged to the Gôtama Gôtra. In the commentary a lengthy legend is given how Gautama came to want this instruction. As it is not necessary for understanding the contents of this lecture, I may pass it over.

come to its close); Gautama, be careful all the while! (1)

As a dew-drop dangling on the top of a blade of Kusa-grass lasts but a short time, even so the life of men; Gautama, be careful all the while! (2)

As life is so fleet and existence so precarious, wipe off the sins you ever committed; Gautama, &c. (3)

A rare chance, in the long course of time, is human birth for a living being; hard are the consequences of actions; Gautama, &c. (4)

When the soul has once got into an earth-body[1], it may remain in the same state as long as an Asa*m*khya[2]; Gautama, &c. (5)

When the soul has once got into a water-body, &c. (all as in verse 5). (6)

When a soul has once got into a fire-body, &c. (all as in verse 5). (7)

When the soul has once got into a wind-body, &c. (all as in verse 5). (8)

When the soul has once got into a vegetable-body, it remains long in that state, for an endless time, after which its lot is not much bettered[3]; Gautama, &c. (9)

When the soul has once got into a body of a Dvîndriya (i.e. a being possessing two organs of

---

[1] Verses 5–9 treat of the êkêndriyas or beings which possess but one organ of sense, that of touch. A full description of them as well as of the dvîndriyas, &c. is given in the last lecture.

[2] The periods called asa*m*khya are measured by utsarpi*n*îs and avasarpi*n*îs which correspond to the kalpas of the Hindus, but greatly exaggerated. An asa*m*khya is the longest time (ukkôsa*m* = utkarsha*m*) which a soul may be doomed to live in earth-bodies; see below, XXXVI, 81 ff.

[3] This is, according to the commentary, the meaning of duranta.

sense), it may remain in the same state as long as a period called sa*m*khyêya[1]; Gautama, &c. (10)

When the soul has once got into a body of a Trîndriya (i.e. a being possessing three organs of sense), it, &c. (all as in verse 10). (11)

When the soul has once got into a body of a *K*aturindriya (i.e. a being possessing four organs of sense), it, &c. (all as in verse 10). (12)

When the soul has once got into a body of a Pa*ñk*êndriya (i.e. a being possessing five organs of sense), it may remain in the same state as long as seven or eight births; Gautama, &c. (13)

When the soul has once got into the body of a god or of a denizen of hell, it may remain in that state one whole life; Gautama, &c. (14)

Thus the soul which suffers for its carelessness, is driven about in the Sa*m*sâra by its good and bad Karman; Gautama, &c. (15)

Though one be born as a man, it is a rare chance to become an Ârya; for many are the Dasyus and Mlê*kkh*as; Gautama, &c. (16)

Though one be born as an Ârya, it is a rare chance to possess all five organs of sense; for we see many who lack one organ or other; Gautama, &c. (17)

Though he may possess all five organs of sense, still it is a rare chance to be instructed in the best Law; for people follow heretical teachers; Gautama, &c. (18)

Though he may have been instructed in the right Law, still it is a rare chance to believe in it; for many people are heretics; Gautama, &c. (19)

---

[1] A sa*m*khi*gg*a, i.e. sa*m*khyêya, is a period which can be measured by thousands of years.

Though one believe in the Law, he will rarely practise it; for people are engrossed by pleasures; Gautama, &c. (20)

When your body grows old, and your hair turns white, the power of your ears decreases; Gautama, &c. (21)

When your body grows old, and your hair turns white, the power of your eyes decreases; Gautama, &c. (22)

When your body grows old, and your hair turns white, the power of your nose decreases. (23)

When your body grows old, and your hair turns white, the power of your tongue decreases. (24)

When your body grows old, and your hair turns white, the power of your touch decreases. (25)

When your body grows old, and your hair turns white, all your powers decrease. (26)

Despondency, the king's evil, cholera, mortal diseases of many kinds befall you; your body wastes and decays; Gautama, &c. (27)

Cast aside from you all attachments, as the (leaves of) a lotus let drop off the autumnal[1] water, exempt from every attachment, Gautama, be careful all the while! (28)

Give up your wealth and your wife; you have entered the state of the houseless; do not, as it were, return to your vomit; Gautama, &c. (29)

Leave your friends and relations, the large fortune you have amassed; do not desire them a second time; Gautama, &c. (30)

---

[1] This attribute is here given to 'water,' because in autumn the water becomes pure, and even the purest water has no hold upon the leaves of a lotus; thus a saint should give up even the best and dearest attachment.

There is now no *G*ina[1], but there is a highly esteemed guide to show the way; now being on the right path, Gautama, be careful all the while! (31)

Now you have entered on the path from which the thorns have been cleared, the great path; walk in the right path; Gautama, &c. (32)

Do not get into an uneven road like a weak burden-bearer; for you will repent of it afterwards; Gautama, &c. (33)

You have crossed the great ocean; why do you halt so near the shore? make haste to get on the other side; Gautama, &c. (34)

Going through the same religious practices as perfected saints[2], you will reach the world of perfection, Gautama, where there is safety and perfect happiness; Gautama, &c. (35)

The enlightened[3] and liberated monk should control himself, whether he be in a village or a town, and he should preach to all[4] the road of peace; Gautama, &c. (36)

Having heard the Buddha's[5] well-delivered

---

[1] As this assertion cannot be put in the mouth of Mahâvîra, this verse must be set down as a later addition—or perhaps as a blunder of the poet similar to that noted before, in IX, 42.

[2] This seems, according to the commentary, to be the meaning of the phrase akalêvarasê*n*im ûsiyâ. Akalêvara*s*rê*n*î is said to mean as much as kshapaka*s*rê*n*î.

[3] Buddha.

[4] Bûhaê = v*rim*hayêt; literally, propagate.

[5] Here the word buddha is used as a title; but its use is very restricted, scarcely going beyond that of a common epithet. This is just what we otherwise should have to assume in order to explain the use by the Bauddhas of that word to denote the founder of their sect. In the Sûtrak*ri*tâṅga II, 6, 28 Buddha, in the plural, actually denotes the prophets of the Buddhists.

sermon, adorned by illustrations, Gautama cut off love and hatred and reached perfection. (37)

Thus I say.

ELEVENTH LECTURE.

THE VERY LEARNED.

I shall explain, in due order, the right discipline of a houseless monk who has got rid of all worldly ties. Listen to me. (1)

He who is ignorant of the truth, egoistical, greedy, without self-discipline, and who talks loosely, is called ill-behaved and void of learning. (2)

There are five causes which render wholesome discipline impossible: egoism, delusion, carelessness, illness, and idleness: (3)

For eight causes discipline is called virtue, viz.: not to be fond of mirth, to control one's self, not to speak evil of others, not to be without discipline, not to be of wrong discipline, not to be covetous, not to be choleric, to love the truth; for their influence discipline is called virtue. (4, 5)

A monk who is liable to the following fourteen charges, is called ill-behaved, and does not reach Nirvâ*n*a: (6)

If he is frequently angry; if he perseveres in his wrath; if he spurns friendly advice; if he is proud of his learning; if he finds fault with others; if he is angry even with friends; if he speaks evil even of a good friend behind his back; if he is positive in his assertions; if he is malicious, egoistical, greedy, without self-discipline; if he does not share with others; if he is always unkind: then he is called ill-behaved. (7-9)

But for the following fifteen good qualities he is called well-behaved: if he is always humble, steady, free from deceit and curiosity; if he abuses nobody; if he does not persevere in his wrath; if he listens to friendly advice; if he is not proud of his learning; if he does not find fault with others; if he is not angry with friends; if he speaks well even of a bad friend behind his back; if he abstains from quarrels and rows; if he is enlightened, polite, decent, and quiet: then he is called well-behaved. (10-13)

He who always acknowledges his allegiance to his teacher[1], who has religious zeal and ardour for study, who is kind in words and actions, deserves to be instructed. (14)

As water put into a shell shines with a doubled brilliancy, so do the piety, fame, and knowledge of a very learned monk. (15)

As a trained Kambô*g*a-steed, whom no noise frightens[2], exceeds all other horses in speed, so a very learned monk is superior to all others[3]. (16)

As a valiant hero bestriding a trained horse, with heralds singing out to his right and left, (has no equal)[4], neither has a very learned monk. (17)

---

[1] Literally, who always remains in his teacher's kula.

[2] Kanthaka. The horse of Buddha is called Kanthaka; our passage shows that the word is not a proper noun, but an appellative.

[3] This is the burden of all verses down to verse 30.

[4] I have supplied these words here and in the following verses. The commentators try to do without them, and labour to point out qualities of the monk, which correspond to the attributes of the subject of the comparison.

As a strong and irresistible elephant of sixty years, surrounded by his females, (has no equal), neither has a very learned monk. (18)

As a sharp-horned, strong-necked bullock, the leader of the herd, is a fine sight, so is a very learned monk. (19)

As a proud lion with sharp fangs, who brooks no assault, is superior to all animals, so is a very learned monk (superior to all men). (20)

As Vâsudêva, the god with the conch, discus, and club, who fights with an irresistible strength, (has no equal), neither has a very learned monk. (21)

As a universal monarch with his fourfold army and great power, the possessor of the fourteen attributes of a king, (has no equal), neither has a very learned monk. (22)

As *S*akra the thousand-eyed, the wielder of the thunderbolt, the fortress-destroyer, the king of gods, (has no equal), neither has a very learned monk. (23)

As the rising sun, the dispeller of darkness, who burns as it were with light, (has no equal), neither has a very learned monk. (24)

As the moon, the queen of the stars, surrounded by the asterisms, when she is full at full-moon, (has no equal), neither has a very learned monk. (25)

As a well-guarded storehouse of merchants, which is filled with grain of many kinds, (has no equal), neither has a very learned monk. (26)

As the best of *G*ambû[1] trees, called Sudar*s*anâ,

---

[1] Eugenia Jambu. According to the commentators the very tree is meant from which *G*ambûdvîpa took its name. They make of the presiding (â*n*â*dh*iya) deity, the god Anâd*ri*ta. I am not prepared to say that there is such a god as Anâd*ri*ta. The name looks suspicious. I think â*n*â*dh*iya is equal to â*gñ*âsthita.

which is the abode of the presiding deity, (has no equal), neither has a very learned monk. (27)

As the best of rivers, the ocean-flowing stream *S*îtâ[1] with its dark waters, (has no equal), neither has a very learned monk. (28)

As the best of hills, high mount Mandara, on which various plants shed a bright lustre, (has no equal), neither has a very learned monk. (29)

As the ocean of inexhaustible water, the delight of Svayambhû[2], which is full of precious things of many kinds, (has no equal), neither has a very learned monk. (30)

Monks who equal the ocean in depth, who are difficult to overcome, are frightened by nobody (or nothing), and are not easily assailed, who are full of extensive learning and take care of themselves, will go to the highest place, after their Karman has been annihilated. (31)

Therefore, seeker after the highest truth, study the sacred lore, in order to cause yourself and others to attain perfection. (32)

Thus I say.

[1] According to the cosmography of the *G*ainas the *S*îtâ is a river which takes its rise in the Nîla range and falls into the Eastern ocean. The Nîla is the fourth of the six parallel mountain-barriers, the southernmost of which is the Himâlaya. (Trailôkya Dîpikâ, Umâsvâtis' Tattvârthâdhigama Sûtra, &c.)

[2] This epithet apparently refers to Vish*n*u's sleeping on the ocean.

TWELFTH LECTURE[1].

HARIKÊ*S*A.

Harikê*s*a-Bala was born in a family of *S*vapâkas (*K*â*nd*âlas); he became a monk and a sage, possessed of the highest virtues, who had subdued his senses. (1)

He observed the rules with regard to walking, begging, speaking, easing nature, and receiving and keeping (of things necessary for a monk)[2], controlled himself, and was always attentive (to his duty). (2)

He protected from sin his thoughts, speech, and body[3], and subdued his senses.

---

[1] The commentators relate a legend of the principal figure in the following lecture. We may skip his former births and begin with his last. Near the Ganges lived Balakôsh*th*a, chief of a *K*â*nd*âla tribe, called Harikê*s*a (the yellow-haired). With his wife Gaurî he had a son Bala, who in the course of time became a *G*aina monk and a great *Ri*shi. On his wanderings he once stayed in the Tinduga-grove near Benares, the presiding deity of which, a Yaksha, became his most fervent follower. One day Bhadrâ, king Kausalika's daughter, came to the Yaksha's shrine and paid homage to the idol. But seeing the dirty monk, she did not conceal her aversion. The Yaksha, however, to punish her for her want of respect for the holy man, possessed her. As no physician or conjurer could cure her madness, the Yaksha, by whom she was possessed, said she would recover only if she were offered as bride to Bala, the monk. The king agreeing, Bhadrâ became sound as before and went to the monk to choose him for her husband. Bala of course refused her. She was then married by the king to his Purôhita, Rudradêva, whose sacrifice-enclosure is the scene of the occurrences related in the Twelfth Lecture.

[2] These are the five Samitis. Compare Bhandarkar, Report on the Search for Sanskrit Manuscripts for 1883–84, p. 98, note †.

[3] These are the three Guptis. Compare Bhandarkar, loc. cit. p. 100, note *.

Once on his begging tour, he approached the enclosure of a Brahmanical sacrifice. (3)

When (the priests) saw him coming up, emaciated by austerities, in a miserable condition, and with the poorest outfit, they laughed at him, the ruffians. (4)

Stuck up by pride of birth, those killers of animals, who did not subdue their senses, the unchaste sinners, made the following speech: (5)

'Who is that dandy coming there? he is swarthy, dreadful, with a turned-up nose, miserably clad, a very devil[1] of a dirty man, with a filthy cloth put on his neck? (6)

'Who are you, you monster? or for what purpose have you come here? you miserably clad devil of a dirty man! go, get away! why stand you there?' (7)

At this turn the Yaksha, who lived in the Tinduka-tree, had compassion on the great sage, and making his own body invisible spoke the following words: (8)

"I am a chaste *S*rama*n*a, controlling myself; I have no property, nothing belonging to me, and do not cook my food; I have come for food which is dressed for somebody else at the time when I call. (9)

"You give away, eat, and consume plenty of food; know that I subsist by begging; let the mendicant get what is left of the rest." (10)

'The dinner has been prepared for Brâhma*n*as, it has been got ready especially for ourselves and for

---

[1] Pi*s*â*k*a. A full description of a Pi*s*â*k*a is given in the Uvâsaga Dasâo, § 94 of Hoernle's edition.

us exclusively; we shall not give you such food and drink; why stand you there?' (11)

"The husbandmen throw the corn on high ground and on low ground[1], hoping (for a return). For the like motive give unto me; I may be the field which may produce merit (as the return for your benevolence)." (12)

'All the world knows that we are (as it were) the field on which gifts sown grow up as merit; Brâhma*n*as of pure birth and knowledge are the blessed fields.' (13)

"Those who are full of anger and pride, who kill, lie, steal, and own property, are Brâhma*n*as without pure birth and knowledge; they are very bad fields. (14)

"You are only the bearer of words as it were, you do not understand their meaning, though you have learned the Vêdas. The saints call at high and lowly (houses); they are the blessed fields." (15)

'Detractor of the learned doctors, how dare you speak thus in our presence! This food and drink should rather rot, than we should give it you, Nirgrantha[2].' (16)

"If you do not give me what I ask for, I who observe the Samitis, who am protected by the Guptis[3], who subdue my senses, what benefit, then, will you gain by your sacrifices?" (17)

'Are here no Kshattriyas, no priests who tend the fire, no teachers with their disciples, who will

---

[1] This reminds one of the biblical parable of the sower.

[2] The word Nirgrantha has here, besides its common meaning, *G*aina monk, another derived from its etymological meaning, 'without any tie, without restraint,' i.e. shameless.

[3] For Samiti and Gupti see notes 2 and 3 on p. 50.

beat him with a stick, or pelt him with a nut, take him by the neck, and drive him off?' (18)

On these words of the teachers, many young fellows rushed forward, and they all beat the sage with sticks, canes, and whips. (19)

At that turn king Kausalika's daughter, Bhadrâ, of faultless body, saw that the monk was beaten, and appeased the angry youngsters. (20)

'He is the very man to whom the king, impelled by the devil (who possessed me), had given me, but who would not think of me; he is the sage whom princes and gods adore, who has refused me. (21)

'He is that austere ascetic, of noble nature, who subdues his senses and controls himself; the chaste man, who would not accept me when my own father, king Kausalika, gave me to him. (22)

'He is the man of great fame and might, of awful piety and power; do not injure him who cannot be injured, lest he consume you all by the fire (of his virtue).' (23)

When the Yakshas heard these well-spoken words of (the Purôhita's) wife Bhadrâ, they came to the assistance of the sage, and kept the young men off. (24)

Appearing in the air with hideous shapes, the Asuras beat the people. When Bhadrâ saw them with rent bodies spitting blood, she spoke again thus: (25)

'You may as well dig rocks with your nails, or eat iron with your teeth, or kick fire with your feet, as treat contemptuously a monk. (26)

'Like a poisonous snake is a great sage of severe austerities, of tremendous piety and power; like a swarm of moths you will rush into a fire, if you beat a monk on his begging tour. (27)

'Prostrate yourself before him for protection, you together with all of them, if you want to save your life and your property; for in his wrath he might reduce the world to ashes.' (28)

When the Brâhma*n*a saw the disciples bowing their back and head, and holding out their hands, not minding their occupation; with streaming eyes, spitting blood, looking upwards, their eyes and tongues protruding, like as many logs of wood, he became heartbroken and dejected, and together with his wife he appeased the sage: 'Forgive us our injury and abuse, sir! (29, 30)

'Forgive, sir, these ignorant, stupid boys, that they injured you; sages are exceedingly gracious, nor are the saints inclined to wrath.' (31)

"There is not the least hatred in me, neither now, nor before, nor in future. The Yakshas attend upon me, therefore they have beaten the boys." (32)

'You know the truth and the Law; you are not angry, compassionate sage; we take refuge at your feet, we together with all of them. (33)

'We worship you, mighty sir; there is nothing in you that we do not worship; eat this dish of boiled rice seasoned with many condiments. (34)

'I have got plenty of food; eat it to do us a favour!' The noble (monk) said 'yes,' and took food and drink after having fasted a whole month. (35)

At that moment the gods caused a rain of perfumed water and flowers, and showered down heavenly treasures; they struck the drums, and in the air they praised the gift. (36)

'The value of penance has become visible, birth

appears of no value! Look at the holy Harikê*s*a, the son of a *S*vapâka, whose power is so great.' (37)

"O Brâhma*n*as, why do you tend the fire, and seek external purity by water? The clever ones say that external purity which you seek for, is not the right thing. (38)

"You (use) Ku*s*a-grass, sacrificial poles, straw and wood, you touch water in the evening and in the morning; thereby you injure living beings, and in your ignorance you commit sins again and again." (39)

'How should we sacrifice, O monk, and how avoid sinful actions? Tell us, ascetic, whom the Yakshas hold in honour, what do the clever ones declare to be the right method of sacrificing?' (40)

"Doing no injury to living beings of the six orders, abstaining from lying and from taking what is not freely given, renouncing property, women, pride, and deceit, men should live under self-restraint. (41)

"He who is well protected by the five Sa*m*varas [1] and is not attached to this life, who abandons his body [2], who is pure and does not care for his body, wins the great victory, the best of offerings." (42)

'Where is your fire, your fireplace, your sacrificial ladle? where the dried cowdung (used as fuel)? Without these things, what kind of priests can the monks be? What oblations do you offer to the fire?' (43)

---

[1] Sa*m*vara is preventing, by means of the Samitis and Guptis, the âsrava, or flowing in of the Karman upon the soul. Bhandarkar, loc. cit. p. 106.

[2] This is the Kâyôtsarga, the posture of a man standing with all his limbs immovable, by which he fortifies himself against sins, &c.

"Penance is my fire; life my fireplace; right exertion is my sacrificial ladle; the body the dried cowdung; Karman is my fuel; self-control, right exertion, and tranquillity are the oblations, praised by the sages, which I offer." (44)

'Where is your pond, and where the holy bathing-place? how do you make your ablutions or get rid of impurity? Tell us, O restrained monk whom the Yakshas hold in honour; we desire to learn it from you.' (45)

"The Law is my pond, celibacy my holy bathing-place, which is not turbid, and throughout clear for the soul[1]; there I make ablutions; pure, clean, and thoroughly cooled I get rid of hatred[2] (or impurity). (46)

"The clever ones have discovered such bathing, it is the great bath praised by the seers, in which the great seers bathe, and, pure and clean, they obtain the highest place." (47)

Thus I say.

THIRTEENTH LECTURE.

*K*ITRA AND SAMBHÛTA[3].

Being contemptuously treated for the sake of his birth (as a *K*â*nd*âla) Sambhûta took, in Hastinâpura,

---

[1] Attapasannalêsa = âtmaprasannalê*s*ya, 'in which the Lê*s*yâ is favourable for the soul.' The Lê*s*yâ is comparable to the subtile body of the orthodox philosophy. The theory of the Lê*s*yâ forms the subject of the Thirty-fourth Lecture.

[2] Dôsa, which means hatred (dvêsha) and impurity (dôsha).

[3] The stories about *K*itra and Sambhûta and the fate they

the sinful resolution (to become a universal monarch in some later birth); descending from the heavenly region Padmagulma, he was born of *K*ulanî in Kâmpilya as Brahmadatta; *K*itra, however, was born in the town Purimatâla in the great family of a merchant; when he had heard the Law, he entered the order. (1, 2)

In the town Kâmpilya, both Sambhûta and *K*itra (as they were called in a former birth) met again and told each other the reward they had realised for their good and bad actions. (3)

The universal monarch Brahmadatta, the powerful and glorious king, respectfully addressed the following words to him (who had been) his brother (in a former birth): (4)

'We were brothers once, kind to each other, loving each other, wishing well to each other. (5)

'We were slaves in the country of the Da*s*âr*n*as, then antelopes on mount Kâla*ñg*ara, then geese on the shore of M*ri*tagaṅgâ, and *S*vapâkas in the land of Kâ*s*i. (6)

'And we were gods having great power, in the regions of the gods. This is our sixth birth, in which we are separated from each other.' (7)

"Karman is produced by sinful thoughts, and you have entertained them, O king; it is by the influence of this Karman that we were separated." (8)

underwent in many births are common to Brahmans, *G*ainas, and Buddhists. The whole subject has been exhaustively dealt with by Prof. Leumann in two learned papers in the Wiener Zeitschrift für die Kunde des Morgenlandes, vol. v, pp. 1 ff., 111 ff., where an analysis of the various documents which relate this legend is given, and the Prâk*ri*t text of the Thirteenth and Fourteenth Lectures together with a German translation is published. For all details, therefore, the reader is referred to Prof. Leumann's papers.

'I had done actions derived from truth and purity, and now I enjoy their effect; is this also true in your case, *K*itra?' (9)

"Every good deed will bear its fruit to men; there is no escape from the effect of one's actions. Through riches and the highest pleasures my soul has got the reward for its virtues. (10)

"Know, Sambhûta, that you have got the reward of your virtues in the shape of great wealth and prosperity; but know, O king, that is just so with *K*itra; he also obtained prosperity and splendour. (11)

"A song of deep meaning condensed in words has been repeated in the midst of a crowd of men, (having heard) which monks of piety and virtues exert themselves in this (religion): I have become a *S*rama*n*a." (12)

'Renowned are my beautiful palaces U*kk*a, Udaya, Madhu, Karka, and Brahman: this house, full of treasures and containing the finest products of the Pa*ñk*âlas, O *K*itra[1], regard it as your own! (13)

'Surround yourself with women who dance, and sing, and make music; enjoy these pleasures, O monk; I deem renunciation a hard thing.' (14)

As the virtuous *K*itra, for old friendship's sake, loved the king who was attached to sensual pleasures, and as he had at heart his welfare, he spoke to him the following words: (15)

"All singing is but prattle, all dancing is but

---

[1] The commentator constructs *K*itra with dha*n*appabhûya: full of manifold treasures; but Prof. Leumann is probably right in taking it as a vocative.

mocking, all ornaments are but a burden, all pleasures produce but pains. (16)

"O king, pleasures which the ignorant like, but which produce pains, do not delight pious monks who care not for pleasure, but are intent on the virtues of right conduct. (17)

"Excellent king, the lowest caste of men is that of the *S*vapâkas, to which we twice belonged; as such we were loathed by all people, and we lived in the hamlets of *S*vapâkas. (18)

"In that miserable birth we lived in the hamlets of *S*vapâkas, detested by all people; then we acquired the Karman (the fruit of which we now enjoy). (19)

"You are now a king of great power and prosperity, enjoying the reward of your good actions; put from you the transitory pleasures, and enter the order for the sake of the highest good[1]! (20)

"He who in this life has done no good actions and has not practised the Law, repents of it in the next world when he has become a prey to Death. (21)

"As a lion takes hold of an antelope, so Death leads off a man in his last hour; neither mother, nor father, nor brother will, at that time, save a particle (of his life). (22)

"Neither his kinsmen, nor his friends, nor his sons, nor his relations will share his suffering, he alone has to bear it; for the Karman follows the doer. (23)

"Leaving behind bipeds and quadrupeds, his fields, his house, his wealth, his corn, and everything;

---

[1] Âdâna, explained *k*aritradharma.

against his will, and accompanied only by his Karman [1], he enters a new existence, either a good or a bad one. (24)

"When they have burned with fire on the funeral pile his forlorn, helpless corpse, his wife and sons and kinsfolk will choose another man to provide for them. (25)

"Life drags on (towards death) continuously [2]; old age carries off the vigour of man. King of the Pa*ñk*âlas, mark my words: do no fearful actions." (26)

'I, too, know just as well as you, O saint, what you have told me in your speech: pleasures will get a hold on men and are not easily abandoned by such as we are, sir. (27)

'O *K*itra, in Hastinâpura [3] I saw the powerful king (Sanatkumâra), and I took that sinful resolution in my desire for sensual pleasures. (28)

'And since I did not repent of it, this has come of it, that I still long for sensual pleasures, though I know the Law. (29)

'As an elephant, sinking down in a quagmire,

---

[1] This might be translated, as Professor Leumann suggests: possessing Karman as the germ (of his future destiny); still I prefer the meaning vouched for by the commentators, because karmabî*g*a generally means the germ, i. e. cause of Karman, see below, Thirty-second Lecture, verse 7.

[2] See Professor Leumann's remarks on this verse, l. c., p. 137 f.

[3] When Sunandâ, wife of Sanatkumâra, paid homage to Sambhûta, then a *G*aina monk, and touched his feet with the curls of her soft hair, he was possessed by the desire to become a universal monarch in reward for his penances. This is the nidâna of which the text speaks, and what I render in this connection by 'taking a resolution.' For the story itself, see my Ausgewählte Erzählungen in Mâhârâsh*t*rî, p. 5 f.

sees the raised ground but does not get to the shore, so do we who long for sensual pleasures, not follow the path of monks. (30)

'Time elapses and quickly pass the days; the pleasures of men are not permanent; they come to a man and leave him just as a bird leaves a tree void of fruit.' (31)

"If you are unable to abandon pleasure, then do noble actions, O king; following the Law, have compassion on all creatures: then you will become a god on entering a new existence. (32)

"If you have no intention of abandoning pleasure, and still long for undertakings and property, my long talk has been to no purpose. I go, king, farewell." (33)

And Brahmadatta, king of the Pa*ñk*âlas, did not act on the counsel of the saint; he enjoyed the highest pleasure, and (afterwards) sank into the deepest hell. (34)

But *K*itra the great sage, of excellent conduct and penance, was indifferent to pleasure; after he had practised the highest self-control, he reached the highest place of perfection. (35)

Thus I say.

FOURTEENTH LECTURE.

ISHUKÂRA.

Having been gods in a former existence and lived in the same heavenly region, some were born (here below) in the ancient, wealthy, and famous town called Ishukâra[1], which is beautiful like heaven. (1)

By a remnant of the merit they had acquired in their former life, they were born in noble families. Disgusted with the world and afraid of the Sa*m*sâra, they abandoned (pleasures, &c.) and took refuge in the path of the *G*inas. (2)

Two males remained bachelors, (the third became) the Purôhita (Bh*ri*gu), (the fourth) his wife Ya*s*â, (the fifth) the widely-famed king Ishukâra, and (the sixth) his wife Kamalâvatî. (3)

Overcome by fear of birth, old age, and death, their mind intent on pilgrimage, and hoping to escape the Wheel of Births, they examined pleasures and abandoned them. (4)

Both dear sons of the Brahmanical Purôhita, who was intent on works, remembered their former birth, and the penance and self-control they had then practised. (5)

Averse to human and heavenly pleasures, desiring liberation, and full of faith, they went to their father and spoke thus: (6)

'Seeing that the lot of man is transitory and precarious, and that his life lasts not long, we take no delight in domestic life; we bid you farewell: we shall turn monks.' (7)

In order to dissuade them from a life of austerities, the father replied to those (would-be) monks: 'Those versed in the Vêdas say that there will be no better world for men without sons. (8)

'My sons, after you have studied the Vêdas, and fed the priests, after you have placed your own sons

[1] In Prâk*ri*t Usuyâra (or Isuyâra). According to the Prâk*ri*t legend given in the commentary it was in the Kuru country.

at the head of your house, and after you have enjoyed life together with your wives, then you may depart to the woods as praiseworthy sages.' (9)

The young men perceiving that the Purôhita was wholly consumed, as it were, by the fire of grief, which was fed by his individual inclinations and blown into a huge flame by the wind of delusion; that he suffered much and talked a great deal in many ways; that he tried to persuade them by degrees, and that he would even bribe them with money and with objects of desire, (spoke) these words: (10, 11)

"The study of the Vêdas will not save you; the feeding of Brâhma*n*as will lead you from darkness to darkness, and the birth of sons will not save you. Who will assent to what you said? (12)

"Pleasures bring only a moment's happiness, but suffering for a very long time, intense suffering, but slight happiness; they are an obstacle to the liberation from existence, and are a very mine of evils. (13)

"While a man walks about without abandoning pleasures, and grieves day and night, while he is anxious about other people, and seeks for wealth, he comes to old age and death. (14)

"I have this, and I have not that; I must do this, and I should not do that! While he talks in this strain, the robbers (viz. time) drag him away. What foolishness is this!" (15)

'Great wealth and women, a family and exquisite pleasures: for such things people practise austerities. All this you may have for your asking.' (16)

"What avail riches for the practice of religion, what a family, what pleasures? We shall become

*S*rama*n*as, possessed of many virtues, and wander about collecting alms." (17)

'As fire is produced in the Ara*n*i-wood, as butter in milk, and oil in sesamum seed, so, my sons, is the soul[1] produced in the body; (all these things) did not exist before, they came into existence, and then they perish; but they are not permanent.' (18)

"(The soul) cannot be apprehended by the senses, because it possesses no corporeal form[2], and since it possesses no corporeal form it is eternal. The fetter of the soul has been ascertained to be caused by its bad qualities, and this fetter is called the cause of worldly existence. (19)

"Thus being ignorant of the Law, we formerly did sinful actions, and through our wrong-mindedness we were kept back and retained (from entering the order). We shall not again act in the same way. (20)

"As mankind is harassed (by the one), and taken hold of (by the other), and as the unfailing ones go by, we take no delight in the life of a householder." (21)

'Who harasses the world? who takes hold of it?

[1] Sattâ in the original; it is rendered sattva by the commentators. Perhaps sattâ is the Prâk*ri*t for svâtmâ; at any rate, the context of the next verse proves that soul is intended.

[2] Amûrta. In later philosophy mûrtatva is defined as the possessing of definite and limited form (pari*kkh*innaparimâ*n*avattvam) or the possessing of action (kriyâvattvam or vegavattvam). Amûrta dravya are with the Vai*s*eshikas: the air (âkâ*s*a), time, space, and Âtman. These are also called nityadravya. Amûrta is here apparently synonymous with arûpin, formless, compare XXXVI, 4, where dharma, adharma, akâ*s*a, and kâla are enumerated as the 'formless things without life.'

whom do you call unfailing? My sons, I am anxious to learn this.' (22)

"Mankind is harassed by Death; it is taken hold of by Old Age; the days[1] are called unfailing: know this, Father! (23)

"The day that goes by will never return; the days elapse without profit to him who acts contrary to the Law. (24)

"The day that goes by will never return; the days elapse with much profit to him who acts up to the Law." (25)

'Having lived together in one place, and both parties[2] having acquired righteousness, we shall, O my sons, afterwards go forth (as monks) and beg alms from house to house.' (26)

"He who can call Death his friend, or who can escape him, or who knows that he will not die, might perhaps decide: this shall be done to-morrow. (27)

"We will even now adopt the Law, after the adoption of which we shall not be born again. The future has nothing in store for us (which we have not experienced already). Faith will enable us to put aside attachment." (28)

(Bh*ri*gu speaks to his wife Vâsish*th*î.) 'Domestic

---

[1] Literally, the nights. It seems to have been the custom at the time when the Sûtras were composed, to reckon the time by nights, though the reckoning by days is not quite uninstanced in the Sûtras.

[2] This is the explanation of duhaô by the commentators, who apparently think that the parents and the sons are meant. The word in question is originally an adverb, but it is also (cf. Thirteenth Lecture, verse 18) taken by the commentator as a numeral, and rendered dvayô*h*. A genitive of the dual occurs in XIX, 90.

life ceases (to have attraction) for one who has lost his sons; Vâsish*th*î, the time has arrived for me to turn mendicant friar. As long as a tree retains its branches, it is really a tree; when they are lopped off, it is called a trunk. (29)

'As a bird without its wings, as a king in battle without his followers, as a merchant on a boat without his goods, even so am I without my sons.' (30)

"You have brought together all these objects of desire, and have collected many exquisitely pleasant things. Let us, therefore, fully enjoy the pleasures; afterwards we shall go forth on the road of salvation." (31)

'We have finished enjoying pleasures, my dear; our life is drawing to its close. I do not abandon pleasures for the sake of an unholy life; but looking with indifference on gain and loss, on happiness and suffering, I shall lead the life of a monk.' (32)

"May you not remember your brothers (when it is too late) like an old goose swimming against the current. Enjoy the pleasures together with me. A mendicant's life is misery." (33)

'My dear, as a snake casts off the slough of its body and goes along free and easy, even so have my sons abandoned pleasure. Why should I, being left alone, not follow them? (34)

'As the fish Rôhita[1] breaks through a weak net, even so wise men of exemplary character and famous for their austerities abandon pleasure and live as mendicants. (35)

"As the herons fly through the air and the geese too, who had rent the net, even so my sons and

[1] Cyprinus Rohita.

my husband depart. Why should I, being left alone, not follow them?" (36)

When the queen had heard that the Purôhita with his wife and sons had entered the order, abandoning pleasures and all his large property, she spoke to the king: (37)

'A man who returns, as it were, to the vomit, is not praised; but you want to confiscate[1] the property left by the Brâhma*n*a. (38)

'If the whole world and all treasures were yours, you would still not be satisfied, nor would all this be able to save you. (39)

'Whenever you die, O king, and leave all pleasant things behind, the Law alone, and nothing else in this world, will save you, O monarch. (40)

'As a bird dislikes the cage, so do I (dislike the world). I shall live as a nun, without offspring, poor, upright, without desire, without love of gain, and without hatred. (41)

'As when by a conflagration of a forest animals are burned, other beasts greatly rejoice, being under the influence of love and hate; even so we, fools that we are, being attached to pleasure, do not perceive that the world is consumed by the fire of love and hatred. (42, 43)

'Those who have enjoyed pleasures, and have renounced them, move about like the wind, and go wherever they please, like the birds unchecked in their flight. (44)

'When they[2] are caught, and held by my hand,

---

[1] It was considered a privilege of the king to confiscate the property of a man who had no heir; compare Gautama XXVIII, 42, Vasish*th*a XVII, 83–86, &c.

[2] This apparently refers to the birds mentioned in the last verse.

sir, they struggle; we shall be like them, if we are attached to pleasures. (45)

'As an unbaited (bird)[1] sees a baited one caught in the snare, even so shall we avoid every bait and walk about, not baited by anything. (46)

'Being aware that pleasures are causes for the continuance of worldly existence, as illustrated in (the above) similes of the greedy man, one should be cautious and stir as little as possible, like a snake in the presence of Suparna. (47)

'Like an elephant who has broken his fetters, go to your proper destination. O great king Ishukâri; this is the wholesome truth I have learned. (48)

'Leave your large kingdom and the pleasures which are so dear to all; abandon what pleases the senses, and what attracts; be without attachment and property; learn thoroughly the Law and give up all amusements; then practise famous and severe penance, being of firm energy[2].' (49, 50)

The commentators labour to interpret them as 'pleasures,' but that will not make good sense.

[1] Kulala in the original. Kulâla in Sanskrit denotes the wild cock, Phasianus Gallus. The word seems to be derived from kulâya by assimilation of the y to the preceding consonant, compare salilâ for saliyâ = saritâ = sarit. In the sense of bird the word kulâla seems to be used in the well-known stanza of Bhartrihari: brahmâ yena kulâlavan niyamito brahmândabhândôdare, unless here kulâla is an early corruption for kulâyin.

[2] The commentators assign these verses to the two sons of Bhrigu; but then the verses do not construe. Besides the mention of the 'large kingdom' in the first line seems to prove that the king, and not the Brahmans, is to be understood as the person addressed. In the last line I separate pagigghaha kkhâyam (scil. tavam), instead of pagiggh*ahakkhâyam. It is, however, just possible that the next verse is to be connected with the preceding ones; in that case, we must read pagiggh* and interpret it in conformity with the scholiast as a gerund.

In this way all (these) professors of the Law gradually obtained enlightenment, being frightened by birth and death, and seeking for the end of misery. (51)

Their doubts about the true doctrine were dispersed, and they realised the Bhâvanâs[1]; in a short time they reached the end of misery. (52)

The king and the queen, the Brahmanical Purôhita, his wife, and his sons, they all reached perfection. (53)

Thus I say.

FIFTEENTH LECTURE.

THE TRUE MONK[2].

He who adopts the Law in the intention to live as a monk, should live in company (with other monks), upright, and free from desire; he should abandon his former connections, and not longing for pleasures, he should wander about as an unknown beggar: then he is a true monk. (1)

Free from love he should live, a model of

---

[1] The bhâvanâs are certain meditations which are conducive to the purity of the soul. They are treated at length in a work by Hêma*k*andra, called Bhavabhâvanâ, which seems to be rather popular with the *S*vêtâmbaras. The Digambaras seem to call them Anuprêkshâs. A work in Prâk*ri*t by *S*ubha*k*andra, called Kârttikêyânuprêkshâ, is epitomised in Bhandarkar's Report for 1883–84, p. 113 ff.

[2] The name of this lecture, sa bhikkhû, is derived from the burden which runs through the whole of it and winds up every verse.

righteousness [1], abstaining from sins, versed in the sacred lore, protecting his soul (from every wrong), wise, hardy, observing everything; he who is attached to nothing, is a true monk. (2)

Ignorant of abuse and injury, a steadfast monk should be a model of righteousness, always protecting his soul (from sins), neither rash nor passionate; when he endures everything, then he is a true monk. (3)

He who is content with lowly beds and lodgings, bears heat and cold, flies and gnats, is neither rash nor passionate, and endures everything, he is a true monk. (4)

He does not expect respectful treatment, nor hospitality, nor reverence, nor, indeed, praises; he controls himself, keeps the vows, practises austerities, lives together with other monks, meditates on his soul; this is a true monk. (5)

If he does not care for his life, or abandons every delusion, if he avoids men and women, always practises austerities, and does not betray any curiosity, then he is a true monk. (6)

He who does not profess and live on divination from cuts and shreds [2], from sounds on the earth or in the air, from dreams, from diagrams, sticks, and

---

[1] Lâ*dh*ê, explained sada*n*ush*th*ânatayâ pradhâna*h*. Lâ*dh*a is also the name of a country in western Bengal, inhabited, at Mahâvîra's time, by uncivilised tribes, see part i, p. 84, note 1. The etymology of both words is doubtful.

[2] Compare the note on p. 161 of part i. The 71st chapter of Varâha Mihira's B*ri*hat Sa*m*hitâ treats of vastra*kh*êda, rents, &c. of clothes; the 51st, of aṅgavidyâ, forebodings from the body; and the 53rd, of vâstuvidyâ, property of buildings; chapters 88, 90, and 95 are devoted to the forebodings from the cries of birds, female jackals, and crows.

properties of buildings, from changes in the body, from the meaning[1] of the cries (of animals)—he is a true monk. (7)

Spells, roots, every kind of medical treatment, emetics, purgatives, fumigation, anointing of the eye, and bathing, the patient's lamentation, and his consolation—he who abstains from all these things, is a true monk. (8)

He who does not praise, or pay attention to, the warriors, Ugras[2], princes, Brâhma*n*as, Bhôgas, and artists of all sorts, who abstains from this, he is a true monk. (9)

He who does not, for earthly gain, improve his acquaintance with householders, with whom he fell in as a monk, or was in friendly relation before that time, he is a true monk. (10)

A Nirgrantha is forbidden to take from householders, if they do not give it themselves, bed, lodging,

---

[1] A conjectural rendering of vi*g*aya, which cannot be taken in its ordinary meaning 'victory.' The commentary explains it *s*ubhâ*s*ubhanirûpa*n*âbhyâsa*h*.—Notice the absence of astrology from the above list of prophetical arts practised by strolling friars apparently to insinuate themselves into the good graces of laymen and women. If Greek nativity had already risen to importance, it certainly would have been mentioned. For it has ever since held a firm hold on the Hindu mind.—This remark also applies to XX, 45. But in Sûtrak*ri*tâṅga I, 12, 9, astrology (sa*m*va*kkh*ara) is mentioned; it is, however, the ancient astrology of the Hindus, not the Greek one.

[2] The Ugras and Bhôgas were Kshattriyas. The former were, according to the *G*ainas, descendants of those whom *Ri*shabha, the first Tîrthakara, appointed to the office of kô*t*wals or prefects of towns, while the Bhôgas were descendants from those whom *Ri*shabha acknowledged as persons deserving of honour. Comp. Hoernle, Uvâsaga Dasâo, Appendix, p. 58, and my edition of the Kalpa Sûtra, p. 103, note on § 18.

drink, food, or any dainties and spices; he who is not angry at such occasions, he is a true monk. (11)

If a monk gets any food and drink, or dainties and spices, and does not feel compassion (on a sick fellow-monk) in thoughts, words, and deeds, (then he is not a true monk)[1]; but if he has his thoughts, words, and acts under strict discipline, then he is a true monk. (12)

Dish-water[2], barley-pap, cold sour gruel[3], water in which barley has been washed: such loathsome food and drink he should not despise, but call at the lowliest houses (for alms); then he is a true monk. (13)

There are many voices on the earth, of gods, of men, and of beasts, dreadful, frightful, and awful noises; if he hears them without trembling, then he is a true monk. (14)

He who understands all religious disputations, [who lives together with fellow-monks][4], who practises self-discipline[5], who meditates on his soul, who is wise, hardy, and observes everything, who

---

[1] The commentators supply these words; something to that purport is wanted to make out a consistent meaning, but there is not so much as a hint of it in the text itself. As it stands now, the meaning would be just the opposite of that given in the translation, which is in better accordance with the established custom.

[2] Âyâmaga, it is rendered â*k*âmaka in Sanskrit, and explained ava*s*râva*n*a, i.e. avasrâva*n*a. See also Leumann, Aupapâtika Sûtra, Glossar s.v.

[3] Sauvîra, explained kâ*ñg*ika, the water of boiled rice in a state of spontaneous fermentation.

[4] This is a later addition, proved to be such by the metre, though the commentators comment upon it.

[5] Khêyâ*n*ugaê. The commentators explain khêda by sa*m*yama.

is calm, and does not hurt anybody, he is a true monk. (15)

He who, not living by any art, without house, without friends, subduing his senses, free from all ties, sinless, and eating but little, leaves the house and lives single, he is a true monk. (16)

Thus I say.

SIXTEENTH LECTURE.

THE TEN CONDITIONS OF PERFECT CHASTITY.

O long-lived (*G*ambûsvâmin)! I (Sudharman) have heard the following Discourse from the Venerable (Mahâvîra):

Here[1], indeed, the venerable Sthaviras have declared ten conditions for the realisation of celibacy, by hearing and understanding which the monks will reach a high degree of self-discipline, of Sa*m*vara[2], and of contemplation, will be well protected (by the three Guptis), will guard their senses, guard their chastity, and will thus never be remiss (in the attendance on their religious duties).

What, then, are those ten conditions for the realisation of celibacy as declared by the venerable Sthaviras, by hearing and understanding which the monks will reach a high degree of self-discipline, of

---

[1] The word 'here' is explained as meaning 'in this religion of the *G*ainas.' See p. 8, note 5.

[2] Sa*m*vara is the stopping of the âsravas by means of the Samitis and Guptis, see above, p. 55, note 1.

Sa*m*vara, and of contemplation, will be well protected (by the three Guptis), will guard their senses, guard their chastity, and will thus never be remiss (in the attendance on their religious duties)?

These, then, are the ten conditions for the realisation of celibacy, &c. (all down to) duties.

1. A Nirgrantha may occupy various places for sleep or rest[1]; but a Nirgrantha should not occupy places, for sleep or rest, frequented by women, cattle, or eunuchs. The preceptor has explained the reason for this. If a Nirgrantha occupies places for sleep or rest, frequented by women, cattle, or eunuchs, then, though he be chaste, there may arise a doubt with regard to his chastity, or a sensual desire, or a feeling of remorse, or he will break the rules, or he will become a slave to passion, or he will acquire a dangerous illness of long duration, or he will desert the faith which the Kêvalin has proclaimed. Therefore a Nirgrantha should not occupy places, for sleep or rest, frequented by women, cattle, or eunuchs.

2. A Nirgrantha should not converse with women[2]. The preceptor has explained the reason for this. If a Nirgrantha converses with women &c. (all as above).

3. A Nirgrantha should not sit together with women on the same seat. The preceptor has explained the reason for this. If a Nirgrantha sits on the same seat with women, &c. (all as above).

---

[1] Literally, beds and seats.

[2] This might also be rendered: he should not talk about women.

4. A Nirgrantha should not look at, or contemplate, the charms and beauties of women. (The rest similar as above.)

5. A Nirgrantha should not, behind a screen, or curtain, or wall, listen to the screeching or screaming or singing or laughing or giggling or crying of women. (The rest similar as above.)

6. A Nirgrantha should not recall to his memory the pleasure and amusements which in the past he enjoyed together with women. (The rest similar as above.)

7. A Nirgrantha should not eat well-dressed food. (The rest similar as above.)

8. A Nirgrantha should not eat or drink to excess. (The rest similar as above.)

9. A Nirgrantha should not wear ornaments. The preceptor has explained the reason for this. If he wears ornaments, or adorns his body, he might become an object of desire to women. When he is an object of desire to women, then, &c. (the rest as in 1).

10. A Nirgrantha should not care for sounds, colours, tastes, smells, and feelings. (The rest similar as above.)

Here are some verses (to the same effect)[1]:

A monk should take up a detached lodging, free from, and not frequented by women, to preserve his chastity. (1)

A chaste monk should avoid talking with women, which delights the mind and foments love and passion. (2)

---

[1] The preceding part of this lecture is in prose.

A chaste monk should always avoid the company of, and frequent conversation with women. (3)

A chaste monk should avoid observing the body, limbs, and figure of women, their pleasant prattle and oglings. (4)

A chaste monk should avoid listening to the screeching, screaming, singing, laughing, giggling, and crying of women. (5)

A chaste monk should never recall to his mind how he had laughed and played with women, and had enjoyed them, how they became jealous, and what tricks he played to frighten them. (6)

A chaste monk should always avoid well-dressed food and drink which will soon raise his sensuality. (7)

A chaste monk should always eat his food, collected according to the rules, for the sustenance of life, in the prescribed quantity, and at the right time; concentrated in his thoughts he should not eat to excess. (8)

A chaste monk should abstain from ornaments, he should not adorn his body after the fashion of amorous people. (9)

He should always abstain from the five orders of pleasant things: sounds, colours, smells, tastes, and feelings of touch. (10)

A lodging frequented by women, their pleasant talk, their company, and looking at their charms; (11)

Their screeching, screaming, singing, and laughing, eating and sleeping together with them; well-dressed food and drink, or partaking of them to excess; (12)

And ornaments and finery[1]: these pleasant things,

---

[1] I*tth*a*m* *k*a, i.e. ish*t*a*m* *k*a. The commentators connect the

which are hard to leave, are like the poison Tâlapu*t*a[1], for a man who seeks after the true Self. (13)

He should, once for all, abandon pleasant things which are hard to leave; and concentrated in his thoughts he should avoid whatever casts a doubt on his chastity. (14)

A monk should be the steadfast charioteer, as it were, of the Law in the park of the Law[2], a vessel of righteousness, content, restrained, attentive to the duties of a chaste monk. (15)

The gods, Dânavas, Gandharvas, Yakshas, Râkshasas, and Kinnaras pay homage to a chaste monk who performs his difficult duties. (16)

This unchangeable, permanent, and eternal Law has been proclaimed by the *G*inas; through it the Siddhas have reached perfection, and others will reach it. (17)

Thus I say.

SEVENTEENTH LECTURE.

THE BAD *S*RAMA*N*A.

A Nirgrantha who has entered the order, who has learned the Law, who has received religious

---

words with the second part of the sentence. By giving to *k*a the meaning of api they interpret the two words in question as meaning 'though very pleasant.'

[1] Tâlau*d*a. According to the Dîpikâ it is a poison which kills by merely touching the palate (tâlukaspar*s*anamâtrâd êva); but this is a mere guess prompted by a wrong etymology. Tâlau*d*a stands perhaps for tâlakû*t*a, which may have been a variant of kâlakû*t*a, the deadly poison swallowed by *S*iva.

[2] Here we have twice the same word dhammârâmê, which

discipline, and who has obtained the benefit of Bôdhi which is difficult to obtain, may perhaps afterwards begin to live as he likes. (1)

(He will say:) I have a good bed and wherewithal to cover me; I obtain food and drink; I know everything that comes to pass, friend; why then should I study, sir? (2)

He who, after entering the order, always sleeps, eats, and drinks as much as he likes, and lives comfortably, is called a bad *S*rama*n*a. (3)

The sinner who despises the learning and discipline which his preceptor and teachers have taught him, is called a bad *S*rama*n*a. (4)

He who does not, as he should, strive to please his preceptor and teachers, and does not, in his arrogance, treat them with respect, is called a bad *S*rama*n*a. (5)

He who hurts living beings, seeds, and sprouts, who does not control himself, though he believes himself well-controlled, is called a bad *S*rama*n*a. (6)

He who uses a bed, a plank, a chair, a seat, or his duster[1], without having well wiped these things, is called a bad *S*rama*n*a. (7)

He who walks with great haste and without care, being overbearing and fierce, is called a bad *S*rama*n*a. (8)

I have once translated 'park of the Law,' and then 'vessel of righteousness.' It is obvious that a play on this word is intended, though I may have failed to hit the meaning of the author.

[1] Pâdakambala, usually called ra*g*ôhara*n*a. One commentator suggests, as a possible rendering, pâtrakambala 'a cloth to cover his almsbowl.'

He who carelessly inspects things[1], throwing down his duster at random, not being attentive to the inspection of things, is called a bad *S*rama*n*a. (9)

He who carelessly inspects things, his attention being absorbed by what he hears, who always slights his teachers, is called a bad *S*rama*n*a. (10)

He who is deceitful, talkative, arrogant, greedy, who does not control himself, nor share (his food, &c. with those who are in want), and is not of an amiable disposition, is called a bad *S*rama*n*a. (11)

He who is a controversialist, and ill-behaved, who perverts the truth, and delights in quarrels and contentions, is called a bad *S*rama*n*a. (12)

He who sits down on a weak, shaking seat wherever he lists, and is not careful in sitting down, is called a bad *S*rama*n*a. (13)

He who sleeps with dusty feet and does not inspect his couch, being careless about his bed, is called a bad *S*rama*n*a. (14)

He who eats milk, curds, and other things produced from milk, and does not practise austerities, is called a bad *S*rama*n*a. (15)

He who eats after sunset, and when admonished, makes an angry reply, is called a bad *S*rama*n*a. (16)

He who leaves his own teacher, and follows heretical ones, who continuously changes his school[2], being of a bad disposition, is called a bad *S*rama*n*a. (17)

---

[1] It is a monk's duty closely to inspect everything that he uses or comes in contact with, in order to avoid hurting inadvertently anything considered to possess life. This is called pa*d*ilêhâ.

[2] Gâ*n*a*m*ga*n*ika, according to the commentators one who attaches himself to another ga*n*a every half-year.

He who has left his own house, and busies himself in another's house, who lives by fortune-telling, is called a bad *S*rama*n*a. (18)

He who eats the food of his relations, and does not like living by alms[1], who reposes on the seat of the householder, is called a bad *S*rama*n*a. (19)

Such a monk, who, like the heretics[2], does not protect himself from sins, who though having the appearance (of a monk) is the lowest among his worthy brethren, is despised in this world like poison; he is nobody in this world and in that beyond. (20)

But he who always avoids these sins, and is pious amongst his brethren, is welcomed in this world like nectar; he conquers this world and the next[3]. (21)

Thus I say.

EIGHTEENTH LECTURE.

SA*Ñ*GAYA[4].

In the town of Kâmpilya there was a king, named Sa*ñ*gaya, who possessed numerous troops and war-chariots; once he went a-hunting. (1)

---

[1] Sâmudâ*n*iya, explained bhaiksham.

[2] Pa*ñk*akus*î*la, literally, those who practise the five wrong *s*îlas, whereby probably those are denoted who do not keep the five great vows of the *G*ainas. Note that the Buddhists too have their pa*ñk*as*î*la. They could therefore have been called pa*ñk*akus*î*la by the *G*ainas.

[3] The text is not settled in the last line; but there can be no doubt about the meaning.

[4] The commentators Sanskritise this name in Sa*m*yata. But however appropriate it may be to a *G*aina, it certainly does not

He was surrounded on all sides by a large host of horses, elephants, chariots, and footmen. (2)

He chased the deer on horseback in the Kêsara-park of Kâmpilya; and intent on his sport he killed there the frightened deer. (3)

Now in the Kêsara-park there was a houseless ascetic intent on sacred study and meditating on the Law. (4)

Annihilating sinful inclinations[1], he meditated in the Âsphôta-bower[2]. But the king killed the deer that fled to him. (5)

Now the king on horseback came quickly there; he saw the killed deer and saw the monk there. (6)

The king in his consternation (thought) 'I had nearly hurt the monk; ill-fated and cruel me that is mad for the sport.' (7)

Having dismissed his horse, the king bowed respectfully to the monk's feet (saying), 'Forgive me this, Reverend sir.' (8)

But the venerable monk, being plunged in silent meditation, made no reply to the king, who, therefore, was seized with fear. (9)

'I am Sañgaya; answer me, Reverend sir; a monk might by the fire of his wrath reduce millions of men to ashes.' (10)

'Be without fear, O king; but grant safety to others also; in this transient world of living beings, why are you addicted to cruelty? (11)

---

look like a king's name. The Sanskrit form of the name was probably Sañgaya or Sriñgaya, both of which frequently occur in Sanskrit literature.

[1] To render âsrava.

[2] Apphôva in the original; there are several plants which are called âsphôta.

'As you must, of necessity, one day part with everything, in this transient world of living beings, why do you cling to kingly power? (12)

'Transient like a stroke of lightning are life and beauty, which you love so much; you do not comprehend what will benefit you in the next life. (13)

'Wives and children, friends and relations, all are dependent on a man during his life; but they will not follow him in death. (14)

'The sons, in great sorrow, will remove the corpse of their father (to the cemetery); and so will parents do with their sons and relations; O king, do penance! (15)

'O king, other men, glad, and pleased, and well attired, will enjoy the riches (the deceased) had amassed, and will dally with the wives he had so well guarded. (16)

'And whatever actions he has done, good or wicked ones, with their Karman he will depart to his next existence.' (17)

Then the king was taught the Law by this monk, and was filled with a great desire for purity, and disregard of worldly objects. (18)

Sa*ñg*aya gave up his kingly power and adopted the faith of the *G*inas in the presence of the venerable monk Gardabhâli. (19)

A Kshattriya, who had abandoned his kingdom and had turned monk, said to him: 'As you look so happy in outward appearance, you must have peace of mind. (20)

'What is your name, to which Gôtra do you belong, and why have you become an ascetic[1]?

[1] Literally, a Brahman.

How do you venerate the enlightened ones [1], and how did you come to be called a well-behaved (monk)?' (21)

"My name is Sañgaya; I belong to the Gôtra of Gôtama; my teacher is Gardabhâli, who is conversant with the sacred lore and good conduct. (22)

"O great sage, the man of limited knowledge talks foolishly on these four heads [2], viz. the existence of the soul, its non-existence, idolatry, and the inefficiency of knowledge. (23)

"This has been declared by him who is enlightened, wise, liberated, conversant with the sacred lore and good conduct, who is truthful and of right energy. (24)

"Men who commit sins will go to hell; but those who have walked the road of righteousness, will obtain a place in heaven. (25)

"All this delusive talk (of the heretics) is untrue and without any meaning; I live and walk about according to the rules of self-control. (26)

---

[1] Buddhê, explained âkâryân, preceptors.

[2] These are the four great heresies: (1) that of the kriyâvâdinas, who maintain that the soul exists; (2) that of the akriyâvâdinas, who hold the reverse of the preceding doctrine; (3) that of the vainayikas, which seems to be identical with salvation by bhakti; (4) that of the agñânavâdinas, who contend that knowledge is not necessary for salvation, but tapas; this seems identical with the karmapatha. The commentators explain kriyâvâdinah 'those who believe the soul or âtman to be characterised by the verb to be (i.e. by a permanent and unchangeable existence), and ascribe to it such qualities as ubiquity or non-ubiquity, activity or non-activity.' This they treat as heresy, but from Mahâvagga VI, 31, 2 (vol. xvii, p. 109) it is evident that the Gainas were considered kriyâvâdins. The akriyâvâda is also identified with the kshanikavâda or doctrine, usually ascribed to Buddhists, that everything has but a momentary existence and is in the next moment replaced by a facsimile of itself. About these heresies compare the Sûtrakritânga I, 12; II, 2, 77.

"I know all these heresies to be contemptible; I know that there will be a life hereafter, and I know my Self. (27)

"I was an illustrious god in the Mahâprâ*n*a heaven, and reached old age as we here would say of a man who is a hundred years old; but in heaven, hundred years consist of as many Mahâpâlîs of Pâlîs [1]. (28)

"Descending from the Brahmalôka, I was born as a man. I know exactly the length of my life as well as that of other men. (29)

"A monk should abandon the manifold doctrines (of heretics), and his own fancies, and such deeds as are productive of evil everywhere. One should live up to this wisdom [2]. (30)

"I keep clear of the (superstitious) questions and the spells of laymen, exerting myself day and night (in the true religion). Thinking thus, one should practise austerities. (31)

"And what you of a pure mind asked me just now, that has been revealed by the enlightened one [3]; such knowledge makes part of the creed of the *G*inas. (32)

"A wise man believes in the existence of the soul [4],

---

[1] According to the commentary a pâlî seems to be what is commonly called palyôpamâ, and mahâpâlî a sâgarôpamâ. However the longest life of a god in Brahmalôka is but ten Sâgarôpamâs, see below, XXXVI, 225. The construction of the verse is very involved, but the drift of it cannot be mistaken.

[2] ii vi*gg*âm a*n*usa*mk*arê. I believe that vi*gg*âm here stands for vidvân, as in the following verse. The meaning would then be, 'knowing this one should live as a monk.'

[3] Buddha.

[4] The *G*ainas do not deny the existence of the soul, but the unalterable character of the soul. Hence they object to the kriyâvâda.

he avoids the heresy of the non-existence of the soul; possessing true faith one should practise the very difficult Law according to the faith. (33)

"Having learned this pure creed, which is adorned by truth and righteousness, Bharata[1] gave up Bharatavarsha and all pleasures, and entered the order. (34)

"King Sagara[2] also gave up the ocean-girt Bharatavarsha and his unrivalled kingly power, and reached perfection through his compassion. (35)

"After having given up Bharatavarsha, the famous universal monarch of great power, called Maghavan[3], entered the order. (36)

"King Sanatkumâra[4], a universal monarch of great power, placed his son on the throne, and then practised austerities. (37)

"*S*ânti[5], a universal monarch of great power, the

[1] Bharata was the eldest son of *Ri*shabha, the first Tîrthakara. He became the first *K*akravartin, or universal monarch, and resided in Ayôdhyâ. At his renunciation he was ordered by Indra himself to pluck out five handfuls of his hair as is the custom of *G*aina monks on entering the order.

[2] Sagara, king of Ayôdhyâ, was, according to the legend contained in the commentary (see R. Fick, Eine jainistische Bearbeitung der Sagara-Sage, Kiel, 1889), the younger brother of A*g*ita, the second Tîrthakara. He became the second *K*akravartin, and, in the end, he was ordained by A*g*ita. The *G*aina legend seems to be but a strangely distorted version of the story of Sagara told in the first book of the Râmâya*n*a.

[3] Maghavan, son of king Samudravi*g*aya of *S*râvastî, and his wife Bhadrâ, became the third *K*akravartin.

[4] Sanatkumâra, son of king A*s*vasêna of Hastinâpura, and his wife Sahadêvî, became the fourth *K*akravartin. The adventures of Sanatkumâra are told in a Prâk*ri*t legend, which I have published in my Ausgewählte Erzählungen in Mâhârâsh*t*rî, Leipzig, 1886, p. 20 ff.

[5] *S*ânti was the sixteenth Tîrthakara, Kunthu the seventeenth, and

bringer of peace to the world, gave up Bharatavarsha and reached perfection. (38)

"King Kunthu, the bull of the Aikshvâka race, the widely famed lord, reached perfection. (39)

"King Ara, after he had given up the sea-girt Bharatavarsha, reached perfection on becoming exempt from defilement. (40)

"After having given up his large kingdom, his army and war-chariots, his exquisite pleasures, Mahâpadma[1] practised austerities. (41)

"Having brought the (whole) earth under his sceptre, king Harishê*n*a[2], who humbled the pride (of other kings), reached perfection. (42)

"*G*aya[3], together with thousands of kings, renouncing the world, practised self-restraint. He

Ara the eighteenth Tîrthakara. Kunthu sounds strange for a proper name. I think it just possible that it is a popular or Prâk*ri*t corruption of Kakutstha, who was an Aikshvâka. As is well known, Râma is frequently called after him Kâkutstha, and so are other kings of the same line, in which he stands as the twenty-fifth according to the list in the Râmâya*n*a I, 70.

[1] Mahâpadma was the ninth *K*akravartin. His elder brother was Vish*n*ukumâra, who was ordained by Suvrata, a disciple of Munisuvrata, the twentieth Tîrthakara. He wrenched the sovereignty of the world from Namu*k*i, minister of his father Padmôttara, who had ascended the throne, by making him promise as much of his territory as he could cover with three strides. This is the Brahmanical story of Vish*n*u and Bali, for whom the *G*ainas have substituted Namu*k*i. According to them the minister Namu*k*i was, in a disputation, defeated by the *G*aina monks, and to revenge himself on them, he ordered them to quit his kingdom as soon as he got it.—Mahâpadma's residence was Hastinâpura.

[2] Harishê*n*a, son of king Mahâhari of Kâmpilya, became the tenth *K*akravartin.

[3] *G*aya, son of king Samudravi*g*aya of Râ*g*ag*ri*ha, became the eleventh *K*akravartin.

reached perfection which has been taught by the *G*inas. (43)

"Da*s*âr*n*abhadra[1], giving up his flourishing kingdom of Dasâr*n*a, turned monk; he renounced the world, being directed to do so by *S*akra himself. (44)

"Karaka*nd*u was king of Kaliṅga; Dvimukha, of Pa*ñk*âla; Nami, of Vidêha; Naggati (or rather Nagna*g*it), of Gândhâra[2]. (45)

"Nami humbled himself, being directed to do so by *S*akra himself; the king of Vidêha left the house and became a *S*rama*n*a. (46)

"These bulls of kings have adopted the faith of the *G*inas; after having placed their sons on the throne, they exerted themselves as *S*rama*n*as. (47)

"Udâya*n*a[3], the bull of the kings of Sauvîra, renounced the world and turned monk; he entered the order and reached perfection. (48)

"And thus the king of Kâ*s*i[4], exerting himself for the best truth, abandoned all pleasures, and hewed down, as it were, his Karman like a forest. (49)

"And thus king Vi*g*aya[5], whose sins were not quite annihilated[6], turned monk after he, the famous man, had quitted his excellent kingdom. (50)

---

[1] King Da*s*âr*n*abhadra was a contemporary of Mahâvîra.

[2] These are the four Pratyêkabuddhas; see p. 35, note 2.

[3] The story of Udâya*n*a (or perhaps Uddâyana) will be found in my Ausgewählte Erzählungen in Mâhârâsh*t*rî, p. 28 ff. He was contemporary with Mahâvîra.

[4] He was Nandana, the seventh Baladêva, son of king Agni*s*ikha of Benares.

[5] He was the son of king Brahmarâ*g*a of Dvârakâvatî, and eldest brother of the Vâsudêva Dvip*ri*sh*t*a or Dvipush*t*i.

[6] To render a*n*a*tth*âkitti, of which the commentators offer several explanations, rendering it anârttâkîrti and anash*t*akîrti. A various reading â*n*a*tth*âkitti is mentioned, and explained â*gñ*â-artha-âk*ri*ti.

"And thus the royal seer Mahâbala[1] practised severe penance with an undistracted mind, and took upon himself the glory (of self-control). (51)

"Why should a wise man, for bad reasons, live on earth like a madman, since those persons (mentioned above) who reached eminence, exerted themselves strongly? (52)

"I have spoken true words able to promote virtue; some have been saved, some are being saved, and some will be saved. (53)

"Why should a wise man, for bad reasons, bring affliction upon himself? He who has become free from all ties and sins, will reach perfection." (54)

Thus I say.

NINETEENTH LECTURE.

THE SON OF M*RI*GÂ.

In the pleasant town of Sugrîva, which is adorned with parks and gardens, there was the king Balabhadra and M*ri*gâ, the principal queen. (1)

Their son Bala*s*rî, also known as M*ri*gâputra (i. e. son of M*ri*gâ), the darling of his father and mother, was crown-prince, a (future) lord of ascetics. (2)

In his palace Nandana he dallied with his wives, like the god Dôgundaga[2], always happy in his mind. (3)

---

[1] Mahâbala was the son of king Bala of Hastinâpura. He lived at the time of Vimala, the thirteenth Tîrthakara.

[2] According to the commentators the Dôgundaka gods are the trâyastri*ms*a gods. The Sanskrit of dôgundaga would be dvikundaka.

Standing at a window of his palace[1], the floor of which was inlaid with precious stones and jewels, he looked down on the squares, places, and roads of the town. (4)

Once he saw pass there a restrained *S*rama*n*a, who practised penance, self-restraint, and self-control, who was full of virtues, and a very mine of good qualities. (5)

M*ri*gâputra regarded him with fixed eyes, trying to remember where he had seen the same man before. (6)

While he looked at the saint, and his mind became pure, the remembrance of his former birth came upon him as he was plunged in doubt. (7)

When the remembrance of his former birth came upon the illustrious M*ri*gâputra, he remembered his previous birth and his having been then a *S*rama*n*a. (8)

Being not delighted with pleasures, but devoted to self-control, he went to his father and mother, and spoke as follows: (9)

'I have learned the five great vows; (I know) the suffering (that awaits the sinner) in hell or in an existence as a brute; I have ceased to take delight in the large ocean (of the Sa*m*sâra); therefore, O mother, allow me to enter the order. (10)

'O mother, O father, I have enjoyed pleasures which are like poisonous fruit: their consequences are painful, as they entail continuous suffering. (11)

'This body is not permanent, it is impure and of

[1] I separate the words pâsây*-*âlôya*n*a*tth*iô. The commentators take them for a compound; but then the preceding part of the sentence would not construe. It is an irregular sandhi, instances of which, however, are not unfrequent.

impure origin; it is but a transitory residence (of the soul) and a miserable vessel of suffering. (12)

'I take no delight in this transitory body which one must leave sooner or later, and which is like foam or a bubble. (13)

'And this vain human life, an abode of illness and disease, which is swallowed up by old age and death, does not please me even for a moment. (14)

'Birth is misery, old age is misery, and so are disease and death, and ah, nothing but misery is the Sa*m*sâra, in which men suffer distress. (15)

'Leaving behind my fields, house, and gold, my son and wife, and my relations, leaving my body I needs must, one day, depart. (16)

'As the effect of Kimpâka-fruit[1] is anything but good, so the effect of pleasures enjoyed is anything but good. (17)

'He who starts on a long journey with no provisions, will come to grief on his way there, suffering from hunger and thirst. (18)

'Thus he who without having followed the Law, starts for the next world, will come to grief on his way there, suffering from illness and disease. (19)

'He who starts on a long journey with provisions, will be happy on his way there, not suffering from hunger and thirst. (20)

'Thus he who after having followed the Law, starts for the next world, will be happy on his journey there, being exempt from Karman and suffering. (21)

'As when a house is on fire, the landlord carries away valuable things and leaves behind those of

[1] Cucumis Colocynthus.

no value; so when the whole world is on fire, as it were, by old age and death, I shall save my Self, if you will permit me.' (22, 23)

To him his parents said: "Son, difficult to perform are the duties of a *S*rama*n*a; a monk must possess thousands of virtues. (24)

"Impartiality towards all beings in the world, whether friends or enemies, and abstention from injury to living beings throughout the whole life: this is a difficult duty. (25)

"To be never careless in abstaining from falsehood, and to be always careful to speak wholesome truth: this is a difficult duty. (26)

"To abstain from taking of what is not given, even of a toothpick, &c.; and to accept only alms free from faults: this is a difficult duty. (27)

"To abstain from unchastity after one has tasted sensual pleasures, and to keep the severe vow of chastity: this is a very difficult duty. (28)

"To give up all claims on wealth, corn, and servants, to abstain from all undertakings, and not to own anything: this is a very difficult duty. (29)

"Not to eat at night any food of the four kinds[1], not to put away for later use or to keep a store (of things one wants): this is a very difficult duty. (30)

"Hunger and thirst, heat and cold, molestation by flies and gnats, insults, miserable lodgings, pricking grass, and uncleanliness, blows and threats, corporal punishment and imprisonment, the mendicant's life and fruitless begging: all this is misery. (31, 32)

"Such a life is like that of pigeons (always afraid of

---

[1] I.e. food, drink, dainties, and spices.

dangers); painful is the plucking out of one's hair; difficult is the vow of chastity and hard to keep (even) for a noble man. (33)

"My son, you are accustomed to comfort, you are tender and cleanly[1]; you are not able, my son, to live as a *S*rama*n*a. (34)

"No repose as long as life lasts; the great burden of duty is heavy like a load of iron, which is difficult to be carried, O son. (35)

"As it is difficult to cross the heavenly Ganges, or to swim against the current, or to swim with one's arms over the sea, so it is difficult to get over the ocean of duties. (36)

"Self-control is untasteful like a mouthful of sand, and to practise penance is as difficult as to walk on the edge of a sword. (37)

"It is difficult (always to observe the rules of) right conduct with one's eyes for ever open like (those of) a snake[2], O son; it is difficult to eat iron grains, as it were. (38)

"As it is very difficult to swallow burning fire, so is it difficult for a young man to live as a *S*rama*n*a. (39)

"As it is difficult to fill a bag[3] with wind,

---

[1] Literally, well washed or bathed.

[2] This appears to be the meaning of the words ahîv*ê*ganta-di*tth*îê. We might perhaps take ahîv* for ahiva*m* = ahivat, in which case the construction of the sentence would be grammatically correct. An alternative rendering would be: '(A monk) like a snake must have his eyes always open on the difficult conduct, O son.' It is a well-known fact that snakes cannot shut their eyes as other animals.

[3] Kotthala, a Dê*s*î-word for ku*s*ûla, granary, see Hêma*k*andra, Dê*s*î Kôsha 2, 48. The commentators render it by 'cloth.'

so is it difficult for a weak man to live as a *S*ramana. (40)

"As it is difficult to weigh Mount Mandara in a balance, so it is difficult to live as a *S*ramana with a steady and fearless mind. (41)

"As it is difficult to swim over the sea with one's arms, so it is difficult for one whose mind is not pacified, (to cross) the ocean of restraint. (42)

"Enjoy the fivefold[1] human pleasures. After you have done enjoying pleasures, O son, you may adopt the Law." (43)

He answered: 'O father and mother, it is even thus as you have plainly told; but in this world nothing is difficult for one who is free from desire. (44)

'An infinite number of times have I suffered dreadful pains of body and mind, repeatedly misery and dangers. (45)

'In the Samsâra, which is a mine of dangers and a wilderness of old age and death, I have undergone dreadful births and deaths. (46)

'Though fire be hot here, it is infinitely more so there (viz. in hell)[2]; in hell I have undergone suffering from heat. (47)

'Though there may be cold here, it is of infinitely greater intensity there; in hell I have undergone suffering from cold. (48)

---

[1] Viz. those of the five senses.

[2] The description of hell is a favourite theme with the monks of all ages and all religions; and the *G*aina monks are not behind others in the treatment of this gruesome subject. A detailed description of the different hells will be found in the fifth lecture of the first book of the Sûtrak*ri*tânga. I remember a yati showing me, with much complacency, a manuscript of the latter work adorned with lively illustrations of the most exquisite tortures.

'An infinite number of times have I been roasted over a blazing fire in an oven, screaming loud, head down and feet aloft. (49)

'In the desert which is like a forest on fire, on the Va*g*ravâlukâ and the Kadambavâlukâ[1] rivers, I have been roasted an infinite number of times. (50)

'Being suspended upside down over a boiler, shrieking, with no relation to help me, I was cut to pieces with various saws[2], an infinite number of times. (51)

'I have suffered agonies when I was fastened with fetters on the huge *S*âlmalî tree, bristling with very sharp thorns, and then pushed up and down. (52)

'An infinite number of times have I been crushed like sugar-cane in presses, shrieking horribly, to atone for my sins, great sinner that I was. (53)

'By black and spotted wild dogs[3] I have, ever so many times, been thrown down, torn to pieces, and lacerated, screaming and writhing. (54)

'When I was born in hell for my sins, I was cut, pierced, and hacked to pieces with swords and daggers, with darts and javelins. (55)

'I have been forcibly yoked to a car of red-hot iron full of fuel[4], I have been driven on with a goad

---

[1] These are two rivers in hell; the sand of the one consists of va*g*ra (either steel-filings or diamonds), and that of the other, of turmeric.

[2] Karavattakarakayâîhi*m* = karapattrakraka*k*âdibhi*h*.

[3] Kôlasu*n*aya, explained by *s*ûkara*s*van, hog-dog, which may be a kind of hog or dog, probably the latter.

[4] Samilâ *g*ue. The commentators render *g*ue by yuga and yuta, and do not explain samilâ, which they treat as a Sanskrit word. I think it is the Prâk*ri*t of samidh, compare vi*gg*ulâ = vidyut, salilâ = sarit.

and thongs, and have been knocked down like an antelope[1]. (56)

'On piles, in a blazing fire, I have forcibly been burnt and roasted like a buffalo, in atonement for my sins. (57)

'An infinite number of times have I violently been lacerated by birds whose bills were of iron and shaped like tongs, by devilish vultures[2]. (58)

'Suffering from thirst I ran towards the river Vaitaranî to drink its water, but in it I was killed (as it were) by blades of razors[3]. (59)

'When suffering from the heat, I went into the forest in which the trees have a foliage of daggers; I have, ever so many times, been cut to pieces by the dropping dagger-leaves. (60)

'An infinite number of times have I suffered hopelessly from mallets and knives, forks and maces, which broke my limbs. (61)

'Ever so many times have I been slit, cut, mangled, and skinned with keen-edged razors, knives, and shears. (62)

'As[4] an antelope I have, against my will, been

---

[1] Roggho = risya, see Hêmakandra, Dêsî Kôsha 7, 12.

[2] Dhaṅka gridhra. The commentators offer no explanation of dhaṅka, but only say that they are not real vultures as there are no animals in hell. Therefore they must be vaikriya, i. e., in our case, demons who have adopted the shape of vultures.

[3] The water of the river Vaitaranî consists of a very caustic acid.

[4] Here and in the following verses the suffering of Mrigâputra as an animal and a plant seems to be described. But in verse 68 the scene is again laid in hell. The first word in verse 63, &c., 'as,' would literally be 'like' (viva in the original text), but in rendering it by 'like,' we have to assume that as a denizen of hell he is treated in the manner described, which seems rather strained.

caught, bound, and fastened in snares and traps, and frequently I have been killed. (63)

'As a fish I have, against my will, been caught with hooks and in bow-nets; I have therein been scraped, slit, and killed, an infinite number of times. (64)

'As a bird I have been caught by hawks, trapped in nets, and bound with bird-lime, and I have been killed, an infinite number of times. (65)

'As a tree I have been felled, slit, sawn into planks, and stripped of the bark by carpenters with axes[1], hatchets, &c., an infinite number of times. (66)

'As iron I have been malleated, cut, torn, and filed by blacksmiths[2], an infinite number of times. (67)

'I have been made to drink hissing molten copper, iron, tin, and lead under horrid shrieks, an infinite number of times. (68)

'You like meat minced or roasted; I have been made to eat, ever so many times, poisoned meat, and red-hot to boot. (69)

'You like wine, liquor, spirits, and honey[3]; I have been made to drink burning fat and blood. (70)

'Always frightened, trembling, distressed, and suffering, I have experienced the most exquisite pain and misery. (71)

'I have experienced in hell sharp, acute and

---

[1] Kuhâ*d*â = ku*th*âra; comp. piha*d*a = pi*th*ara. The form kuhârâ occurs in Guzeratî, Sindhî, and Panjâbî.

[2] Kumâra; this is obviously the modern kamâr 'blacksmith' (derived from karmakâra); and it is of interest to find this form in an old text like the Uttarâdhyayana.

[3] To render surâ, sîdhu, mairêya, and madhu.

severe, horrible, intolerable, dreadful, and formidable pain. (72)

'O father, infinitely more painful is the suffering in hell than any suffering in the world of men. (73)

'In every kind of existence I have undergone suffering which was not interrupted by a moment's reprieve.' (74)

To him his parents said: "Son, a man is free to enter the order, but it causes misery to a *S*rama*n*a that he may not remedy any ailings." (75)

He answered: 'O father and mother, it is even thus as you have plainly told; but who takes care of beasts and birds in the woods? (76)

'As a wild animal[1] by itself roams about in the woods, thus I shall practise the Law by controlling myself and doing penance. (77)

'When in a large forest a wild animal falls very sick at the foot of a tree, who is there to cure it? (78)

'Or who will give it medicine? or who will inquire after its health? or who will get food and drink for it, and feed it? (79)

'When it is in perfect health, it will roam about in woods and on (the shores of) lakes in search of food and drink. (80)

'When it has eaten and drunk in woods and lakes, it will walk about and go to rest according to the habits of wild animals. (81)

'In the same way a pious monk goes to many places and walks about just as the animals, but afterwards he goes to the upper regions. (82)

[1] Miga = m*ri*ga, literally 'antelope;' but here as frequently the word has apparently the more general meaning 'wild animal.'

'As a wild animal goes by itself to many places, lives in many places, and always gets its food; thus a monk on his begging-tour should not despise nor blame (the food he gets). (83)

'I shall imitate this life of animals.' "Well, my son, as you please." With his parents' permission he gave up all his property. (84)

'I shall imitate this life of animals, which makes one free from all misery, if you will permit me.' "Go, my son, as you please." (85)

When he had thus made his parents repeat their permission, he gave up for ever his claims in any property, just as the snake casts off its slough. (86)

His power and wealth, his friends, wives, sons, and relations he gave up as if he shook off the dust from his feet, and then he went forth. (87)

He observed the five great vows, practised the five Samitis, and was protected by the three Guptis[1]; he exerted himself to do mental as well as bodily penance. (88)

He was without property, without egoism, without attachment, without conceit[2], impartial towards all beings, whether they move or not. (89)

He was indifferent to success or failure (in begging), to happiness and misery, to life and death, to blame and praise, to honour and insult. (90)

He turned away from conceit and passions, from injurious, hurtful, and dangerous actions[3], from gaiety and sadness; he was free from sins and fetters. (91)

---

[1] See notes 2 and 3 on p. 50.

[2] Gârava = gaurava or garva. Dîpikâ: *ri*ddhigârava-rasagârava-sâtâgârava iti garvatrayarahita*h*.

[3] To render da*n*dasallabhaêsu.

He had no interest in this world and no interest in the next world; he was indifferent to unpleasant and pleasant things [1], to eating and fasting. (92)

He prevented the influx of Karman (âsrava) through all bad channels [2]; by meditating upon himself he obtained praiseworthy self-purification and sacred knowledge. (93)

Thus he thoroughly purified himself by knowledge, right conduct, faith, penance, and pure meditations, and after having lived many years as a *S*rama*n*a, he reached perfection after breaking his fast once only every month. (94, 95)

Thus act the enlightened ones, the learned, the clever; like M*ri*gâputra they turn away from pleasures. (96)

When you have heard the words of the illustrious and famous son of M*ri*gâ, his perfect practise of austerities, and his liberation, famous in the three worlds, you will despise wealth, the cause of misery, and the fetter of egoism, the cause of many dangers, and you will bear the excellent and pleasant yoke of the Law that leads to the great happiness of Nirvâ*n*a. (97, 98)

Thus I say.

---

[1] Vâsî*k*anda*n*akappô. The author of the Ava*k*ûri explains this phrase thus: he did not like more a man who anoints himself with sandal than a mason. Apparently he gives to vâsa the meaning 'dwelling;' but I think that the juxtaposition of *k*andana calls for a word denoting a bad-smelling substance, perhaps 'ordure.'

[2] Literally 'door.' The meaning of the line will be fully rendered and the simile at least partially be preserved by the following less literal translation: he shut the door, as it were, to evil influences. For the âsrava, see above, p. 55, note 1.

TWENTIETH LECTURE.

THE GREAT DUTY OF THE NIRGRANTHAS.

Piously adoring the perfected and the restrained saints, listen to my true instruction which (teaches the real) profit (of men), religion, and liberation[1]. (1)

King *S*rê*n*ika[2], the ruler of Magadha, who possessed many precious things, once made a pleasure-excursion to the Ma*nd*ikukshi *K*aitya[3]. (2)

It was a park like Nandana[4], with trees and creepers of many kinds, peopled by various birds, and full of various flowers. (3)

There he saw a restrained and concentrated saint sitting below a tree, who looked delicate and accustomed to comfort. (4)

When the king saw his figure, his astonishment at that ascetic's figure was very great and unequalled. (5)

'O his colour, O his figure, O the loveliness of the noble man, O his tranquillity, O his perfection, O his disregard for pleasures!' (6)

---

[1] Atthadhammagai*m* = arthadharmagati. I think this equal to artha dharma môksha, though the commentators offer a different explanation by making gati mean *gñ*âna. The phrase is derived from the typical expression kâmârthadharmamôksha by leaving out kâma, which of course could not be admitted by ascetics.

[2] He is identical with Bimbisâra of the Buddhists; see my edition of the Kalpa Sûtra, introduction, p. 2.

[3] The following verses prove that *k*aitya denotes park here as the word is explained by the scholiast in IX, 9.

[4] Nandana is Indra's park.

Adoring his feet and keeping him on his right side (he sat down), neither too far off nor too close by, and asked him with his hands clasped : (7)

'Though a young nobleman, you have entered the order ; in an age fit for pleasure you exert yourself as a *S*rama*n*a, O ascetic ; I want to hear you explain this.' (8)

"I am without a protector, O great king ; there is nobody to protect me, I know no friend nor any one to have sympathy with me." (9)

Then king *S*rê*n*ika, the ruler of Magadha, laughed : 'How should there be nobody to protect one so accomplished as you ?' (10)

'I am the protector of religious men[1] ; O monk ; enjoy pleasures together with your friends and relations ; for it is a rare chance to be born as a human being.' (11)

"You yourself are without a protector, *S*rê*n*ika, ruler of Magadha ; and as you are without a protector, how can you protect anybody else ?" (12)

When the saint had addressed this unprecedented speech to the king, who was greatly moved and astonished, and struck with astonishment, (he answered)[2] : (13)

'I have horses, elephants, and subjects, a town and a seraglio, power and command : enjoy human pleasures. (14)

'In possession of so great means, which permit the owner to enjoy all pleasures, how could he be

---

[1] Bhadantâ*n*a*m*.

[2] The verb is wanting in this verse, and there is an apparent tautology in the words as they now stand. This is an obvious mark of a corruption in the text, which, however, I do not know how to remove by a plausible conjecture.

without protection? Reverend sir, you speak untruth.' (15)

"O king, you do not know the meaning and origin[1] of (the word) 'without protection,' nor how one comes to be without protection or with protection, O ruler of men. (16)

"Hear, O great king, with an undistracted mind in what way a man can be said to be 'without protection,' and with what purpose I have said all this. (17)

"There is a town Kau*s*âmbî by name, which is among towns what Indra[2] is (among the gods); there lived my father, who possessed great wealth. (18)

"In my childhood, O great king, I caught a very bad eye-disease and a severe burning fever in all my limbs, O ruler of men. (19)

"My eyes ached as if a cruel enemy thrust a sharp tool in the hollow of my body. (20)

"In the back, the heart[3], and the head, I suffered

[1] Pottha*m* or po*kkh*a*m*. The commentators are at a loss to give an etymology of this word, or rather have a choice of them to offer, which comes to the same thing, and proves that nothing certain was known. If potthâ is the correct form, it may be derived from pra+ut+sthâ, and mean 'origin;' if po*kkh*â or pu*kkh*â is the right spelling it is p*ri**kkh*â, and may mean 'etymology.'

[2] Purâ*n*a purabhêda*n*î. As usual the commentators give a purely etymological explanation. But it is obvious that purabhêdana must have a similar meaning as purandara = Indra, or purabhid *S*iva. The latter word occurs in later literature only, and, besides, *S*iva does not yet seem to have been generally acknowledged as the supreme god, when and where the *G*aina Sûtras were composed. The Vedic word pûrbhid, 'destroyer of castles,' also presents itself as an analogy; though it is not yet the exclusive epithet of a god, it is frequently applied to Indra.

[3] To render antari*kkh*a or antarittha. The Guzeraty translation renders it h*ri*daya.

dreadful and very keen pains equal to a stroke of lightning. (21)

"Then the best physicians came to my help, who cure by their medical art and by spells, who were versed in their science, and well knew spells and roots. (22)

"They tried to cure me according to the fourfold science[1] which they had been taught; but they could not rid me of my pains: hence I say that I am without protection. (23)

"My father would have spent all he possessed, for my sake; but he could not rid me of my pains, hence I say that I am without protection. (24)

"My mother, O great king, was agonized with grief about her son; but she could not, &c. (25)

"O great king, my own brothers, the elder and younger ones, could not rid me of my pains, &c. (26)

"O great king, my own sisters, the elder and younger ones, could not, &c. (27)

"O great king, my loving and faithful wife moistened my breast with the tears of her eyes. (28)

"The poor lady did not eat, nor drink, nor bathe, nor use perfumes, wreaths, and anointment, with my knowledge or without it. (29)

"O great king, she did not leave[2] my side even for a moment; but she could not rid me of my pains, hence I say that I am without protection. (30)

"Then I said: It is very hard to bear pains again and again in the endless Circle of Births. (31)

---

[1] *K*âuppâya=*K*atu*h*pâda. Four branches of medical science are intended.

[2] Phi*tt*ai=bhra*s*yati, Hêma*k*andra's Prâk*ri*t Grammar, iv, 177.

"If I, for once, shall get rid of these great pains, I shall become a houseless monk, calm, restrained, and ceasing to act. (32)

"While I thought so, I fell asleep, O ruler of men; and after that night my pains had vanished. (33)

"Then in the morning of the next day I took leave of my relations and became a houseless monk, calm, restrained, and ceasing to act. (34)

"Thus I became the protector of myself and of others besides, of all living beings, whether they move or not. (35)

"My own Self is the river Vaitara*n*î, my own Self the *S*âlmalî tree[1]; my own Self is the miraculous cow Kâmaduh, my own Self the park Nandana. (36)

"My own Self is the doer and undoer of misery and happiness; my own Self, friend and foe, according as I act well or badly. (37)

"But there is still another want of protection, O king; hear, therefore, O king, attentively with concentrated thoughts, how some easily discouraged men go astray after having adopted the Law of the Nirgranthas[2]. (38)

"If an ordained monk, through carelessness, does not strictly keep the great vows, if he does not restrain himself, but desires pleasure, then his fetters will not be completely cut off. (39)

"One who does not pay constant attention to his walking, his speaking, his begging, his receiving and keeping (of things necessary for a monk), and his

---

[1] See above, p. 94.

[2] The verses 38–53 are apparently a later addition because (1) the subject treated in them is not connected with that of the foregoing part, and (2) they are composed in a different metre.

easing nature [1], does not follow the road trod by the Lord. (40)

"One who for a long time wears a shaven crown and mortifies himself, but who is careless with regard to the vows, and neglects penance and self-control, will not be a winner in the battle (of life). (41)

"He is empty like a clenched [2] fist, (of no value) like an uncoined [3] false Kârshâpa*n*a or like a piece of glass resembling turquoise, he is held lightly by men of discernment. (42)

"He who has the character of a sinner, though he lays great stress on the outward signs of his calling [4] as a means of living; he who does not control himself, though he pretends to do so; will come to grief for a long time. (43)

"As the poison Kâlakû*t*a kills him who drinks it; as a weapon cuts him who awkwardly handles it; as a Vêtâla kills him who does not lay him; so the Law harms him who mixes it up with sensuality. (44)

"He who practises divination from bodily marks and dreams, who is well versed in augury and superstitious rites, who gains a sinful living by practising magic tricks [5], will have no refuge at the time (of retribution). (45)

"The sinner, always wretched, goes from darkness

---

[1] These are the five Samitis, see above, p. 50.

[2] Pollâ or pullâ, explained anta*h*-sushira 'hollow in the middle.'

[3] Ayantita = ayantrita. My translation is but conjectural. Perhaps the regular coins are not meant, but stamped lumps of metal, which were current long before coins were introduced.

[4] Literally, 'the flag of the seers;' the broom &c. are meant.

[5] Kuhê*d*aviggâ.

to darkness, to utter misery; the unholy man who breaks the rules of monks, rushes, as it were, to hell, and to be born again as a brute. (46)

"He who accepts forbidden alms, viz. such food as he himself asks for, as has been bought for his sake, or as he gets regularly (as by right and custom), who like fire devours everything, will go to hell from here, after having sinned. (47)

"A cut-throat enemy will not do him such harm as his own perversity will do him; the man without pity will feel repentance in the hour of death. (48)

"In vain he adopts nakedness, who errs about matters of paramount interest; neither this world nor the next will be his; he is a loser in both respects in the world. (49)

"Thus the self-willed sinner who leaves the road of the highest *G*inas, who with the appetite of an osprey is desirous of pleasure, will grieve in useless sorrow. (50)

"A wise man who hears this discourse, an instruction full of precious wisdom, and who deserts every path of the wicked, should walk the road of the great Nirgranthas. (51)

"He who possesses virtuous conduct and life, who has practised the best self-control, who keeps from sinful influences[1], and who has destroyed his Karman, will reach (in the end) the greatest, best, and permanent place (viz. mukti)." (52)

Thus the austere and calm, great ascetic and great sage who kept great vows and possessed great fame, preached at great length this great sermon: the great duty of the Nirgranthas. (53)

---

[1] Nirâsava = nirâsrava. For the âsravas, see p. 55, note 1.

And king *S*rê*n*ika, pleased, spoke thus: 'You have truly shown what it is to be without protection. (54)

'You have made the best use of human birth, you have made a true gain, O great sage, you are a protector (of mankind at large) and of your relations, for you have entered the path of the best *G*inas. (55)

'You are the protector of all unprotected beings, O ascetic; I ask you to forgive me: I desire you to put me right. (56)

'That by asking you I have disturbed your meditation, and that I invited you to enjoy pleasures, all this you must forgive me.' (57)

When the lion of kings had thus, with the greatest devotion, praised the lion of houseless monks, he, together with his wives, servants, and relations, became a staunch believer in the Law, with a pure mind. (58)

The ruler of men, with the hair on his body joyfully erected, bowed his head (to the monk), keeping him on his right side, and departed. (59)

And the other, rich in virtues, protected by the three Guptis, and abstaining from injuring (living beings) in the three ways (viz. by thought, words, and acts), travelled about on the earth, free like a bird, and exempt from delusion. (60)

Thus I say.

TWENTY-FIRST LECTURE.

SAMUDRAPÂLA.

In *K*ampâ there lived a *S*râvaka, the merchant Pâlita, who was a disciple of the noble and venerable Mahâvîra. (1)

As a *S*râvaka he was well versed in the doctrines of the Nirgranthas. Once he went by boat to the town of Pihu*nd*a on business. (2)

A merchant gave him his daughter while he was doing business in Pihu*nd*a. When she was big with child, he took her with him on his returning home. (3)

Now the wife of Pâlita was delivered of a child at sea; as the boy was born at sea (samudra), he was named Samudrapâla. (4)

Our merchant, the *S*râvaka, went leisurely to *K*ampâ, to his house; in his house the boy grew up surrounded by comfort. (5)

He studied the seventy-two arts, and acquired knowledge of the world[1]; he was in the bloom of youth, and had a fine figure and good looks. (6)

His father procured him a beautiful wife, Rûpi*n*î, with whom he amused himself in his pleasant palace, like a Dôgundaga god[2]. (7)

Once upon a time he saw from the window of his palace a man sentenced to death, dressed for execution, on his way to the place of execution. (8)

---

[1] To render nîtikôvida.

[2] For Dôgundaga, see above, p. 88, note 2.

Agitated by what he saw, Samudrapâla spoke thus: 'Of wicked actions this is the bad result.' (9)

He became enlightened at once, the venerable man, and he was immensely agitated; he took leave of his parents, and entered the state of houselessness. (10)

Abandoning the great distress to which the worldly[1] are liable, the great delusion, and whatever causes fear, one should adopt the Law of monks[2], the vows, the virtues, and the (endurance of) calamities. (11)

One should keep the five great vows, viz. not to kill, to speak the truth, not to steal, to be chaste, to have no property whatever; a wise man should follow the Law taught by the *G*inas. (12)

A monk should have compassion on all beings, should be of a forbearing character, should be restrained and chaste, and abstaining from everything sinful; he should live with his senses under control. (13)

Now and then[3] he should travel in one country,

---

[1] Saggantha = sagrantha, which is obviously the opposite of nirgrantha. The commentators correct sa*m*ga*m*tha in sa*m*ga*m* *k*a. The original reading is in MS. B. A. has sa*m*ga*m*tha, and so had C. originally, but it corrects the tha into *k*a. According to the commentators we should translate: abandoning worldly attachment which causes great distress, great delusion, black (Lê*s*yâ), and dangers, one should, &c.

[2] Paryâya-dharma. Paryâya means a state under which a substance presents itself. Here is meant the state of the soul in pravra*g*yâ, i.e. *s*râma*n*ya-paryâya; compare the expressions *kh*admastha-paryâya and kêvali-paryâya. Paryâya-dharma is here equal to pravra*g*yâ-dharma, Law of the monks.

[3] Kâlê*n*a kâla*m*, the commentators supply kurvan, and explain the passage as follows: kâlêna, i.e. in a paurushî (four

taking into consideration its resources and his own ability; like a lion he should not be frightened by any noise; and whatever words he hears, he should not make an improper reply. (14)

In utter indifference he should walk about, and bear everything, be it pleasant or unpleasant; he should not approve of everything everywhere, nor care for[1] respectful treatment or blame. (15)

There are many opinions here among men, which a monk places in their true light; there will rise many dangerous and dreadful calamities, caused by gods, men, or animals, which are difficult to be borne and cause easily-discouraged men to sink under them; but a monk who comes in contact with them will not be afraid, like a stately elephant at the head of the battle. (16, 17)

Cold and heat, flies and gnats, unpleasant feelings, and many diseases attack the body; without flinching[2] he should bear them, and should

---

hours) less one quarter of it, kâlam, i.e. what is proper for the time. The meaning would be 'doing at every time what is proper or prescribed to do at it.' But this explanation looks very artificial; I think that the expression kalê*n*a kâla*m* is an adverb of the same type as ma*ggh*a*m* ma*ggh*ê*n*a and many others.

[1] Sa*mg*ae. This word may be sa*m*yata in this place; but in verse 20, where the same line occurs again, it cannot be so interpreted, because there the word sa*mg*ae occurs twice; once it has the meaning of sa*mg*ata, but in the passage under discussion it must be a verb, and it is rendered there sa*ñg*ayet=saṅga*m* kuryât by the commentators.

[2] Akukkuô, translated akukû*g*a, derived from the root kû*g* 'to warble, to groan;' it would therefore mean 'without complaint.' But in I, 30 we have appakukkuê, derived from the root ku*k* 'to bend, to be crooked,' and it is rendered alpaspandana. The same meaning applies in the present case.

not recall to his memory the pleasures he once enjoyed. (18)

Giving up love, hatred, and delusion, a monk who is always careful and who is steadfast even as Mount Mêru cannot be shaken by the storm, should bear calamities, guarding himself. (19)

A great sage should be neither too elevated by pride nor too humble, he should not care for respectful treatment nor blame; an ascetic who has ceased (to act), will by means of his simplicity enter the path of Nirvâ*n*a. (20)

He is neither grieved nor pleased (by anything)[1], he abandons his relations with men, he ceases (to act), is intent on the benefit of his soul, he strives for the highest good (viz. mukti), and uses the means to reach it, free from sorrow, egoism, and any kind of property. (21)

A merciful (monk) should use beds distant from others, which are not got ready for his sake[2] nor strewn (with leaves or things considered to be possessed of life); he should sustain such hardships as the sages are accustomed to. (22)

The great sage (Samudrapâla), understanding the sacred lore and practising completely the best Law, shone forth like the sun in the sky, being possessed of the highest knowledge and glory. (23)

Having annihilated his Karman both meritorious

---

[1] This is the meaning commonly given to the frequently occurring phrase arairaisahe. Another interpretation is: sa*m*yamâsa*m*yamavishayê, tâbhyâ*m* na bâdhatê.

[2] Nirôvalêvâi = nirupalipta. By upalêpa may be meant 'dirt,' but the author of the Ava*k*ûri explains upalêpa as consisting in abhishvaṅga 'affection.' It is almost impossible to render satisfactorily so vague an expression.

and sinful, being steadfast[1], and free from all fetters, Samudrapâla crossed the ocean-like Flood of worldly existence and obtained exemption from transmigration. (24)

Thus I say.

TWENTY-SECOND LECTURE.

RATHANÊMI.

In the town of *S*auryapura[2] there was a powerful king, Vasudêva by name, who possessed the characteristic marks of a king. (1)

He had two wives, Rôhi*n*î and Dêvakî; each of them had a beloved son, Râma and Kê*s*ava. (2)

In the town of *S*auryapura there was (another) powerful king, Samudravi*g*aya by name, who possessed the characteristic marks of a king. (3)

His wife was *S*ivâ by name; and her famous son was the venerable Arish*t*anêmi, the saviour of the world and the lord of ascetics. (4)

This Arish*t*anêmi, who was gifted with an excellent voice and possessed the thousand and eight lucky marks of the body, was a Gautama, and his skin was black. (5)

His body was strong like that of a bull, and hard

---

[1] Nirangana = sa*m*yamê nis*k*ala, immovable with regard to self-control.

[2] According to the Brahmanical account Vasudêva lived in Mathurâ. The name given to the town by the *G*ainas is apparently derived from *S*auri, an epithet of K*r*ish*n*a, whose grandfather was *S*ûra. Soriyapura may be *S*aurikapura or *S*auryapura. The latter rendering adopted by our commentators is based on a wrong etymology.

like steel; he was well proportioned, and had a belly like that of a fish.

Kêsava asked the girl Râgîmatî[1] in marriage for him. (6)

Now this daughter of an excellent king[2] was virtuous and well looking; she possessed all lucky marks of the body, and shone forth like the lightning Saudâmanî. (7)

Her father said to the powerful Vâsudêva: 'Let the prince come here that I may give him my daughter.' (8)

He had taken a bath containing all (lucky) herbs, and had performed the customary ceremonies; he wore a suit of heavenly clothes and was decked out with ornaments. (9)

Riding on the best mast elephant[3] of Vâsudêva he looked beautiful, like a jewel worn on the head. (10)

He sat under a raised umbrella, fanned by two chowries, and he was surrounded on all sides by a host of Dasârhas[4] and by a complete army drawn

---

[1] Râîmaî, Râimaî, and Râyamatî are the forms of her name in Prâkrit; the spellings Râgimatî and Râgamatî are also met with in Sanskrit.

[2] Viz. Ugrasêna. He was placed on the throne by Krishna on the death of Kamsa, cf. Vishnu Purâna V, 21. He and Dêvaka were the sons of Âhuka, Kamsa was a son of Ugrasêna, and Dêvakî a daughter of Dêvaka, loc. cit. IV, 14. According to the legend of Krishna, as told by the Brahmans and Gainas, Garâsandha afterwards repeatedly attacked Mathurâ. Krishna therefore built Dvârakâ on the shore of the western ocean, and sent thither the Yâdava tribe, loc. cit. V, 22 and 23. The events narrated in the text must be understood to have occurred in Dvârakâ, as is evident from verse 21.

[3] Gandhahastin, an elephant of the best class, whose very smell is sufficient, as is believed, to frighten common elephants, see verse 15.

[4] Dasâra in Prâkrit. They are a clan descended from Yadu.

up in rank and file, while the heavenly sound of musical instruments reached the sky. (11, 12)

With such pomp and splendour the hero of the V*ri*sh*n*is started from his own palace. (13)

On his way he saw animals, kept in cages and enclosures, overcome by fear and looking miserable. (14)

Seeing them on the point of being killed for the sake of their flesh, and to be eaten afterwards, the great sage spoke to his charioteer[1] thus: (15)

'Why are[2] all these animals, which desire to be happy, kept in cages and enclosures?' (16)

Then the charioteer answered: 'Lucky are these animals because at thy wedding they will furnish food for many people.' (17)

Having heard these words, which announced the slaughter of many animals, the great sage, full of compassion and kindness to living beings, meditated thus: (18)

'If for my sake many living beings are killed, I shall not obtain happiness in the next world.' (19)

Then the famous man presented the charioteer with his pair of earrings, his neck-chain, and all his ornaments. (20)

When he had formed his resolution, the gods

---

[1] In verse 10 Arish*t*anêmi rides on an elephant, but in the sequel he is supposed to travel in a car. Unless the poet can be charged with having made this blunder, which I think just possible, verse 10 must be considered a later addition.

[2] The form of the verb a*kkh*ahi*m* for a*kkh*anti is worthy of note, because hi*m* as ending of the third person plural belongs to Apabhra*ms*a. It is interesting to find a true Apabhra*ms*a form in a text so old as ours, for it seems to prove that at all times Apabhra*ms*a went along with the common Prâk*ri*t, a vulgar or low with a high middle-Indian language.

descended (from heaven), according to the established custom, to celebrate, with great pomp together with their retinue, the event of his renunciation. (21)

Surrounded by gods and men, and sitting on an excellent palankin, the Venerable One left Dvârakâ and ascended mount Raivataka[1]. (22)

On arriving at the park he descended from his excellent palankin, surrounded by a crowd of thousands, and then his renunciation took place, while the moon was in conjunction with *K*itrâ[2]. (23)

Then he himself plucked out his delightfully-perfumed, soft, and curled hair in five handfuls. (24)

And Vâsudêva said to that subduer of the senses, who had plucked out his hair: 'O lord of ascetics, may you soon obtain what you wish and desire. (25)

'Increase in knowledge, faith, and right conduct, in forbearance and perfection!' (26)

In this manner Râma and Kêsava, the Da*s*ârhas, and many people paid homage to Arish*t*anêmi and then returned to the town of Dvârakâ. (27)

When the daughter of the king heard of the ordination of the *G*ina, laughter and gaiety forsook her, and she was overwhelmed with affliction[3]. (28)

---

[1] Raivataka is mount Girnâr in Ka*th*iawâ*d*. The hill is one of the most sacred places of the *G*ainas, and is covered with temples of the *G*inas. It is also sacred to the Hindus on account of its connection with the history of K*ri*sh*n*a. The poetical description of mount Raivataka forms the subject of the fourth sarga of the *S*i*s*upâlavadha by Mâgha.

[2] The lunar mansion, the chief star of which is Spica or α Virginis.

[3] The lamentation of Râ*g*îmatî on her husband's becoming an ascetic forms the subject of a curious Sanskrit poem called Nêmidûtakâvya, by Vikrama, son of Sangha*n*a, which has been edited in

Râgîmatî thought: 'Shame upon my life, that I have been forsaken by him! it is better I should turn nun.' (29)

Firm and decided she cut off her tresses which were black like bees and dressed with a brush and comb[1]. (30)

And Vâsudêva said to her who had cut off her hair, and subdued her senses: 'Lady, cross the dreadful ocean of the Samsâra without difficulty!' (31)

When she had entered the order, the virtuous and very learned lady induced there many people, her relations and servants, to enter the order too. (32)

On her way to mount Raivataka it began to rain; her clothes being wet, she entered a cave and waited there in the darkness while it was raining. (33)

She took off her clothes and was naked as she was born, thus she was seen by Rathanêmi[2], whose

---

the Kâvyamâlâ of 1886. It is what is technically called a samasyâpûrana or gloss. The last line of each stanza is taken from the Mêghadûta of Kâlidâsa, and the first three lines are added by the poet to make the whole fit the circumstances of his tale.

[1] Kukkaphanaga, in Sanskrit kûrkaphanaka. According to the scholiasts phanaka is a comb made of bamboo.—I have translated, 'cut off her tresses,' but literally it is: 'plucked out her hair.' However, I do not think that women also are to pluck out their hair.

[2] Rathanêmi was her husband's elder brother. According to a legend told in Haribhadra's *T*îkâ of the Dasavaikâlika Sûtra (see Leumann in the Journal of the German Oriental Society, vol. 46, p. 597), Rathanêmi fell in love with Râgîmatî. But that lady in order to make him see his wrong, vomited a sweet beverage she had drunk, in a cup and offered it him. On his turning away with disgust she explained to him her meaning: she too had been vomited, as it were, by Arishtanêmi, notwithstanding which he wanted to have her. She then taught him the *G*aina creed, and he became a monk.

(peace of) mind became (thereby) disturbed; and afterwards she saw him. (34)

She was frightened when she discovered herself alone with the monk; folding her arms over her breast she sank down trembling. (35)

When the prince, Samudravi*g*aya's son, saw her frightened and trembling, he spoke the following words: (36)

'I am Rathanêmi, O dear, beautiful, sweetly-speaking lady! Do accept me for your lover, O slender one[1], you shall have no cause to complain. (37)

'Come, let us enjoy pleasures, for it is a rare chance to be born a human being; after we have enjoyed pleasures, we shall enter on the path of the *G*inas.' (38)

When Râ*g*îmatî perceived that Rathanêmi's strength of will was broken, and temptation had got the better of him, she did not lose her presence of mind and defended her Self on that occasion. (39)

The daughter of the best king, true to self-control and her vows, maintained the honour of her clan and family, and her virtue, and spoke to him: (40)

'If you owned the beauty of Vai*s*rama*n*a[2], the pleasing manners of Nalakûbara[3], if you were like Purandara[4] himself, I should have no desire for you. (41)

Suya*n*u = sutanu. This may, however, be a proper name, a synonym of Râ*g*îmatî, for according to the Hariva*ms*a 2029 and the Vish*n*u Purâ*n*a IV, 14, Sutanu was a daughter of Ugrasêna.

[2] Vai*s*rama*n*a is a Prâk*ri*t spelling for Vai*s*rava*n*a = Kubêra.

[3] Nalakûbara is Vai*s*rama*n*a's son.

[4] Indra.

'Fie upon you, famous knight, who want to quaff the vomited drink for the sake of this life; it would be better for you to die[1]. (42)

'I am the daughter of the Bhôga-king[2], and you are an Andhakav*ri*sh*n*i; being born in a noble family let us not become like Gandhana-snakes[3]; firmly practise self-control! (43)

'If you fall in love with every woman you see, you will be without hold like the Ha*th*a-plant[4], driven before the wind. (44)

'As a herdsman or a keeper of goods does not own the things (he has the care of), so you will not truly own *S*rama*n*ahood.' (45)

Having heard these well-spoken words of the virtuous lady, he returned to the Law like an elephant driven by the hook[5]. (46)

Protected in thoughts, words, and acts, subduing his senses and keeping the vows, he practised true *S*rama*n*ahood throughout life. (47)

---

[1] The verses 42, 43, 44, 46 have been received in the Da*s*avaikâlika Sûtra II, 7-10, see Leumann's edition of that Sûtra quoted in the note, p. 116. A metrical German translation will be found in the same place.

[2] On the Bhôgas see p. 71, note 2. It is perhaps here misspelt for Bhô*g*a. In the Vish*n*u Purâ*n*a, Ka*m*sa, Ugrasêna's son, is twice called Bhô*g*arâ*g*a (see Wilson's translation, ed. Hall, vol. iv, pp. 260, 271), in contradiction to the common tradition which makes him an Andhaka, compare Patañ*g*ali on Pâ*n*ini IV, 1, 114.

[3] There are said to be two kinds of snakes, the gandhana and the agandhana. The former can be made to suck the poison from the wound they have inflicted; the other will rather die than do so. Cf. Leumann, loc. cit., p. 597, note *.

[4] Pistia Stratiotes, an aquatic plant.

[5] Dêvêndra here refers to the story of the Nûpurapa*nd*ita, of which he gives a small portion in Prâk*ri*t. The whole story is related in the Pari*s*ish*t*aparvan of Hêma*k*andra, see the introduction to my edition of that work in the Bibliotheca Indica.

After practising severe austerities both of them became Kêvalins, and having completely annihilated their Karman, they reached the highest perfection. (48)

Thus act the enlightened, the wise, the clever ones; they turn from pleasures as did this best of men[1]. (49)

Thus I say.

TWENTY-THIRD LECTURE[2].

KÊSI AND GAUTAMA.

There was a *G*ina, Pâr*s*va[3] by name, an Arhat, worshipped by the people, who was thoroughly enlightened and omniscient, a prophet of the Law, and a *G*ina. (1)

And there was a famous disciple of this Light of

---

[1] Compare the last verse of the Ninth Lecture.

[2] In this lecture we have a very interesting legend about the way in which the union of the old church of Pâr*s*va and the new church of Mahâvîra was brought about. A revival of this ancient difference seems to have caused the united church afterwards to divide again into the present *S*vêtâmbara and Digambara sects. They do not continue the two primitive churches, but seem to have grown out of the united church.

[3] Pâr*s*va is the last but one Tîrthakara, his Nirvâ*n*a took place 250 years before that of Mahâvîra. This statement, which has been generally accepted, is, however, in seeming contradiction to the account of our text, according to which a disciple of Pâr*s*va, who is called a young monk kumâra-*s*rama*n*a, met Gautama, i.e. Sudharman, the disciple of Mahâvîra. We therefore must take the word disciple, sîse, as paramparâ*s*ishya, that is not in its literal sense. See note 3, p. 122.

the World, the young *S*rama*n*a Kê*s*i, who had completely mastered the sciences and right conduct. (2)

He possessed the light of *S*ruta and Avadhi knowledge[1], and was surrounded by a crowd of disciples; wandering from village to village he arrived in the town of *S*râvastî. (3)

In the district of that town there is a park, called Tinduka; there he took up his abode in a pure place to live and sleep in. (4)

Now at that time there lived the Prophet of the Law, the *G*ina, who in the whole world is known as the venerable Vardhamâna. (5)

And there was a famous disciple of this Light of the World, the venerable Gautama by name, who had completely mastered the sciences and right conduct. (6)

He knew the twelve Aṅgas, was enlightened, and was surrounded by a crowd of disciples; wandering from village to village he too arrived in *S*râvastî. (7)

In the district of that town there is a park Kôsh*th*aka; there he took up his abode in a pure place to live and sleep in. (8)

The young *S*rama*n*a Kê*s*i and the famous Gautama, both lived there, protecting themselves (by the Guptis) and being careful. (9)

The pupils of both, who controlled themselves, who practised austerities, who possessed virtues, and who protected their Self, made the following reflection: (10)

---

[1] These are the second and third kinds of knowledge according to the *G*aina classification. *S*ruta is the knowledge derived from the sacred books, and avadhi is limited or conditioned knowledge. See Bhandarkar, Report, p. 106.

'Is our Law the right one, or is the other Law[1] the right one? are our conduct and doctrines right, or the other? (11)

'The Law as taught by the great sage Pârsva, which recognises but four vows[2], or the Law taught by Vardhamâna, which enjoins five vows? (12)

'The Law which forbids clothes (for a monk), or that which (allows) an under and upper garment? Both pursuing the same end, what has caused their difference?' (13)

Knowing the thoughts of their pupils, both Kêsi and Gautama made up their minds to meet each other. (14)

Gautama, knowing what is proper and what is due to the older section (of the church), went to the Tinduka park, accompanied by the crowd, his pupils. (15)

When Kêsi, the young monk, saw Gautama approach, he received him with all becoming attention. (16)

He at once offered Gautama the four pure kinds of straw and hay[3] to sit upon. (17)

Kêsi, the young *S*rama*n*a, and the famous Gautama, sitting together, shone forth with a lustre like that of sun and moon. (18)

There assembled many heretics out of curiosity, and many thousands of laymen; (19)

Gods, Dânavas, Gandharvas, Yakshas, Râkshasas,

---

[1] Viz. the Law of Pârsva or the Law of Mahâvîra.

[2] Hence it is called kâu*gg*âma *k*âturyâma. Chastity (maithunavirama*n*a) was not explicitly enumerated, but it was understood to be contained in the fourth commandment: to have no property (aparigraha).

[3] The four kinds of straw are: sâlî vîhî koddava râlaga, to which is added hay: ra*nn*e ta*n*â*n*i.

and Kinnaras (assembled there), and there came together invisible ghosts[1] too. (20)

Kêsi said to Gautama, 'I want to ask you something, holy man.' Then to these words of Kêsi Gautama made the following reply: "Sir, ask whatever you like." Then with his permission Kêsi spoke to Gautama: (21, 22)

'The Law taught by the great sage Pârsva, recognises but four vows, whilst that of Vardhamâna enjoins five. (23)

'Both Laws pursuing the same end, what has caused this difference? Have you no misgivings about this twofold Law, O wise man?' (24)

Then to these words of Kêsi Gautama made the following reply: "Wisdom recognises the truth of the Law and the ascertainment of true things. (25)

"The first[2] saints were simple but slow of understanding, the last saints prevaricating and slow of understanding, those between the two simple and wise; hence there are two forms of the Law[3]. (26)

---

[1] Bhûya = bhûta, explained Vyantara. The vantara or vânamantara are a class of ghosts. The second part of the word apparently is tara 'crossing,' and the first seems to contain an accusative vam or vânamam which may be connected with viha or vyôman 'air.'

[2] Those under the first Tîrthakaras.

[3] The meaning of this explanation is as follows. As the vow of chastity is not explicitly mentioned among Pârsva's four vows, but was understood to be implicitly enjoined by them, it follows that only such men as were of an upright disposition and quick understanding would not go astray by observing the four vows literally, i. e. by not abstaining from sexual intercourse, as it was not expressly forbidden.—The argumentation in the text presupposes a decay of the morals of the monastic order to have occurred between Pârsva and Mahâvîra, and this is possible only on the assumption of a sufficient interval of time having

"The first could but with difficulty understand the precepts of the Law, and the last could only with difficulty observe them, but those between them easily understood and observed them." (27)

'Well, Gautama, you possess wisdom, you have destroyed my doubt; but I have another doubt which you must explain to me, Gautama. (28)

'The Law taught by Vardhamâna forbids clothes, but that of the great sage Pârsva allows an under and upper garment. (29)

'Both Laws pursuing the same end, what has caused this difference? Have you no misgivings about this twofold Law, O wise man?' (30)

To these words of Kêsi Gautama made the following reply: "Deciding the matter by their superior knowledge, (the Tîrthakaras) have fixed what is necessary for carrying out the Law. (31)

"The various outward marks (of religious men) have been introduced in order that people might recognise them as such; the reason for the characteristic marks is their usefulness for religious life and their distinguishing character. (32)

"Now the opinion (of the Tîrthakaras) is that knowledge, faith, and right conduct are the true causes of final liberation, (and not the outward marks)." (33)

'Well, Gautama, you possess wisdom, you have destroyed my doubt; but I have another doubt, which you must explain to me, Gautama. (34)

'Gautama, you stand in the midst of many

elapsed between the last two Tîrthakaras. And this perfectly agrees with the common tradition that Mahâvîra came 250 years after Pârsva.

thousand (foes) who make an attack on you; how have you vanquished them[1]?' (35)

"By vanquishing one, five are vanquished; by vanquishing five, ten are vanquished; by this tenfold victory, I vanquish all foes." (36)

Kêsi said to Gautama: 'Whom do you call a foe?' To these words of Kêsi Gautama made the following reply: (37)

"Self is the one invincible foe, (together with the four) cardinal passions[2], (viz. anger, pride, deceit, and greed, they are five) and the (five) senses (make ten). These (foes), O great sage, I have regularly vanquished." (38)

'Well, Gautama, &c. (as in verse 28). (39)

'We see many beings in this world who are bound by fetters; how have you got rid of your fetters and are set free, O sage?' (40)

"Having cut off all fetters, and having destroyed them by the right means, I have got rid of my fetters and am set free, O sage." (41)

Kêsi said to Gautama: 'What do you call fetters?'

---

[1] This question does not refer to the difference in doctrines between Pârsva and Mahâvîra, but is discussed here, as the commentator states, for the benefit of the pupils of both sages who are engaged in conversation. I think, however, that this and the following questions are asked and answered here by the disciples of the two Tîrthakaras for a better reason than that given by the scholiast. For in them the leading topics of Gainism are treated in a symbolical way. Gautama at once understands the true meaning of the similes and interprets them to the satisfaction of Kêsi. In this way the unity in doctrine subsisting between the Law of Pârsva and that of Mahâvîra is demonstrated to the hearers of the dispute, after the differences had been explained away.

[2] Kashâya.

To these words of Kê*s*i Gautama made the following reply: (42)

"Love, hatred, &c., are heavy fetters, attachment is a dangerous one; having regularly destroyed them, I live up to the rules of conduct." (43)

'Well, Gautama, &c. (as in verse 28). (44)

'O Gautama, in the innermost heart there grows a plant which brings forth poisonous fruit; how have you torn it out?' (45)

"I have thoroughly clipped that plant, and torn it out altogether with its roots; thus I have got rid of the poisonous fruit." (46)

Kê*s*i said to Gautama, 'What do you call that plant?' To these words of Kê*s*i Gautama made the following reply: (47)

"Love of existence is that dreadful plant which brings forth dreadful fruit; having regularly torn it out, I live pleasantly." (48)

'Well, Gautama, &c. (as in verse 28). (49)

'Gautama, there is blazing up a frightful fire which burns[1] the embodied beings; how have you put it out?' (50)

"Taking water, excellent water, from (the river) produced by the great cloud, I always pour it over my body; thus sprinkled the fire does not burn me." (51)

Kê*s*i said to Gautama, 'What do you call the fire?' To these words of Kê*s*i Gautama made the following reply: (52)

"The passions are the fire; knowledge, a virtuous life, and penances are the water; sprinkled

[1] In the original 'fire' is put in the plural because the four kashâyas or cardinal passions are denoted by it.

with the drops of knowledge the fire of the passions is extinguished and does not burn me." (53)

'Well, Gautama, &c. (as in verse 28). (54)

'The unruly, dreadful, bad horse, on which you sit, runs about, Gautama! how comes it to pass that it does not run off with you?' (55)

"I govern it well in its course by the bridle of knowledge; it does not go astray with me, it keeps to the right path." (56)

Kêsi said to Gautama, 'What do you call this horse?' To these words of Kêsi Gautama made the following reply: (57)

"The mind is that unruly, dreadful, bad horse; I govern it by the discipline of the Law (so that it becomes a well-) trained Kambôga-steed[1]." (58)

'Well, Gautama, &c. (as in verse 28). (59)

'There are many bad roads in this world, which lead men astray; how do you avoid, Gautama, going astray as you are on the road?' (60)

"They all are known to me, those who are in the right path and those who have chosen a wrong path; therefore I do not go astray, O sage!" (61)

Kêsi said to Gautama, 'What do you call the path?' To these words of Kêsi Gautama made the following reply: (62)

"The heterodox and the heretics have all chosen a wrong path; the right path is that taught by the Ginas; it is the most excellent path." (63)

'Well, Gautama, &c. (as in verse 28). (64)

'Is there a shelter, a refuge, a firm ground for the beings carried away by the great flood of water? do you know the island, O Gautama?' (65)

---

[1] Kanthaka, see above, p. 47, note 2.

"There is a large, great island in the midst of water, which is not inundated by the great flood of water." (66)

Kêsi said to Gautama, 'What do you call this island?' To these words of Kêsi Gautama made the following reply: (67)

"The flood is old age and death, which carry away living beings; Law is the island, the firm ground, the refuge, the most excellent shelter." (68)

'Well, Gautama, &c. (as in verse 28). (69)

'On the ocean with its many currents there drifts a boat; how will you, Gautama, on board of it reach the opposite shore?' (70)

"A boat that leaks will not reach the opposite shore; but a boat that does not leak, will reach it." (71)

Kêsi said to Gautama, 'What do you call this boat?' To these words of Kêsi Gautama made the following reply: (72)

"The body is the boat, life is the sailor, and the Circle of Births is the ocean which is crossed by the great sages." (73)

'Well, Gautama, &c. (as in verse 28). (74)

'In this dreadfully dark gloom there live many beings; who will bring light into the whole world of living beings?' (75)

"The spotless sun has risen which illuminates the whole world; he will bring light into the whole world of living beings." (76)

Kêsi said to Gautama, 'What do you call this sun?' To these words of Kêsi Gautama made the following reply: (77)

"Risen has he who put an end to the Circle of

Births, the omniscient *G*ina, the luminary, who brings light into the whole world of living beings." (78)

'Well, Gautama, &c. (as in verse 28). (79)

'Do you, O sage, know a safe, happy, and quiet place for living beings which suffer from pains [1] of body and mind?' (80)

"There is a safe place in view of all, but difficult of approach, where there is no old age nor death, no pain nor disease." (81)

Kê*s*i said to Gautama, 'What is this place called?' To these words of Kê*s*i Gautama made the following reply: (82)

"It is what is called Nirvâ*n*a, or freedom from pain, or perfection, which is in view of all; it is the safe, happy, and quiet place which the great sages reach. (83)

"That is the eternal place, in view of all, but difficult of approach. Those sages who reach it are free from sorrows, they have put an end to the stream of existence." (84)

'Well, Gautama, you possess wisdom, you have destroyed my doubt; obeisance to you, who are not troubled by doubts, who are the ocean, as it were, of all Sûtras.' (85)

After his doubt had been solved, Kê*s*i, of enormous sanctity, bowed his head to the famous Gautama. (86)

And in the pleasant (Tinduka park) he sincerely adopted the Law of the five vows, which was proclaimed by the first Tîrthakara, according to the teaching of the last Tîrthakara. (87)

---

[1] Mâ*n*asê dukkhê stands for mâ*n*asêhi*m* dukkhêhi*m*. It is an interesting instance of the dropping of case affixes, which probably was more frequent in the vernacular.

In that meeting of Kêsi and Gautama, knowledge and virtuous conduct were for ever brought to eminence, and subjects of the greatest importance were settled. (88)

The whole assembly was greatly pleased and fixed their thoughts on the right way. They praised Kêsi and Gautama: 'May the venerable ones show us favour!' (89)

Thus I say.

TWENTY-FOURTH LECTURE.

THE SAMITIS.

The eight articles[1] of the creed are the Samitis and the Guptis; there are five Samitis and three Guptis. (1)

The Samitis[2] are: 1. îryâ-samiti (going by paths trodden by men, beasts, carts, &c., and looking carefully so as not to occasion the death of any living creature); 2. bhâshâ-samiti (gentle, salutary, sweet, righteous speech); 3. êshanâ-samiti (receiving alms in a manner to avoid the forty-two faults that are laid down); 4. âdâna-samiti (receiving and keeping of the things necessary for

[1] The word I have rendered 'article' is mâyâ, the Sanskrit form of which may be mâtâ or mâtrâ. The word is derived from the root mâ 'to find room in,' and denotes that which includes in itself other things, see verse 3. The word may also mean mâtri 'mother,' as Weber understands it. But this is an obviously intentional double meaning.

[2] The definitions placed in parentheses in the text are taken from Bhandarkar's Report for 1883-1884, p. 98, note †, p. 100, note *.

religious exercises, after having carefully examined them); 5. u*kk*âra-samiti (performing the operations of nature in an unfrequented place). The three Guptis (which are here included in the term Samiti in its wider application) are: 1. mano-gupti (preventing the mind from wandering in the forest of sensual pleasures by employing it in contemplation, study, &c.); 2. vâg-gupti (preventing the tongue from saying bad things by a vow of silence, &c.); 3. kâya-gupti (putting the body in an immovable posture as in the case of Kâyôtsarga). (2)

The eight Samitis are thus briefly enumerated, in which the whole creed taught by the *G*inas and set forth in the twelve Aṅgas, is comprehended. (3)

1. The walking of a well-disciplined monk should be pure in four respects: in respect to 1. the cause[1]; 2. the time; 3. the road; 4. the effort[2]. (4)

The cause is: knowledge, faith, and right conduct; the time is day-time; the road excludes bad ways. (5)

The effort is fourfold, viz. as regards: 1. substance, 2. place, 3. time, and 4. condition of mind. Hear me explain them. (6)

With regard to substance: the (walking monk) should look with his eyes; with regard to place: the space of a yuga (i.e. four hastas or cubits); with regard to time: as long as he walks; and with regard to condition of mind: carefully[3]. (7)

He walks carefully who pays attention only to

---

[1] Âlambana, literally support; explained: supported by which the mind becomes pure.

[2] *G*âya*n*â = yatna; it consists chiefly in compassion with living creatures (*g*îvadayâ).

[3] Upayukta.

his walk and his body (executing it), whilst he avoids attending to the objects of sense, but (minds) his study, the latter in all five ways[1]. (8)

2. To give way to: anger, pride, deceit and greed, laughter, fear, loquacity and slander[2]; these eight faults should a well-disciplined monk avoid; he should use blameless and concise speech at the proper time. (9, 10)

3. As regards begging[3], a monk should avoid the faults in the search[4], in the receiving[5], and in the use[6] of the three kinds of objects, viz. food, articles of use, and lodging. (11)

A zealous monk should avoid in the first (i.e. in the search for alms) the faults occasioned either by the giver (udgama) or by the receiver (utpâdana); in the second (i.e. in the receiving of alms) the faults inherent in the receiving; and in the use of the articles received, the four faults[7]. (12)

---

[1] The 'five ways' are vâ*k*anâ, &c., as explained in the Twenty-ninth Lecture, §§ 19–23, below, p. 165 f. The commentators supply kuryât 'he should carry on his study.'

[2] Vikahâ = vikathâ, which does not occur in common Sanskrit. Perhaps it stands for vikatthâ 'boasting.'

[3] Êsha*n*â. [4] Gavêsha*n*â. [5] Graha*n*aisha*n*â.

[6] Paribhôgaisha*n*â.

[7] There are altogether forty-six faults to be avoided. As they are frequently alluded to in the sacred texts, a systematical enumeration and description of them according to the Dîpikâ will be useful.

There are sixteen udgama-dôshas by which food, &c. becomes unfit for a *G*aina monk:

1. Âdhâkarmika, the fault inherent in food, &c., which a layman has prepared especially for religious mendicants of whatever sect.

2. Auddê*s*ika, is food, &c., which a layman has prepared for a particular monk.

4. If a monk takes up or lays down the two kinds of things belonging to his general and supple-

3. Pûtika, is food, &c., which is pure on the whole, but contains particles impure on account of the first fault.

4. Unmi*s*ra, is food, &c., of which a part only had been especially prepared for the monk in question.

5. Sthâpanâkarmika, is food, &c., which has been reserved for the monk.

6. Prâbh*ri*tika, is food, &c., which has been prepared for some festivity.

7. Prâdu*h*kara*n*a, when the layman has to light a lamp in order to fetch the alms for the monk.

8. Krîta, when he has to buy the things.

9. Prâmitya, when he has to fetch a ladle (? uddhâraka) in order to draw out the food, &c.

10. Parâv*ri*tti, when he replaces bad particles of the food by good ones, and vice versa.

11. Adhyâh*ri*ta, when he has to fetch the food, &c., from some distance.

12. Udbhinna, when he has to open locks before he gets at the food, &c.

13. Mâlâh*ri*ta, when he has to take the food, &c., from some raised or underground place.

14. Â*kkh*idya, when the food, &c., was taken by force from somebody.

15. Anis*ri*sh*t*a, when a man gives from a store he possesses in common with other men, without asking their permission.

16. Adhyavapûra, when the mendicant calls while the dinner is being cooked, and for his sake more food is put in the pot on the fire.

(Some of these faults are enumerated in the Aupapâtika Sûtra, § 96, III.)

There are sixteen utpâdana-dôshas; or such faults as are occasioned by the monk's using some means to make the layman give him alms:

1. Dhâtrîkarman, when the monk plays with the layman's children.

2. Dûtakarman, when he gives him information about what his people are doing.

3. Nimitta, when he speaks in praise of almsgiving.

4. Â*g*îvikâ, when he makes his birth and family known to him.

mentary[1] outfit, he should proceed in the following way. (13)

5. Vapanîka, when he expatiates upon his misery.

6. *K*ikitsâ, when he cures sick people.

7. Krôdhapi*nd*a, when he extorts alms by threats.

8. Mânapi*nd*a, when he tells the layman that he has laid a wager with other monks that he would get alms from him.

9. Mâyâpi*nd*a, when he employs tricks or buffoonery in order to procure alms.

10. Lôbhapi*nd*a, when he goes begging from a desire of good fare.

11. Sa*m*stava-pi*nd*a, when he flatters the layman.

12. Vidyâpi*nd*a, when he makes a show of his learning; or when he conjures a god from whom to get alms.

13. Mantradôsha, when he obliges the layman in some way or other.

14. *K*ûr*n*ayôga, when he makes himself invisible and then takes away the food, &c.

15. Yôgapi*nd*a, when he teaches people spells, tricks, &c.

16. Mûlakarman, when he teaches them how to obviate evils by roots, charms, &c.

There are ten faults of graha*n*aisha*n*â:

1. *S*añkita, when a monk accepts alms from a frightened layman.

2. Mrakshita, when the food is soiled (khara*nt*ita) by animate or inanimate matter.

3. Nikshipta, when the food is placed among animate things.

4. Pihita, when animate food is covered with inanimate matter, and vice versa.

5. Sa*m*h*ri*ta, when the layman has to take out the thing to be given from one vessel and puts it into another.

6. Dâyaka, when the condition or occupation of the giver forbids accepting alms from him.

7. Unmi*s*rita, when the layman mixes up pure with impure food.

8. Aparita (?), when one joint possessor gives away from the store against the other's will.

9. Lipta, when the layman gives food, &c., with a ladle or his hand, soiled with milk, butter, &c.

10. *Kh*ardita, when in giving alms he spills milk, &c.

[1] See next page.

A zealous monk should wipe the thing after having inspected it with his eyes, and then he should take it up or put it down, having the Samiti in both respects[2]. (14)

5. Excrements, urine, saliva, mucus, uncleanliness of the body, offals of food, waste things, his own body (when he is about to die), and everything of this description (is to be disposed of in the way to be described). (15)

[A place may be not frequented and not seen (by people), or not frequented but seen, or frequented and not seen, or frequented and seen. (16)][3]

In a place neither frequented nor seen by other people, which offers no obstacles to self-control, which is even, not covered with grass or leaves[4], and has

---

There are four faults of paribhôgaisha*n*â:

1. Sa*m*yô*g*anâ, when the monk puts together the ingredients for a good meal.

2. Apramâ*n*a, when he accepts a greater than the prescribed quantity of food.

3. Iṅgâla, when he praises a rich man for his good fare, or dhûma, when he blames a poor man for his bad fare.

4. Akâra*n*a, when he eats choice food on other occasions than those laid down in the sacred texts.

[1] Aughika and aupagrahika. The former is explained sâmudâyika, the other denotes such things as are wanted occasionally only, as a stick. I cannot make out with certainty from the commentaries whether the broom is reckoned among the former or the latter.

[2] This means, according to the commentator, either in taking up or putting down, or with respect to the ôgha and aupagrahika outfit, or with respect to substance and condition of mind.

[3] This verse, which is in a different metre (Âryâ), is apparently a later addition, and has probably been taken from an old commentary, the *K*û*r*n*i or the Bhâshya.

[4] A*gg*h*usirê = asushirê, not perforated, not having holes. I translate according to the author of the Ava*k*ûri. The literal

been brought into its present condition[1] not long ago, which is spacious, has an inanimate surface-layer[2], not too near (the village, &c.), not perforated by holes, and is exempt from insects and seeds—in such a place he should leave his excrements, &c. (17, 18)

The five Samitis are thus briefly enumerated, I shall now explain in due order the three Guptis[3]. (19)

1. There is, 1. truth; 2. untruth; 3. a mixture of truth and untruth; 4. a mixture of what is not true, and what is not untrue. The Gupti of mind refers to all four[4]. (20)

A zealous monk should prevent his mind from desires for the misfortune of somebody else[5], from thoughts on acts which cause misery to living beings[6], and from thoughts on acts which cause their destruction[7]. (21)

2. The Gupti of speech is also of four kinds (referring to the four divisions as in verse 20). (22)

A zealous monk should prevent his speech from (expressing) desires, &c. (as in verse 21). (23)

3. In standing, sitting, lying down, jumping, going, and in the use of his organs, a zealous monk should prevent his body from intimating obnoxious desires,

---

translation would give a wrong idea, as it would come to the same as the word bilavar*g*ita in the next verse.

[1] I. e. where the ground has been cleared not long ago by burning the grass, &c.

[2] Ôgâ*dh*ê, where the animate ground is covered by at least five digits of inanimate matter.

[3] Viz. of mind (20, 21), of speech (22, 23), and of the body (24, 25).

[4] See part i, p. 150, note 2.

[5] Sa*m*rambha.

[6] Samârambha.

[7] Ârambha.

from doing acts which cause misery to living beings, or which cause their destruction. (24, 25)

These are the five Samitis for the practice of the religious life, and the Guptis for the prevention of everything sinful. (26)

This is the essence of the creed, which a sage should thoroughly put into practice; such a wise man will soon get beyond the Circle of Births. (27)

Thus I say.

TWENTY-FIFTH LECTURE.

THE TRUE SACRIFICE.

There was a famous Brâhma*n*a, *G*ayaghôsha by name, who was born in a Brâhmanical family, but who was pledged to the performing of the yamas[1]. (1)

This great sage, who subdued all his senses, and who walked on the right road, came, on his wandering from village to village, to the town of Benares. (2)

There outside of Benares he took up his lodgings in a pleasant park; there he took up his abode in a pure place to live and sleep in. (3)

At the same time a Brâhma*n*a, versed in the Vêdas, Vi*g*ayaghôsha by name, offered a sacrifice in that town. (4)

Now this houseless (monk) at the end of a fast of a month's duration, went to the sacrifice of Vi*g*ayaghôsha to beg alms. (5)

---

[1] Yama etymologically means 'restraint;' here it denotes the great vows of the *G*ainas; cf. XXIII, 12, p. 121 and note 2.

The priest wanted to turn the approaching monk off: 'I shall not give you alms, mendicant, beg somewhere else. (6)

'Priests who are versed in the Vêdas and are chaste as behoves offerers, who are versed in the *G*yôtishâṅga[1] and are well grounded in the sacrificial science, who are able to save themselves and others, such priests ought to be presented with food and all they desire.' (7, 8)

When the great sage was thus refused by the priest, he was neither angry nor pleased, as he always strove for the highest good. (9)

Not to obtain food, or drink, or whatever else he wanted, but to save these people he spoke the following words: (10)

"You do not know what is most essential[2] in the Vêdas, nor in sacrifices, nor in the heavenly bodies[3], nor in duties[4]. (11)

"Nor do you know those who are able to save themselves and others; but if you do, then speak out!" (12)

The priest did not make a reply to defend himself against his insinuation; but he and all there assembled joined their hands and questioned the great sage: (13)

'Tell us the most essential subject in the Vêdas, and tell us what is most essential in the sacrifice;

---

[1] It is worthy of note that, according to the opinion of our author, the knowledge of astronomy, as taught in the *G*yôtisha, was one of the principal accomplishments of a priest. This quality of a priest must therefore have been more conspicuous to an outsider than Brâhmanical books would make us believe.

[2] To render muha = mukha.

[3] Nakshatra.

[4] Dharma.

tell us the first of the heavenly bodies, and tell us the best of dharmas. (14)

'Who are able to save themselves and others (viz. tell me). I ask you to solve this my doubt, O saint.' (15)

"The most essential subject in the Vêdas is the agnihôtra, and that of the sacrifice is the purpose of the sacrifice[1]; the first of the heavenly bodies is the moon, and the best of dharmas is that of Kâ*s*yapa (i.e. *Ri*shabha). (16)

"The beautiful (gods) with joined hands praise and worship the highest Lord (i.e. the Tîrthakara) as the planets, &c., (praise) the moon. (17)

"The ignorant (priests) pretend to know the sacrifice, those whose Brâhmanical excellence consists in (false) science; they shroud themselves in study and penance, being like fire covered by ashes. (18)

"He who is called by people a Brâhma*n*a and is worshipped like fire (is no true Brâhma*n*a). But him we call a true Brâhma*n*a, whom the wise point out as such. (19)

"He who has no worldly attachment after entering the order, who does not repent of having become a monk[2], and who takes delight in the noble words, him we call a Brâhma*n*a. (20)

"He who is exempt from love, hatred, and fear,

---

[1] *G*anna*tth*î vêyasâ muham = ya*gñ*ârthî vedasâm mukham. According to the Dîpikâ sacrifice here means the ten virtues: truth, penance, content, patience, right conduct, simplicity, faith, constancy, not injuring anything, and Sa*m*vara.

[2] According to the commentators we should translate: He who does not embrace (his people) on meeting them, and is not sorry on leaving them.

(and who shines forth) like burnished gold, purified in fire[1], him we call a Brâhma*n*a. (21)

"A lean, self-subduing ascetic, who reduces his flesh and blood, who is pious and has reached Nirvâ*n*a, him we call a Brâhma*n*a. (22)

"He who thoroughly knows living beings, whether they move or not, and does not injure them in any of the three ways[2], him we call a Brâhma*n*a. (23)

"He who does not speak untruth from anger or for fun, from greed or from fear, him we call a Brâhma*n*a. (24)

"He who does not take anything that is not given him, be it sentient or not sentient, small or large, him we call a Brâhma*n*a. (25)

"He who does not carnally love divine, human, or animal beings, in thoughts, words, or acts, him we call a Brâhma*n*a. (26)

"He who is not defiled by pleasures as a lotus growing in the water is not wetted by it, him we call a Brâhma*n*a. (27)

"He who is not greedy, who lives unknown, who has no house and no property, and who has no friendship with householders, him we call a Brâhma*n*a. (28)

"He who has given up his former connections (with his parents, &c.), with his kinsmen and relations, and who is not given to pleasure, him we call a Brâhma*n*a. (29)

---

[1] Niddhantamalapâvaga*m*. The commentator assumes a transposition of the members in this compound. Such irregular compounds are not unfrequent in our Prâk*ri*t. If, however, pâvaga stands for pâpaka, the compound would be regular, and would refer not to 'gold,' but to the person described. In that case we must translate: whose impurities and sins had been annihilated.

[2] I. e. by thoughts, words, and acts.

"The binding of animals (to the sacrificial pole), all the Vêdas, and sacrifices, being causes of sin, cannot save the sinner; for his works (or Karman) are very powerful. (30)

"One does not become a *S*rama*n*a by the tonsure, nor a Brâhma*n*a by the sacred syllable ôm, nor a Muni by living in the woods, nor a Tâpasa by wearing (clothes of) Ku*s*a-grass and bark. (31)

"One becomes a *S*rama*n*a by equanimity, a Brâhma*n*a by chastity, a Muni by knowledge, and a Tâpasa by penance. (32)

"By one's actions one becomes a Brâhma*n*a, or a Kshattriya, or a Vai*s*ya, or a *S*ûdra. (33)

"The Enlightened One has declared these (good qualities) through which one becomes a (true) Snâtaka[1]; him who is exempt from all Karman, we call a Brâhma*n*a. (34)

"The most excellent twice-born men[2] who possess these good qualities, are able to save themselves and others." (35)

When thus his doubt had been solved, Vi*g*ayaghôsha, the Brâhma*n*a, assented[3] to the great sage *G*ayaghôsha and to his (speech). (36)

Vi*g*ayaghôsha, pleased, folded his hands and spoke

---

[1] Snâtaka denotes a Brahman who has finished his studies; it here means as much as 'a perfect sage.'

[2] A various reading in one MS. adds, '*G*inas and Brâhma*n*as' before dvi*g*as.

[3] Samudâya taya*m* ta*m* tu. The text is evidently corrupted. Samudâya stands, according to the commentators, for samâdâya, but there is no finite verb with which to construe the absolute participle, either expressed or easily supplied. Perhaps we must read samuvâya vaya*m* = samuvâ*k*a va*k*as; for the perfect is retained in some cases. However, if this conjecture be right, the next line would be superfluous.

as follows: 'You have well declared to me what true Brâhma*n*ahood consists in. (37)

'You are a sacrificer of sacrifices, you are the most learned of those who know the Vêdas, you know the *G*yôtishâṅga, you know perfectly the Law. (38)

'You are able to save yourself and others; therefore do us the honour to accept our alms, O best of monks.' (39)

"I do not want any alms; but, O Brâhma*n*a, enter the order at once, lest you should be drifted about on the dreadful ocean of the Sa*m*sâra, whose eddies are dangers. (40)

"There is glue (as it were) in pleasure: those who are not given to pleasure, are not soiled by it; those who love pleasures, must wander about in the Sa*m*sâra; those who do not, will be liberated. (41)

"If you take two clods of clay, one wet, the other dry, and fling them against the wall, the wet one will stick to it. (42)

"Thus foolish men, who love pleasure, will be fastened (to Karman), but the passionless will not, even as the dry clod of clay (does not stick to the wall)." (43)

When Vi*g*ayaghôsha had learned the excellent Law from the houseless *G*ayaghôsha, he entered the order. (44)

*G*ayaghôsha and Vi*g*ayaghôsha both annihilated their Karman by self-control and penance, and reached the highest perfection. (45)

Thus I say.

TWENTY-SIXTH LECTURE.

THE CORRECT BEHAVIOUR.

I shall declare the correct behaviour (sâmâ*k*ârî) which causes freedom from all misery; by practising it the Nirgranthas have crossed the ocean of Sa*m*sâra. (1)

The correct behaviour of monks consists of (the following) ten parts: 1. âva*s*yikâ; 2. naishêdhikî; 3. âp*rikkh*anâ; 4. pratip*rikkh*anâ; 5. *kh*andanâ; 6. i*kkh*âkâra; 7. mithyâkâra; 8. tathâkâra; 9. abhyutthâna; 10. upasampad. (2–4)

The âva*s*yikâ is required when he leaves a room (or the presence of other monks on some necessary business); the naishêdhikî, on entering a place; âp*rikkh*anâ, (or asking the superior's permission) for what he is to do himself; pratip*rikkh*anâ, for what somebody else is to do; *kh*andanâ, (or placing at the disposal of other monks) the things one has got; i*kkh*âkâra, in the execution (of one's intention by oneself or somebody else); mithyâkâra, in the blaming oneself (for sins committed); tathâkâra, (assent) in making a promise; abhyutthâna, in serving those who deserve respect; and upasampad, in placing oneself under another teacher. Thus the twice fivefold behaviour has been declared. (5–7)

After sunrise during the first quarter (of the first Paurushî)[1] he should inspect (and clean) his things and pay his respects to the superior. (8)

Then, with his hands joined, he should ask him:

[1] The southern half of the sky or horizon, between east and west, is divided into four quarters, each of which corresponds in time to a paurushî, the fourth part of a day or a night.

'What shall I do now? I want to be employed, sir, in doing some work or in studying.' (9)

If he is ordered to do some work, he should do it without tiring; if he is ordered to study, he should do it without allowing himself to be affected by any pains. (10)

A clever monk should divide the day into four (equal) parts (called paurushî), and fulfil his duties (uttaragu*n*a) in all four parts. (11)

In the first Paurushî he should study, in the second he should meditate, in the third he should go on his begging-tour, and in the fourth he should study again. (12)

In the month Âshâ*dh*a the Paurushî (of the night) contains two feet (pada)[1]; in the month Pausha, four; in the months *K*aitra and Â*s*vayu*g*a, three. (13)

(The Paurushî) increases or decreases a digit[2] (aṅgula) every week, two digits every fortnight, four digits every month. (14)

The dark fortnight of Âshâ*dh*a, Bhâdrapada, Kârttika, Pausha, Phâlguna, and Vai*s*âkha are known as avamarâtrâs[3]. (15)

---

[1] A paurushî is the fourth part of a day or a night; about the time of the equinoxes, when the day as well as the night contains twelve hours, the paurushî contains three hours. At the same time, in the months *K*aitra and Â*s*vina, as we learn from our verse, the paurushî has three feet, padas. The pada therefore is equal to one hour exactly. The duration of the night at the summer solstice was therefore estimated at eight hours and at the winter solstice at sixteen, just as in the Vedic *G*yôtisha.

[2] A digit, aṅgula, is apparently the twelfth part of a foot, pada = one hour. The digit is therefore equal to five minutes.

[3] The fortnights, mentioned in the text, consist of fourteen days only, the remaining ones of fifteen days. In this way the lunar year is made to consist of 354 days.

In the quarter of the year comprising the three months *G*yêsh*th*âmûla, Âshâ*dh*a, and *S*râva*n*a, the (morning-) inspection is to last six digits (beyond ¼ Paurushî); in the second quarter, eight; in the third, ten; in the fourth, eight[1]. (16)

A clever monk should divide the night too into four parts, and fulfil his duties (uttaragu*n*a) in all four parts. (17)

In the first Paurushî he should study, in the second he should meditate, in the third he should leave off sleep, and in the fourth he should study again. (18)

When the nakshatra which leads the night[2] has reached the first quarter of the heaven, at dawn he should cease to study. (19)

When a small part of the quarter is left[3], in which the (leading) nakshatra stands, during that space of time, being considered intermediate[4] (between two) days, a monk should watch. (20)

In the first quarter (of the first Paurushî) he should inspect (and clean) his things, pay his respects to his superior, and then begin to study, not allowing himself to be affected by any pains[5]. (21)

---

[1] Or thirty, forty, fifty, forty minutes respectively.

[2] I.e. the nakshatra which is in opposition to the sun, and accordingly rises at the same time with the setting sun, and sets with the rising sun, compare Râmâya*n*a III, 16, 12.

[3] I.e. is about to set.

[4] Vêrattiya, translated vairâtrika; but there is no such word in Sanskrit. It apparently stands for dvairâtrika, belonging to two days. As the Hindus reckon the day from sunrise, the time immediately preceding it may be considered to belong to two days.

[5] Compare verse 8.

In the (last) quarter of the first Paurushî, after paying his respect to the Guru, a monk should inspect his almsbowl, without, however, performing the Kâla-pratikrama*n*a[1]. (22)

He should first inspect his mouth-cloth[2], then his broom[3], and taking the broom in his hand he should inspect his cloth. (23)

Standing upright he holds his cloth firmly and inspects it first leisurely, then he spreads it, and at last he wipes it. (24)

(He should spread the cloth) without shaking or crushing it, in such a way as to make the folds disappear, and to avoid friction of its parts against each other; he should fold it up six times in length, and nine times in breadth, and then he should remove living beings with his hand (spreading the cloth on the palm of his hand)[4]. (25)

He must avoid want of attention: 1. in beginning his work; 2. in taking up the corners of the cloth; 3. in folding it up; 4. in shaking out the dust; 5. in putting it down (on some other piece of cloth); 6. in sitting upon the haunches[5]. (26)

---

[1] I.e. expiation of sins concerning time, cf. Bhandarkar's Report, p. 98, note ‡. It seems to consist in Kâyôtsarga.

[2] This is a piece of muslin which the *G*aina monks place before their mouth in speaking, in order to prevent insects being drawn in the mouth by the breath.

[3] It is here called gô*kkh*aga = gu*kkh*aka, originally a bunch of peacocks' feathers, it is so still, if I am not mistaken, with the Digambaras, whilst the *S*vêtâmbaras use other materials, especially cotton threads.

[4] Much in my translation is conjectural. There are some technicalities in these verses which I fail to understand clearly, notwithstanding the explanations of the scholiasts.

[5] Vêdikâ.

(One must further avoid) to hold the cloth loosely, or at one corner, or so as to let it flap, or so as to subject it to friction, or so as to shake it in different ways, or if one has made a mistake in the number of foldings (see verse 25) to count (aloud or with the help of the fingers, &c.)[1] (27)

There should be neither too little nor too much of inspection, nor an exchange (of the things to be inspected); this is the right way to do (the inspection), all other methods are wrong:— (28)

(This is) if one engaged in inspecting his things converses or gossips (with anybody), renounces something[2], teaches another his lesson, or receives his own lesson from another, (he neglects his inspection). (29)

He who is careful in the inspection, protects the six kinds of living beings, viz. the earth-bodies, water-bodies, fire-bodies, wind-bodies, plants, and animals. (30)

He who is careless in the inspection, injures the six kinds of living beings (just enumerated)[3]. (31)

In the third Paurushî he should beg food and drink, (he may do so) for any of the following six reasons: (32)

---

[1] I am not sure of having hit the true meaning. The commentators reckon this counting as a fault, while the text itself seems to enjoin it.

[2] Dêi pa*kk*akkhâna*m*. The meaning is, I believe, that during the time of inspection one should not make up one's mind to abstain from this or that because one is to devote one's whole attention to the inspection of one's things.

[3] The Dîpikâ places this verse before the last and construes it with verse 29, making out the following meaning: if one, engaged in inspecting his things, converses or gossips, &c., then, being careless in the inspection, he injures, &c.

1. To prevent an illness; 2. to serve the Guru; 3. to be able to comply with the rules about walking[1]; 4. to be able to comply with the rules of self-control[2]; 5. to save one's life; 6. to be able to meditate on the Law. (33)

A zealous Nirgrantha or Nirgranthî may omit to beg food for the following six reasons, when it will not be considered a transgression of his duties: (34)

1. In case of illness; 2. in case of a disaster; 3. to preserve one's chastity and the Guptis; 4. out of compassion for living beings; 5. in the interest of penance; 6. to make an end of one's life[3]. (35)

Taking his whole outfit a monk should inspect it with his eye; he then may walk about, but not beyond half a Yô*g*ana. (36)

In the fourth Paurushî he should put away his almsbowl (after having eaten his meal), and then begins his study which reveals all existent things. (37)

In the last quarter of the fourth Paurushî he should pay his reverence to the Guru, and after having performed Kâla-pratikrama*n*a[4], he should inspect his lodging. (38)

A zealous monk should also inspect the place where to discharge his excrements and urine, and then (till the sun sets) he should go through Kâyôtsarga without allowing himself to be affected by any pains. (39)

---

[1] Iriya*tth*âê; for one will not be careful about walking (îryâsamitî) if too hungry or thirsty.

[2] For one might eat forbidden food if too hungry.

[3] It may be remarked here that the verses 15, 16, 19, 20, 24, 26, 27, 29, 33, 34, 35 are in the Âryâ-metre while the rest of the lecture is in *S*lôka.

[4] Compare note 1, p. 145.

Then he should, in due order, reflect on all transgressions he has committed during the day, with regard to knowledge, faith, and conduct. (40)

Having finished Kâyôtsarga, and paid his reverence to the Guru, he should, in due order, confess his transgressions committed during the day. (41)

Then having recited the Pratikrama*n*a Sûtra[1], and having annihilated his sins, he should pay his reverence to the Guru (asking absolution)[2], and go through Kâyôtsarga without allowing himself to be affected by any pains. (42)

Having finished Kâyôtsarga, and paid his reverence to the Guru, he should pronounce the customary (three) praises, and then wait for the proper time. (43)

In the first Paurushî (of the night) he should study; in the second he should meditate; in the third he should leave off sleep; and in the fourth he should study again[3]. (44)

In the fourth Paurushî he should wait for the proper time and then begin to study without waking the householders. (45)

In the last quarter of the fourth Paurushî he should pay his reverence to the Guru, and performing Kâla-pratikrama*n*a[4] he should wait for the proper time. (46)

When the (time for) Kâyôtsarga has arrived, he

---

[1] Pa*d*ikamittu = pratikramya, explained pratikrama*n*a-sûtram uktvâ.

[2] According to the Dîpikâ: having repeated the three Gâthâs beginning âriyauva*ggh*âya.

[3] This verse is the same as verse 18, except a verbal difference in the last line.

[4] Pa*d*ikamittu kâlassa, see p. 145, note 1. The Dîpikâ here explains this phrase by: doing acts proper for that time.

should go through it, without allowing himself to be affected by any pains. (47)

Then he should, in due order, reflect on all transgressions he has committed during the night with regard to knowledge, faith, and conduct. (48)

Having finished Kâyôtsarga and paid his reverence to the Guru, he should, in due order, confess his transgressions committed during the night. (49)

Then having recited the Pratikrama*n*a Sûtra &c. (see verse 41). (50)

He should consider what kind of austerities he will undertake. Having finished his Kâyôtsarga, he pays his reverence to the Guru. (51)

Having finished Kâyôtsarga and paid his reverence to the Guru, he should practise those austerities which he has decided upon, and praise the perfected saints. (52)

Thus has been summarily declared the correct behaviour, by practising which many souls have crossed the ocean of Sa*m*sâra. (53)

Thus I say.

TWENTY-SEVENTH LECTURE.

THE BAD BULLOCKS.

There was a Sthavira and Ga*n*adhara[1], the learned sage Garga. This leader of the Ga*n*a once made the following reflections: (1)

'He who rides in a car, crosses a wilderness; he

[1] Ga*n*a seems to correspond to the modern Ga*kkh*a; see part i, p. 288, note 2. Ga*n*adhara, therefore, does not denote here, as usual, a disciple of Tîrthakara.

who rides, as it were, in (the car of) religious exercise, crosses the Sa*m*sâra. (2)

'But he who puts bad bullocks[1] before his car, will be tired out with beating them; he will feel vexation, and his goad will be broken (at last). (3)

'(A bad bullock) will bite its mate in the tail; it will wound the other[2]; it will break the pin of the yoke[3], or it will leave the road. (4)

'It will fall down on its side, or sit down, or lie down; it will jump up or caper, or it will obstinately make for a young cow. (5)

'It will furiously advance with its head lowered for an attack, or angrily go backward; it will stand still as if dead, or run at full speed. (6)

'The cursed beast[4] will rend asunder the rope, or in its unruliness break the yoke; and roaring it will break loose and run off. (7)

'Just as bad bullocks are when put before a car, so are bad pupils when yoked, as it were, to the car of the Law; they break down through want of zeal. (8)

'Some attach great importance[5] to their success;

---

[1] Khalu*m*ka = galivr*i*shabha. Gali is explained in the dictionaries: a strong but lazy bull. In verse 16 we meet with galigaddaha = galigardabha, as synonymous with khalu*m*ka.

[2] The commentator understands the first line of this verse as having reference to the angry driver. But though an angry driver will perhaps, for all I know, put his bullock's tail to his teeth, still it is harder to supply another subject in the first line than in the second, and in the following verses.

[3] Samilâ = yugarandhrakîlaka, Ava*k*ûri.

[4] *Kh*imâla = *g*âra, see Hêma*k*andra, Dê*s*î Kôsha 3, 27. It is a coarse term, which I replace by another, though probably the language of our coach-drivers might supply us with a more idiomatic rendering.

[5] Gârava, cf. p. 98, note 2.

some to their good fare; some to their comfort; some nurse their anger. (9)

'Some are averse to begging; some are afraid of insults and are stuck up; (how can) I convince them by reasons and arguments[1] (?) (10)

'(A bad pupil) makes objections, and points out (imagined) difficulties; he frequently acts in opposition to the words of the superiors. (11)

'(He will say if sent to a lady): "She does not know me, she will give me nothing; I suppose she will be gone out; send some other monk there." (12)

'If sent on an errand, they do not do what they were bidden[2], but stroll about wherever they like; or deporting themselves like servants of the king[3], they knit their brows (when speaking to other people). (13)

'After they have been instructed, admitted into the order, and nourished with food and drink, they disperse in all directions like geese whose wings have grown.' (14)

Now this driver (viz. Garga), who had to deal with bad bullocks, thought: 'What have I to do with bad pupils? I am disheartened. (15)

'As are bad pupils, so are bad bullocks; I shall leave these lazy donkeys, and shall practise severe austerities.' (16)

---

[1] The metre of this verse seems to have originally been Âryâ, but an attempt has been made to change it into Anush*t*ubh. We meet here with the interesting form a*n*usâsammî (read a*n*usasammi) = anu*s*âsmi.

[2] This seems to be the meaning of the word paliu*mk*anti. The commentators say, after other explanations, that they pretend not to have met the person to whom they were sent.

[3] Râ*g*ave*tth*i*m* va mannantâ; ve*tth*i=vish*t*i, hire.

That noble man, who was full of kindness, grave, and always meditating, wandered about on the earth, leading a virtuous life. (17)

Thus I say.

TWENTY-EIGHTH LECTURE.

THE ROAD TO FINAL DELIVERANCE.

Learn the true road leading to final deliverance, which the *G*inas have taught; it depends on four causes and is characterised by right knowledge and faith. (1)

I. Right knowledge; II. Faith; III. Conduct; and IV. Austerities; this is the road taught by the *G*inas who possess the best knowledge. (2)

Right knowledge, faith, conduct, and austerities; beings who follow this road, will obtain beatitude. (3)

I. Knowledge is fivefold: 1. *S*ruta, knowledge derived from the sacred books; 2. Âbhinibôdhika, perception[1]; 3. Avadhi, supernatural knowledge; 4. Mana*h*paryâya[2], knowledge of the thoughts of other people; 5. Kêvala, the highest, unlimited knowledge. (4)

---

[1] This is usually called mati, and is placed before *s*ruta. The same enumeration recurs in XXXIII, 4, p. 193. Umâsvâti in Môksha Sûtra I, 14, gives the following synonyms of mati: smr*i*ti, *k*intâ, abhinibôdha.

[2] Ma*n*anâ*n*am.

This is the fivefold knowledge. The wise ones have taught the knowledge of substances, qualities, and all developments[1]. (5)

Substance is the substrate of qualities; the qualities are inherent in one substance; but the characteristic of developments is that they inhere in either (viz. substances or qualities). (6)

Dharma, Adharma, space, time, matter, and souls (are the six kinds of substances[2]); they make up this world, as has been taught by the *G*inas who possess the best knowledge. (7)

Dharma, Adharma, and space are each one substance only; but time, matter, and souls are an infinite number of substances. (8)

The characteristic of Dharma is motion, that of Adharma immobility, and that of space[3], which contains all other substances, is to make room (for everything)[4]. (9)

The characteristic of time is duration[5], that of soul the realisation[6] of knowledge, faith, happiness, and misery. (10)

The characteristic of Soul is knowledge, faith, conduct, austerities, energy, and realisation (of its developments). (11)

The characteristic of matter is sound, darkness,

---

[1] Dravya, gu*n*a, paryâya (pa*gg*ava in *G*aina Prâk*ri*t). Gu*n*a, quality, is generally not admitted by the *G*ainas as a separate category, see *S*îlâṅka's refutation of the Vai*s*êshika doctrines at the end of his comments on Sûtrak*ri*tâṅga I, 12 (Bombay edition, p. 482).

[2] They are frequently called astikâyas, or realities.

[3] It is here called nabhas instead of âkâ*s*a.

[4] Avagâha.

[5] Vartanâ.

[6] Upayôga.

lustre (of jewels, &c.), light, shade, sunshine; colour, taste, smell, and touch. (12)

The characteristic of development is singleness, separateness[1], number, form, conjunction, and disjunction. (13)

1. *g*îva, Soul; 2. a*g*îva, the inanimate things; 3. bandha, the binding of the soul by Karman; 4. pu*n*ya, merit; 5. pâpa, demerit; 6. âsrava, that which causes the soul to be affected by sins; 7. sa*m*vara, the prevention of âsrava by watchfulness; 8. the annihilation of Karman; 9. final deliverance: these are the nine truths (or categories). (14)

He who verily believes the true teaching of the (above nine) fundamental truths, possesses righteousness. (15)

II. Faith is produced by 1. nisarga, nature; 2. upadê*s*a, instruction; 3. â*gñ*â, command; 4. sûtra, study of the sûtras; 5. bî*g*a, suggestion; 6. abhigama, comprehension of the meaning of the sacred lore; 7. vistâra, complete course of study; 8. kriyâ, religious exercise; 9. sa*m*kshêpa, brief exposition; 10. dharma, the Law. (16)

1. He who truly comprehends, by a spontaneous effort of his mind[2], (the nature of) soul, inanimate things, merit, and demerit, and who puts an end to sinful influences[3], (believes by) nature. (17)

He who spontaneously believes the four truths (explicitly mentioned in the last verse), which the

---

[1] Singleness (êkatva) makes a thing appear as one thing, separateness (p*ri*thaktva) as different from others.

[2] Sahasamuiya = svaya*m*samudita. It is usually rendered sahasammati.

[3] Âsravasa*m*vara, see above, verse 14, 6 and 7.

*G*inas have taught, (thinking) they are of this and not of a different nature, believes by nature. (18)

2. But he who believes these truths, having learned them from somebody else, either a *Kh*admastha [1] or a *G*ina, believes by instruction. (19)

3. He who has got rid of love, hate, delusion, and ignorance, and believes because he is told to do so, believes by command. (20)

4. He who obtains righteousness by (the study of) the Sûtras, either Aṅgas or other works [2], believes by the study of Sûtras. (21)

5. He who by correctly comprehending one truth arrives at the comprehension of more—just as a drop of oil expands on the surface of water—believes by suggestion. (22)

6. He who truly knows the sacred lore, viz. the eleven Aṅgas, the Prakîr*n*as [3], and the D*ri*sh*t*ivâda, believes by the comprehension of the sacred lore. (23)

7. He who understands the true nature of all substances by means of all proofs (pramâ*n*a) and nayas [4], believes by a complete course of study. (24)

8. He who sincerely performs (all duties implied)

---

[1] A *kh*admastha is one who has not yet obtained Kêvala, or the highest knowledge; he is in the two gu*n*asthânas (the fourteen stages in the development of the soul from the lowest to the highest) characterised as 1. upa*s*ântamôha, and 2. kshî*n*a-môha; viz. 1. that in which delusion is only temporarily separated from the soul, and 2. that in which delusion is finally destroyed.

[2] Bâhira; apparently the same works are intended which are elsewhere called anaṅgapravish*t*a.

[3] The original has the singular.

[4] The seven nayas are 'points of view or principles with reference to which certain judgments are arrived at or arrangements made.' Bhandarkar, Report, p. 112.

by right knowledge, faith, and conduct, by asceticism and discipline, and by all Samitis and Guptis, believes by religious exercise. (25)

9. He who though not versed in the sacred doctrines[1] nor acquainted with other systems[2], holds no wrong doctrines, believes by brief exposition. (26)

10. He who believes in the truth[3] of the realities[4], the Sûtras, and conduct, as it has been explained by the *G*inas, believes by the Law. (27)

Right belief depends on the acquaintance with truth[5], on the devotion to those who know the truth, and on the avoiding of schismatical and heretical tenets. (28)

There is no (right) conduct without right belief[6], and it must be cultivated (for obtaining) right faith; righteousness and conduct originate together, or righteousness precedes (conduct). (29)

Without (right) faith there is no (right) knowledge, without (right) knowledge there is no virtuous conduct[7], without virtues there is no deliverance[8], and without deliverance there is no perfection. (30)

(The excellence of faith depends on the following) eight points: 1. that one has no doubts (about the truth of the tenets); 2. that one has no preference (for heterodox tenets); 3. that one does not doubt

---

[1] Prava*k*ana. [2] E. g. that of Kapila, &c., Comm.

[3] Dharma. [4] Astikâya; see note on verse 7.

[5] I. e. true things as soul, &c.

[6] Sa*m*yaktva 'righteousness.'

[7] *K*ara*n*agu*n*a. The commentators make this a dvandva compound, and interpret *k*ara*n*a as vratâdi, and gu*n*a as pi*nd*avi*s*uddhi, &c.

[8] By deliverance I have rendered môksha, and by final perfection nirvâ*n*a. Môksha denotes freedom from Karman, a condition which in Brâhmanical philosophy is called *g*îvanmukti.

its saving qualities[1]; 4. that one is not shaken in the right belief (because heretical sects are more prosperous); 5. that one praises (the pious); 6. that one encourages (weak brethren); 7. that one supports or loves the confessors of the Law; 8. that one endeavours to exalt it. (31)

III. Conduct, which produces the destruction of all Karman, is 1. sâmâyika[2], the avoidance of everything sinful; 2. *kh*êdôpasthâpana, the initiation of a novice; 3. parihâravi*s*uddhika, purity produced by peculiar austerities[3]; 4. sûkshma samparâya, reduction of desire; 5. akashâya yathâkhyâta, annihilation of sinfulness according to the precepts of the Arhats, as well as in the case of a *Kh*admastha as of a *G*ina. (32, 33)

IV. Austerities are twofold: external and internal; both external and internal austerities are sixfold. (34)

By knowledge one knows things, by faith one believes in them, by conduct one gets (freedom from Karman), and by austerities one reaches purity. (35)

Having by control and austerities destroyed their Karman, great sages, whose purpose is to get rid of all misery, proceed to (perfection).

Thus I say.

---

[1] Nivvitigi*kkh*â=nirvi*k*ikitsa. According to the commentary it may stand for nir-vid-*g*ugupsâ 'without loathing the saints.'

[2] See Bhandarkar, Report, p. 98, note ‡.

[3] The Dîpikâ contains the following details. Nine monks resolve to live together for eighteen months. They make one of their number their superior, kalpasthita, four become parihârikas, and the remaining four serve them (anuparihârikas). After six months the parihârikas become anuparihârikas and vice versa. After another six months the kalpasthita does penance and all the other monks serve him as anuparihârikas.

TWENTY-NINTH LECTURE.

THE EXERTION IN RIGHTEOUSNESS.

O long-lived (*G*ambûsvâmin)! I (Sudharman) have heard the following discourse from the venerable (Mahâvîra).

Here, forsooth, the Venerable Ascetic Mahâvîra, of the Kas*y*apa Gôtra, has delivered this lecture called the exertion in righteousness. Many creatures, who truly believe in the subject (taught in this lecture), put their faith in it, give credence to it, accept it, practise it, comply with it, study it, understand it, learn it, and act up to it according to the precept (of the *G*inas)[1]—have obtained perfection, enlightenment, deliverance, final beatitude, and have put an end to all misery.

This lecture treats of the following subjects:

1. sa*m*vêga, longing for liberation;
2. nirvêda, disregard of worldly objects;
3. dharmas*r*addhâ, desire of the Law;
4. gurusâdharmikas*u*s*r*ûsha*n*â, obedience to co-religionists and to the Guru.
5. âlô*k*anâ, confession of sins before the Guru;
6. nindâ, repenting of one's sins to oneself;
7. garhâ, repenting of one's sins before the Guru;

[1] Here we have no less than ten verbs, many of which are synonyms, with probably no well-defined difference in their meaning. This heaping of synonymous words is a peculiarity of the archaic style. The commentators always labour hard to assign to each word an appropriate meaning, but by sometimes offering different sets of explanations they show that their ingenuity of interpretation was not backed by tradition.

8. sâmâyika, moral and intellectual purity of the soul;

9. *k*aturvi*ms*atistava, adoration of the twenty-four *G*inas;

10. vandana, paying reverence to the Guru;

11. pratikrama*n*a, expiation of sins;

12. kâyôtsarga, a particular position of the body;

13. pratyâkhyâna, self-denial;

14. stavastutimaṅgala, praises and hymns;

15. kâlasya pratyupêksha*n*â, keeping the right time;

16. prâya*sk*ittakara*n*a, practising penance;

17. kshamâpa*n*a, begging forgiveness;

18. svâdhyâya, study;

19. vâ*k*anâ, recital of the sacred texts;

20. parip*rikkh*anâ, questioning (the teacher);

21. parâvartanâ, repetition;

22. anuprêkshâ, pondering;

23. dharmakathâ, religious discourse;

24. *s*rutasyârâdhanâ, acquisition of sacred knowledge;

25. êkâgramana*h*sannivê*s*anâ, concentration of thoughts;

26. sa*m*yama, control;

27. tapas, austerities;

28. vyavadâna, cutting off the Karman;

29. sukhâ*s*âta, renouncing pleasure;

30. apratibaddhatâ, mental independence;

31. vi*k*itra*s*ayanâsanasêvanâ, using unfrequented lodgings and beds;

32. vinivartanâ, turning from the world;

33. sambhôgapratyâkhyâna, renouncing collection of alms in one district only;

34. upadhipratyâkhyâna, renouncing articles of use;

35. âhârapratyâkhyâna, renouncing food;

36. kashâyapratyâkhyâna, conquering the passions;

37. yôgapratyâkhyâna, renouncing activity;

38. *s*arîrapratyâkhyâna, renouncing the body;

39. sahâyapratyâkhyâna, renouncing company;

40. bhaktapratyâkhyâna, renouncing all food;

41. sadbhâvapratyâkhyâna, perfect renunciation;

42. pratirûpatâ, conforming to the standard;

43. vaiyâv*ri*tya, doing service;

44. sarvagu*n*asampûr*n*atâ, fulfilling all virtues;

45. vîtarâgatâ, freedom from passion;

46. kshânti, patience;

47. mukti, freedom from greed;

48. âr*g*ava, simplicity;

49. mârdava, humility;

50. bhâvasatya, sincerity of mind;

51. kara*n*asatya, sincerity of religious practice;

52. yôgasatya, sincerity of acting;

53. manôguptatâ, watchfulness of the mind;

54. vâg-guptatâ, watchfulness of the speech;

55. kâyaguptatâ, watchfulness of the body;

56. mana*h*samâdhâra*n*â, discipline of the mind;

57. vâksamâdhâra*n*â, discipline of the speech;

58. kâyasamâdhâra*n*â, discipline of the body;

59. *gñ*ânasampannatâ, possession of knowledge;

60. dar*s*anasampannatâ, possession of faith;

61. *k*âritrasampannatâ, possession of conduct;

62. *s*rôtrêndriyanigraha, subduing the ear;

63. *k*akshurindriyanigraha, subduing the eye;

64. ghrâ*n*êndriyanigraha, subduing the organ of smell;

65. *g*ihvêndriyanigraha, subduing the tongue;

66. spar*s*anêndriyanigraha, subduing the organ of touch;

67. krôdhavi*g*aya, conquering anger;

68. mânavi*g*aya, conquering pride;

69. mâyâvi*g*aya, conquering deceit;

70. lôbhavi*g*aya, conquering greed;

71. prêmadvêshamithyâdar*s*a*n*avi*g*aya, conquering love, hate, and wrong belief;

72. *s*ailê*s*î, stability;

73. akarmatâ, freedom from Karman.

1. Sir, what does the soul obtain by the longing for liberation? By the longing for liberation the soul obtains an intense desire of the Law; by an intense desire of the Law he quickly arrives at an (increased) longing for liberation; he destroys anger, pride, deceit, and greed, which reproduce themselves infinitely; he acquires no (bad) Karman, and ridding himself of wrong belief which is the consequence of the latter, he becomes possessed of right faith; by the purity of faith some will reach perfection after one birth; nobody, however, who has got this purity, will be born more than thrice before he reaches perfection. (1)

2. Sir, what does the soul obtain by disregard of worldly objects[1]? By disregard of worldly objects the soul quickly feels disgust for pleasures enjoyed by gods, men, and animals; he becomes indifferent to

[1] Or aversion to the Circle of Births.

all objects; thereby he ceases to engage in any undertakings, in consequence of which he leaves the road of Sa*m*sâra and enters the road to perfection. (2)

3. Sir[1], what does the soul obtain by the desire of the Law? By the desire of the Law the soul becomes indifferent to pleasures and happiness to which he was attached; he abandons the life of householders, and as a houseless monk he puts an end to all pains of body and mind, which consist in (the suffering of) cutting, piercing, union (with unpleasant things), &c.; and he obtains unchecked happiness. (3)

4. By obedience to co-religionists and to the Guru the soul obtains discipline (vinaya). By discipline and avoidance of misconduct (towards the teacher[2]) he avoids being reborn as a denizen of hell, an animal, a (low) man, or a (bad) god; by zealous praise of, devotion to, and respect for (the Guru) he obtains birth as a (good) man or god, gains perfection and beatitude, does all praiseworthy actions prescribed by discipline, and prevails upon others to adopt discipline. (4)

5. By confession of sins (before the Guru) the soul gets rid of the thorns, as it were, of deceit, misapplied austerities[3], and wrong belief, which obstruct the way to final liberation and cause an endless migration of the soul; he obtains simplicity, whereby the soul which is free from deceit does not acquire that Karman which results in his having a carnal desire for a woman or eunuch[4], and annihilates such Karman as he had acquired before. (5)

---

[1] In this way all paragraphs up to § 72 open with a question of always the same form. I drop the question in the sequel.

[2] Atyâ*s*âtana.

[3] Nidâna, cf. p. 60, n. 2.

[4] This is the meaning of the words itthîvêya napu*m*saga-

6. By repenting of one's sins to oneself the soul obtains repentance, and becoming indifferent by repentance he prepares for himself an (ascending) scale of virtues [1], by which he destroys the Karman resulting from delusion. (6)

7. By repenting of one's sins before the Guru the soul obtains humiliation; feeling humiliated, he will leave off all blameable occupations [2], and apply himself to praiseworthy occupations, whereby a houseless monk will stop infinite disabling [3] developments. (7)

8. By moral and intellectual purity (literally, equilibrium) the soul ceases from sinful occupations. (8)

9. By the adoration of the twenty-four *G*inas the soul arrives at purity of faith. (9)

10. By paying reverence (to the Guru) the soul destroys such Karman as leads to birth in low families, and acquires such Karman as leads to birth in noble families; he wins the affection of people, which results in his being looked upon as an authority, and he brings about general goodwill. (10)

11. By expiation of sins he obviates transgressions of the vows; thereby he stops the Âsravas, preserves a pure conduct, practises the eight articles [4], does not neglect (the practice of control), and pays great attention to it. (11)

---

vêya*m* = strîvêda, napu*m*sakavêda, as explained by the commentators on XXXII, 102.

[1] Kara*n*agu*n*a*s*rêdhîm pratipadyatê. It is difficult to render this phrase adequately; the meaning is that by successively destroying moral impurities one arrives at higher and higher virtues.

[2] Yôga, i.e. the cause of the production of Karman.

[3] Ghâti, compare Bhandarkar, Report, p. 93, note *

[4] See Twenty-fourth Lecture, p. 129 ff.

12. By Kâyôtsarga he gets rid of past and present (transgressions which require) Prâyas*k*itta[1]; thereby his mind is set at ease like a porter who is eased of his burden; and engaging in praiseworthy contemplation he enjoys happiness. (12)

13. By self-denial he shuts, as it were, the doors of the Âsravas; by self-denial he prevents desires rising in him; by prevention of desires he becomes, as it were, indifferent and cool towards all objects. (13)

14. By praises and hymns he obtains the wisdom consisting in knowledge, faith, and conduct; thereby he gains such improvement, that he will put an end to his worldly existence[2], (or) be born afterwards in one of the Kalpas and Vimânas[3]. (14)

15. By keeping the right time he destroys the Karman which obstructs right knowledge. (15)

16. By practising Prâyas*k*itta[1] he gets rid of sins, and commits no transgressions; he who correctly practises Prâyas*k*itta, gains the road and the reward of the road[4], he wins the reward of good conduct. (16)

17. By begging forgiveness he obtains happiness of mind; thereby he acquires a kind disposition towards all kinds of living beings[5]; by this

---

[1] Expiatory rites, âlô*k*anâ, &c.

[2] Antakriyâ, explained by mukti.

[3] The Kalpas and the Vimânas are the heavens of the Vaimânika gods, see below, p. 226.

[4] By road is meant the means of acquiring right knowledge, and by the reward of the road, right knowledge. The reward of good conduct is mukti.

[5] Savvapâ*n*abhûyag*î*vasattâ. The prâ*n*as possess from two to four organs of sense, the g*î*vas five, the bhûtas are plants, and the sattvas are all remaining beings.

kind disposition he obtains purity of character and freedom from fear. (17)

18. By study he destroys the Karman which obstructs right knowledge. (18)

19. By the recital of the sacred texts he obtains destruction of Karman, and contributes to preserve the sacred lore, whereby he acquires the Law of the Tîrtha [1], which again leads him to the complete destruction of Karman, and to the final annihilation of worldly existence. (19)

20. By questioning (the teacher) he arrives at a correct comprehension of the Sûtra and its meaning, and he puts an end to the Karman which produces doubts and delusion. (20)

21. By repetition he reproduces the sounds (i.e. syllables) and commits them to memory. (21)

22. By pondering (on what he has learned) he loosens the firm hold which the seven kinds of Karman, except the Âyushka [2] (have upon the soul); he shortens their duration when it was to be a long one; he mitigates their power when it was intense; (he reduces their sphere of action when it was a wide one) [3]; he may either acquire Âyushka-karman or not, but he no more accumulates Karman which

---

[1] According to the commentaries, by Tîrtha are meant the Ga*n*adharas.

[2] Concerning the eight kinds of Karman, see XXXIII, 2 and 3, p. 192. Âyushka is that Karman which determines the length of time which one is to live. A somewhat different explanation of this Karman is given by Bhandarkar, loc. cit., p. 97, note.

[3] The passage in question is an addition in some MSS., as the commentators tell us. The meaning seems to be that the Karman which was attached to many parts of the soul is restricted to fewer places by the influence of the purity superinduced on the soul by pondering.

produces unpleasant feelings, and he quickly crosses the very large forest of the fourfold Sa*m*sâra, which is without beginning and end. (22)

23. By religious discourses he obtains destruction of the Karman; by religious discourses he exalts the creed, and by exalting the creed he acquires Karman, which secures, for the future, permanent bliss. (23)

24. By acquisition of sacred knowledge he destroys ignorance, and will not be corrupted by worldliness. (24)

25. By concentration of his thoughts he obtains stability of the mind. (25)

26. By control he obtains freedom from sins. (26)

27. By austerities he cuts off the Karman[1]. (27)

28. By cutting off the Karman he obtains (the fourth stage of pure meditation characterised by) freedom from actions, by doing no actions he will obtain perfection, enlightenment, deliverance, and final beatitude, and will put an end to all misery. (28)

29. By renouncing pleasures he obtains freedom from false longing, whereby he becomes compassionate, humble, free from sorrow, and destroys the Karman produced by delusion regarding conduct. (29)

30. By mental independence he gets rid of attachment, whereby he will concentrate his thoughts (on the Law), and will for ever be without attachment and fondness (for worldly things). (30)

31. By using unfrequented lodgings and beds he obtains the Gupti of conduct, whereby he will use

---

[1] Vyavadâna is the cutting off of the Karman and the subsequent purity of the soul.

allowed food, be steady in his conduct, be exclusively delighted with (control), obtain a yearning for deliverance, and cut off the tie of the eightfold Karman. (31)

32. By turning from the world he will strive to do no bad actions, and will eliminate his already acquired Karman by its destruction; then he will cross the forest of the fourfold Sa*m*sâra. (32)

33. By renouncing collection of alms in one district only[1] he overcomes obstacles[2]; unchecked by them he exerts himself to attain liberation; he is content with the alms he gets, and does not hope for, care for, wish, desire, or covet those of a fellow-monk; not envying other monks he takes up a separate, agreeable lodging[3]. (33)

34. By renouncing articles of use[4] he obtains successful study; without articles of use he becomes exempt from desires, and does not suffer misery. (34)

35. By renouncing (forbidden) food he ceases to act for the sustenance of his life; ceasing to act for the sustenance of his life he does not suffer misery when without food. (35)

36. By conquering his passions he becomes free from passions; thereby he becomes indifferent to happiness and pains. (36)

37. By renouncing activity he obtains inactivity, by ceasing to act he acquires no new Karman, and destroys the Karman he had acquired before. (37)

38. By renouncing his body he acquires the pre-eminent virtues of the Siddhas, by the possession

---

1 Sambhôga = êkama*nd*alyâm âhârakara*n*am.

2 Âlambanâ, glânatâdi.

3 Du*kk*am suhase*gg*am uvasa*m*pa*gg*ittâ*n*a*m* viharai.

4 Except such as are obligatory, e.g. his broom, the mukhavastrikâ, &c.

of which he goes to the highest region of the universe, and becomes absolutely happy. (38)

39. By renouncing company he obtains singleness; being single and concentrating his mind, he avoids disputes, quarrels, passions, and censoriousness, and he acquires a high degree of control, of Sa*m*vara, and of carefulness[1]. (39)

40. By renouncing all food he prevents his being born again many hundreds of times. (40)

41. By perfect renunciation[2] he enters the final (fourth stage of pure meditation), whence there is no return; a monk who is in that state, destroys the four remnants of Karman which even a Kêvalin possesses, viz. vêdanîya, âyushka, nâman, and gôtra[3]; and then he will put an end to all misery. (41)

42. By conforming to the standard of monks[4] he obtains ease, thereby he will be careful, wear openly the excellent badges of the order, be of perfect righteousness, possess firmness and the Samitis, inspire all beings with confidence, mind but few things[5], subdue his senses, and practise, in a high degree, the Samitis and austerities. (42)

43. By doing service he acquires the Karman

---

[1] Samâhiê = samâhita or sa*m*âdhimân.

[2] Sadbhâva pratyâkhyâna. The Dîpikâ gives the following explanation: he makes the renunciation in such a way that he need not make it a second time.

[3] Vêdanîya is that Karman which produces effects that must be experienced, as pleasure or pain; âyushka is the Karman that determines the length of life; nâman and gôtra cause him to be born as such or such an individual in this or that family; see Thirty-third Lecture, verses 2 and 3, p. 192 f.

[4] Explained: sthavirakalpasâdhuvêshadhâritvam.

[5] Appa*d*ilêha = alpapratyupêksha; he has to inspect few things, because he uses only few.

which brings about for him the nâman and gôtra of a Tîrthakara. (43)

44. By fulfilling all virtues he secures that he will not be born again; thereby he will become exempt from pains of the body and mind. (44)

45. By freedom from passion he cuts off the ties of attachment and desire; thereby he becomes indifferent to all agreeable and disagreeable sounds, touches, colours, and smells. (45)

46. By patience he overcomes troubles. (46)

47. By freedom from greed he obtains voluntary poverty, whereby he will become inaccessible to desire for property. (47)

48. By simplicity he will become upright in actions, thoughts, and speech, and he will become veracious; thereby he will truly practise the Law. (48)

49. By humility he will acquire freedom from self-conceit; thereby he will become of a kind and meek disposition, and avoid the eight kinds of pride. (49)

50. By sincerity of mind he obtains purity of mind, which will cause him to exert himself for the fulfilment of the Law which the *G*inas have proclaimed; and he will practise the Law in the next world too. (50)

51. By sincerity in religious practice he obtains proficiency in it; being proficient in it he will act up to his words. (51)

52. By sincerity of acting he will become pure in his actions. (52)

53. By watchfulness[1] of the mind he concentrates his thoughts; thereby he truly practises control. (53)

[1] Gupti.

54. By watchfulness of speech he keeps free from prevarication; thereby he enables his mind to act properly. (54)

55. By watchfulness of the body he obtains Samvara[1]; thereby he prevents sinful Âsravas. (55)

56. By discipline of the mind he obtains concentration of his thoughts; thereby he obtains development of knowledge, which produces righteousness and annihilates wrong belief. (56)

57. By discipline of the speech he obtains development of faith, whereby he acquires facility of becoming enlightened, and destroys preventing causes. (57)

58. By discipline of the body he obtains development of conduct, which causes him to conduct himself according to the regulation; thereby he destroys the four remnants of Karman which even a Kêvalin possesses[2]; after that he obtains perfection, enlightenment, deliverance, and final beatitude, and he puts an end to all misery. (58)

59. By possession of knowledge he acquires an understanding of words and their meaning; thereby he will not perish in the forest of the fourfold Samsâra; as a needle with its thread will not be lost, thus the soul possessing the sacred lore[3] will not be lost in the Samsâra; he performs all prescribed actions relating to knowledge, discipline, austerities, and conduct, and well versed in his

[1] For Samvara and Âsrava, see above, p. 55, note 1, and p. 73, note 2.

[2] See above, § 41.

[3] Here is a pun on the word sutta=sûtra, which means thread and Sûtra, sacred lore, or knowledge acquired by the study of the Sûtras.

own and in heterodox creeds he will become invincible. (59)

60. By possession of faith he annihilates wrong belief which is the cause of worldly existence, and he will not lose his inner light; but he endues his Self with the highest knowledge and faith, and purifies it[1]. (60)

61. By possession of conduct he obtains a stability like that of the king of mountains[2] (viz. Mêru), whereby a houseless monk destroys the four remnants of Karman which even a Kêvalin possesses; after that he obtains perfection, enlightenment, deliverance, and final beatitude, and puts an end to all misery. (61)

62. By subduing the organ of hearing he overcomes his delight with or aversion to all pleasant or unpleasant sounds, he acquires no Karman produced thereby, and destroys the Karman he had acquired before. (62)

63–66. (All this applies also to his) subduing the organs of sight, of smelling, of tasting, and of touch (with regard to) pleasant colours, smells, tastes, and touches. (63–66)

67. By conquering anger he obtains patience; he acquires no Karman productive of anger[3], and destroys the Karman he had acquired before. (67)

68. By conquering pride he obtains simplicity, &c. (as in 67, substituting pride for anger). (68)

69. By conquering deceit he obtains humility, &c. (as in 67, substituting deceit for anger). (69)

---

[1] I.e. makes it contain nothing foreign to its own nature.

[2] Sêlêsî = *s*ailê*s*î; *s*ailê*s*a is Mêru, and its avasthâ, or condition, is *s*ailê*s*î.

[3] Or, perhaps, which results in experiencing anger.

70. By conquering greed he obtains content, &c. (as in 67, substituting greed for anger). (70)

71. By conquering love, hate, and wrong belief he exerts himself for right knowledge, faith, and conduct, then he will cut off the fetters of the eightfold Karman; he will first destroy the twenty-eight kinds[1] of Karman, which are productive of delusion; (then) the five kinds of obstruction to right knowledge[2], the nine kinds of obstruction to right faith[3], and the five kinds of obstacles (called Antarâya): the last three remnants of Karman he destroys simultaneously; afterwards he obtains absolute knowledge and faith, which is supreme, full, complete, unchecked, clear, faultless, and giving light (or penetrating) the whole universe; and while he still acts[4], he acquires but such Karman as is inseparable from religious acts[5]; the pleasant feelings (produced by it) last but two moments: in the first moment it is acquired, in the second it is experienced, and in the third it is destroyed; this Karman is produced, comes into contact (with the soul), takes rise, is experienced, and is destroyed; for all time to come he is exempt from Karman. (71)

72. Then[6] when his life is spent up to less than

---

[1] There are sixteen kashâyas, nine nô-kashâyas, and three môhanîyas.

[2] These are the obstacles to the five kinds of knowledge: mati, sruta, avadhi, manahparyâya, kêvala.

[3] They are: the obstacles to kakshurdarsana, to akakshurdarsana, to avadhidarsana, and to kêvaladarsana, and five kinds of sleep (nidrâ). Concerning Antarâya, see p. 193.

[4] Sayôgin, i.e. while he has not yet reached the fourteenth gunasthâna, the state of a Kêvalin.

[5] Airyapathika.

[6] I.e. when he has become a Kêvalin, as described in the preceding paragraph.

half a muhûrta, he discontinues to act, and enters upon the (third degree of) pure meditation [1], from which there is no relapse (to lower degrees), and which requires most subtile functions only (of his organs); he first stops the functions of his mind, then the functions of speech, then those of the body, at last he ceases to breathe. During the time required for pronouncing five short syllables, he is engaged in the final pure meditation, in which all functions (of his organs) have ceased, and he simultaneously annihilates the four remnants of Karman, viz. vêdanîya, âyushka, nâman, and gôtra [2]. (72)

73. Then having, by all methods, got rid of his audârika, kârma*n*a (and tai*g*asa) bodies, the soul takes the form of a straight line, goes in one moment, without touching anything and taking up no space, (upwards to the highest Âkâ*s*a), and there develops into its natural form, obtains perfection, enlightenment, deliverance, and final beatitude, and puts an end to all misery. (73)

This indeed is the subject of the lecture called exertion in righteousness, which the Venerable Ascetic Mahâvîra has told, declared, explained, demonstrated. (74)

Thus I say.

---

[1] *S*ukladhyâna. [2] See note on § 41.

THIRTIETH LECTURE.

THE ROAD OF PENANCE.

Now hear with concentrated mind, how a monk destroys by austerities the bad Karman which he had acquired by love and hatred. (1)

By abstaining 1. from destroying life; 2. from lying; 3. from taking anything which is not given; 4. from all sexual indulgence; 5. from having any property; and 6. from eating at night, the soul becomes free from Âsravas[1]. (2)

By possessing the five Samitis and the three Guptis, by freedom from passions, by subduing the senses, by vanquishing conceit[2], and by avoiding delusions, the soul becomes free from Âsravas. (3)

Hear attentively how a monk destroys (the Karman) acquired by love and hatred in the absence of the above-mentioned (virtues). (4)

As a large tank, when its supply of water has been stopped, gradually dries up by the consumption of the water and by evaporation, so the Karman of a monk, which he acquired in millions[3] of births, is annihilated by austerities, if there is no influx of bad Karman. (5, 6)

Austerities are of two kinds: external and internal;

---

[1] Karmôpâdânahêtavas, that through which the soul becomes affected by Karman.

[2] Agârava = agaurava; but it is here explained, free from garva, cf. p. 98, note 2.

[3] Literally krores, i.e. ten millions.

external austerities are of six kinds, and internal are of six kinds [1]. (7)

External austerities are:

1. anasana, fasting; 2. avamôdarikâ, abstinence [2]; 3. bhikshâkaryâ, collecting alms; 4. rasaparityâga, abstention from dainty food; 5. kâyaklêsa, mortification of the flesh; 6. samlînatâ, taking care of one's limbs [3]. (8)

1. Fasting is of two kinds: *a.* itvara, temporary, and *b.* maranakâla, fasting which precedes, and ends with death. Temporary fasting is either such in which a desire (for food) is present, or such in which no such desire exists. (9)

a. The temporary fasting is briefly of six kinds: 1. in the form of a line [4]; 2. in the form of a square; 3. in the form of a cube; 4. of a sixth power; 5. of a twelfth power; 6. of any arrangement. Temporary fasting (can be practised) for different objects which one has in mind. (10, 11)

---

[1] Comp. Aupapâtika Sûtra, ed. Leumann, p. 38 ff. The general division is the same, but the subdivision differs in many details.

[2] Gradual reduction of food, from a full meal of thirty-two morsels to one of one morsel.

[3] Aṅgôpâṅgâdikam samvritya pravartanam, *T*îkâ.

[4] The meaning of this singular statement is as follows. If four fasts of two, three, four, and five days are performed in this order, they form a line. If this set of fasts is four times repeated, each time beginning with a different number, we get sixteen fasts; they form a square, viz.:

1 . 2 . 3 . 4
2 . 3 . 4 . 1
3 . 4 . 1 . 2
4 . 1 . 2 . 3

The next class contains 64 fasts, the fourth 4,096, the fifth 16,777,216 fasts. Fasts of the last class require 700,000 years at least, and must be assumed to be restricted to former Tîrthakaras, whose lives lasted enormous periods of time.

b. Fasting which is to precede death, is of two kinds with regard to the motions of the body: with change (of position) and without change. (12)

And again it is twofold: admitting of relief[1], or not; one may either leave the place (which one has chosen to die in), or not leave it; in both cases one may not take any food. (13)

2. Abstinence is briefly of five kinds: with regard to *a*. substance; *b*. place; *c*. time; *d*. state of mind; *e*. development. (14)

a. He who takes less food than he usually does[2], in the extreme case but one mouthful, performs abstinence with regard to substance. (15)

b. (Place means) a village, a scotfree town[3], a capital, a camp of merchants[4], a mine, a settlement of a wild tribe[5], a place with an earth wall[6], a poor town[7], a town with a harbour[8], a large town[9], an isolated town[10], and an open town[11]. (16)

---

[1] Saparikarma = vaiyâvrityasahita. This leads to inginîmarana and bhaktapratyakhyâna; the aparikarma to pâdapôpagamana (i.e. prâyôpagamana); comp. part i, p. 72.

[2] Thirty-two mouthfuls is the usual quantity of food of men, twenty-eight that of women. A mouthful is of the size of an egg.

[3] Nagara, where no taxes (na kara) are levied, while villages pay eighteen taxes.

[4] Nigama, or a place where many merchants dwell.

[5] Pallî.

[6] Khê*t*a.

[7] Karva*t*a. According to the dictionary, it means 'market-town;' but the commentators render it by kunagâra, or say that it is karva*t*a*g*anâvâsa, the dwelling-place of the Karva*t*a people.

[8] Drô*n*amukha, a town to which there is access by water and land, like Bh*ri*guka*kkh*a or Tâmralipti.

[9] Pa*tt*ana.

[10] Ma*t*amba, a town which is more than three and a half yô*g*anas distant from the next village.

[11] Sambâdha, prabhûta*k*âturvar*n*yanivâsa.

In a hermitage, a vihâra[1], a halting-place for procession[2], a resting-place for travellers[3], a station of herdsmen, a camp on high ground, a caravan's camp, a fortified place of refuge. (17)

In gardens, on roads, in houses—all this is meant by place. In these and similar places he may (wander about). In this way he performs abstinence with regard to place. (18)

1. pê*t*â, 2. ardhapê*t*â, 3. gômûtrikâ, 4. pataṅgavîthikâ, 5. *s*ambûkâvartta, 6. âyata*m*-gatvâ-pratyâgata[4]. (19)

c. Abstinence with reference to time (is observed by him) who goes about in that time of the four Paurushîs of the day (which he selects for that purpose). (20)

Or if he collects alms in a part of the third Paurushî, or in its last quarter, then he observes abstinence with reference to time. (21)

d. Abstinence with reference to state of mind (is observed by him) who accepts alms from a woman or man, from an adorned or unadorned person, from one of any age or dress, of any temper or colour: if that person does not change his disposition or condition[5]. (22, 23)

---

[1] A dwelling-place of Bhikshus, or a dêvag*ri*ha.

[2] Sannivê*s*a.

[3] Samâ*g*a.

[4] These are terms for different kinds of collecting alms; it is called pê*t*â (box), when one begs successively at four houses forming the corners of an imaginary square; gômûtrikâ, when he takes the houses in a zigzag line; pataṅgavîthikâ (cricket's walk), when he goes to houses at a great distance from one another; *s*ambûkâvartta (the windings of a conch), when he goes in a spiral line, either toward the centre (abhyantara) or from the centre outward (bahis); âyata*m*-gatvâ-pratyâgata, when he first goes straight on and then returns.

[5] I give the traditional explanation of the verses, as handed

e. A monk who observes abstinence according to the particulars which have been enumerated with regard to substance, place, time, and state of mind, observes abstinence with regard to development[1] too. (24)

3. With regard to collecting alms there are the eight principal ways[2] how to collect them; the seven êsha*n*âs (or modes of begging) and other self-imposed restrictions. (25)

4. Abstention from dainty food means abstention from such highly nourishing[3] food and drink as milk, curds, ghee, &c. (26)

5. Mortification of the flesh consists in the different postures as Vîrâsana, &c., which benefit the soul, and which are difficult to perform. (27)

6. Using unfrequented lodgings and beds consists in living and sleeping in separate and

---

down in the commentaries. If we might set it aside, I should translate: abstinence with reference to disposition is observed by him who in collecting alms preserves the same disposition, whether he has to do with a woman or man, &c.

[1] For development (pa*gg*ava = paryâya) denotes any form or phase of existence which anything can assume. Therefore all particulars of place, e.g. are developments of Place. As all restrictions of place, &c., indirectly diminish the food obtainable by a monk, they also come under the head Abstinence.

[2] According to the commentator, these are the six kinds enumerated in verse 19. *S*ambûkâvartta is of two kinds, as explained in the note; the eighth kind is *rig*vî, or the common way of begging. These eight ways have reference to the houses in which they collect alms. The seven êsha*n*âs refer to the quality or quantity of the food; their names are given in the *T*îkâ, partly in Prâk*ri*t, partly in Sanskrit: 1. sa*m*sa*tth*â; 2. asa*m*sa*tth*â; 3. uddha*d*â; 4. alpalêpikâ; 5. udg*ri*hîtâ; 6. prag*ri*hîtâ; 7. u*ggh*itadharmâ. According to another passage: 1. is sa*m*sp*ri*sh*t*a, 3. uddhrita, 5. avag*ri*hîta.

[3] Pra*n*îta, explained push*t*ikara.

unfrequented places where there are neither women nor cattle. (28)

Thus external austerities have been briefly explained; I shall now explain internal austerities in due order. (29)

Internal austerities are:

1. prâyas*k*itta, expiation of sins;
2. vi*n*aya, politeness;
3. vaiyâv*ri*tya, serving the Guru;
4. svâdhyâya, study;
5. dhyâna, meditation;
6. vyutsarga[1], abandoning of the body. (30)

1. Expiation of sins is tenfold, what must be confessed[2], &c.; this is to be strictly observed by a monk; this is called expiation of sins. (31)

2. Politeness consists in rising (from one's seat), folding of the hands, offering of a seat, loving the Guru, and cordial obedience. (32)

3. There are ten[3] kinds of service, as serving the Â*k*ârya, &c.[4]; doing service consists in giving one's assistance as well as one is able. (33)

4. Study is fivefold: 1. saying or learning one's lesson; 2. (questioning the teacher about it); 3. repetition; 4. pondering; 5. religious discourse. (34)

---

[1] Viôsagga, viussaga, viusagga. It is usually rendered vyutsarga, but the Sanskrit prototype is vyavasarga, as Leumann has pointed out, l.c., p. 152.

[2] Compare Aupapâtika Sûtra, ed. Leumann, p. 40.

[3] Ibidem, p. 42.

[4] They are enumerated in the following Gâthâ: âyariya-uva*ggh*âê thêra-tavassî-gilâ*n*a-sêhâ*n*a | sâhammiya-kula-ga*n*a-saṅgha-sa*m*gaya*m* tam iha kâyavva*m*. The ten persons or body of persons entitled to 'service' are: 1. â*k*ârya; 2. upâdhyâya; 3. sthavira; 4. tapasvin; 5. glâna; 6. *s*aiksha; 7. sâdharmika; 8. kula; 9. ga*n*a; 10. saṅgha.

5. Abstaining to meditate on painful and sinful things[1], one should, with a collected mind, engage in pure meditations on the Law; this the wise call meditation. (35)

6. If a monk remains motionless when lying down, sitting, or standing upright, this is called abandoning of the body, which is the sixth kind (of internal austerities). (36)

If a sage truly performs these two kinds of austerities, he will soon be thoroughly released from the Circle of Births. (37)

Thus I say.

THIRTY-FIRST LECTURE.

MODE OF LIFE[2].

I shall declare the mode of life that benefits the soul; by practising it many souls have crossed the ocean of Sa*m*sâra. (1)

One should desist from one thing, and practise another: desist from neglect of self-control, and practise self-control. (2)

Love and hatred are two evils which produce bad

---

[1] This is the ârtaraudradhyâna.

[2] This lecture offers many difficulties to the translator, as it contains scarcely more than a dry list of articles of the *G*aina faith. To fully understand or interpret it would require an accurate knowledge of the complete religious system of the *G*ainas, to which we can lay no claim at present. The order in which the articles are given follows the number of their subdivisions. In some cases the number is not given in the Sûtra, but is supplied by the commentary.

Karman; if a monk always avoids them, he will not stand within the circle (of transmigration). (3)

A monk who always avoids the thrice threefold hurtful, conceited, and delusive acts [1], will not stand in the circle (of transmigration). (4)

A monk who well bears calamities produced by gods, animals, or men, will not stand, &c. (5)

A monk who always avoids the (four) different kinds of praises [2], passions, expressions (of the emotions) [3], and (of the four) meditations the two sinful ones, will not stand, &c. (6)

A monk who always exerts himself [4] with regard to the (five) vows, the (five) objects of sense, the (five) Samitis, and (five) actions [5], will not stand, &c. (7)

A monk who always exerts himself with regard to the six lêsyâs [6], the six kinds of bodies, and the six (regular functions as) eating [7], will not stand, &c. (8)

A monk who always exerts himself with regard to the (seven) rules of accepting alms [8], and the seven causes of danger (to other men) will not stand, &c. (9)

---

[1] Compare XIX, 91, and XXX, 3. Hurtful acts (da*n*d*a) are threefold, as referring to thoughts, words, and acts; conceited acts (gârava), as pride of riches, of taste (rasa), and of pleasure or fashion (sâtâ); delusive acts (*s*alya), as mâyâ, nidâna, and mithyâdar*s*ana.

[2] Vikatthâ. [3] Sa*m*g*ñ*â.

[4] Yatatê 'exerts himself;' supply 'to avoid, to know, or to do,' as the case may require.

[5] Kriyâ; they are: 1. kâyikî; 2. adhikara*n*ikî; 3. prâdvêshikî; 4. paritâpanikî, and 5. prâ*n*âtipâtikî.

[6] On the lêsyâs see Thirty-fourth Lecture, p. 196 ff.

[7] From the commentaries I learn two more of these six kâra*n*as: vêdana and vaiyâv*ri*tya. I cannot say which are the remaining three.

[8] They are enumerated in note 2 on XXX, 25, p. 178.

A monk who always exerts himself with regard to the (eight) objects of pride[1], to that which protects his chastity[2], and to the tenfold Law of the monks[3]. (10)

A monk who always exerts himself with regard to the (eleven) duties of the upâsakas, and the (twelve) duties of the bhikshus[4], will not stand, &c. (11)

A monk who always exerts himself with regard to the (thirteen) actions (productive of Karman), to the various (fourteen) kinds of living beings, and the (fifteen) places of punishment of the wicked[5], will not stand, &c. (12)

A monk who always exerts himself with regard to the sixteen Gâthâs[6], and to the (seventeen kinds of) neglect of self-control, will not stand, &c. (13)

A monk who always exerts himself with regard to the (eighteen kinds of) continence, to the (nineteen) *gñ*âtâdhyayanas[7], and the (twenty) cases for not concentrating one's thoughts, will not, &c. (14)

---

[1] Viz. caste, family, beauty, &c.; see Sûtrak*ri*t. II, 2, 17.

[2] Brahmagupti. This is of nine kinds.

[3] Bhikshudharma. It consists of Nos. 46–49, 26, 27, of Lecture XXIX, truth, purity, poverty, and chastity.

[4] The details given in the commentary (Dêvêndra) partly differ from the description of the twelve duties of *S*râvakas, and the ten duties of Bhikshus given by Bhandarkar from the Kârttikêyânuprêkshâ, see his Report, p. 114 ff.

[5] Paramâdhârmika. My translation is based on the enumeration of fifteen words, among which the names of some well-known hells occur.

[6] The sixteen lectures of the first part of the Sûtrak*ri*tâṅga, the last of which is called Gâthâ, are meant by the sixteen Gâthâs. The whole book contains twenty-three lectures as stated in verse 16.

[7] The first *s*rutaskandha of the *Gñ*âtâdharmakathâ, which contains nineteen adhyayanas, is intended by *gñ*âtâdhyayana.

A monk who always exerts himself with regard to the twenty-one forbidden[1] actions, and the twenty-two troubles[2], will not stand, &c. (15)

A monk who always exerts himself with regard to the twenty-three (lectures of the) Sûtrak*ri*tâṅga, and to the gods whose number exceeds by an unit[3] (the number of the lectures of the Sûtrak*ri*tâṅga), will not stand, &c. (16)

A monk who always exerts himself with regard to the twenty-five clauses[4], and (to the recitation of the twenty-six) chapters of the Da*s*âs, &c.[5], will not stand, &c. (17)

A monk who always exerts himself with regard to the (twenty-seven) virtues of the laity, and the (twenty-eight lectures of the) Prakalpa[6], will not stand, &c. (18)

A monk who always exerts himself with regard to the (twenty-nine) causes of wrong knowledge, and the (thirty) causes of delusion, will not stand, &c. (19)

A monk who always exerts himself with regard to the (thirty-one) qualities of Siddhas, &c., the (thirty-

---

[1] *S*abala, because they 'variegate' the conduct. The actions meant are sitting on an unwiped seat, &c.

[2] Parîsaha, see above, p. 9 ff.

[3] Rûpa. The twenty-four gods are: ten Bhavanapatis, eight Vyantaras, five *G*yôtishkas, one Vaimânika; or the 24 prophets.

[4] Bhâvanâ, the subdivisions of the five great vows, see part i, p. 189 ff.

[5] The Da*s*â*s*rutaskandha, B*ri*hat Kalpa, and Vyavahâra Sûtras are meant, which together contain twenty-six uddê*s*as.

[6] I.e. the Â*k*ârâṅga Sûtra; it now contains but twenty-four lectures, but is said to have originally contained four more, see part i, introduction, p. xlix f. These four lectures were: Mahâparinnâ, Ugghâya, A*n*ugghâya, Ârôva*n*â.

two) Yôgas[1], and thirty-three Âsâtanâs[2], will not stand, &c. (20)

A clever monk who always exerts himself with regard to the above-mentioned points, will soon be thoroughly released from the Circle of Births (21)

Thus I say.

THIRTY-SECOND LECTURE.

THE CAUSES OF CARELESSNESS.

With attentive mind hear me explain for your benefit the deliverance from the beginningless time, together with its causes[3], and from all misery: a truly wholesome subject. (1)

By the teaching of true[4] knowledge, by the avoidance of ignorance and delusion, and by the destruction of love and hatred, one arrives at final deliverance which is nothing but bliss. (2)

This is the road to it: to serve the Gurus and the old (teachers), to avoid throughout foolish people, to

---

[1] The pure operations of mind, speech, and body.

[2] As far as I can make out from the enumeration in the commentary, they are articles regulating the intercourse between monks, especially pupils and teacher.

[3] By beginningless time the Sa*m*sâra is meant; its causes are the kashâyas or cardinal passions, and avirati.

[4] Sa*kk*assa = satyasya. This is a various reading; the received text has savvassa. The commentators give the following explanation: by the property of knowledge to make everything known—this indicates that knowledge is the cause of môksha.

apply oneself earnestly to study, and to ponder zealously on the meaning of the Sûtras. (3)

A *S*rama*n*a engaged in austerities, who longs for righteousness[1], should eat the proper quantity of allowed food, should select a companion of right understanding, and should live in a place suited to seclusion. (4)

If he does not meet with a clever companion who surpasses or equals him in virtue, he should live by himself, abstaining from sins and not devoted to pleasures. (5)

As the crane[2] is produced from an egg, and the egg is produced from a crane, so they call desire[3] the origin of delusion, and delusion the origin of desire. (6)

Love and hatred are caused by Karman, and they say that Karman has its origin in delusion; Karman is the root of birth and death, and birth and death they call misery. (7)

Misery ceases on the absence of delusion, delusion ceases on the absence of desire, desire ceases on the absence of greed, greed ceases on the absence of property. (8)

I shall explain in due order the means which must be adopted by him who wants to thoroughly uproot love, hatred, and delusion. (9)

Pleasant food[4] should not be enjoyed with preference, for it generally makes men over-strong[5]; and desires rush upon the strong, like birds upon a tree with sweet fruits. (10)

---

[1] Samâdhi; the Dîpikâ explains it by *g*ñ*â*nadar*s*ana*k*âritralâbha.

[2] Balâka. [3] T*ri*sh*n*â. [4] Rasâ. [5] D*ri*ptikara.

As in a forest, full of fuel, a fire fanned by the wind cannot be extinguished, so the fire (as it were) of the senses of him who eats as he lists; it does not benefit any chaste man. (11)

The mind of those who always live in unfrequented lodgings, who eat low food, and who subdue their senses, will not be attacked by the foe, Love, who is vanquished as disease is by medicine. (12)

As it is not safe for mice to live near the dwelling of a cat, so a chaste (monk) cannot stay in a house inhabited by women. (13)

A *S*rama*n*a, engaged in penance, should not allow himself to watch the shape, beauty, coquetry, laughter, prattle, gestures, and glances of women, nor retain a recollection of them in his mind. (14)

Not to look at, nor to long for, not to think of, nor to praise, womankind: this is becoming the meditation of the noble ones, and it is always wholesome to those who delight in chastity. (15)

Though those who possess the three Guptis, cannot be disturbed even by well-adorned goddesses, still it is recommended to monks to live by themselves, as this is wholesome in every way. (16)

To a man who longs for liberation, who is afraid of the Sa*m*sâra, and lives according to the Law, nothing in the world offers so many difficulties[1] as women who delight the mind of the ignorant. (17)

To those who have overcome the attachment (to women), all others will offer no difficulties[2]; even as to those who have crossed the great ocean, no river, though big like the Ganges, (will offer any difficulty). (18)

---

[1] Duttara.

[2] Suuttara.

From desire of pleasure arises the misery of the whole world, the gods included; whatever misery of body and mind there is, the dispassionate will put an end to it. (19)

As the fruit of the Kimpâka[1] is beautiful in taste and colour, when eaten; but destroys the life when digested, (being) poison; similar in their effect are pleasures. (20)

A *S*rama*n*a, engaged in austerities, who longs for righteousness[2], should not fix his thoughts on the pleasant objects of the senses, nor turn his mind from them, if they be unpleasant. (21)

'Colour' attracts the eye; it is the pleasant cause of Love, but the unpleasant cause of Hatred[3]; he who is indifferent to them (viz. colours), is called dispassionate. (22)

The eye perceives 'colour,' and 'colour' attracts the eye; the cause of Love is pleasant, and the cause of Hatred is unpleasant. (23)

He who is passionately fond of 'colours,' will come to untimely ruin; just as an impassioned moth which is attracted by the light rushes into death. (24)

He who passionately hates (a colour), will at the same moment suffer pain. It is the fault of an undisciplined man that he is annoyed (by a colour); it is not the 'colour' itself that annoys him. (25)

[1] Trichosanthes Palmata, or Cucumis Colocynthus.

[2] Compare verse 4.

[3] Love and Hatred must of course be understood in their widest meaning. The same remark applies to the term 'colour,' which according to Hindu terminology denotes everything that is perceived by the eye. The first three sentences are, in the original, dependent on verbs as vadanti, âhus. I have, here and elsewhere, dropped them in the translation.

He who is very fond of a lovely 'colour,' hates all others; hence a fool will suffer misery, but a dispassionate sage is not affected by it. (26)

He who has a passion for 'colours[1],' will kill many movable and immovable beings; a passionate fool, intent on his personal interest, pains and torments those beings in many ways. (27)

How can a man who passionately desires 'colours[2],' be happy while he gets, keeps, uses, loses, and misses (those things). Even when he enjoys them, he is never satisfied. (28)

When he is not satisfied with those 'colours,' and his craving for them grows stronger and stronger, he will become discontented, and unhappy by dint of his discontent; misled by greed he will take another's property. (29)

When he is overcome by violent desire, takes another's property, and is not satisfied with those 'colours' and their possession, then his deceit and falsehood increase on account of his greed; yet he will not get rid of his misery. (30)

After and before he has lied[3], and when he is on the point of lying, he feels infinitely unhappy. Thus when he takes another's property, and is (after all) not satisfied by the 'colours' (he has

---

[1] Rûvâ*n*ugâsâ*n*uga = rûpa-anuga-â*s*â-anuga. This division of the compound looks artificial; I should prefer to divide rûva-a*n*ugâsa-a*n*uga = rûpa-anukarsha-anuga; literally, possessed of attraction by colours.

[2] Rûva*n*uvâê*n*a pariggahê*n*a. Parigraha is explained as the desire to possess them.

[3] Instead of 'lying,' we can also adopt the rendering 'stealing,' as the word in the original môsa may stand either for m*ri*shâ, or for môsha.

obtained), he becomes unhappy, and nobody will protect him[1]. (31)

How, then, can a man who is devoted to 'colours,' ever derive any happiness from anything? He suffers pain at the time of their enjoyment to procure which he had suffered misery. (32)

In the same way he who hates 'colours,' incurs a long succession of pains; when his mind is filled with hatred, he accumulates Karman which in the end again produces misery. (33)

But a man who is indifferent to 'colours,' is free from sorrows; though still in the Sa*m*sâra, he is not affected by that long succession of pains, just as the leaf of the Lotus (is not moistened) by water. (34)

[The whole set of verses 22–34 is, with few alterations, five times repeated in the original in order to apply to the other organs of sense.

Verses 35–47 treat of sounds; 'sound' is to be substituted for 'colour,' 'ear' for 'eye.'

The last line of verse 37, which corresponds to verse 24, runs thus:

As an impassioned deer allured (by a song) rushes into death, without being satisfied with the sound.

In the same way verses 48–60 apply to 'smells'; substitute 'smell' and 'organ of smell.'

Verses 61–73 apply to tastes; substitute 'tastes' and 'tongue.'

Verses 74–86 apply to touches; substitute 'touches' and 'body.'

Verses 87–99 apply to feelings; substitute 'feelings' and 'mind.'

---

[1] A*n*issa = ani*s*ra. Ni*s*râ does not occur in common Sanskrit; it is rendered avash*t*ambha by the commentators.

The lines corresponding to the comparison in verse 24, run as follows:

Just as an impassioned snake which is allured by the smell of a drug, when it comes out of its hole. (50)

Just as an impassioned fish which is eager to swallow the bait, has its body transfixed by a hook. (63)

Just as an impassioned buffalo who dives in cold water, is taken hold of by a crocodile and dies. (76)

Just as an impassioned elephant who is inflamed by carnal desires, is turned from his way by a female elephant (and is captured and at last killed in battle). (89)]

Thus the objects of the senses and of the mind cause pain to passionate men, but they never in the least cause any pain to the dispassionate. (100)

Pleasant things (by themselves) do not cause indifference nor emotions (as anger, &c.); but by either hating or loving them, a man undergoes such a change through delusion. (101)

Anger, pride, deceit, greed; disgust, aversion to self-control and delight in sensual things [1]; mirth, fear, sorrow, carnal desire for women, men, or both; all these manifold passions arise in him who is attached to pleasures; and so do other emotions produced by those (before mentioned) arise in him who is to be pitied, who (ought to be) ashamed of himself, and who is hateful. (102, 103)

---

[1] Arati and rati. Compare note on XXI, 21, where I have adopted another translation suited to the context. The first four numbers contain the cardinal passions; the rest the emotions which are called nô-kashâya.

A monk should not desire a companion, not (even) one who is able to perform his religious duties; nor, if he regrets having taken the vows, (should he desire for) a worldly reward of his austerities[1]. Such emotions of an infinite variety arise in one who is the slave of his senses. (104)

Desiring happiness and being submerged in the ocean of delusion, he forms many plans for warding off misery; and for their sake an impassioned man exerts himself. (105)

But all kinds of objects of the senses, sounds, &c., will cause to the indifferent neither a pleasant nor an unpleasant feeling. (106)

He who endeavours to recognise the vanity of all desires[2], will arrive at perfect indifference. When he ceases to desire the objects (of the senses), his desire for pleasures will become extinct. (107)

The dispassionate man who has performed all duties will quickly remove the obstructions to right knowledge and to right faith, and whatever Karman produces obstruction (to righteousness). (108)

Then he knows and sees all things, he is free from delusion and hindrances, his Âsravas have gone,

---

[1] My translation follows the interpretation of the commentators. The original runs thus: Kappa*m* na i*kkh*igg*a* sahâyali*kkh*û pa*kkh*â*n*utâvê*n*a tavappabhâva*m*. The meaning they have made out is very unsatisfactory. There is a remarkable various reading in MS. C not noticed by the scholiasts: sahâyala*kkh*i*m* = svabhâvalakshmî*m*. If this was the original reading, the meaning of the line, in which however I must leave the word kappam untranslated, would come to this: a monk who regrets having taken the vows should not desire personal power as the reward for his penance. Kalpa, according to the commentators, is one who is able to perform his religious duties; a kalpa is contrasted with a *s*ishya, novice.

[2] Sa*m*kalpavikalpanâsu upasthitasya.

and he is proficient in meditation and concentration of thoughts, and being pure he will arrive at beatitude when his life is spent. (109)

He will get rid of all misery which always afflicts mankind; recovered from the long illness, as it were, and glorious, he becomes infinitely happy, and obtains the (final) aim. (110)

We have taught the way how to become exempt from all misery which arises since time without beginning; those beings who follow it will in their time become infinitely happy. (111)

Thus I say.

THIRTY-THIRD LECTURE.

THE NATURE OF KARMAN.

I shall now in due order explain the eight kinds of Karman, bound by which the soul turns round and round in the Circle of Births. (1)

The eight kinds of Karman are briefly the following:

1. *G*ñânâvara*n*îya (which acts as an obstruction to right knowledge);
2. Dar*s*anâvara*n*îya (which acts as an obstruction to right faith);
3. Vêdanîya (which leads to experiencing pain or pleasure);
4. Môhanîya (which leads to delusion);
5. Âyu*h*karman (which determines the length of life);

6. Nâman (which determines the name or individuality of the embodied soul) ·

7. Gôtra (which determines his Gôtra);

8. Antarâya (which prevents one's entrance on the path that leads to eternal bliss[1]). (2, 3)

1. Obstruction of knowledge is fivefold (viz. obstruction to):

a. *S*ruta, knowledge derived from the sacred books;

b. Âbhinibôdhika, perception;

c. Avadhi*gñ*âna, supernatural knowledge;

d. Mana*h*paryâya, knowledge of the thoughts of other people;

e. Kêvala, the highest, unlimited knowledge. (4)

2. The nine kinds of obstruction to right faith are: 1. sleep; 2. activity; 3. very deep sleep; 4. a high degree of activity[2]; 5. a state of deep-rooted greed; 6–9 refer to faith in the objects of the first three and the last kinds of knowledge. (5, 6)

3. Vêdanîya is twofold, pleasure and pain; there are many subdivisions of pleasure and so there are of pain also. (7)

4. Môhanîya is twofold as referring to faith and to conduct; the first is threefold, the second twofold. (8)

The three kinds of Môhanîya referring to faith are: 1. right faith; 2. wrong faith; 3. faith partly right and partly wrong. (9)

---

[1] Compare Bhandarkar, Report, p. 93, note *.

[2] Nos. 1–4 are nidrâ, pra*k*alâ, nidrânidrâ, pra*k*alâpra*k*alâ; I render the etymological meaning of these words. According to the Dîpikâ, however, they have a different meaning: nidrâ means the state of agreeable waking; pra*k*alâ, the slumber of a standing or sitting person; nidrânidrâ, deep sleep; pra*k*alâpra*k*alâ, sleep of a person in motion. Nos. 6 and 7 are here called *k*akkhu and a*k*akkhu, instead of âbhinibôdhika and *s*ruta.

The two kinds of Môhanîya referring to conduct are: 1. what is experienced in the form of the four cardinal passions; 2. what is experienced in the form of feelings different from them. (10)

The first kind of this Karman is sixteenfold, the second sevenfold or ninefold[1]. (11)

5. Âyushka is fourfold as referring to 1. denizens of hell; 2. brute creation; 3. men; 4. gods. (12)

6. Nâman is twofold, good and bad; there are many subdivisions of the good variety, and so there are of the bad one also[2]. (13)

7. Gôtra is twofold, high and low; the first is eightfold, and so is the second also. (14)

8. Antarâya is fivefold as preventing: 1. gifts; 2. profit; 3. momentary enjoyment; 4. continuous enjoyment[3]; and 5. power. (15)

Thus the division of Karman and the subdivisions have been told.

Now hear their number of atoms[4], place, time, and development. (16)

---

[1] The divisions of the second Karman are the feelings or emotions enumerated in the 102nd verse of the last lecture, from disgust onward. There are seven of them, if desire for women, men, or both, is reckoned as one item, but nine, if it is reckoned as three. The sixteen divisions of the Karman produced by the cardinal passions are arrived at by subdividing each of the four passions with reference to 1. anantânubandha; 2. pratyâkhyâna; 3. apratyâkhyâna; 4. sa*mg*valana.

[2] In the Dîpikâ 103 subdivisions are enumerated; they correspond to our genera.

[3] 3. Bhôga, 4. upabhôga; bhôga is enjoyment of flowers, food, &c.; upabhôga, that of one's house, wife, &c. The Karman in question brings about an obstruction to the enjoyment, &c., though all other circumstances be favourable.

[4] The Karman is considered to consist, like other substances, of atoms, here called prade*s*a point. The word I have translated

The number of atoms of every Karman is infinite; it is (infinitely) greater than (the number) of fettered[1] souls, but less than that of the perfected ones. (17)

The Karman in the six directions of space[2] binds all souls, and it binds the whole soul in all its parts in every possible way. (18)

The longest duration (of Karman) is thirty Krores of Krores of Sâgarôpamâs[3], and the shortest a part of a muhûrta. (19)

This holds good with both Âvara*n*îyas, with Vêdanîya and Antarâya. (20)

The longest duration of Môhanîya is seventy Krores of Krores of Sâgarôpamâs, and the shortest a part of a muhûrta. (21)

The longest duration of Âyushka is thirty-three Krores of Krores of Sâgarôpamâs, and the shortest a part of a muhûrta. (22)

The longest duration of Nâman and Gôtra is twenty Krores of Krores of Sâgarôpamâs, and the shortest eight muhûrtas. (23)

The number of perfected souls is infinite, and that

---

number of atoms is paêsagga*m* = pradê*s*âgram, which is rendered paramâ*n*uparimâ*n*a.

[1] Ga*nth*iyasatta = granthigasattva.

[2] The six directions of space are the four cardinal points, zenith and nadir. The commentators quote scripture that êkêndriyas, or beings with one organ of sense, are bound by Karman in three and more directions. The true meaning of this statement is beyond my grasp.—The Dîpikâ explains how Karman acts on the soul. The soul absorbs all material particles of a suitable nature (especially the karmapudgalas) with which it comes into contact, i.e. all that are in the same space with the soul, and assimilates them in the form of *gñ*ânâvara*n*îya, &c., just as fire consumes everything within its reach, but nothing beyond it.

[3] I.e. 3,000,000,000,000,000 Sâgarôpamâs.

of the subdivisions of Karman[1] is also (infinite); the number of atoms in all these (subdivisions) exceeds (the number) of all souls. (24)

Therefore a wise man should know the different subdivisions of these Karmans, and should exert himself to prevent and to destroy them. (25)

Thus I say.

THIRTY-FOURTH LECTURE.

ON LÊSYÂ[2].

I shall deliver in due order the Lecture on Lêsyâ; hear the nature of the six Lêsyâs (produced by) Karman. (1)

---

[1] Anubhâga, explained karmarasavisêsha.

[2] The lêsyâs (adhyavasâya visêshâh) are different conditions produced in the soul by the influence of different Karman; they are therefore not dependent on the nature of the soul, but on the Karman which accompanies the soul, and are, as it were, the reflection of the Karman on the soul, as stated in the following verse from the Avakûri: krishnâdidravyasâkivyât parinâmô ya âtmanah ı spatikasyêva tatrâyam lêsyâsabdah pravartate ıı 'The alteration produced on the soul, just as on a crystal by the presence of black things, &c., is denoted by the word lêsyâ.' The Lêsyâ, or, according to the above explanation, what produces Lêsyâ, is a subtile substance accompanying the soul; to it are attributed the qualities described in this lecture.—The word lêsâ is derived from klêsa; this etymology appears rather fanciful, but I think it may be right. For the Lêsyâs seem to be the Klêsas, which affect the soul, conceived as a kind of substance. The Sanskrit term Lêsyâ is of course a hybrid word. It must, however, be stated that lêsâ occurs also in the meaning 'colour,' e.g. Sûtrakrit. I, 6, 13, and that the Prâkrit of klêsa is kilêsa.

Hear 1. the names, 2. colours, 3. tastes, 4. smells, 5. touches, 6. degrees, 7. character, 8. variety, 9. duration, 10. result, and 11. life of the Lêsyâs. (2)

1. They are named in the following order: black, blue, grey, red, yellow, and white. (3)

2. The black Lêsyâ has the colour of a rain-cloud, a buffalo's horn, (the fruit of) Rish*t*aka[1], or the eye of the wagtail. (4)

The blue Lêsyâ has the colour of the blue Asôka[2], the tail of the *K*âsha[3], or of lapis lazuli. (5)

The grey Lêsyâ has the colour of the flower of Atasî[4], the feathers of the Kôkila, or the collar of pigeons. (6)

The red Lêsyâ has the colour of vermilion, the rising sun, or the bill of a parrot. (7)

The yellow Lêsyâ has the colour of orpiment, turmeric, or the flowers of *S*a*n*a[5] and Asana[6]. (8)

The white Lêsyâ has the colour of a conch-shell, the aṅka-stone[7], Kunda-flowers[8], flowing milk, silver, or a necklace of pearls. (9)

3. The taste of the black Lêsyâ is infinitely more bitter than that of Tumbaka[9], (the fruit of the) Nimb-tree[10], or of Rôhi*n*î. (10)

---

[1] Sapindus Detergens.

[2] It is not the common Asôka, Jonesia Asoka, which has red flowers.

[3] Corarias Indica, blue jay; according to some, a kingfisher.

[4] Linum Usitatissimum, whose flowers are blue.—The word for grey is kâû = kâpôta; in the comm., however, it is described as ki*mk*it k*ri*sh*n*â, ki*mk*il lôhitâ, which would be rather brown. But the description given in our verse leaves no doubt that grey colour is intended.

[5] Crotolaria Juncea.

[6] Terminalia Tomentosa.

[7] Aṅka, ma*n*ivisêsha.

[8] Jasminum Multiflorum.

[9] The gourd Lagenaria Vulgaris.

[10] Azadirachta Indica.

The taste of the blue Lêsyâ is infinitely more pungent than Trika*t*uka [1] and Hastipippalî. (11)

The taste of grey Lêsyâ is infinitely sourer than that of unripe Mango and Kapittha[2]. (12)

The taste of red Lêsyâ is infinitely more pleasant than that of ripe Mango and Kapittha. (13)

The taste of yellow Lêsyâ is infinitely better than that of excellent wine and various liquors, honey and Mairêyaka[3]. (14)

The taste of white Lêsyâ is infinitely better than that of dates, grapes, milk, candied and pounded sugar. (15)

The smell of the bad Lêsyâs (viz. the three first) is infinitely worse than that of the corpse of a cow, dog, or snake. (16)

The smell of the three good Lêsyâs is infinitely more pleasant than that of fragrant flowers and of perfumes when they are pounded. (17)

5. The touch of the bad Lêsyâs is infinitely worse than that of a saw, the tongue of a cow, or leaf of the Teak tree. (18)

The touch of the three good Lêsyâs is infinitely more pleasant than that of cotton, butter, or *S*irîsha-flowers[4]. (19)

6. The degrees[5] of the Lêsyâs are three, or nine,

---

[1] The aggregate of three spices, &c., black and long pepper and dry ginger.

[2] Feronia Elephantum.

[3] A kind of intoxicating drink, extracted from the blossoms of Lythrum Fructicosum, with sugar, &c.

[4] Acacia Sirisa.

[5] The Lêsyâs may possess their qualities in a low, middle, or high degree; each of these degrees is again threefold, viz. low, middle, and high. In this way the subdivision is carried on up to 243.

or twenty-seven, or eighty-one, or two hundred and forty-three. (20)

7. A man who acts on the impulse of the five Âsravas[1], does not possess the three Guptis, has not ceased to injure the six (kinds of living beings), commits cruel acts, is wicked and violent, is afraid of no consequences[2], is mischievous and does not subdue his senses—a man of such habits develops the black Lêsyâ. (21, 22)

A man of the following qualities: envy, anger, want of self-control, ignorance, deceit, want of modesty, greed, hatred, wickedness, carelessness, love of enjoyment; a man who pursues pleasures and does not abstain from sinful undertakings, who is wicked and violent—a man of such habits develops the blue Lêsyâ. (23, 24)

A man who is dishonest in words and acts, who is base, not upright, a dissembler and deceiver[3], a heretic, a vile man, a talker of hurtful and sinful things, a thief, and full of jealousy—a man of such habits develops the grey Lêsyâ. (25, 26)

A man who is humble, steadfast, free from deceit and inquisitiveness, well disciplined, restrained, attentive to his study and duties[4], who loves the Law and keeps it, who is afraid of forbidden things and strives after the highest good—a man of such habits develops the red Lêsyâ. (27, 28)

A man who has but little anger, pride, deceit, and greed, whose mind is at ease, who controls himself,

---

[1] I.e. commits the five great sins.—The following verses give the character—lakshana—of the Lêsyâs.

[2] This is, according to the comm., the meaning of the word niddhamdhasaparinâmô.

[3] Paliuññkaga-uvahiya = pratikuññkaka-upadhika.

[4] Yôgavân upadhânavân.

who is attentive to his study and duties, who speaks but little, is calm, and subdues his senses—a man of such habits develops the yellow Lê*s*yâ. (29, 30)

A man who abstains from constant thinking about his misery and about sinful deeds, but engages in meditation on the Law and truth only[1], whose mind is at ease, who controls himself, who practises the Samitis and Guptis, whether he be still subject to passion or free from passion, is calm, and subdues his senses—a man of such habits develops the white Lê*s*yâ. (31, 32)

8. There are as many varieties[2] of Lê*s*yâs as there are Samayas[3] in the innumerable Avasarpi*n*îs and Utsarpi*n*îs, and as there are countless worlds. (33)

9. Half a muhûrta is the shortest, and thirty-three Sâgarôpamâs plus one muhûrta is the longest duration of the black Lê*s*yâ. (34)

Half a muhûrta is the shortest, and ten Sâgarôpamâs plus one Palyôpamâ and a part of an Asa*m*khyêya is the longest duration of the blue Lê*s*yâ. (35)

Half a muhûrta is the shortest, and three Sâgarôpamâs plus one Palyôpamâ and a part of an Asa*m*khyêya is the longest duration of the grey Lê*s*yâ. (36)

Half a muhûrta is the shortest, and two Sâgarôpamâs plus one Palyôpamâ and a part of an Asa*m*khyêya is the longest duration of the red Lê*s*yâ. (37)

Half a muhûrta is the shortest, and ten Sâgarôpamâs plus one muhûrta is the longest duration of the yellow Lê*s*yâ. (38)

---

[1] Literally: who avoids the ârta and raudra dhyânas, and practises the dharma and *s*ukla dhyânas. These terms cannot be adequately translated; the reader may therefore be referred for details to Bhandarkar's Report, p. 110 ff.

[2] *Th*â*n*ai*m* sthânâni.

[3] Samaya is the smallest division of time = instant, moment.

Half a muhûrta is the shortest, and thirty-three Sâgarôpamâs plus one muhûrta is the longest duration of the white Lê*s*yâ. (39)

I have described above the duration of the Lê*s*yâs generally; I shall now detail their duration in the four walks of mundane existence[1]. (40)

The shortest duration of the grey Lê*s*yâ (of a denizen of hell) is ten thousand years, the longest three Sâgarôpamâs plus one Palyôpamâ and part of an Asa*m*khyêya. (41)

The shortest duration of the blue Lê*s*yâ (of a denizen of hell) is three Sâgarôpamâs plus one Palyôpamâ and a part of an Asa*m*khyêya, the longest ten Sâgarôpamâs plus one Palyôpamâ and a part of an Asa*m*khyêya. (42)

The shortest duration of the black Lê*s*yâ (of a denizen of hell) is ten Sâgarôpamâs plus one Palyôpamâ and a part of an Asa*m*khyêya, the longest thirty-three Sâgarôpamâs. (43)

I have described the duration of the Lê*s*yâs of denizens of hell; I shall now describe that of animals, men, and gods. (44)

The duration of any of the Lê*s*yâs except the best (viz. white one) is less than a muhûrta for (the lowest organisms), animals, and men[2]. (45)

Half a muhûrta is the shortest duration of the white Lê*s*yâ (of animals and men), and the longest a Krore of former years[3] less nine years. (46)

[1] Viz. as denizens of hell, brutes, men, and gods. Only the three first Lê*s*yâs lead to being born in hell.

[2] The consequence of this statement appears to be that at the expiration of the Lê*s*yâ a new one is produced. The commentators, however, are not explicit on this head.

[3] About the former years, see above, p. 16, note 1.

I have described the duration of the Lêsyâs of animals and men, I shall now describe that of the gods. (47)

The shortest duration of the black Lêsyâ is ten thousand years, the longest a Palyôpamâ and (a part of) an Asamkhyêya. (48)

The shortest duration of the blue Lêsyâ is equal to the longest of the black one plus one Samaya; the longest is one Palyôpamâ plus a (greater part of) an Asamkhyêya. (49)

The shortest duration of the grey Lêsyâ is equal to the longest of the blue one plus one Samaya; the longest is one Palyôpamâ plus (a still greater part of) an Asamkhyêya. (50)

I shall now describe the red Lêsyâ as it is with gods, Bhavanapatis, Vyantaras, Gyôtishkas, and Vaimânikas. (51)

The shortest duration of the red Lêsyâ is one Palyôpamâ, the longest two Sâgarôpamâs plus one Palyôpamâ and a part of an Asamkhyêya[1]. (52)

The shortest duration of the red Lêsyâ is ten thousand years, the longest two Sâgarôpamâs plus one Palyôpamâ and a part of an Asamkhyêya. (53)

The longest duration of the red Lêsyâ plus one Samaya is equal to the shortest of the yellow Lêsyâ; its longest, however, is ten muhûrtas longer. (54)

The longest duration of the yellow Lêsyâ plus one Samaya is equal to the shortest of the white Lêsyâ; the longest, however, is thirty-three muhûrtas longer. (55)

10. The black, blue, and grey Lêsyâs are the

[1] This verse seems to lay down the duration of the Lêsyâ in the case of common gods, while the next one applies to Bhavanapatis, &c.

lowest Lêsyâs; through them the soul is brought into miserable courses of life. (56)

The red, yellow, and white Lêsyâs are the good Lêsyâs; through them the soul is brought into happy courses of life. (57)

11. In the first moment of these Lêsyâs when they are joined (with the soul), the latter is not born into a new existence[1]. (58)

In the last moment of all these Lêsyâs when they are joined (with the soul), the latter is not born into a new existence. (59)

While the last muhûrta is running and a part of it is still to come, the souls with their Lêsyâs developed, go to a new birth. (60)

A wise man should, therefore, know the nature of these Lêsyâs; he should avoid the bad ones and obtain the good ones. (61)

Thus I say.

THIRTY-FIFTH LECTURE.

THE HOUSELESS MONK.

Learn from me, with attentive minds, the road shown by the wise ones[2], which leads a monk who follows it, to the end of all misery. (1)

---

[1] The question treated rather darkly in the next three verses is, according to the comm., the following:—Every individual dies in the same Lêsyâ in which he is born. When his Lêsyâ ends with his life, then the soul must get a new Lêsyâ. Our verses state at which time the new Lêsyâ comes into existence or is joined with the soul.

[2] Buddhêhi.

Giving up the life in a house, and taking Pravragyâ, a sage should know and renounce those attachments which take hold of men. (2)

A restrained monk should abstain from killing, lying, stealing, carnal intercourse, from desire, love, and greed. (3)

Even in his thoughts a monk should not long for a pleasant painted house filled with the fragrance of garlands and frankincense, secured by doors, and decorated with a white ceiling-cloth[1]. (4)

For in such a dwelling a monk will find it difficult to prevent his senses from increased desire and passion. (5)

He should be content to live on a burial-place, in a deserted house, below a tree, in solitude, or in a place which had been prepared for the sake of somebody else[2]. (6)

A well-controlled monk should live in a pure place, which is not too much crowded, and where no women live. (7)

He should not build a house, nor cause others to erect one; for many living beings both movable and immovable, both subtile and gross, are seen to be killed when a house is being built; therefore a monk should abstain from building a house. (8, 9)

The same holds good with the cooking of food and drink, or with one's causing them to be cooked. Out of compassion for living beings one should not cook nor cause another to cook. (10)

Beings which live in water, corn, or in earth and

---

[1] Ullôva = ullô*k*a.

[2] Paraka*d*a = parak*ri*ta, explained parair âtmârtha*m* k*ri*ta.

wood, are destroyed in food and drink; therefore a monk should cause nobody to cook. (11)

There is nothing so dangerous as fire, for it spreads in all directions and is able to destroy many beings; one should therefore not light a fire. (12)

Even in his thoughts a monk should not long for gold and silver; indifferent alike to dirt and gold he abstains from buying and selling. (13)

If he buys, he becomes a buyer; if he sells, he becomes a merchant; a monk is not to engage in buying and selling. (14)

A monk who is to live on alms, should beg and not buy; buying and selling is a great sin; but to live on alms is benefitting. (15)

He should collect his alms in small parts according to the Sûtras and so as to avoid faults; a monk should contentedly go on his begging-tour, whether he get alms or not. (16)

A great sage should not eat for the sake of the pleasant taste (of the food) but for the sustenance of life, being not dainty nor eager for good fare, restraining his tongue, and being without cupidity. (17)

Even in his thoughts he should not desire to be presented with flowers, to be offered a seat, to be eloquently greeted, or to be offered presents, or to get a magnificent welcome and treatment. (18)

He should meditate on true things only[1], committing no sins and having no property; he should walk about careless of his body till his end arrives. (19)

Rejecting food when the time of his death arrives,

---

[1] *S*ukla dhyâna, see note 1, p. 200.

and leaving the human body, he becomes his own master[1], and is liberated from misery. (20)

Without property, without egoism, free from passions and the Âsravas, he obtains absolute knowledge, and reaches eternal beatitude. (21)

Thus I say.

THIRTY-SIXTH LECTURE.

ON LIVING BEINGS AND THINGS WITHOUT LIFE[2].

Now learn from me with attentive minds the division of Living Beings and Things without life[3], which a monk must know who is to exert himself in self-control. (1)

---

[1] By the destruction of the vîryântarâya.

[2] It will perhaps not be amiss to give a systematic list of the subjects treated in this lecture. The numbers refer to the verses.

- A. Things without life, 3–48.
  - (1) Without form, 5–9.
  - (2) With form, 10–48.
- B. Living Beings, 48–246.
  - (1) Perfected souls, 50–68.
  - (2) Mundane Beings, 69–246.
    - *a.* Immovable Beings, 71–106.
      - *α.* Earth Lives, 71–84.
      - *β.* Water Lives, 85–92.
      - *γ.* Plants, 93–106.
    - *b.* Movable Beings, 108–246.
      - *α.* Fire Lives, 109–117.
      - *β.* Wind Lives, 118–126.
      - *γ.* Beings with an organic body, 127–246.

[3] See next page.

The Living Beings and the Things without life make up this world (Lôka); but the space where only Things without life are found is called the Non-world (Alôka). (2)

The Living Beings and the Things without life will be described with reference to 1. substance, 2. place, 3. time, and 4. development. (3)

A. Things without life.

Things without life are 1. possessing form, 2. formless; the formless things are of ten kinds, those possessing form are of four kinds. (4)

(1) The ten kinds of formless things: 1. Dharma, 2. its divisions, 3. its indivisible parts; 4. Adharma, 5. its divisions, 6. its indivisible parts; 7. space,

---

i. With two organs of sense, 128–136.
ii. With three organs of sense, 137–145.
iii. With four organs of sense, 146–155.
iv. With five organs of sense, 156–246.
a. Denizens of hell, 157–170.
b. Animals (vertebratae), 171–193.
1. Aquatic, 171–178.
2. Terrestrial, 179–186.
3. Aerial, 187–193.
c. Men, 194–202.
d. Gods, 203–246.
1. Bhavanavâsin, 205, 218.
2. Vyantara, 206, 219.
3. *G*yôtishka, 207, 220.
4. Vaimânika, 208, 221–246.
a'. Living in Kalpas, 209, 210, 221–232.
b'. Living above the Kalpas, 211.
α'. Graivêyakas, 212, 213, 233–241.
β'. Anuttaras, 214–217, 242, 243.
Appendix, 247–267.

[3] *G*îva and a*g*îva. The former is defined in the Dîpikâ as upayôgavân in accordance with our text, XXVIII, 10; the latter is also called pudgala.

8. its divisions, 9. its indivisible parts, and 10. time[1]. (5, 6)

Dharma and Adharma are co-extensive with the World (Lôka); space fills the World and the Non-world (Alôka); time exists in what is called the place of time[2]. (7)

Dharma, Adharma, and Space are ever without beginning and end. (8)

And time also, if regarded as a continuous flow[3], is called so (i. e. without beginning and end); but with regard to an individual thing it has a beginning and an end. (9)

(2) The four kinds of things possessing form are 1. compound things, 2. their divisions, 3. their indivisible parts, and 4. atoms[4]. (10)

Compound things and atoms occur as individual things and apart (or different from others)[5], in the whole world and in parts of the world; this is their distribution with regard to place. (11)

Subtile things occur all over the world, gross things only in a part of it.

---

[1] It is here called addhâ-samaya, which may be translated real-time. It has no divisions or parts as the other things, because of time only the present moment is existent. And a moment cannot be divided.

[2] Time is only present in the two and a half continents inhabited by men, and the oceans belonging to them; beyond this sphere there is no time or, as the Dîpikâ correctly remarks, no divisions of time.

[3] Sa*m*tati*m* pappa = sa*m*tatim prâpya.

[4] According to the Dîpikâ, we should have but two divisions, viz.: 1. compound things (skandha, aggregates of atoms), and 2. not aggregated atoms; for Nos. 2 and 3 of our text are but subdivisions of No. 1.

[5] Êgattê*n*a puhuttê*n*a = êkatvêna p*ri*thaktvêna.

I shall now give their fourfold division with regard to time. (12)

With regard to the continuous flow (or development of a thing) it is without beginning and without end; but with regard to its existence (as an individual thing) it has both a beginning and an end[1]. (13)

The longest duration of Things without life possessing form is an immeasurable[2] period; the shortest one Samaya. (14)

The longest interruption[3] in the existence of Things without life possessing form is an endless time; the shortest one Samaya. (15)

Their development is fivefold: with regard to 1. colour, 2. smell, 3. taste, 4. touch, and 5. figure. (16)

Those which develop with regard to colour are of five kinds: 1. black, 2. blue, 3. red, 4. yellow, 5. white. (17)

Those which develop with regard to smell are of two kinds: 1. sweet-smelling substances, and 2. of bad smell. (18)

Those which develop with regard to taste are of five kinds: 1. bitter, 2. pungent, 3. astringent, 4. sour, and 5. sweet. (19)

Those which develop with regard to touch are of eight kinds: 1. hard, 2. soft, 3. heavy, 4. light, 5. cold, 6. hot, 7. smooth, and 8. rough.

---

[1] The meaning of this verse is that a thing, as far as its material cause is concerned, has always existed, and will ever exist under one form or other, but that the individual thing in its present form has but a limited existence.

[2] Asa*m*khakâlam. See above, p. 42, note 2.

[3] Antaram; the interval between the thing being removed from its proper scene and reaching it again (Ava*k*ûri and Dîpikâ).

In this way the substances have been declared, which develop with regard to touch. (20, 21)

Those which develop with regard to figure are of five kinds: 1. globular, 2. circular, 3. triangular, 4. square, and 5. long. (22)

Things of black colour are subdivided with regard to smell, taste, touch, and figure. (23)

The same subdivision holds good with blue, red, yellow, and white things. (24–27[1])

Things of sweet smell are subdivided with regard to colour, taste, touch, and figure; things of bad smell are similarly subdivided. (28, 29)

Things of bitter taste are subdivided with regard to colour, smell, touch, and figure. (30)

The same subdivision holds good with pungent, astringent, sour, and sweet things. (31–34)

Things of hard touch are subdivided with regard to colour, smell, taste, and figure. (35)

The same subdivision holds good with soft, heavy, light, cold, hot, smooth, and rough things. (36–42)

Things of globular figure are subdivided with regard to colour, smell, taste, and touch. (43)

The same subdivision holds good with circular, triangular, square, and long things. (44–47)

Thus the division of Things without life has briefly been told.

B. Living Beings.

I shall now, in due order, deliver the division of living beings. (48)

Living beings are of two kinds: 1. those still

[1] Each verse has the same form as 23, only that another colour is substituted for black. In the same way the subdivisions of smells, &c., are given. I give the first verse of each class and abbreviate the rest.

belonging to the Sa*m*sâra, and 2. the perfected souls (siddhas). The latter are of many kinds; hear me explain them. (49)

(1) The perfected souls are those of women, men, hermaphrodites, of orthodox, heterodox, and householders. (50)

Perfection is reached by people of the greatest, smallest, and middle size [1], on high places, underground, on the surface of the earth, in the ocean, and in water (of rivers, &c.). (51)

Ten hermaphrodites reach, at the same time, perfection, twenty women, one hundred and eight men; four householders, ten heterodox, and one hundred and eight orthodox monks. (52, 53)

Two individuals of the greatest size reach perfection (simultaneously), four of the smallest size, and one hundred and eight of the middle size. (54)

Four individuals reach perfection (simultaneously) on high places, two in the ocean, three in water, twenty underground, and one hundred and eight on the surface of the earth. (55)

From where are the perfected souls debarred? Where do the perfected souls reside? Where do they leave their bodies, and where do they go, on reaching perfection? (56)

Perfected souls are debarred from the non-world (Alôka); they reside on the top of the world; they leave their bodies here (below), and go there, on reaching perfection. (57)

Twelve Yô*g*anas above the (Vimâna) Sarvârtha is

[1] The greatest size (ôgâha*n*â) of men is 500 dhanus, or 2,000 cubits, the smallest one cubit.

the place called Îshatprâgbhâra [1], which has the form of an umbrella; (there the perfected souls go). (58)

It is forty-five hundred thousand Yô*g*anas long, and as many broad, and it is somewhat more than three times as many in circumference. (59)

Its thickness is eight Yô*g*anas, it is greatest in the middle, and decreases [2] toward the margin, till it is thinner than the wing of a fly. (60)

This place, by nature pure, consisting of white gold, resembles in form an open umbrella, as has been said by the best of *G*inas. (61)

(Above it) is a pure blessed place (called *S*îtâ), which is white like a conch-shell, the aṅka-stone [3], and Kunda-flowers; a Yô*g*ana thence is the end of the world. (62)

The perfected souls penetrate the sixth part [4] of the uppermost Krô*s*a of the (above-mentioned) Yô*g*ana. (63)

There at the top of the world reside the blessed perfected souls, rid of all transmigration, and arrived at the excellent state of perfection. (64)

The dimension of a perfected soul is two-thirds of the height which the individual had in his last existence. (65)

The perfected souls, considered singly, (as individuals) have a beginning but no end; considered

---

[1] Similar details are given in the Aupapâtika Sûtra (ed. Leumann, § 163 f.).

[2] According to the commentator, who quotes scripture, it decreases an aṅgula every Yô*g*ana.

[3] Compare XXXIV, 9 and note. The commentators here treat aṅka as a separate substance without offering any explanation. The Dîpikâ writes sîtâ instead of *s*îtâ.

[4] Or $333\frac{1}{3}$ dhanus.

collectively[1] (as a class) they have neither a beginning nor an end. (66)

They have no (visible) form, they consist of Life throughout, they are developed into knowledge and faith, and they possess paramount happiness which admits of no comparison. (67)

They all dwell in one part of the world, and have developed into knowledge and faith, they have crossed the boundary of the Sa*m*sâra, and reached the excellent state of perfection. (68)

(2) Living beings which still belong to the Sa*m*sâra, are of two kinds: *a.* movable, and *b.* immovable ones: the immovable ones are of three kinds: (69)

α. Earth Lives, *β.* Water Lives, and *γ.* plants; these are the three kinds of immovable living beings; now learn from me their subdivision. (70)

α. The Earth Lives are of two kinds: subtile and gross; and both of them are either fully developed or undeveloped. (71)

The gross and fully developed are of two kinds: viz. smooth or rough. The smooth ones are of seven kinds: (72)

Black, blue, red, yellow, white, pale dust, and clay.

The rough ones are of thirty-six kinds: (73)

Earth, gravel, sand, stones, rocks, rock-salt[2], iron, copper, tin, lead, silver, gold, and diamond; (74)

Orpiment, vermilion, realgar, Sâsaka[3], antimony,

---

[1] The words translated, 'considered singly' and 'considered collectively,' are êgattê*n*a and puhuttê*n*a = êkatvêna and p*ri*thaktvêna. Their usual meaning has been given in verse 11.

[2] Lava*n*âsê?

[3] Not in our dictionaries; the commentators only say that it is a kind of mineral, dhâtuvi*s*êsha. I give the Sanskrit names of

coral, Abhrapa*t*ala, Abhravâluka; these are varieties of gross (Earth-) bodies and kinds of precious stones. (75)

Hyacinth, natron, Aṅka, crystal, Lôhitâksha, emerald, Masâragalla, Bhu*g*amô*k*aka, and sapphire; (76)

*K*andana, red chalk, Ha*m*sagarbha, Pulaka[1], and sulphur; *K*andraprabha, lapis lazuli, *G*alakânta, and Sûryakânta[2]. (77)

These thirty-six kinds of 'rough earth' have been enumerated. The 'subtile earth' is but of one kind, as there is no variety. (78)

The subtile species is distributed all over the world, but the gross one (is found) in a part of the world only.

I shall now give their fourfold division with regard to time. (79)

With regard to the continuous flow (or development of an earth-body) it is without a beginning and end; but with regard to its existence in its present form it has both a beginning and end. (80)

Twenty-two thousand years is the longest duration of the Earth Lives; its shortest is less than a muhûrta. (81)

The longest duration of the body of Earth Lives, if they do not leave that (kind of) body[3], is an

---

the stones, which cannot be identified with certainty, or are not contained in the index of R. Garbe's work on the Indian minerals, Leipzig, 1882.

[1] A medicinal earth, commonly called Kaṅkush*th*a.

[2] The enumeration contains thirty-nine, instead of thirty-six items, as stated in verses 73 and 76.

[3] The meaning seems to be that souls of earth-bodies live in

immeasurable time; the shortest is less than one muhûrta. (82)

The longest interval between an Earth Life's leaving its body (till its return to it), is an endless time; the shortest less than one Muhûrta. (83)

Their varieties, caused by (difference of) colour, smell, taste, touch, figure, and place, are (counted) by thousands. (84)

β. The Water Lives are of two kinds: subtile and gross ones; and both of them are either fully developed or undeveloped. (85)

The gross and fully developed ones are of five kinds: pure water, dew, exudations, fog, and ice. (86)

The 'subtile water' is of one kind, as there is no variety. The subtile species is distributed all over the world, but the gross one (is found) in a part of the world only. (87)

With regard to the continuous flow, &c. (as in verse 80).

Seven thousand years is the longest duration of the life of Water Lives, &c. (as in verse 81). (All that has been said of Earth Lives in verses 82–84 is verbally repeated here of 'Water Lives.') (88–92)

γ. Plants are of two kinds: subtile and gross ones; and both of them are either fully developed or undeveloped. (93)

The gross and fully developed plants are of two kinds: either many have one body in common, or each has its own body. (94)

Those who severally have their own body are of

earth-bodies, the time stated in verse 82, while the length of each separate existence is determined in verse 81.

many kinds: trees, shrubby plants[1], shrubs[2], big plants[3], creeping plants[4], grass[5]; (95)

Palms[6], plants of knotty stems or stalks[7], mushrooms[8], water-plants, annual plants[9], and herbs[10]. These are called plants possessing severally their own body. (96)

Those plants of which many have one body in common are of many kinds[11]: Âluya[12], Mûlaya[13], ginger; (97)

Harilî, Sirilî, Sassirilî, *G*âvaî, Kêyakandalî[14], onion, garlic, plantain-tree, Ku*d*uvvaya[15]; (98)

---

[1] Gu*kkh*a; it is explained to denote such plants from the single root or bulb of which come forth many stalks, e.g. V*ri*ntâka, Solanum Melongena.

[2] Gulma, similar to the preceding class, but bringing forth twigs or stems, instead of stalks, e.g. Navamâlikâ, Jasminum Sambac, Ka*n*avîra, &c.

[3] Latâ, as Lotus, Pandanus, &c.

[4] Vallî, as gourds, Piper Betel, &c.

[5] T*ri*na, grass. But of the two examples given in the commentary, *g*u*ñg*uka is not in our dictionaries, and Ar*g*una denotes usually a tree, Terminalia Arjuna.

[6] Valaya; so called from their foliation.

[7] Parvaga, as sugar-cane.

[8] Kuha*n*a, plants which cause the earth to burst, as sarpa*kkh*atra, mushroom (toad-stool).

[9] Ôshadhi, such plants as die after having brought forth seed, as rice, &c.

[10] Haritakâya, as ta*nd*ulêya, &c.

[11] The plants in the following list are, according to the commentary, mostly bulbs, 'well known in the countries where they grow.' Many of them are not in our dictionaries. I give the Prâk*ri*t form of their names, and note the Sanskrit equivalent when it can be identified.

[12] Âluka, Amorphophallus Campanulatus. [13] Mûlaka, radish.

[14] A various reading has for the last two words (which might be differently divided), âpaikkêikandalî. The Kandalî, the plantain-tree, occurs in the next line again.

[15] A various reading is Ku*d*ambaya.

Lôhi*n*îhûya, Thîhûya, Tuhaga, Ka*n*ha[1], Va*gg*a-kanda[2], Sûra*n*aya[3]; (99)

Assaka*nn*î[4], Sîhaka*nn*î, Musu*ndh*î, turmeric, and many others besides. (100)

The subtile plants are of one kind, as there is no variety. Subtile plants are distributed all over the world, gross plants (are found) in a part of the world only. (101)

With regard to the continuous flow, &c. (as in verse 80). (102)

Ten thousand years is the longest duration of the life of plants, &c. (All as in verses 81–84. Substitute plants, which are here called vanaspati and panaka, for Earth-bodies.) (103–106)

Thus the three kinds of immovable living beings have briefly been told. I shall now explain in due order the three kinds of movable living beings. (107)

b. The movable beings are *α.* the Fire Lives, *β.* the Wind Lives, and *γ.* those with an organic body; these are the three kinds of movable beings. Learn from me their subdivision. (108)

α. The Fire Lives are of two kinds: subtile and gross ones; and both of them are either fully developed or undeveloped. (109)

The gross and fully developed ones are of many kinds: coal, burning chaff, fire, and flame of fire; (110)

Meteors, and lightning, and many other kinds besides.

---

[1] K*ri*sh*n*akanda, Nymphaea Rubra.

[2] Va*g*rakanda of the Sanskrit Koshas.

[3] *S*ûra*n*a, Arum Campanulatum.

[4] A*s*vakar*n*â. A*s*vakar*n*a is a tree, Vatika Robusta.

The subtile Fire Lives are but of one kind, as there is no variety. (111)

The subtile species, &c. (see verses 79–84. Substitute Fire Lives for Earth Lives. In verses 114 f., corresponding to verses 81, 89, and 103, read: 'the longest duration of the life of Fire Lives is three days,' &c.; the rest as above). (112–117)

β. The Wind Lives are of two kinds, &c. (as in verse 109). (118)

The gross and fully developed ones are of five kinds: squalls[1], whirlwinds[2], thick winds[3], high winds, low winds; (119)

And the Sa*m*vartaka[4] wind, &c.; thus they are of many kinds[5].

The subtile Wind Lives are but of one kind, as there is no variety. (120)

The subtile species, &c. (as above 79–84. Substitute Wind Lives for Earth Lives. In verse 123, corresponding to 114, read: 'the longest duration of the life of Wind Lives is three thousand years;' the rest as above). (121–126)

---

[1] Utkalikâ, intermittent winds. [2] Ma*nd*alikâ = vâtôlî.

[3] According to the comm. these winds blow on the oceans which are situated below the Ratnaprabhâ-hell, or which support the heavenly Vimânas, and have the density of snow. Perhaps the notion is similar to that of the Hindu astronomers, who fancied that the heavenly bodies were set in motion by cords of wind called pravaha. See Sûrya Siddhânta II, 3.

[4] This seems to be the hurricane which causes the periodical destruction of the world. But Dêvêndra says: 'Sa*m*vartaka is a wind which carries grass, &c., from the outside into a particular place.'

[5] Though in the preceding verse it was said that there are five kinds of wind, six are enumerated, and more are implied by the '&c.'

γ. Movable beings with organic bodies (i.e. animals) are of four kinds: i. those possessing two organs of sense, ii. those with three organs, iii. those with four organs, iv. those with five organs. (127)

i. Beings with two organs of sense are of two kinds: subtile and gross ones. Both are either fully developed or undeveloped. Learn from me their subdivision[1]. (128)

Worms, Sômaṅgala, Alasa[2], Mâivâhaya[3], Vâsîmuha[4], shells, conches, Saṅkhâ*n*aga[5]; (129)

Pallôya, A*n*ullaya, cowries, leeches, *G*âlaga, and *K*anda*n*a[6]. (130)

These and others are the many kinds of beings with two organs of sense. All of them live in a part of the world only, they do not live everywhere. (131)

With regard to the continuous flow, &c. (as in verse 80). (132)

---

[1] As many of these lower animals are not known to us, I give the Prâk*ri*t names of those which I cannot identify. Dêvêndra says: 'Some of them are well known, the remaining ones are to be explained according to tradition.' The explanation of this passage in the Ava*k*ûri is fuller.

[2] A small poisonous animal. Petersburg Dictionary, s. v. According to the *G*îvavi*k*âra V*ri*tti V, 16, they are earth-snakes (bhûnâga), which originate in the rainy season when the sun is in A*s*leshâ, i.e. about the beginning of July.

[3] Mât*ri*vâhaka. According to the description of the Ava*k*ûri, the larvae of Phryganeae seem intended. According to the *G*îvavi*k*âra V*ri*tti, they are called *k*û*d*êlî in Guzeratî..

[4] Vâsîmukha, explained: Whose mouth is like a chisel or adze. There are many insects, e.g. the Curculionidae, which suit this description.

[5] *S*aṅkhânaka, 'very small, conch-like animals.'

[6] *K*anda*n*a = Akâv*ri*ksha (?). According to the *G*îvavi*k*âra V*ri*tti V, 16, they are animals living in water and on land, and are called Aksha in the vernacular (samayabhâshâ).

The duration of the life of beings with two organs of sense is twelve years at the utmost; the shortest is less than a muhûrta. (133)

The longest duration of the body of beings with two organs of sense is a Sa*m*khyêya (or measurable time) if they do not leave that (kind of) body; the shortest is less than one muhûrta. (134)

135, 136 = 83, 84. Substitute 'beings with two organs of sense' for Earth Lives.

ii. Beings with three organs of sense are of two kinds: subtile and gross ones. Both are either fully developed or undeveloped. Learn from me their subdivision. (137)

Kunthu[1], ants, bugs, Ukkala, white ants, Ta*n*ahâra, Ka*tth*ahâra, Mâlûga[2], Pattahâraga; (138)

Duga shining like lead, which originate in the kernel of the cotton-seed, Sadâvarî, centipedes, Indagâiya; (139)

Cochineal, &c. Thus they are of many kinds.

All of them live in a part of the world only, they do not live everywhere. (140)

141–145 = 132–136. (Substitute 'beings with three organs of sense.' The longest duration, &c., is forty-nine days, verse 142 = 133.)

iii. Beings with four organs of sense are of two kinds: subtile and gross ones. Both are either

---

[1] Kunthu or animalcules are also called A*n*uddharî, see concerning them, Kalpa Sûtra, Rules for Yatis, § 44, part i, p. 304.—I give in the text the Prâk*ri*t form of the words I cannot identify.

[2] Mâlûka is the name of a plant, Ocimum Sanctum. It must, of course, here denote some animal.—The *G*îvavi*k*âra enumerates many other animals, lice, bugs, different kinds of larvae living in dung, corn, &c.—The *tri*n*a*hâra, kâsh*th*ahâra, and patrahâra seem to denote different kinds of ants.

developed or undeveloped. Learn from me their subdivision. (146)

Andhiya, Pottiyâ, flies, mosquitoes, bees, moths, Dhiṅka*n*a and Kaṅka*n*a; (147)

Kukku*d*a[1], Siṅgirî*d*î, Nandâvatta[2], scorpions, *D*ôla, crickets, Viralî, A*kkh*ivêhaya; (148)

A*kkh*ila, Sâhaya A*kkh*irô*d*aya, Vi*k*itta, Vi*k*ittapattaya[3], Uhi*m*galiyâ, *G*alakârî, Nîyâ, and Tantavagâiyâ. (149)

These and others are the beings with four organs of sense. All of them, &c. (the rest as in verses 131–136. Substitute 'beings with four organs of sense.' The longest duration, &c., is six months, verse 152 = 133). (150–155)

iv. Beings with five organs of sense are of four kinds: denizens of hell, animals[4], men, and gods. (156).

a. Denizens of hell are of seven kinds according to the seven hells; they are called Ratnâbha, *S*arkarâbha, Vâlukâbha; (157)

Paṅkâbha, Dhûmâbha, Tamâ, and Tamatamâ. Thus the seven kinds of denizens of hell have been enumerated. (158)

All the (denizens of hell) live in a part of the

---

[1] Kukku*t*a is given in the dictionaries as the name of a small lizard.

[2] Nandyâvarta occurs elsewhere as the name of a particular fish, and of a shell. It can be neither of these in our passage, as both animals belong to other classes than the *K*aturindriyas.

[3] Etymologically: with many-coloured wings. Probably butterflies are intended.

[4] Tirikkha = tiryak. Apparently only the higher animals are intended by this term, the lower animals, from the insects downwards, being enumerated in the preceding classes of beings.

world only; they do not live everywhere, &c. (as in verses 79 and 80). (159, 160)

In the first hell the longest duration of their life is one Sâgarôpamâ; the shortest is ten thousand years. (161)

In the second hell the longest duration of their life is three Sâgarôpamâs; the shortest is one Sâgarôpamâ[1]. (162)

In the third hell the longest duration of their life is seven Sâgarôpamâs; the shortest is three Sâgarôpamâs. (163)

In the fourth hell the longest duration of their life is ten Sâgarôpamâs; the shortest is seven Sâgarôpamâs. (164)

In the fifth hell the longest duration of their life is seventeen Sâgarôpamâs; the shortest is ten Sâgarôpamâs. (165)

In the sixth hell the longest duration of their life is twenty-two Sâgarôpamâs; the shortest is seventeen Sâgarôpamâs. (166)

In the seventh hell the longest duration of their life is thirty-three Sâgarôpamâs; the shortest is twenty-two Sâgarôpamâs. (167)

The length of the life of denizens of hell is also that of their continuance in the same kind of body, with regard both to the longest and shortest duration of it. (168)

Verses 169, 170 = 83, 84. (Substitute, denizens of hell.)

b. The animals which possess five organs of sense are of two kinds, those which originate by gene-

[1] It will be seen that the longest duration of life in each hell is always equal to the shortest in the preceding one.

ratio aequivoca[1], and those which are born from the womb. (171)

Either of them are again of three kinds: 1. aquatic, 2. terrestrial, and 3. aerial animals. Learn from me their subdivision. (172)

1. Fishes, tortoises, crocodiles, Makaras, and Gangetic porpoises are the five kinds of aquatic animals. (173)

174, 175 = 159, 160.

The longest duration of the life of aquatic animals is one Krore of former years[2]; the shortest is less than one muhûrta. (176)

The longest duration of the aquatic animals' continuance in the (same kind of body) is from two to nine[3] Krores of former years. (177)

178 = 83.

2. Quadrupeds and reptiles are the two kinds of terrestrial animals. The quadrupeds are of four kinds; listen to my description of them: (179)

(1) Solidungular animals, as horses, &c.;
(2) Biungular animals, as cows, &c.;
(3) Multiungular animals, as elephants, &c.;
(4) Animals having toes with nails, as lions, &c. (180)

The reptiles are of two kinds: 1. those which walk on their arms, as lizards, &c., and 2. those which move on their breast, as snakes, &c. Both are again of many kinds. (181)

---

[1] Sammûr*kh*ima. They grow by assimilating the materials in their surrounding. According to a second explanation, their internal organ does not fully develop.

[2] See page 16, note 1.

[3] This is, according to the Ava*k*ûri, the meaning of puhutta*m* pr*i*thaktvam.

182, 183 = 159, 160.

The longest duration of the life of terrestrial animals is three Palyôpamâs; the shortest is less than one muhûrta. (184)

The longest duration of the terrestrial animals' continuance in the (same kind of) body is three Palyôpamâs plus from two to nine Krores of former years; the shortest is less than one muhûrta. (185)

186 = 83.

3. Winged animals are of four kinds: those with membranous wings[1], those with feathered wings, those with wings in the shape of a box[2], and those (which sit on) outspread wings[3]. (187)

188, 189 = 159, 160.

The longest duration of the life of aerial animals is an Asa*m*khyêya-part of a Palyôpamâ[4]; the shortest is less than one muhûrta. (190)

The longest duration (of the aerial animals' continuance in the same kind of body) is an Asa*m*khyêya-part of a Palyôpamâ plus from two to nine Krores of former years; the shortest is less than one muhûrta. (191)

192, 193 = 159, 160.

c. Men are of two kinds; listen to my description of them: men originating by generatio aequivoca[5], and men born from the womb. (194)

Those who are born from the womb are of three

---

[1] E.g. the *k*arma*k*a*t*akas or bats.

[2] Samudga. These interesting birds are said to live outside the Mânushôttara, or world inhabited by men.

[3] The comm. do not tell us what kind of birds is intended.

[4] The comm. do not explain this expression; the meaning, therefore, is doubtful. I give a literal translation of it in this and the next verse.

[5] See page 223, note 1, on verse 171.

kinds: those living in the Karmabhûmi[1], those living in the Akarmabhûmi, and those living on the minor continents[2]. (195)

They have, in the same order, fifteen[3], thirty[4], and twenty-eight subdivisions. These are the numbers handed down. (196)

Men originating by generatio aequivoca are of as many kinds. They all live but in a part of the world. (197)

Verses 198–202 = 183–186. (Substitute, 'men' for 'terrestrial animals.')

d. Gods are of four kinds; listen to my description of them: 1. Bhaumêyikas; 2. Vyantaras; 3. *G*yôtishkas; 4. Vaimânikas. (203)

There are ten kinds of Bhavanavâsins (= Bhaumêyikas), eight of those who live in woods (= Vyantaras), five of *G*yôtishkas, and two of Vaimânikas. (204)

1. The Bhavanavâsins are: the Asura-, Nâga-, Suvar*n*a-, Vidyut-, Agni-, Dvîpa-, Udadhi-, Vâta-, and Gha*n*ika-(Kumâras[5]). (205)

2. The eight kinds of Vyantaras are: Pi*s*â*k*as,

---

[1] Concerning Karmabhûmi, see part i, p. 195, note 1. The Ava*k*ûri places the Akarmabhûmi first, but the next verse proves that it originally stood in the second place.

[2] These are seven groups of islands situated off the eastern and western ends of the Himâlaya, which are inhabited by fabulous races.

[3] According to the Ava*k*ûri, there are five kinds in Bharata, five in Airâvata, and five in Vidêha.

[4] Viz. five in each of the six Akarmabhûmis: Haimavata, Harivarsha, Haira*n*yavata, Dêvakuru, and Uttarakuru.

[5] According to the commentaries the word kumâra is to be supplied after each of the ten names.

Bhûtas, Yakshas, Râkshasas, Kinnaras, Kimpurushas, Mahôragas, and Gandharvas. (206)

3. The moons, the suns, the Nakshatras, the planets, and the hosts of stars are the fivefold dwellings of the *G*yôtishkas. (207)

4. The Vaimânika gods are of two kinds: *a*′. those who are born in the heavenly Kalpas, and *b*′. those who are born in the regions above them[1]. (208)

a′. The former are of twelve kinds: those who live in (the following Kalpas, after which they are named): Saudharma, Î*s*âna, Sanatkumâra, Mâhêndra, Brahmalôka, and Lantaka; (209)

Mahâ*s*ukla, Sahasrâra, Ânata, Prâ*n*ata[2], Âra*n*a, and A*k*yuta. These are the gods who are born in Kalpas. (210)

b′. The gods who are born in the regions above the Kalpas are of two kinds: *α*′. the Graivêyakas[3], and *β*′. the Anuttaras[4]. The Graivêyakas are of nine kinds. (211)

α′. The lowest of the lowest, the middle of the lowest, the highest of the lowest, the lowest of the middle; (212)

The middle of the middle, the highest of the middle, the lowest of the highest, the middle of the highest; (213)

The highest of the highest. These are the Graivêyaka gods.

---

[1] They are termed Kalpôpaga and Kalpâtîta.

[2] I am not sure that these are the correct Sanskrit forms of the two last Kalpas; the original has Â*n*aya and Pâ*n*aya.

[3] I.e. those who live on the neck (grîva), i.e. on the upper part of the universe.

[4] I.e. those above whom there dwell no other gods.

β′. The Vi*g*ayas, the Vai*g*ayantas, the *G*ayantas, the Aparâ*g*itas (214)
And the Sarvârthasiddhas: these are the five kinds of Anuttara gods.

These and others besides are the many kinds of Vaimânika gods. (215–217 = 159–160)

The longest duration of the life of the Bhaumêyika gods is somewhat more than a Sâgarôpamâ, the smallest ten thousand years. (218)

The longest duration of the life of the Vyantaras is one Palyôpamâ, the shortest is ten thousand years. (219)

The longest duration of the life of the *G*yôtishkas is one Palyôpamâ plus one hundred thousand years, the shortest is the eighth part of a Palyôpamâ. (220)

The longest duration of life in the Saudharmakalpa is two Sâgarôpamâs, the shortest is one Palyôpamâ. (221)

(In the same way (*a*) the longest, and (*b*) the shortest duration of life in the remaining Kalpas and heavenly regions is given in the original. I give in the sequel the substance only of each verse.)

In Î*s*âna Kalpa (*a*) is somewhat more than a Sâgarôpamâ, (*b*) somewhat more than a Palyôpamâ. (222)

In Sanatkumâra Kalpa (*a*) is seven, (*b*) two Sâgarôpamâs. (223)

In Mâhêndra Kalpa (*a*) is somewhat more than seven Sâgarôpamâs, (*b*) somewhat more than two. (224)

In Brahmalôka Kalpa (*a*) is ten Sâgarôpamâs, (*b*) seven. (225)

In Lantaka Kalpa (*a*) is fourteen Sâgarôpamâs, (*b*) ten. (226)

In Mahâsukla Kalpa (*a*) is seventeen Sâgarôpamâs, (*b*) fourteen[1]. (227)

In Sahasrâra Kalpa (*a*) is eighteen Sâgarôpamâs, (*b*) seventeen. (228)

In Ânata Kalpa (*a*) is nineteen Sâgarôpamâs, (*b*) eighteen. (229)

In Prâ*n*ata Kalpa (*a*) is twenty Sâgarôpamâs, (*b*) nineteen. (230)

In Âra*n*a Kalpa (*a*) is twenty-one Sâgarôpamâs, (*b*) twenty. (231)

In A*k*yuta Kalpa (*a*) is twenty-two Sâgarôpamâs, (*b*) twenty-one. (232)

In the first (Graivêyika region) (*a*) is twenty-three Sâgarôpamâs, (*b*) twenty-two. (233)

In the second (Graivêyika region) (*a*) is twenty-four Sâgarôpamâs, (*b*) twenty-three. (234)

In the third (Graivêyika region) (*a*) is twenty-five Sâgarôpamâs, (*b*) twenty-four. (235)

In the fourth (Graivêyika region) (*a*) is twenty-six Sâgarôpamâs, (*b*) twenty-five. (236)

In the fifth (Graivêyika region) (*a*) is twenty-seven Sâgarôpamâs, (*b*) twenty-six. (237)

In the sixth (Graivêyika region) (*a*) is twenty-eight Sâgarôpamâs, (*b*) twenty-seven. (238)

In the seventh (Graivêyika region) (*a*) is twenty-nine Sâgarôpamâs, (*b*) twenty-eight. (239)

In the eighth (Graivêyika region) (*a*) is thirty Sâgarôpamâs, (*b*) twenty-nine. (240)

In the ninth (Graivêyika region) (*a*) is thirty-one Sâgarôpamâs, (*b*) thirty. (241)

In the four heavens (of the Anuttara gods), be-

[1] From this verse to verse 241 the length of life increases by one Sâgarôpamâ in each following class of gods.

ginning with Vigaya[1], (*a*) is thirty-three Sâgarôpamâs, (*b*) thirty-one. (242)

In the great Vimâna Sarvârtha(siddha) there is no difference between the longest and shortest duration of life, but it is always thirty-three Sâgarôpamâs. (243)

The longest and shortest duration of the gods' (continuance in the same kind of) body is equal to that which has been given for their life. (244, 245[2], 246 = 159, 160)

We have described the Living Beings, the worldly and the perfected ones, and we have described the Lifeless Things, those possessing form and those without form. (247)

Having thus learned (the nature of) living beings and lifeless things which is in accordance with the principles of reasoning[3], and believing in it, a sage should delight in self-control. (248)

After having lived as a *S*rama*n*a many years, a sage should mortify himself[4] by the following religious exercises. (249)

The longest duration of the mortification is twelve years; the middle, one year; and the shortest, six months. (250)

---

[1] Viz. Vigaya, Vaigayanta, *G*ayanta, and Aparâgita.

[2] Two MSS. (A and D) insert after verses 245 the following two verses: The longest interval between a Graivêyika's leaving his rank in Ânata, &c., and being again born to it, is an endless time, the shortest is from two to nine years. In the case of Anuttara gods the longest interval is a Sâgarôpamâ plus one Sa*m*khyêya, the shortest is from two to nine years.

[3] Naya.

[4] The last self-mortification, sa*m*lekhanâ, which is to end with death, is intended here. Some details about it will be found in part i, p. 74 ff.

In the first four years he should abstain from dressed food[1], in the second four years he should keep various fasts. (251)

During two years he should eat Â*k*âmla[2] at the end of every second fast; in the following half year he should keep not too long fasts. (252)

In the second half of the year he should keep long fasts. During the whole year he should eat but small portions of Â*k*âmla[2]. (253)

During the (last) year a sage should make the ends of two consecutive fasts meet[3], and should break his fast after half a month or a whole month, (till he dies). (254)

The following (Bhâvanâs), Kandarpa-, Âbhiyôgika-, Kilvisha-, Môha-, and Asuratva-(Bhâvanâs[4]), will lead to evil ways (i. e. bad births); they are obnoxious at the time of death. (255)

Those souls who cherish heretical opinions, commit sins, and kill living beings, will not reach Bôdhi at the time of death. (256)

Those souls who cherish orthodox opinions, do not commit sins, and are enveloped in white Lê*s*yâ, will reach Bôdhi at the time of death. (257)

---

[1] Vigaî-ni*gg*ûha*n*a. The meaning is that at the end of his fasts a monk should eat â*k*âmla, nirvik*ri*tika, &c. In the Ava*k*ûri a verse from the Ni*s*îtha*k*ûrni is quoted, which gives the same rule for the second four years.

[2] Âyâma = â*k*âmla. Is this the same thing as the âyâmaga = â*k*âmaka mentioned XV, 13? See above, p. 72, note 2.

[3] Kô*d*îsahiyam âyamam = kô*t*isahitam â*k*âmlam. The commentators give two explanations of this phrase: (1) Having fasted one day, one should take â*k*âmla on the next day; (2) one should on the second day continue to abstain from â*k*âmla.

[4] The definition of these technical terms is given below, verses 262 ff.

Those souls who cherish heretical opinions, commit sins, and are enveloped in black Lêsyâ, will not reach Bôdhi at the time of death. (258)

Those who love the creed of the *G*inas and piously practise it, will be pure and free from the soil (of passions), and will (in due time) get out of the Circle of Births. (259)

The miserable men who do not know the creed of the *G*inas, will many times commit unholy suicide and die against their will. (260)

Those who are well versed in the sacred lore and possess much knowledge, who awaken piety (in others) and appreciate their good qualities, are for this very reason worthy to hear the doctrine of salvation[1]. (261)

He who by ribaldry and buffoonery, by his comical habits and appearance, by jests and words amuses other people, realises the Kandarpa-Bhâvanâ. (262)

Those who practise spells and besmear their body with ashes for the sake of pleasure, amusement, or power, realise the Âbhiyôgika-Bhâvanâ[2]. (263)

The deceitful man who reviles the sacred lore, the Kêvalins, the teacher of the Law, the Saṅgha, and the monks, realises the Kilvishika-Bhâvanâ. (264)

He who is continuously angry, and who puts his faith in prognostics, realises the Asuratva-Bhâvanâ. (265)

Those who use weapons, eat poison, throw them-

---

[1] Âlôkanâ = *s*rama*n*aphalam. The Ava*k*ûri renders the last phrase: 'They are able to bring about the salvation of others.' The original, however, has sôu*m*, 'to hear.'

[2] The Abhiyôgidêvas are genii who serve the gods. This Bhâvanâ leads to being born as an Abhiyôgidêva; the next two Bhâvanâs, as a Kilvishadêva and an Asura.

selves into fire or water, and use things not prescribed by the rules of good conduct, are liable to be born and to die again and again. (Such persons realise the Môha-Bhâvanâ.) (266)

The enlightened and liberated *Gñ*â*tri*(putra) has thus delivered Thirty-six Lectures of the Uttarâdhyayana[1], which the pious[2] approve of. (267)

---

[1] Uttara*ggh*âê in the original. The commentators give uttara here the meaning pradhâna, 'best, prominent.' The same explanation is given by the scholiast on the Nandî (Weber, Sacred Literature of the Jains, p. 124). Perhaps the name refers to the tradition that Mahâvîra recited at the time of his death the thirty-six apu*tth*a-vâgara*n*âi*m*, which are identified by one commentator of the Kalpa Sûtra (Lives of the *G*inas, § 147) with the Uttarâdhyayana; for uttara also means 'last.'

[2] Bhavasiddhîya=bhavasiddhika, explained by bhavya.

SÛTRAK*RI*TÂṄGA.

SÛTRAKR*I*TÂṄGA.

FIRST BOOK[1].

FIRST LECTURE,

CALLED

THE DOCTRINE[2].

FIRST CHAPTER.

One should know what causes the bondage of Soul, and knowing (it) one should remove[3] it.

(*G*ambûsvâmin asked Sudharman):

What causes the bondage (of Soul) according to Mahâvîra? and what must one know in order to remove it? (1)

(Sudharman answered):

He who owns even a small property in living or lifeless things[4], or consents to others holding it, will not be delivered from misery. (2)

---

[1] *S*rutaskandha. Its Sanskrit title mentioned by *S*îlâṅka is Gâthâshô*d*a*s*aka, i.e. the book whose Sixteenth Lecture is called Gâthâ. It is mentioned in the Uttarâdhyayana XXXI, 13 by the name of the sixteen Gâthas; see above, p. 182.

[2] Samaya. This title is not found in MSS. at the end of the lecture, but it is given by the author of the Niryukti (verse 29). The subject of this lecture is more fully treated in §§ 15–33 of the First Lecture of the Second Book.

[3] Tiu*tt*igg*â*. The commentators translate this word trô*t*ayêt, but the true Sanskrit original is ativartêta, as is evident from the form atiu*tt*anti in I, 2, 22.

[4] Living and lifeless things as we understand these words, not

If a man kills living beings, or causes other men to kill them, or consents to their killing them, his iniquity will go on increasing. (3)

A sinner who makes the interests of his kinsmen[1] and companions his own, will suffer much; for the number of those whose interest he takes to heart constantly increases. (4)

All this, his wealth and his nearest relations, cannot protect him (from future misery); knowing (this) and (the value of) life, he will get rid of Karman. (5)

Some men[2], *S*rama*n*as and Brâhma*n*as, who ignore and deny these true words[3], adhere (to their own tenets), and are given to pleasures. (6)

Some[4] profess (the exclusive belief in) the five gross elements: earth, water, fire, wind, and air. (7)

'These five gross elements (are the original causes of things), from them arises another (thing, viz. âtman)[5]; for on the dissolution of the (five elements) living beings cease to exist. (8)

as the *G*ainas do. The original has: *k*ittamanta*m* a*k*itta*m* vâ, beings possessed of intellect, and things without intellect. The latter are, according to *G*aina notions, living beings *g*îva as well as inanimate matter.

[1] Literally, those in whose family he is born. *S*îlâṅka, the author of the oldest *T*ikâ on the Sûtrak*ri*tâṅga, names the Râsh*t*rakû*t*as or Râ*th*ors in order to illustrate what is meant by family.'

[2] According to *S*îlâṅka the Bauddhas, Bârhaspatyas, and others are intended.

[3] Grantha, passage in a book. The verses 2-5 are intended.

[4] They are the Nâstikas or *K*ârvâkas.

[5] In other words: the Âtman is produced by the elements. But there is, it would seem, but one Âtman, for in verses 11, 12, we have another heretical philosophy which acknowledged a plurality of transient âtmans.

'And as the Earth, though it is but one pile, presents many forms, so the intelligent (principle, viz. the âtman) appears under various forms as the universe[1].' (9)

Thus say some fools. (But how can they explain on their theory that) the man engaging in undertakings, who has committed a sin, will himself suffer severe pain[2]? (10)

'Everybody, fool or sage, has an individual soul. These souls exist (as long as the body), but after death they are no more; there are no souls which are born again. (11)

'There is neither virtue nor vice, there is no world beyond; on the dissolution of the body the individual ceases to be.' (12)

'When a man acts or causes another to act, it is not his soul (âtman) which acts or causes to act[3].' Thus they (viz. the adherents of the Sâṅkhya philosophy) boldly proclaim. (13)

How can those who hold such opinions explain (the variety of existence in) the world? They go from darkness to utter darkness, being fools and engaged in works. (14)

Some[4] say that there are five elements and that

[1] This is the doctrine of the Vêdântins.

[2] If there were but one âtman common to all men, the fruit of works done by one man might accrue to another. For the âtman is the substratum of merit and demerit.

[3] Though there is no doubt about the meaning of this passage, still the construction is so elliptic that I may have failed to understand the connection of the parts of the sentence.

[4] This is the opinion expressed by *K*araka and in the early law-books, see Professor Jolly's paper in the Transactions of the Ninth International Congress of Orientalists, vol. i, p. 456. *S*îlâṅka ascribes it to the Sâṅkhyas and *S*aivâdhikârins.

the soul is a sixth (substance), but they contend that the soul and the world (i.e. the five elements) are eternal. (15)

'These (six substances) do not perish neither (without nor with a cause); the non-existent does not come into existence, but all things are eternal by their very nature[1].' (16)

Some fools[2] say that there are five skandhas of momentary existence. They do not admit that (the soul) is different from, nor identical[3] with (the elements), that it is produced from a cause (i.e. the elements), nor that it is without a cause (i.e. that it is eternal). (17)

The *G*â*n*ayas[4] say that there are four elements: earth, water, fire, and wind, which combined form the body (or soul?). (18)

(All these heretics say): 'Those who dwell in houses, in woods, or on hills, will be delivered from all misery if they adopt our creed.' (19)

---

[1] Niyatîbhâvam âgayâ. Niyatî is explained by nityabhâva.

[2] Viz. the Bauddhas. The five skandhas are explained in the commentary as follows: 1. rûpaskandha, or substances and their qualities; 2. vêdanâskandha, feelings, as pleasure and pain; 3. vi*g*ñânaskandha, perceptions of the qualities of things; 4. sa*m*g*ñ*âskandha, perception and knowledge of things; 5. sa*m*skâraskandha, merit and demerit.

[3] Identical, i.e. a product of the elements as the *K*ârvâkas maintain.

[4] *G*â*n*aya, which is explained in the Dîpikâ by *g*ñânaka = pa*nd*ita*m*manya, denotes the Bauddhas. I think that the word may be derived from yâna 'vehicle,' which the Buddhist used to designate the two sections of the church, viz. the Hînayâna and Mahâyâna schools. The commentator quotes a various reading: âvarê for *g*â*n*ayâ, and explains it as referring to another sect of Bauddhas than those spoken of in the preceding verse. *S*ilâṅka comments on the reading avvarê first, and then on *g*â*n*aya.

But they do not cross the Flood of Life, who, ignoring the true relation of things, and not versed in the true Law, hold the above heretical opinions. (20)

They do not reach the end of the Sa*m*sâra, who, ignoring, &c. (21)

They do not reach the end of transmigration, who, &c. (22)

They do not put an end to birth, who, &c. (23)

They do not put an end to misery, who, &c. (24)

They do not put an end to death, who, &c. (25)

They will again and again experience manifold pains in this ring[1] of the earth, which is full of death, disease, and old age. (26)

The highest *G*ina, Mahâvîra the *G*ñâtr*i*putra, has said that they will undergo births without number, being placed in all sorts of existences. (27)

Thus I say.

SECOND CHAPTER.

Again some[2] say: 'It is proved that there are individual souls; they experience pleasure and pain; and (on dying) they lose their state of life. (1)

'But misery (and pleasure) is not caused by (the souls) themselves; how could it be caused by other (agents, as time, &c.)? Pleasure and misery, final beatitude[3] and temporal (pleasure and pain) are not

---

[1] *K*akravâla.

[2] They are the fatalists whose peculiar opinions are stated in verses 2 and 3.

[3] Sêhiya*m* = saiddhikam, i.e. môkshê bhava*m* sukham. Another explanation of the commentator makes saiddhika those pleasures which depend on external causes, as wreaths, sandal, &c., and asaiddhika the pleasures of the mind.

caused by (the souls) themselves, nor by others; but the individual souls experience them; it is the lot assigned them by destiny.' This is what they (i.e. the fatalists) say. (2, 3)

Those who proclaim these opinions, are fools who fancy themselves learned; they have no knowledge, and do not understand that things depend partly on fate, and partly on human exertion[1]. (4)

Thus (say) some heretics[2]; they are very bold men; if they act up to their principles, they will never be delivered from misery. (5)

As the swift deer who are destitute of protection, are frightened where there is no danger, and not frightened where there is danger; (6)

(As) they dread safe places, but do not dread traps; they are bewildered by ignorance and fear, and run hither and thither; (7)

If they did jump over the noose or pass under it, they would escape from the snare; but the stupid animal does not notice[3] it; (8)

The unhappy animal, being of a weak intellect, runs into the dangerous (place), is caught in the snare, &c., and is killed there; (9)

So some unworthy *S*rama*n*as who hold wrong doctrines are afraid of what is free from danger, and are not afraid of real dangers. (10)

The fools dread the preaching of the Law, but

---

[1] To render niyatâniyata*m*.

[2] Pâsattha, usually translated pâr*s*vastha 'outsider,' those who do not acknowledge true arguments; another rendering is pâ*s*astha 'held in bondage.'

[3] Dêhati = pa*s*yati. The form dekkhati occurs in the Prâk*ri*t of plays.

they do not dread works, being without discernment and knowledge. (11)

Shaking off greed[1], pride[2], deceit[3], and wrath[4], one becomes free from Karman. This is a subject (which an ignorant man, like) a brute animal, does not attend to. (12)

The unworthy heretics who do not acknowledge this, will incur death an endless number of times, like deer caught in a snare. (13)

All Brâhma*n*as and *S*rama*n*as contend that they possess the knowledge (of the truth), but the creatures in the whole world do not know anything. (14)

As a Mlê*kkh*a[5] repeats what an Ârya has said, but does not understand the meaning, merely repeating his words, so the ignorant, though pretending to possess knowledge, do not know the truth, just as an uninstructed Mlê*kkh*a. (15, 16)

The speculations of the Agnostics cannot lead to knowledge; they cannot reach the truth by themselves, still less teach it to other men. (17)

As when a man in a wood who does not know it, follows a guide who also does not know it, both being unacquainted (with the place), come to great trouble; (18)

As when one blind man is the guide of another, the man walks a great distance, loses his way, or follows a wrong way; (19)

Thus some who search after salvation and pretend

---

1 Savvappaga = sarvâtmaka, lôbha.

2 Viukkassa = vyutkarsha, mâna.

3 Nûma = mâyâ. 4 Appattiya = krôdha.

5 It is worthy of note that the Mlê*kkh*as here are represented as not understanding the language of the Âryas.

to practise the (true) Law, follow the false Law and do not arrive at the thoroughly right (thing, viz. self-control). (20)

Thus some (wrong philosophers) do not apply to others for arguments, but they continue to err because they believe their own arguments to be right[1]. (21)

Thus arguing according to their light, and ignorant about what is right and wrong, they do not get out of misery as birds do not get out of their cage. (22)

They praise their own creed and blame that of their opponents, but those who act in this respect the part of philosophers, will be kept confined in the Circle of Births[2]. (23)

There is the doctrine of the Kriyâvâdins[3], which has been previously explained; it augments the misery of worldly existence of those who do not well consider the nature of acts. (24)

'He who intends (to kill) a living being but does not do it by (an act of) his body, and he who unknowingly kills one, both are affected by that act through a slight contact (with it) only, but the demerit (in their case) is not fully developed[4].' (25)

---

[1] The last part of the verse might also be translated: 'because these fools believe the subject to be cleared up (mañgû) by their own arguments.'

[2] There is a play on the words viussanti and viussiyâ, in the last line of this verse viussanti is a denominative verb from viusa=vidvân, and is translated vidvân ivâ karati. Viussiya =vi+ut+srita.

[3] See above, p. 83. Silâṅka defines the Kriyâvâdins here as men who contend that the principal means of reaching Môksha is kaityakarma, the construction of sanctuaries.

[4] An intentional killing of a living being must actually take place in order to induce the Karman on the soul. If one of the essential conditions which constitute the guilt of slaughter (himsâ),

'There are three ways of committing sins: by one's own activity, by commission, by approval (of the deed). (26)

'These are the three ways of committing sins. Thus by purity of the heart one reaches Nirvâ*n*a. (27)

'A layman may kill his son (during a famine) and eat him; a wise (monk) who partakes of the meat, will not be defiled by the sin[1].' (28)

The mind of those who sin in thoughts is not pure; they are wrong, they do not conduct themselves carefully[2]. (29)

Men attached to pleasure, who think that the above-mentioned doctrines will save them, commit sins. (30)

As a blind-born man getting into a leaky boat, wants to reach the shore, but is drowned during the passage[3], so some unworthy, heretical *S*rama*n*as wish to get beyond the Circle of Births, but they are whirled round in it. (31, 32)

Thus I say.

THIRD CHAPTER.

If a monk should eat forbidden food which a pious (layman) has prepared for some guest, and which food has been mixed up with even thousand (times more

is wanting the Karman is still produced; however, it does not take a firm hold of the soul, but merely 'touches' it. This is of course the opinion of the Kriyâvâdins.

[1] According to *S*îlâṅka the father too would not be guilty; but this interpretation is against good sense and grammar.

[2] This is the answer of the Siddhântin to the foregoing propositions.

[3] The same verse recurs below, I, 11, 30.

pure food)[1], he would be neither monk nor layman. (1)

*S*rama*n*as who do not comprehend this and do not know what is dangerous, who care for the pleasures of the moment only, will suffer death an endless number of times, like big[2] fishes who when the water rises are by the water (deposited) on dry land and are killed (there), poor things, by hungry *dh*aṅkas and herons. (2-4)

We hear also of another error of some (philosophers): some say that the world has been created (or is governed)[3] by the gods, others, by Brahman. (5)

Some[4] say that it has been created by the Îsvara, others that it was produced from chaos, &c., this world with living beings and lifeless things, with its variety of pleasure and pain. (6)

The great *Ri*shi[5] said, that the world has been created by Svayambhû; Mâra originated Mâyâ, therefore the world (appears to be) uneternal. (7)

Some Brâhma*n*as and *S*rama*n*as say that the

---

[1] This might also be translated: 'though the food passes through the hands of a thousand men before he accepts it.'

[2] Vêsâliya = vai*s*âlika. The commentators offer three explanations of this word, (1) marine, vi*s*âla*h* samudras tatrabhavâ*h*; (2) belonging to the genus called vi*s*âla; (3) big, vi*s*âla.

[3] Dêvautté. This is either dêvair upta*h*, sown, i.e. produced by the gods, or dêvair gupta*h*, governed by the gods.

[4] The adherents of the Yôga and Sâṅkhya philosophy, or the theistical and atheistical followers of the latter, are apparently meant by 'some' and 'others.'

[5] The commentators unfortunately have not preserved the name of the great *Ri*shi; they identify Svayambhû with Vish*n*u 'or some one else.' This Svayambhû, afraid that the earth should become overcrowded, called to help Yama, alias Mâra, who with the help of Mâyâ makes the creatures appear to die.

universe was produced from the (primeval) egg, and He (Brahman) created the things. These ignorant men speak untruth. (8)

Those who on arguments of their own maintain that the world has been created, do not know the truth. Nor will (the world) ever perish. (9)

Know that misery arises from wicked deeds[1]. How can those who do not know the origin (of misery) know its prevention? (10)

Some say that the soul (of him who is) pure will become free from bad Karman (on reaching beatitude), but that in that state it will again become defiled through pleasant excitement or hate. (11)

(According to them[2]) he who has lived on earth as a restrained monk, will afterwards become free from Karman. As clear water which was free from defilement becomes again defiled, so (will be the soul). (12)

A wise man should consider that these (heretics) do not lead a life of chastity, and that all these disputants proclaim their own creed in opposition (to the others). (13)

(Others[3] maintain that) perfection can only be reached by their method of religious life, not otherwise; and that even before (that time) they have

---

[1] It is not given us by any of the above-mentioned agents whom the opponents believe to have created the world.

[2] According to *S*îlâṅka the followers of Gô*s*âla and the Trairâ*s*ikas are meant. The latter are the *G*aina followers of the Vai*s*êshika philosophy. The Trairâ*s*ika *S*âkhâ was founded by *Kh*aluka Rôhagupta, see part i, p. 290. The name Trairâ*s*ika is said to have been given to these philosophers because they admit a third state besides those of the bound and of the liberated.

[3] According to *S*îlâṅka the *S*aivas and Ekada*nd*ins are meant.

their senses under control and possess everything to be wished for[1]. (14)

Some say that they will be perfected and sound. On the head of Perfection some men are infatuated with their own doctrines. (15)

But these uncontrolled (men) will whirl round in the beginningless (Circle of Births); after a Kalpa they will rise from their sphere to become the lowest of Asuras[2]. (16)

Thus I say.

Fourth Chapter.

These (philosophers) who are vanquished (by their passions) cannot help you in cases where a sinner perishes[3]; though having given up their former occupations they will give advice in worldly matters. (1)

A wise monk who fully appreciates this, should not mix with those (heretics); without conceit and not attached to them a sage should lead a life equally removed (from love and hate). (2)

Some say that those who own possessions and engage in undertakings (may reach perfection); but a monk should take his refuge to those who neither own possessions nor engage in undertakings. (3)

A wise man should beg food which has been

---

[1] They acquire the eight siddhis or magical powers.

[2] I translate the words *thânâ* âsurakivvisiyâ according to the explanation of the commentary. But they may also mean: from the sphere of Asuras and sinners.

[3] A various reading first commented upon by *S*îlâṅka is: bâlâ pa*nd*itamâ*n*i*n*ô, being ignorant men who fancy themselves learned.

prepared (for somebody else), and he should accept what is freely given him, without greed and passions; he should abstain from overbearing behaviour[1]. (4)

He should know the talk of people: some say things which are the outcome of a wrong understanding and are but opinions of others repeated. (5)

'The world is boundless and eternal, it exists from eternity and does not perish[2]; (another) bold philosopher[3] says that the world is limited, but eternal. (6)

'Some say that the knowledge (of the highest authority) is unlimited; but the same bold philosopher says that it is limited in every way[4].' (7)

Some beings have motion, others not; it depends on certain conditions whether they are in the one state or in the other. (8)

(E.g. big creatures) have one form of bodily existence and then another[5]. But all are subject to pain; hence they should not be killed. (9)

This is the quintessence of wisdom: not to kill anything. Know this to be the legitimate conclusion

---

[1] Omâ*n*a = apamâna.

[2] According to *S*îlâṅka the eternity of things means, with these philosophers, that one thing always retains the same genus or *g*âti, e. g. that he who was a man in this life will again be a man in the next.

[3] According to the commentators Vyâsa is intended. The doctrine referred to in the text is that of the Purâ*n*as.

[4] The commentators interpret this verse as if not two philosophical opinions but only one was spoken of. Unlimited knowledge is according to them different from omniscience; in the second part of the sentence 'limited' refers to the sleep of Brahman during which he is unconscious.

[5] Men are some time embryos, then young men, then old men.

from the principle of the reciprocity with regard to non-killing[1]. (10)

Living (according to the rules of conduct), and without greed, one should take care of the highest good[2].

In walking, in sitting and lying down, and in food and drink: with regard to these three points a monk should always control himself.

And he should leave off pride[3], wrath[4], deceit[5], and greed[6]. (11, 12)

Possessing the Samitis and being protected by the five Sa*m*varas, a pious monk should live, till he reaches perfection, as a man free from fetters among those bound in fetters (viz. the householders). (13)

Thus I say.

---

[1] Ahi*m*sâsamaya*m* = ahi*m*sâsamatâ*m*, viz. as you do not wish to be killed, so others do not wish to be killed. The last part of the sentence might also be translated: know this to be the real meaning of the Law (samaya) of ahi*m*sâ. The same verse recurs I, 11, 10.

[2] Âdâna, right knowledge, right faith, and right conduct.

[3] Ukkasa = utkarsha, mâna.

[4] *G*ala*n*a = *g*valana, krôdha.

[5] Nûma = mâyâ.

[6] Ma*gg*h*attha = madhyastha, lôbha. Compare the similar expressions in I, 1, 2, 12, above, p. 241, notes 1–4, and I, 2, 2, 29, below, p. 257.

SECOND LECTURE[1],

CALLED

THE DESTRUCTION OF KARMAN.

FIRST CHAPTER.

(*Ri*shabha said to his sons):

Acquire perfect knowledge of the Law! why do you not study it? It is difficult to obtain instruction in it after this life. The days (that are gone by) will never return, nor is it easy a second time to obtain human birth. (1)

See, young and old men, even children in the mother's womb die. As a hawk catches a quail, so (life) will end when its time is spent[2]. (2)

---

[1] The name of this lecture, which occurs in its last line, is vêyâlîya, because, as the author of the Niryukti remarks, it treats on vidârika, destruction (of Karman), and because it is composed in the Vaitâlîya metre. For either word, vaidârika (or rather vaidâlika, cf. karmavidalana) and vaitâlîya may, in *G*aina Prâk*ri*t, become vêyâlîya or vêtâlîya. A play of words was apparently intended; it would have been impossible, if both words had not become identical in sound. We may, therefore, conclude that the language of the author obeyed the same phonetic laws as the *G*aina Prâk*ri*t exhibited in our MSS., or in other words, that the text has been written down in about the same language in which it was originally composed. The name of the Fifteenth Lecture leads to the same inference; for it is called *g*amaîya (yamakîya) because each of its verses contains the verbal ornament called yamaka, and because it opens with the words *g*am aîya*m* (yad atîtam).

[2] One MS. here inserts *g*îvâ*n*a *g*îviya*m*, the life of living beings.

(A man) may suffer for the sake of his parents; he will not easily obtain happiness after this life. A pious man should consider these causes of danger and cease to act. (3)

For in this world living beings suffer individually for their deeds; for the deed they have done themselves, they obtain (punishment), and will not get over it before they have felt it. (4)

Even gods, Gandharvas, Râkshasas, and Asuras; animals who live on earth, and snakes; kings, common people, merchants, and Brâhma*n*as: they all must leave their rank and suffer. (5)

Notwithstanding their pleasures and relations, all men must suffer in due time the fruit of their works; as a cocoa-nut detaching itself from its stalk (falls down), so (life) will end when its time is spent. (6)

Even a very learned or virtuous man, or a Brâhma*n*a or an ascetic, will be severely punished for his deed when he is given to actions of deceit[1]. (7)

See, those (heretics) who search for the knowledge of truth, but who do not cross the Sa*m*sâra, talk only about the highest good (without reaching it).

How will you understand what is near you and what is beyond[2]? In the meanwhile you suffer for your deeds. (8)

He who walks about naked and lean, he who eats only once after a month, if he is filled with deceit, will be born an endless number of times. (9)

---

[1] Abhinûma.

[2] According to *S*îlâṅka, this world and the next, or domestic life and monachism, or the Sa*m*sâra and Môksha are meant by the expression 'what is near you and what is beyond.'

Man, cease from sins! For the life of men will come to an end[1]. Men who are drowned (in lust, as it were), and addicted to pleasure will, for want of control, be deluded[2]. (10)

Exert and control yourself! For it is not easy to walk on ways where there are minutely small animals. Follow the commandments which the Arhats have well proclaimed[3]. (11)

Heroes (of faith) who desist (from sins) and exert themselves aright, who subdue wrath, fear, &c., will never kill living beings; they desist from sins and are entirely happy. (12)

It is not myself alone who suffers, all creatures in the world suffer; this a wise man[4] should consider, and he should patiently bear (such calamities) as befall him, without giving way to his passions. (13)

As a wall covered with a plastering (of dried cow-dung)[5] is by a shock made thin, so (a monk) should make his body lean by fasting, &c. He should

---

[1] Paliyantam. Another explanation of this word, preferred by the commentators, is palyôpamasya antar: within, i.e. something shorter than a Palyôpamâ.

[2] Or, acquire Karman which is to result in delusion.

[3] According to the commentators: practise (control) according to the sâsana (i.e. sûtras); this has been well declared by the Arhats.

[4] Sahie. This word is explained sometimes by svahita, intent on his spiritual welfare, sometimes by hitena *g*ñânâdinâ sahita*h*, possessed of knowledge, &c. I translate it 'wise,' and derive the word from Sanskrit sah*ri*daya, the correct Prâk*ri*t for which would be sahiyae.

[5] Cow-dung is stuck, in the form of flat round cakes, against a wall to dry there. When the cakes are dried a little shake is sufficient to make them come down, whereby the wall will be restored to its original shape and dimensions.

abstain from slaughter of living beings. This is the Law proclaimed by the Sage. (14)

As a bird covered with dust removes the grey powder by shaking itself, so a worthy and austere Brâhma*n*a[1], who does penance, annihilates his Karman. (15)

Young and old people claim a houseless *S*rama*n*a as their own, though he begs according to the Law, observes the rules of conduct, and performs austerities. People will even cry themselves hoarse, but they will not captivate him. (16)

Whatever they will do to move his pity, however they will cry about their son, they will not captivate a worthy and virtuous monk or make him return to domestic life. (17)

Though they tempt him with pleasures, and though they should bind him and carry him home, if he does not care for a (worldly) life, they will not captivate him or make him return to domestic life. (18)

His father and mother, his children and wife who claim him, will admonish him: 'See, you are our supporter; care not for the next world in order to support us.' (19)

Some people are (foolishly) attached to others, and are thereby deluded; the unrighteous make them adopt unrighteousness, and they exult in their wickedness. (20)

Therefore a worthy and wise man should be

---

[1] Mâha*n*a = brâhma*n*a. The commentator derives the word from mâ and root han! The word is a synonym of muni, with which it frequently occurs in the same verse and has then been left out in the translation.

careful, ceasing from sin and being entirely happy. The virtuous heroes of faith (have chosen) the great road, the right and certain path to perfection. (21)

He who has entered the road leading to the destruction (of Karman)[1], who controls his mind, speech, and body, who has given up his possessions and relations and all undertakings, should walk about subduing his senses. (22)

SECOND CHAPTER.

A sage thinks that he should leave off sins just as (a snake) leaves its slough; and he is not proud of his Gôtra and other advantages; or is there any use in blaming others? (1)

A man who insults another will long whirl in the Circle of Births; to blame others is not good. Considering this a sage is not conceited. (2)

He who is independent, and he who is the servant of a servant, if they but observe the Vow of Silence[2], they have no reason to be ashamed; (therefore a monk) should behave equally towards all. (3)

Indifferent and pure with regard to every kind of control, a *S*rama*n*a should walk about; he who entertains pure thoughts during his whole life, dies as a worthy and wise man. (4)

The sage who sees the far-off (goal, viz. liberation), past and future things, will practise indifference, though he suffer corporal punishment and be beaten. (5)

Possessing perfect wisdom, a sage always vanquishes (his passions); he correctly expounds the

---

[1] Vêyâliya-maggam. [2] Maunapada.

Law; he never neglects even the smallest (duty); he is neither angry nor proud. (6)

A man who controls himself according to (the Law), which is praised by many people, and is not bound by any worldly ties, who is always pure like a lake, proclaims the Law of Kâsyapa. (7)

Seeing that numerous living beings lead an individual life, and that every one feels (pleasure and pain) just as the others, a wise man who observes the Vow of Silence, leaves off (injuring them). (8)

A sage has completely mastered the Law, and has ceased to do actions; but the selfish grieve, they will not (thereby) recover their (lost) property[1]. (9)

Know that it (viz. property) entails pains in this world, and very great pains[2] in the next. Who will lead a domestic life when he knows that everything must perish? (10)

One should know (and renounce) the great attachment (to the world), and respect and honours on earth; (for conceit) is a very thin thorn difficult to pull out. A wise man, therefore, should abandon worldliness[3]. (11)

A monk should perform postures (as Kâyôtsarga, &c.) alone on his seat, and alone on his couch he should meditate; excelling in the performance of austerities, guarded in words, and restrained in thoughts. (12)

---

[1] *S*îlâṅka quotes a verse which the Nâgâr*g*unîyas insert here; compare part i, p. 32, note 2.

[2] I take duha*m*duha for a kind of intensive form of duha.

[3] This is a rather dark verse. *S*îlâṅka, after explaining it, quotes the verse as it was read by the Nâgâr*g*unîyas, which may be rendered thus: Respect and honours are a great obstacle, this he should know; be the thorn small (or) difficult to pull out, a wise man should remove it by the (means we are about to describe).

An ascetic does not shut the door of a deserted house (where he puts up), nor does he open it; when asked he returns no (rude) answer; he cuts no grass, nor does he strew it (on the ground for a couch). (13)

Where (he is) at sunset, there he calmly (performs his duties); a sage bears pleasant and unpleasant things, be there insects, or wild beasts, or snakes. (14)

He bears the three kinds of calamities arising from beasts, men, and gods. A great sage will not be seized with a shivering, &c.[1], when he stays in a deserted house. (15)

He should not fear for his life, nor should he desire to be praised (for his courage). Fearful things will frighten the mind of a monk who stays in a deserted house. (16)

They say that he who is very well disciplined, who protects others, who lives in a place removed from other people, who is not frightened by dangers, possesses right conduct, &c. (17)

A monk who uses warm or hot water[2], who follows the Law, and loathes (wrong conduct), will by intercourse with bad kings become deficient in his devotion though he be ever so virtuous. (18)

When a monk quarrels and uses very bad language, he will suffer great spiritual loss; therefore a wise man should not quarrel. (19)

He who abstains from cold water[2], who plans (or undertakes) nothing, and has ceased from even the smallest actions, who does not eat food out of the dish of a householder, possesses right conduct, &c. (20)

---

[1] Literally, horripilation. By the '&c.' the other outward signs of horror are indicated.

[2] It should be kept in mind that *G*aina monks are forbidden to use cold water, because it is considered to possess life.

Though life cannot be prolonged, as the saying is[1], still foolish people sin recklessly; a foolish man is filled to the brim (as it were) with sins. Considering this a sage is not conceited. (21)

By self-invented rites common people seek holiness[2], they are full of deceit and shrouded (as it were) in delusion. But a monk is holy[2] through his innocence, he allows no troubles[3] to influence his words, (thoughts, and acts). (22)

As a clever gambler, playing at dice, is not vanquished, since he casts the Krita, but not Kali, nor Trêta, nor Dvâpara; (23)

So adopt for your welfare the best and highest Law which has been proclaimed in this world by the Saviour, as the clever (gambler casts) the Krita, and avoids the other casts. (24)

I have heard that sensual pleasures are said to have the strongest hold on men; but those who abstain from them follow the Law of Kâsyapa. (25)

Those who follow the Law that has been proclaimed by *Gñ*âtrika, the great seer[4], are virtuous and righteous; they confirm each other in the Law. (26)

Take no heed of the seductive (pleasures), endeavour to shake off delusion. Those who are not subdued by the wicked (pleasures), know meditation to be their duty[5]. (27)

---

[1] Compare Uttarâdhyayana IV, 1, above p. 18. The same words recur below, I, 2, 3, 10, p. 259.

[2] Palêti = pralîyatê. [3] Literally, cold and heat.

[4] Mahâvîra.

[5] Âhitam, literally, has been declared. The commentators explain the word as â-hitam, thoroughly good, or âtmani vyavasthitam, placed in the soul.

A monk should not tell stories, nor ask idle questions, nor gossip[1]. But, knowing the highest Law, he should perform his religious duties, and regard nothing his own. (28)

A monk should not indulge deceit[2], greed[3], pride[4], and wrath[5]. Those are virtuous who have arrived at the right understanding of these passions, and who have well practised control[6]. (29)

(A monk) should be free from attachment, wise, controlling himself, seeking the Law, earnest in the performance of austerities, and subduing his senses. It is difficult to obtain the soul's benefit. (30)

Right conduct, &c., which has been taught by the *Gñâtri*ka, the sage who knew everything in the whole world, has either not been learned or not been truly practised (by creatures now in distress). (31)

Many men who thought this Law to be the highest good and conducive to their spiritual welfare, obeyed their preceptors, ceased from works, and have crossed the great flood (of worldly existence). (32)

Thus I say.

THIRD CHAPTER.

If a monk who abstains from actions, suffers pain (for acts done) through ignorance, that Karman will

---

[1] Samprasâraka?

[2] *Kh*anna = mâyâ.

[3] Pasa*m*sa = pra*s*a*m*sâ, lôbha.

[4] Ukkâsa = utkarsha, mâna.

[5] Pagâsa = prakâ*s*a, krôdha.

[6] Dhuya = dhûta. The word preceding this is sug*ô*siya*m* = *g*ush*t*a*m*, sêvita*m*. A various reading is sug*h*ôsiya*m*, which means 'who have well annihilated their Karman (dhûta).'

be annihilated through control. The wise reach (perfection) getting rid of death. (1)

Those who resist the seductions[1] are placed on a line with those who have crossed the Samsâra. Therefore look up (at beatitude as the end in view). Those (virtuous men) regard pleasures as equal to diseases. (2)

Men of princely rank wear precious things imported by merchants; likened (to these precious things) are the excellent great vows together with (the prohibition of) eating at night. (3)

Pleasure-seeking men who are greedy and are absorbed by amusements, are reckless and like the wretched; they do not know that meditation (has been enjoined as) a duty. (4)

As a bullock which is hurt and urged on by the driver[2] becomes weak, and at last, when its strength is exhausted and it is unable to move, sinks down; (5)

So he who knows the pursuit of pleasures, must sooner or later give up their enjoyment (lest they drag him down[3]). He who is still surrounded by pleasant things[4], should not love pleasures, whether he obtains them, or for some reason or other does not obtain them. (6)

Lest the lot of the wicked should fall to you, escape (the influence of the senses), and discipline yourself! The wicked will much and strongly grieve, groan, and wail. (7)

---

[1] Vinnava*n*â = vig*ñ*âpanâ, explained striya*h*.

[2] Instead of 'driver' and 'bullock' we might translate 'hunter' and 'deer.'

[3] He should not be engrossed by them as the bullock sinks down beneath its burden.

[4] To render kâmî.

See, life in this world (is transient); though your life lasts a hundred years, you die as a short-lived man; mind that (your) years swiftly pass. Nevertheless greedy men are attached to pleasures. (8)

Those who engage in undertakings, who work the perdition of their souls, and who kill (living beings), will go to the world of the wicked, to the abode of the Asuras for a long time (to dwell there). (9)

Though life cannot be prolonged, as the saying is [1], still foolish people sin recklessly (thinking): 'We are only concerned with the present time; who has seen the next world and returned thence?' (10)

Believe in the words of him who sees (everything), you who are blind, as it were, you whose sight is blinded, ah, whose sight is obstructed by your works which result in delusion! (11)

The unhappy again and again suffer from delusion; therefore have done with praise and honours! A wise ascetic should consider that living beings are like himself (as regards love of life, aversion to pain, &c.). (12)

The man also who still lives in the house, should, in accordance with his creed [2], be merciful to living beings; we are bidden to be fair and equal with all; (thereby even a householder) goes to the world of the gods. (13)

Being instructed in the creed of the Lord, exert yourself in the truth (i.e. in control)! A monk who has thoroughly subdued his selfishness should collect pure alms. (14)

Knowing the truth, one should live up to it,

---

[1] Compare p. 256, note 1.

[2] Ânupûrvyâ.

seeking the Law, earnest in the performance of austerities, possessing the Guptis, being accomplished, one should always exert oneself, intent on the soul's benefit, and desiring the highest good (viz. liberation). (15)

The fool thinks that his wealth, cattle, and relations will save him; they him, or he them. But they are no help, no protection. (16)

When calamity befalls him, or the end of his life draws near, he must go and come alone; the wise believe that there is nothing to protect him. (17)

All living beings owe their present form of existence to their own Karman; timid, wicked, suffering latent misery, they err about (in the Circle of Births), subject to birth, old age, and death. (18)

He should know that the present time is the best opportunity to mend, and that an awakening is difficult to obtain. A wise man should be aware of this[1]. The (first) *G*ina[2] has said this, and so the remaining ones (will) say it. (19)

O ye monks, the virtuous (*G*inas) that have been and will be, the followers of the Law of Kâ*s*yapa[3], they all have commended these virtues. (20)

Do not kill living beings in the threefold way[4], being intent on your spiritual welfare and abstaining from sins. In this way numberless men have reached

---

[1] A various reading mentioned in the commentary is ahiyâsaê, 'he should bear (all troubles).'

[2] The whole lecture is put by the commentators in the mouth of *Ri*shabha.

[3] The first and last Tîrthakaras belonged to the Kâ*s*yapa Gôtra.

[4] I.e. by your own acts, by order, and by assent; or by thoughts, words, and acts.

perfection, and others, who live now, and who are to come, (will reach it). (21)

Thus spoke the Arhat *Gñ*âtr*i*putra, the reverend, famous native of Vai*s*âlî[1], who possessed the highest knowledge and the highest faith, who possessed (simultaneously) the highest knowledge and faith.

Thus I say.

THIRD LECTURE,

CALLED

THE KNOWLEDGE OF TROUBLES[2].

FIRST CHAPTER.

A man believes himself a hero as long as he does not behold the foe, as did *S*i*s*upâla (before he beheld) the valorously-fighting, great warrior[3]. (1)

They go forward to the head of the battle; but when the fight has begun the mother will not recognise her son, and he will be mangled by his foe. (2)

So a novice, who as yet has not suffered pains and is not yet used to a mendicant's life, believes himself a hero till he practises austerities[4]. (3)

---

[1] See my remarks in part i, Introduction, p. xi. This passage in prose appended to the metrical text seems to contradict the supposition of the commentators that the whole lecture was pronounced by *Ri*shabha.

[2] Compare Uttarâdhyayana II, above, p. 9 ff.

[3] Viz. K*r*ish*n*a. K*r*ish*n*a's victory over *S*i*s*upâla is told in the Mahâbhârata, Sabhâparvan, *S*i*s*upâlavadha (eighth parvan). It forms the subject of Mâgha's famous poem *S*i*s*upâlavadha.

[4] Lûha*m* = rûksham, i.e. sa*m*yamam, control.

When during the winter they suffer from cold and draughts, the weak become disheartened like Kshattriyas who have lost their kingdom. (4)

When they suffer from the heat of summer, sad and thirsty, the weak become disheartened like fish in shallow water. (5)

It is painful never to take anything but what is freely given, and begging is a hard task. Common people say that (men become monks) because they will not work and are wretched. (6)

Weak men who are unable (to bear) these insults in villages or towns, become disheartened like cowards in the battle. (7)

Perchance a snarling dog will bite a hungry monk; in that case the weak will become disheartened like animals burnt by fire. (8)

Some who hate (the monks), revile them: 'Those who lead such a (miserable) life (as monks do), atone but (for their sins in a former life).' (9)

Some call them names, as 'naked, lowest of beggars, baldhead, scabby, filthy, nasty.' (10)

Those who behave in this way and do not know better, go from darkness to utter darkness, being fools and shrouded in delusion [1]. (11)

When bitten by flies and gnats, and unable (to bear) the pricking of grass, (they will begin to doubt), 'I have not seen the next world, all may end with death [2]!' (12)

Some weak men who suffer from the plucking out of the hair, and who are unable to preserve their chastity, will become disheartened like fish transfixed by a spear [3]. (13)

---

[1] Compare I, 1, 1, 14. [2] Compare I, 3, 3, 6.

[3] Kêtana, perhaps 'caught with the hook.'

Some low people who lead a life of iniquity, and entertain heretical opinions, being subject to love and hatred, injure a monk. (14)

Some fools in outlying countries take a pious monk for a spy or a thief, bind him, and insult him with angry words. (15)

A weak monk being hurt with a stick or a fist or a fruit, remembers his (kind) relations, just as a woman who in a passion has left (her husband and house). (16)

All these hardships are difficult to bear; the weak return to their house (when they cannot bear them), like elephants covered with arrows (break down). (17)

Thus I say.

Second Chapter.

There are some tender affections which monks cannot easily overcome. On their account some become disheartened, and are unable to practise control. (1)

His relations on seeing him will surround him and cry: 'Child, we have brought you up, (now) support us! O dear! why will you leave us? (2)

'Child, your father is an old man; your sister is still very young; (and here), O dear, are your own brothers from the same mother; why will you leave us? (3)

'Support your mother and father, thus you will win this world; it is a duty in this world to protect one's mother. (4)

'The old people are kind-spoken; your sons, child, are very young; you have married your wife; (take care) that she will not go to another man. (5)

'Come, child, let us go home; we can do all the work, you need not (do it); the next time we shall take care (that you will not be overburdened with work); child, let us meanwhile go to our house. (6)

'Afterwards you may go again; by this (visit of yours) you will not cease to be a *S*rama*n*a; who will hinder you to practise control when you have done with worldly desires[1]? (7)

'All your outstanding debts we have divided between us, and we shall give you the money (required for) business.' (8)

In this way (his relations) come to him, lamenting, and try to persuade him. Held fast by his attachment for his relations, he quickly returns to his house. (9)

As a creeper encircles a tree growing in the forest, so his relations press him hard that he should leave off control. (10)

He is held fast by his attachment for his relations. So the keepers always follow a newly-caught elephant, and a cow which has just calved never goes far (from the calf). (11)

Men do not (easily) get over this attachment, as (they do not get over) the ocean[2]. For its sake the weak suffer pains, being engrossed by their attachment for their relations. (12)

But a monk should renounce it; for every attachment is but a cause of sin. He should not desire life, having been instructed in the best Law. (13)

There are these whirlpools which have been

---

[1] Akâmagam. Another explanation is, if you are not willing (to do domestic work).

[2] Pâtâla, explained by samudra.

pointed out by Kâ*s*yapa: the wise keep clear of them, but the ignorant go down in them. (14)

Kings and ministers of kings, Brâhma*n*as and Kshattriyas try with pleasant things to seduce a monk who leads a holy life. (15)

(They try to seduce him) with elephants, horses, chariots, and cars, with pleasure-trips (saying to him): 'Enjoy these excellent pleasures, great sage, we worship you! (16)

'Clothes, perfumes, ornaments, women, and beds: enjoy these pleasures, friend, we worship you! (17)

'All the vows which you, holy man, have kept while a monk, are compatible with your living in a house. (18)

'It will be no sin, for you have wandered about long (enough).' In this way they try to tempt him, as men decoy a pig with wild rice. (19)

Weak men who are exhorted to live as monks, but who are unable to practise control, break down like weak (bullocks carrying a heavy burden) uphill. (20)

Unable to practise the rough (i.e. control), and harassed by the austerities, weak men break down, like old oxen in going uphill. (21)

When men who are greedy, attached to women, and who love pleasures, are tempted in the way described above, they return to their houses. (22)

Thus I say.

THIRD CHAPTER.

As at the time of the battle the coward looks behind him for a ditch, thicket, or other hiding-place[1], (thinking that) nobody knows who will win; (1)

---

[1] Nûma = pra*kkh*annam, giriguhâdikam.

'A moment's moment will bring the decision[1]; when we lose, we shall fly.' Thus thinks the coward. (2)

So some *S*rama*n*as, knowing themselves to be weak, have recourse to worldly sciences [2] when they see that they will suffer want. (3)

(They say): 'Who knows what will cause my loss of sanctity, women or water? When we are questioned, we shall speak out (i.e. show our knowledge). We have no (other) resource (in case of need)!' (4)

They are cautious, like those who look out for a ditch, &c. Those who doubt (their ability for control) are like men ignorant of the way. (5)

But famous warriors, leaders of heroes at the time of the battle, do not look behind them; (they think) what if all end with death? (6)

A monk who exerts himself in a similar way, should slip off the ties that bind him to his house. Putting aside all undertakings, he should wander about for the welfare of his soul. (7)

Some revile a monk who leads a holy life. But these revilers are far off from perfection[3]. (8)

(The revilers say), 'You live just as the laymen do, being attached to one another, for (e.g.) you beg alms for a sick man and give it him. (9)

'Therefore you still have an attachment, being obedient to the will of one another; you have not the purity produced by the right path, and have not got beyond the Circle of Births.' (10)

Now a monk who knows (the truth about) Môksha

---

[1] Literally, a moment of a moment of moments will be such.

[2] As grammar, astrology, medicine, &c.

[3] Samâhi, explained môksha, compare first note in the Tenth Lecture.

should answer them[1]: 'You speak thus, wavering between two ways of life (viz. that of householders and monks). (11)

'You eat out of the vessels[2] (of householders, and make them) bring food for a sick brother; you eat seeds and drink cold water[3], and what has been especially prepared (for you when sick). (12)

'You are infected by great faults, you are void of discrimination, and your resolutions are bad. It is not good to scratch a wound too much, for it will grow worse[4].' (13)

They should be instructed in the truth by one who knows it and is free from passions[5]: 'Yours is not the right way, you speak and act without consideration. (14)

'This your talk is weak, like the top of a bamboo, (when you say: a sick brother) may eat the food brought by a householder, but not that brought by a monk! (15)

'(And when you say that) our religious precepts are wholesome only for householders (not for monks, we reply that our prophet had) no such (inconsistent) ideas when he taught (his Law).' (16)

When (these heretics) cannot prove (their assertion) by any arguments they give up the discussion, and fall back on their bold (assertion). (17)

---

[1] According to *S*îlâṅka the Âgîvikas or the Digambaras are intended.

[2] For these heretics carry the principle of absolute poverty so far as to reject even the use of almsbowls.

[3] Bîgôdaka.

[4] The meaning is that the overdoing of the principle of poverty is just as harmful as the scratching of a wound.

[5] Apa*d*inna = aprati*g*ña, explained by râgadvêsharahita.

Overcome by their passions and infected by untruth, (these men) have recourse to bad language, as the (savage) *T*ankana[1] (when beaten) have recourse to their hills. (18)

The argumentation of a monk whose mind is at rest[2] should possess many good qualities. He should proceed in such a way as not to exasperate his opponent. (19)

Following this Law which has been proclaimed by the Kâ*s*yapa, a sound monk should carefully attend a sick brother. (20)

Knowing the beautiful Law, a wise and thoroughly restrained monk should bear all hardships and wander about till he reaches final liberation. (21)

Thus I say.

Fourth Chapter.

Some say that in old times great men, rich in religious penance, have reached perfection though they drank (cold) water (and ate fruits and roots). Ignorant men (who hear such assertions) are led astray (by them). (1)

'Nami, the king of Vidêha, ate nothing, Râmagupta did eat, Bâhuka drank (cold) water, and so did Târâga*n*a[3], the seer. (2)

'Âsila, Dêvala, the great sage Dvîpâyana, and

---

[1] This hill tribe lived somewhere in the north-east of Madhyadê*s*a, see Petersburg Dictionary, s. v.

[2] Attasamâhiê = âtmasamâdhika.

[3] Concerning Nami, see above, p. 35, note 2. Râmagupta may be another name of Râma. Instead of Târâga*n*a *S*îlânka writes Nârâya*n*a.

Pârâsara did drink (cold) water, and did eat seeds and sprouts[1]. (3)

'I have heard that in old times these renowned and well-known great men ate seeds and drank water, and have reached perfection.' (4)

When weak (monks hear such assertions) they become disheartened, as donkeys break down under their burden; in case of danger they retreat (and perish) like men who walk on crutches[2]. (5)

Some[3] say: Pleasant things are produced from pleasant things[4]. (They are those who disdain) the noble path and the renowned highest good. (6)

Do not, by disdaining it, lose much for the sake of little. If you do not give up this (wrong law), you will repent of it as the man did who carried iron (a long way) believing it to be silver. (7)

(And so will) those who kill living beings, who do not abstain from untrue speech, who take what is not freely given them, who enjoy sexual pleasures, and who own property. (8)

---

[1] Âsila is not known from other sources; perhaps Asita is meant, and Âsila Dêvila stands for Asita Dêvala. Concerning Dvîpâyana, the Pârâsara, compare Journal of the German Oriental Society, vol. 42, p. 495. But in the Aupapâtika Sûtra (ed. Leumann, § 76) Pârâsara and Dvîpâyana are two distinct persons.

[2] Pî*dh*asappî = pî*th*asarpin. *S*îlâṅka comments on the reading pi*tth*asappî, i.e. p*ri*sh*t*asarpin; but he makes out no good meaning.

[3] According to the commentators the Buddhists are intended. They quote some verses in illustration of the push*t*imârga of the Buddhists, one of which is not yet known I believe. It runs thus: ma*n*u*nn*a*m* bhôya*n*a*m* bhu*kk*â ma*n*u*nn*a*m* saya*n*âsa*n*a*m* | ma*n*u*nn*a*m*si agâra*m*si ma*n*u*nn*a*m* *gh*âyae mu*n*î || 'Having enjoyed a pleasant dinner, and a pleasant seat and bed, a mu*n*i in a pleasant house meditates on pleasant things.'

[4] Viz. Môksha, a pleasant thing, is arrived at through a comfortable life, another pleasant thing.

Some unworthy heretics[1], slaves of women, ignorant men who are averse to the Law of the *G*inas, speak thus: (9)

'As the squeezing of a blister or boil (causes relief) for some time, (and has no dangerous consequences), so it is with (the enjoyment of) charming women. How could there be any sin in it? (10)

'As a ram drinks the quiet water[2], so, &c. (the rest as in verse 10). (11)

'As the bird Pinga[3] drinks the quiet water (flying), &c. (the rest as in verse 10).' (12)

So say some unworthy heretics who entertain false doctrines, and who long for pleasures, as the ewe[4] for her kid. (13)

Those who do not think of the future, but only enjoy the present, will repent of it afterwards when their life or their youth is gone. (14)

But those who exert themselves at the proper time, feel no remorse afterwards; these heroes who have got rid of their fetters, do not long for life. (15)

As Vaitara*n*î, the river (of hell), is difficult to pass, so in this world women are to the unwise (a temptation) difficult to overcome. (16)

Those who have given up intercourse with women

---

[1] Pâsattha = pâr*s*vastha.

[2] The meaning seems to be that by the ram's drinking the water is not disturbed.

[3] Explained by kapi*ñg*ala, the francoline partridge.

[4] Pûya*n*â (pûtana, who is ever desirous of young), explained either by *s*âkinî 'hog' or ga*dd*arikâ 'ewe.' The commentators relate the following anecdote. In order to find out which animal loved its young ones best, their young ones were placed at the bottom of a well. Their mothers assembled round the brink and howled, but the ewe threw herself recklessly into the well. Therefore the ewe excels the other animals in maternal love.

and have left off adorning themselves, are well established in control, because they have renounced everything. (17)

As merchants go over the sea, so they will cross the flood (of Samsâra), where living beings despond and suffer pains because of their own deeds. (18)

A monk who knows this, will live as a virtuous man guarded by the Samitis; he will abstain from untrue speech, and not take what is not freely given him. (19)

He should cease to injure living beings whether they move or not, on high, below, and on earth. For this has been called the Nirvâna, which consists in peace[1]. (20)

21, 22 = I, 3, 3, 20 and 21.

Thus I say.

FOURTH LECTURE[2],

CALLED

KNOWLEDGE OF WOMEN.

First Chapter.

A monk who has left his mother and father and all worldly ties, (determines) to walk about alone and wise, to abstain from sexual pleasures, and to ask for a secluded place (where to lodge). (1)

---

[1] See below, I, 11, 11.

[2] This whole adhyayana is composed in the archaic form of Âryâ, of which I have treated at length in the thirty-eighth volume of the Journal of the German Oriental Society, p. 594. The same metre occurs also in the Suttanipâta of the Buddhists (ed. Fausböll, 26 f., 170 ff.), a fact which I was not aware of when I wrote the paper just referred to.

With clever pretences women make up to him, however foolish they be; they know how to contrive that some monks will become intimate with them. (2)

They will often sit down at his side; they always put on fine clothes; they will show him the lower part of their body, and the armpit, when lifting up their arms, so that he will follow them about. (3)

And occasionally a woman[1] will tempt him to a comfortable couch or bed. But he should know these things to be as many traps under various disguises. (4)

He should not look at them, nor should he consent to anything inconsiderate, nor walk together with them; thus he will well guard himself. (5)

Inviting a monk and winning his confidence, they offer themselves to him. But he should know, and fly from these temptations[2] in their various forms. (6)

Meekly and politely they approach him with their manifold arts to win his heart; and talking sweetly in confidential conversation they make him do (what they like). (7)

As (men by baiting) with a piece of flesh a fearless single lion get him into a trap, so women may capture an ascetic though he be careful. (8)

And then they make him do what they like, even as a wheelwright gradually turns the felly of a wheel. As an antelope caught in a snare, so he does not get out of it, however he struggles. (9)

Afterwards he will feel remorse like one who has drunk milk mixed with poison; considering the

[1] The original has the plural itthîô, but the metre requires itthî in the singular.

[2] Literally 'sounds,' which stands for objects of the senses in general.

consequences, a worthy monk should have no intercourse with women. (10)

Therefore he should avoid women, knowing them to be like a poisoned thorn. He is no Nirgrantha who without companion (goes into) houses, being a slave (to passion) and preaches (his religion). (11)

Those who are attached to this sinful (intercourse) must be reckoned among the wicked. Even a monk who practises severe austerities should avoid the company of women. (12)

A monk should have no intercourse with his daughters and daughters-in-law, with nurses or female slaves, or with grown-up girls. (13)

When the relations and friends see (the intimacy of a monk with a girl), they become angry (saying): 'All creatures love pleasures; you are a man, protect and support her.' (14)

But some become angry even when they see an innocent *S*rama*n*a, and suspect the fidelity of their wives because of the dishes they serve up[1]. (15)

Those who have intercourse with (women) have already ceased to practise meditation; *S*rama*n*as, therefore, for the benefit of their souls, do not go to the apartments (of women). (16)

Though many leave the house, some (of them) arrive but at a middling position (between householder and monk); they merely talk of the path to perfection. The force of sinners is talking. (17)

In the assembly he pronounces holy (words), yet secretly he commits sins; but the wise know him to be a deceiver and great rogue. (18)

[1] There is a saying in German: Eine verliebte Köchin versalzt den Brei, 'a cook in love spoils the soup.' The commentators put different constructions on the last part of the sentence.

The sinner does not confess his wrong, but rather boasts of it when reprimanded. Though he is admonished not to act as most men do, he becomes weak again and again. (19)

Some men of great intelligence who perform their duties as supporters of women, get into their power, though they be well acquainted with the Strîvêda[1]. (20)

(The adulterers') hands and feet are cut off, their skin and flesh are torn off, they are roasted alive, and acid is poured into their wounds. (21)

Their ears and nose are cut off, and their throats cut; (all this) they will suffer, but though suffering here for their sins they will not promise not to do[2] the same again. (22)

All this some have learned, and it has been well demonstrated in the Strîvêda. Though (people) know it, they do wrong (impelled) by Karman. (23)

One man (women) have in their heart, another in their words, and another still in their actions. Therefore a monk should not trust women, knowing that they are full of deceit. (24)

A young woman, putting on fine ornaments and clothes, will say to a *S*rama*n*a: 'I shall give up (my former way of life) and practise the rough (viz. control). Reverend sir, teach me the Law!' (25)

Or by professing herself a lay-disciple and co-religionist of the *S*rama*n*as, (she will try to make a friend of him). As a pot filled with lac (will melt)

---

[1] I. e. Kâma*s*âstra, or rather the part of it treating on courtezans, Vai*s*ika, that had been composed by Dattaka. He is mentioned by the commentators in an anecdote they relate ad v. 24.

[2] The original has kâhinti 'they will do;' it must be kâha*m* ti 'I shall do.'

near the fire, so even a wise (monk) will fall through intercourse with women. (26)

A pot filled with lac thrown into the fire melts quickly and is destroyed; so monks are lost through intercourse with women. (27)

Some commit sins (with a girl), but when questioned about it, they say: 'I have done no sin; she only slept in my lap (like my daughter).' (28)

This is a second folly of the sinner that he obstinately denies what he has done. He commits a twofold sin, since, for the sake of his reputation, he falls again[1]. (29)

(Some women) will say, by way of invitation, to a good-looking, self-knowing monk: 'Holy man, accept a robe, an almsbowl, food or drink (at our house)!' (30)

He should regard their words like wild rice[2], and should not desire to call at (their) house; for a fool who is bound in the fetters of sensuality will be subject to delusion again and again. (31)

Thus I say.

SECOND CHAPTER.

A monk, living single[3], should not fall in love; if he loves pleasures, he should again become indifferent. Now hear the pleasures of *S*rama*n*as, which some monks enjoy. (1)

When a monk breaks the law, dotes (on a woman), and is absorbed by that passion, she afterwards

[1] Visa*nn*êsî. Visha*nn*a is explained asa*m*yama.

[2] Wherewith pigs are decoyed, see above, p. 265, verse 19.

[3] Ôê = êka*h*, explained: free from love and hate.

scolds him[1], lifts her foot, and tramples on his head. (2)

'O monk, if you will not live with me as a woman who has still her hair, I shall tear it out; but do not live separated from me.' (3)

But when they have captured him, they send him on all sorts of errands[2]: 'Look (for the bodkin to) carve the bottle-gourd[3], fetch some nice fruit. (4)

'(Bring) wood to cook the vegetables, or that we may light a fire at night; paint my feet[4], come and meanwhile rub my back! (5)

'Look after my clothes, bring food and drink, get me some perfume, a broom, a barber[5] (to shave my head)! (6)

'Give me the collyrium-box, my ornaments, the lute, Lôdhra-powder[6], a Lôdhra-flower, the Vê*n*u-palâsika-lute[7], a pill! (7)

'A Utpalakush*t*a[8], Tagara[9]-powder, and aloe pounded together with U*s*îra[10], oil for anointing the

[1] Paribhindiyâ*n*a = paribhidya.

[2] The following verses are interesting as they afford us a glimpse of a Hindu household some 2,000 years ago. We find here a curious list of domestic furniture and other things of common use.

[3] Alâbu*kkh*egg*a* = alâbu*kkh*êdaṁ pippalakâdi *s*astram.

[4] Or, scour my pots.

[5] Kâsavaga = kâ*s*yapa, explained nâpita. The word is probably derived from the root kash 'to scrape.' According to *S*îlâṅka verses 5–6 refer to things used by monks and nuns.

[6] Symplocos Racemosa, the bark of which is used in dyeing.

[7] This is a thin piece of bamboo or bark held between the teeth and with the left hand, and played by the right hand just like a Vî*n*â. (*S*îlâṅka.)

[8] Probably Costus Speciosus. [9] Tabernaemontana Coronaria.

[10] Andropogon Muricatus.

face, baskets of bamboo wickerwork to put my things in! (8)

'Reach me the lip-salve, fetch the umbrella and slippers, the knife to cut the string, have my robe dyed bluish! (9)

'Give me the pot to cook the vegetables in, Myrobalans[1], the jar to fetch water in, the stick to paint the mark upon the forehead, the pin to apply collyrium (to the eyelids), or the fan when it is hot! (10)

'Fetch me the pincers[2], the comb, the ribbon to bind up the hair, reach me the looking-glass, put the tooth-brush near me! (11)

'Fetch me areca-nut and betel, needle and thread, the chamber-pot, the winnowing basket, the mortar, the pot for liquefying natron[3]! (12)

'Give me the vessel (used in worshipping the gods[4]), the water-pot. Friend, dig a privy. Fetch the bow for our son, the bullock for the *S*râma*n*êra! (13)

'The small pot, the drum, and the ball of cloth for the boy (to play with). *S*rama*n*a, the rainy season is at hand, look after the house and the stores! (14)

'(Fetch) the chair with woven twine seat[5], the wooden shoes[6] to walk on!' Pregnant women order

---

[1] They are used in bathing.

[2] To tear out the hair growing in the nose.

[3] Used in India instead of soap for cleaning linen.

[4] *K*andâlaka, a copper vessel used in worship. The name was current in Mathurâ at the time when *S*îlâṅka wrote or the author from whose work he copied this remark.

[5] See Grierson, Bihar Peasant Life, § 632.

[6] Pâulla; either the wooden sandals or slippers made of Mu*ñ*ga grass.

their husbands about like slaves to fulfil their craving. (15)

When a son, the reward (of their wedded life), is born, (the mother bids the father) to hold the baby, or to give it her. Thus some supporters of their sons have to carry burdens like camels. (16)

Getting up in the night they lull the baby asleep[1] like nurses; and though they are ashamed of themselves, they wash the clothes like washermen[2]. (17)

This has been done by many men who for the sake of pleasures have stooped so low; they become the equals of slaves, animals, servants, beasts of burden—mere nobodies. (18)

One should not mind the entreaties of women, but abstain from their friendship and company. These pleasures which are derived therefrom are called causes of blamable actions. (19)

Restraining himself by the thought that these dangerous (pleasures) will not be to his benefit, a monk should abstain from women, and commit no unnatural crime[3]. (20)

A wise and learned monk whose soul is in a pure condition (Lêsyâ), will abstain from doing work for others; in thoughts, words, and actions he will bear all troubles. (21)

The hero (of faith) who has vanquished sin and delusion, has said all this. A monk, therefore, whose soul is pure (and free from sins) should wander about till he reaches final liberation. (22)

Thus I say.

---

[1] *S*îlâṅka gives a specimen of a lullaby without meaning and metre.

[2] Ha*m*sa, explained ra*g*aka.

[3] No itthi*m* no pasu*m* bhikkhû no sayapâ*n*i*n*â nili*gg*e*gg*â.

FIFTH LECTURE,

CALLED

DESCRIPTION OF THE HELLS.

FIRST CHAPTER.

I once asked the Kêvalin, the great sage[1]: What is the punishment in the hells? Knowing it, O sage, tell it me who do not know it! How do sinners go to hell? (1)

When I thus questioned the illustrious Kâsyapa, the omniscient one[2] spoke as follows: I shall describe the truly insupportable pains where there is distress and (the punishment of) evil deeds. (2)

Those cruel sinners who, from a desire of (worldly) life, commit bad deeds, will sink into the dreadful hell which is full of dense darkness and great suffering. (3)

He who always kills movable and immovable beings for the sake of his own comfort, who injures them, who takes what is not freely given, who does not learn what is to be practised (viz. control); (4)

The impudent sinner, who injures many beings without relenting[3], will go to hell; at the end of his life he will sink to the (place of) darkness; head downwards he comes to the place of torture. (5)

They hear the cries of the punishers: Beat, cut,

---

[1] I. e. Mahâvîra. Sudharman speaks to *G*ambûsvâmin.

[2] Âsupanna = âsupra*gñ*a 'quickly comprehending.' I usually render this word 'intelligent,' when it is used of common monks.

[3] Anivvuê = anirv*ri*ta*h*.

split, burn him! The prisoners in hell lose their senses from fright, and do not know in what direction to run. (6)

Going to a place like a burning heap of coals on fire, and being burnt they cry horribly; they remain there long, shrieking aloud. (7)

Have you heard of the horrible (river) Vaitaranî, whose cutting waves are like sharp razors[1]? They cross the horrible Vaitaranî, being urged on by arrows, and wounded with spears. (8)

The punishers pierce them with darts; they go in the boat, losing their memory; others pierce them with long pikes and tridents, and throw them on the ground. (9)

Some, round whose neck big stones are tied, are drowned in deep water. Others again roll about in the Kadambavâlukâ (river)[2] or in burning chaff, and are roasted in it. (10)

And they come to the great impassable hell, full of agony, called Asûrya (i.e. where the sun does not shine), where there is great darkness, where fires, placed above, below, and all around, are blazing. (11)

There, as in a cave, being roasted on the fire, he is burned, having lost the reminiscence (of his sins) and consciousness of everything else; always suffering (he comes) to that miserable hot place that is ever ready (for the punishment of evildoers)[3]. (12)

---

[1] *S*îlânka says that the water of this river is alkali and hot blood; compare Uttarâdhyayana XIX, 59, above p. 95.

[2] See the note on Uttarâdhyayana XIX, 50, above p. 94, note 1.

[3] The last two lines recur in verse 21 with the only difference that there kasi*n*a*m* stands for kalu*n*a*m* in this place; yet the commentators offer a different explanation in the second place. In my translation I follow their interpretation both times.

There the cruel punishers have lighted four fires, and roast the sinners; they are roasted there like fishes put on the fire alive. (13)

The prisoners in hell come to the dreadful place called Santakshaṇa[1] (i.e. cutting), where the cruel punishers tie their hands and feet, and with axes in their hands cut them like wooden planks. (14)

And they turn the writhing victims round, and stew them, like living fishes, in an iron caldron filled with their own blood, their limbs covered with ordure, their heads smashed. (15)

They are not reduced to ashes there, and they do not die of their enormous pains; undergoing this punishment[2], the miserable men suffer for their misdeeds. (16)

And there in the place, where there is constant shivering, they resort to a large burning fire; but they find no relief in that place of torture; the tormentors torture them still[3]. (17)

There is heard everywhere the noise of painfully uttered cries even as in the street of a town. Those whose bad Karman takes effect (viz. the punishers), violently torment again and again those whose bad Karman takes effect also (viz. the punished). (18)

They deprive the sinner of his life; I shall truly tell you how this is done. The wicked (punishers) remind by (similar) punishment (their victims) of all sins they had committed in a former life[4]. (19)

Being killed they are thrown into a hell which is

---

[1] Here and in similar places the commentators do not take the word as a proper name, but as an epithet.

[2] Anubhâga.

[3] Or, with burning fire they roast them.

[4] See Uttarâdhyayana XIX, 69 ff., above p. 96.

full of boiling filth. There they stay eating filth, and they are eaten by vermin. (20)

And there is an always crowded, hot place, which men deserve for their great sins, and which is full of misery[1]. (The punishers) put them in shackles, beat their bodies, and torment them (by perforating) their skulls with drills. (21)

They cut off the sinner's nose with a razor, they cut off both his ears and lips; they pull out his tongue a span's length and torment (him by piercing it) with sharp pikes. (22)

There the sinners dripping (with blood) whine day and night even as the dry leaves of a palm-tree (agitated by the wind). Their blood, matter, and flesh are dropping off while they are roasted, their bodies being besmeared with natron. (23)

Have you heard of the large, erected caldron of more than man's size, full of blood and matter, which is extremely heated by a fresh fire, in which blood and matter are boiling? (24)

The sinners are thrown into it and boiled there, while they utter horrid cries of agony; they are made to drink molten lead and copper when they are thirsty, and they shriek still more horribly. (25)

Those evildoers who have here forfeited their souls' (happiness) for the sake of small (pleasures), and have been born in the lowest births during hundred thousands of 'former years,' will stay in this (hell). Their punishment will be adequate to their deeds. (26)

The wicked who have committed crimes will

[1] Compare note on verse 12. The same lines recur in the next chapter, verse 13. The commentator gives the same explanation there as here.

atone for them, deprived of all pleasant and lovely objects, by dwelling in the stinking crowded hell, a scene of pain, which is full of flesh (&c.). (27)

Thus I say.

SECOND CHAPTER.

I shall now truly tell you another kind of perpetual suffering, how the sinners who have committed crimes suffer for the deeds they have done in their former lives. (1)

Tying their hands and feet the (punishers) cut open their belly with razors and knives; taking hold of the mangled body of the sinner, they forcibly tear the skin off his back. (2)

They cut off his arms at the armpits; they force his mouth wide open and scald it; they yoke the sinner to a car and drive him, and growing angry[1] they pierce his back with a goad. (3)

The (sinners) walk over ground burning and glowing like red-hot iron; scorched they shriek horribly, being urged on with arrows[2] and put to a red-hot yoke. (4)

The sinners are driven over slippery ground which is like a road of red-hot iron; in this dreadful place (the ministers of hell) make them go forward like slaves (beating them) with sticks. (5)

Proceeding in this intolerable (hell) they are crushed by rocks tumbling down. There is the

---

[1] Ârussa = ârushya, here and in a similar passage (verse 15) the commentators explain it, 'making him angry, exasperating him.' They have misunderstood rahamsi in the second line, rendering it rahasi; it is of course = rathê.

[2] Usu = ishu, explained by âravisêsha 'a kind of awl.'

(caldron) Santâpanî[1], where evildoers suffer for a long time. (6)

They throw the sinners into caldrons and boil them; scalded they rise thence again; devilish crows[2] feed on them and (so do) other beasts having claws devour them. (7)

There is a place of smokeless fire in the form of a pile[3] where (the sinners) greatly distressed shriek horribly; head downwards they are lacerated and cut into pieces with iron knives. (8)

Tied up and skinned they are devoured by steel-nebbed birds; it is the hell called Sa*mg*îvanî, where life is long, and where men of an evil mind are tortured. (9)

The (punishers) pierce them with sharp pikes as people do with a captured pig. Transfixed by a pike the (sinners) shriek horribly; suffering both (bodily and mentally) they feel nothing but pains. (10)

There is a great place always on fire, where fires burn without fuel; there for a long time stay the evildoers shrieking aloud. (11)

Setting on fire large piles, they thrust into them (a sinner) who will cry horribly; as butter thrown in the fire melts, so does the evildoer there. (12)

And there is an always crowded, hot place which one deserves for one's great sins, and which is full of misery. There (the punishers) tie (the sinner's)

---

[1] Or, it is (the hell) called Santâpanî. My translation in the text agrees with *S*îlâṅka's interpretation.

[2] Compare Uttarâdhyayana XIX, 58, p. 95.

[3] Samûsiya*m* nâma. This might also be rendered, 'called Samu*kkh*rita.' But the commentators do not take samûsiya for a proper name.

hands and feet, and belabour him with sticks like an enemy. (13)

They break the sinner's back with a weapon, and smash his skull with iron clubs; their bodies are split and sawn like a plank; and tortured with red-hot awls (the sinners) are subjected (to cruelties). (14)

Cruel evildoers[1], urged on with arrows, and put to work (by the punishers), carry burdens in the way of elephants; two or three (punishers) get on one (victim) and growing angry[2] hurt his vital parts. (15)

The sinners are driven over the large, slippery, and thorny ground; tightly bound with straps[3] they lose their senses; the revenging (punishers) cut them into pieces[4], and throw them about like a bali-sacrifice. (16)

There is a dreadful mountain towering high up in the air, called Vaitâlika[5], where the evildoers are tortured for more than a thousand hours. (17)

Tortured, the sinners shriek, suffering day and night; in this horrid, great hell, which is full of implements of torture, they are put to a cruel death. (18)

Full of wrath, like their enemies in a former life,

---

[1] Ruddaasâhukammî = raudra-asâdhu-karmâ*n*a*h*. *S*î-lâṅka thinks that the ministers of hell are meant; but then the verse will not construe.

[2] See note on verse 3.

[3] Vivaddhatappêhi*m*, in a marginal gloss, explained: baddhvâ *k*armabandhanai*h*. But it might also be viv*ri*ddhatâpai*h* 'under increased tortures.'

[4] Ko*tt*a = ku*t*ayitvâ.

[5] Vêtâliya. The commentators render it vaikriya 'produced by magic,' and moreover explain the word as an epithet, not as a proper name.

(the punishers) crush them with hammers and clubs. With mangled bodies, and vomiting blood, they fall to the ground, head foremost. (19)

There are the ever hungry[1], savage, always wrathful, great jackals by whom the evildoers bound with shackles are devoured. (20)

There is the dreadful, slimy river, which is always flowing and full of molten iron; in this very dreadful river (the sinners) must descend one by one[2]. (21)

These pains are suffered without interruption by the sinner who stays there for a long time. There is no escape from the torture; he must, himself and alone, suffer the pains. (22)

Whatever cruelty he has done in a former birth, the same will be inflicted on him in the Circle of Births. Having been born in an extremely miserable state of life, the sufferer experiences infinite pain. (23)

A wise man hearing of these hells should not kill any living being in the whole world; believing in true doctrines and renouncing all property he should know the world, but not become a slave to it. (24)

Knowing the endless Circle of Births[3] with regard to animals, men, and gods, and the reward they will get; knowing all this, (a wise man) should wait for his decease, practising meanwhile self-control. (25)

Thus I say.

---

[1] A*n*âsiyâ, ana*s*itâ*h*. This might also be taken as the name of the jackals.

[2] Êgâyatâ, explained êkakina*h*.

[3] *K*auranta.

SIXTH LECTURE,

CALLED

PRAISE OF MAHÂVÎRA.

*S*rama*n*as and Brâhma*n*as, householders and heretics, have asked (me): Who is he that proclaimed this unrivalled truly wholesome Law, which was (put forward) with true knowledge[1]? (1)

What was the knowledge, what the faith, and what the conduct of the *G*ñâtr*i*putra? If you know it truly, O monk, tell us as you have heard it, as it was told you! (2)

This wise and clever great sage possessed infinite knowledge and infinite faith. Learn and think about the Law and the piety of the glorious man who lived before our eyes[2]! (3)

This wise man had explored all beings, whether they move or not, on high, below, and on earth, as well as the eternal and transient things. Like a lamp he put the Law in a true light. (4)

He sees everything; his knowledge has got beyond (the four lower stages)[3]; he has no impurity; he is virtuous, of a fixed mind, the highest, the

---

[1] The question is supposed to be addressed by *G*ambûsvâmin to Sudharman.

[2] *K*akkhupahê *th*iyassa = *k*akshu*h*pathê sthitasya, literally, 'who stood (or stands) in the path of the eyes.' We are scarcely entitled to infer from this phrase that the author had actually seen Mahâvîra as tradition would make us believe.

[3] Abhibhûya-nâ*n*î. Concerning the five stages or kinds of knowledge, see above, p. 152. The Kêvala knowledge is intended.

wisest in the whole world; he has broken from all ties; he is above danger and the necessity to continue life[1]. (5)

Omniscient, wandering about without a home, crossing the flood (of the Sa*m*sâra), wise, and of an unlimited perception, without an equal, he shines forth (or he does penance) like the sun, and he illumines the darkness like a brilliant fire. (6)

The omniscient[2] sage, Kâ*s*yapa, has proclaimed this highest Law of the *G*inas; he, the illustrious one, is prominent (among men) like the thousand-eyed Indra among the gods of heaven. (7)

His knowledge is inexhaustible like the (water of the) sea; he has no limits and is pure like the great ocean; he is free from passion, unfettered, and brilliant like *S*akra, the lord of the gods. (8)

By his vigour he is the most vigorous; as Sudar*s*ana (Mêru), the best of all mountains, or as heaven, a very mine of delight, he shines forth endowed with many virtues. (9)

(Mêru) a hundred thousand yô*g*anas high, with three tiers[3], with the Pa*nd*aga (-wood) as its flag, rising ninety-nine thousand yô*g*anas above the ground, and reaching one thousand below it; (10)

It touches the sky and is immersed in the earth; round it revolve the suns[4]; it has the colour of gold, and contains many Nandana (parks)[5]; on it the Mahêndras enjoy themselves. (11)

---

[1] To render anâyu*h*.

[2] Âsupanna = â*s*upra*g*ñ*a*, literally, 'quickly witted;' the word is usually explained by kêvalin.

[3] Ka*nd*aka, one of stone, one of gold, and one of turquoise.

[4] As is well known the *G*ainas assume a plurality of suns.

[5] The names of these four parks are, according to the com-

This mountain is distinguished by (many) names; it has the colour of burnished gold; it is the greatest of all mountains, difficult to ascend on account of its rocks; this excellent mountain is like a part of the earth on fire. (12)

The king of mountains, standing in the centre of the earth, is seen in a pure light[1] like that of the sun. With such beauty shines forth this many-coloured, lovely (mountain), which is crowned with radiance. (13)

Thus is described the glory of mount Sudar*s*ana, the great mountain; similar to it is the *S*rama*n*a *Gñ*ât*ri*putra, who is noble, glorious, full of faith, knowledge, and virtue. (14)

As Nishadha[2] is the best of long-stretched mountains, and Ru*k*aka of circular ones, so is he (Mahâvîra) among sages the wisest in the world, according to the declaration of the wise ones. (15)

After having taught the highest Law he practised the highest contemplation[3], which is the purest of pure, pure without a flaw, thoroughly white (as it were) like mother-of-pearl and the moon. (16)

Having annihilated all his Karman, the great sage by his knowledge, virtue, and faith reached

---

mentary, *S*âlavana, Nandanavana, Saumanasavana, and Pa*nd*aka (or Pâ*nd*uka) vana. The first is at the foot of Mêru, the second 500 yô*g*anas above it, the third 62,000 above the second, and the fourth 36,000 above the last, i.e. at the very top.

[1] Suddha-lessê = *s*uddhalê*s*ya. Here lê*s*yâ is equal to tê*g*as.

[2] Nishadha and Ru*k*aka are two fabulous chains of mountains situated beyond *G*ambûdvîpa.

[3] This is the *s*ukla dhyâna. As *s*ukla, which I translate 'pure,' originally means 'white,' the comparison with the moon is natural in the original.

the insurpassable, highest perfection, a state which has a beginning but no end. (17)

As the *S*âlmalî, in which the Supar*n*a[1] gods take their delight, is most famous among trees, as Nandana is among parks, so is the Omniscient most famous through his knowledge and virtue. (18)

As thunder is the loudest of sounds, as the moon is the most glorious of heavenly bodies, as sandal is the best of perfumes, so of monks is he who had renounced all wishes or plans. (19)

As (the ocean on which sleeps) Svayambhû is the best of seas, as Dhara*n*êndra is the best of Nâgas, as the juice of sugarcane is, as it were, the flag of juices, so is he (Mahâvîra) the flag of monks by his austerities. (20)

As Airâva*n*a is the best of elephants, the lion of beasts, Gaṅgâ of rivers, as Garu*d*a, Vê*n*udêva[2], is the best of birds, so is *G*ñât*ri*putra the best of those who have taught the Nirvâ*n*a. (21)

As Vishvaksêna[3] is the most famous of warriors, as the lotus is the best of flowers, as Dantavakra is the best of Kshattriyas, so Vardhamâna is the best of sages. (22)

As giving safety is the best of gifts, as the best of true speeches is that which causes no dis-

---

[1] They belong to the Bhavanapatis, see above, p. 225.

[2] The commentator says that Vê*n*udêva is another name of Garu*d*a. Vê*n*u stands perhaps for ve*n*hu = vish*n*u; but I do not know that Garu*d*a ever was directly identified with Vish*n*u.

[3] Vîsasêna. Vishvaksêna is a name of K*ri*sh*n*a. The commentators make Vi*s*vasêna of Vîsase*n*a, and seem to take it as a synonym of *k*akravartin or universal monarch. Dantavakra is mentioned in my 'Ausgewählte Erzählungen,' p. 35, line 36.

tress, as chastity is the highest of austerities, so is the *S*rama*n*a *G*ñâ*t*r*i*putra the highest of men. (23)

As the Lavasaptamas[1] are the highest of those gods who live very long, as the palace Saudharman is the best of heavenly abodes, as Nirvâ*n*a is the chief object of the Law, so there is no wiser man than *G*ñâ*tr*iputra. (24)

He (bears everything) like the earth; he annihilates (his Karman); he is free from greed; he, the Omniscient, does not keep store (of anything); he has crossed the ocean of life like the sea: he, the Hero, who grants protection to all, and whose perception is infinite. (25)

Having conquered the passions which defile the soul: wrath, pride, deceit, and greed, the Arhat, the great sage, does not commit any wrong, nor does he cause it to be committed. (26)

He understood the doctrines of the Kriyâvâdins, of the Akriyâvâdins, of the Vainayikas, and of the A*g*ñânavâdins[2]; he had mastered all philosophical systems, and he practised control as long as he lived. (27)

He abstained[3] from women, and from eating at night, he practised austerities for the removal of pain, he knew this world and that beyond; the lord renounced[3] everything at every time. (28)

Having heard and believing in the Law, which

---

[1] The commentator identifies them with the fifth class of Anuttara gods (see Uttarâdhyayana XXXVI, 215, above p. 227), and explains the name by saying 'if they lived seven lavas longer, they would reach perfection.'

[2] Concerning these four principal heresies see note on Uttarâdhyayana XVIII, 23, above p. 83.

[3] Vâriya, literally 'forbade.'

has been proclaimed and taught by the Arhat, and has been demonstrated with arguments, people will either make an end of their mundane existence, or they will become like Indra, the king of gods. (29)

Thus I say.

SEVENTH LECTURE,

CALLED

DESCRIPTION OF THE WICKED.

Earth, water, fire, wind; grass, trees, and corn; and the movable beings, (viz.) the oviparous, viviparous, those generated from dirt, and those generated in fluids [1]; (1)

These classes (of living beings) have been declared (by the *G*inas); know and understand that they (all desire) happiness; by (hurting) these beings (men) do harm to their own souls, and will again and again be born as one of them. (2)

Every being born high or low in the scale of the living creation, among movable and immovable beings, will meet with its death. Whatever sins the evildoer commits in every birth, for them he must die [2]. (3)

---

[1] The last two classes are, according to the commentators, (1) lice, bugs, &c.; (2) beings like cotton threads in thick milk, sour barley gruel, &c. Apparently vibrios are meant.

[2] Mi*gg*ati = mîyatê. Another rendering offered by *S*îlânka is 'he will be filled (by Karman).'

In this world or in the next (the sinners suffer themselves what they have inflicted on other beings), a hundred times, or (suffer) other punishment. Living in the Sa*m*sâra they ever acquire new Karman, and suffer for their misdeeds. (4)

Some leave their mother and father to live as *S*rama*n*as, but they use fire; (the prophet) says: 'People are wicked who kill beings for the sake of their own pleasure.' (5)

He who lights a fire, kills living beings; he who extinguishes it, kills the fire. Therefore a wise man who well considers the Law, should light no fire. (6)

Earth contains life, and water contains life; jumping (or flying) insects fall in (the fire); dirt-born vermin[1] (and beings) living in wood: all these beings are burned by lighting a fire. (7)

Sprouts are beings possessed of natural development[2], their bodies (require) nourishment, and all have their individual life. Reckless men who cut them down out of regard for their own pleasure, destroy many living beings. (8)

By destroying seeds, when young or grown up, a careless man does harm to his own soul. (The prophet) says: 'People are wicked who destroy seeds for the sake of their own pleasure.' (9)

---

[1] Viz. insects originated in dung, &c. used as fuel.

[2] Vilambaga; the commentators in explanation of this word say that plants, like men, go through all states of development, youth, ripe age, old age, &c. I think vilambaga is derived from vi*d*ambaka, they imitate (the development of animals). For if I understand *S*îlâṅka aright, a plant contains a great many bhûtas or beings, each localised in a certain part of the plant, as roots, &c. This is, according to him, the meaning of pu*dh*ôsiyâ*n*i, rendered in the text 'have their individual life.'

Men die as embryos, or as babies who do not yet talk, or who do so already; other men, as boys wearing five tufts of hair [1], or as youths, or in middle age: at the expiration of their life all leave the body and die. (10)

Wake up, men! If we look at the dangers (to which he is exposed) a fool has not much chance to obtain human birth; always suffering like men in fever, people will go to utter misery. (11)

Some say that perfection is reached by abstaining from the seasoner of food (viz. salt) [2], others by the use of cold water (i.e. by ablutions) [3], others again by (tending) a fire [4]. (12)

Perfection is not reached by bathing in the morning, nor by abstention from acids and salt; but by drinking liquor or eating meat or garlic men obtain another state of existence (than perfection). (13)

Those who, touching water in the morning and evening, contend that perfection is obtained through water (are easily refuted). For if perfection could be obtained by contact with water, many beings living in water must have reached perfection: (14)

Fishes, tortoises, aquatic snakes, cormorants,

---

[1] Pañkasikha. It usually denotes certain ascetics: but Sîlânka here renders it kumâra 'boy.'

[2] Sîlânka notices two different readings: (1) âhârasappañkagavagganenam, by abstaining from food seasoned with one of the five kinds of salt (viz. saindhava, sauvarkala, vida, rauma, sâmudra); (2) âhâraô pañkaga°, by abstaining from five kinds of food: garlic, onion, young camels' milk, beef, liquor.

[3] Sîlânka mentions the Vâribhadrakas, a subdivision of the Bhâgavatas, as belonging to this category. He states elsewhere that they eat saivala (Vallisneria Octandra) and frequently bathe, wash themselves, and drink water

[4] Viz. Tâpasas and Brâhmanas.

otters[1], and demons living in water. The clever ones declare those to be wrong who maintain that perfection may be obtained through water. (15)

If water did wash off the impure Karman, it must take off merit too. But this (assertion of the heretics) has no foundation but their wish. As a blind man follows a guide (and misses his goal), so a fool (who makes ablutions, &c. as a means of reaching Môksha) kills living beings. (16)

If water did wash off the sins of him who committed them, some would have obtained perfection who killed water-beings. Therefore he is wrong who maintains the attainment of perfection through water. (17)

Those who, lighting fire in the morning and evening, contend that perfection is obtained through fire (are easily refuted). For if thereby perfection could be obtained, mechanics also, who use fire, would be liberated. (18)

Perfection cannot be established by such gratuitous assertions; those who have not learned the truth will come to harm. A wise man, who knows the truth, should know and understand that all beings desire happiness. (19)

All creatures who have committed sins wail, suffer, and tremble. Considering this a wise monk who has ceased to sin, and guards his own self, should abstain from violence with regard to movable and (immovable) beings. (20)

He who keeps a store of rightly-obtained food and eats it; he who makes ablutions with pure water,

---

[1] U*tt*a or u*tth*a, explained as 'a kind of aquatic animal;' the Sanskrit prototype is apparently udra, but the commentators render it ush*t*ra!

contracting his limbs; he who washes and adorns his clothes, is far from being a naked monk. (21)

A wise man, seeing that it is sinful (to use) water, should live of pure water, till he is liberated from the Samsâra[1]; not eating seeds and bulbs, he abstains from bathing, &c., and from women. (22)

He who, after having left father, mother, house, sons, cattle, and wealth, visits houses where he gets nice food, is far from being a *S*rama*n*a. (23)

He who visits houses where he gets nice food, who professes the Law, desirous only of filling his belly, and brags (of himself) for the sake of food, is not equal to the hundredth part of an Ârya. (24)

A miserable man, who becomes a monk in order to get food from others, and a flatterer by the desire of filling his belly, will, in no remote future, come to harm, even as a boar greedy of wild rice[2]. (25)

The servile man says pleasing things for the sake of food, drink, and other things: but wrong belief and bad conduct are worthless like chaff. (26)

He should beg where he is unknown, and maintain himself by it; he should not seek fame and respect by his austerities; he should not desire (pleasant) sounds and colours, but conquer his longing for all kinds of pleasures. (27)

A monk should avoid every attachment and bear every pain, be full (of wisdom), not greedy, wander about homeless, give assurance of safety (to all beings), and be free from passions. (28)

(In order to be able) to practise control[3] a monk should eat; he should desire to get rid of sin; if he

---

[1] Âi = âdi. [2] Cf. p. 265, verse 19.

[3] Bhârassa *g*âyâ = bhârasya (=sa*m*yamasya) yâtrâ.

suffers pain, he should have recourse to control, and subdue the foe at the head of the battle, as it were. (29)

Though beaten he should be like a plank[1]; he should wait for the advent of death; having annihilated his Karman he should not again mix with the world, but be rather like a car whose axle is broken. (30)

Thus I say.

EIGHTH LECTURE,

CALLED

ON EXERTION[2].

It is said that two definitions of exertion are given; but in what does the exertion of the virtuous consist, and how is it defined? (1)

Some say that it consists in works, and the pious (say that it consists) in abstention from works. Men appear divided into two classes from this point of view. (2)

Carelessness is called (the cause of) Karman, carefulness that of the contrary (viz. absence of Karman); when the one or the other is predicated

---

[1] Phalagâvata*tth*i = phalagavad avatash*t*a*h*. *S*îlâṅka gives the following explanation: As a plank planed on both sides becomes thin, so a sâdhu, by reducing his body by exterior and interior tapas, grows thin, of weak body.

[2] Vîrya; it is the power or virtue of a thing.

(of a man, he is called) either a fool or a wise man. (3)

Some learn sciences[1] which teach the destruction of living beings, others study spells for killing all sorts of creatures. (4)

Deceivers practise deceit in order to procure themselves pleasures and amusement; they kill, cut, and dismember (beings) for the sake of their own comfort. (5)

The careless (commit sins) by thoughts, words, and acts, with regard to this and the next world, both (by doing the act themselves and by making others do it). (6)

A cruel[2] man does cruel acts and is thereby involved in other cruelties; but sinful undertakings will in the end bring about misery. (7)

Sinners, subject to love and hate and doing wrong, acquire Karman arising from passions[3] and commit many sins. (8)

Thus the 'exertion leading to works' of the sinners has been described; now learn from me the wise men's 'exertion not leading to works.' (9)

A pious monk, who is free from bonds and has severed all fetters, annihilates his bad Karman, and removes definitely the thorn (of sin). (10)

Following the right doctrine he exerts himself; as one becomes more and more the receptacle

---

[1] Sattha = *s*âstra or *s*astra. On the latter alternative we must translate '(practice of) arms.'

[2] Vêri = vairin, *g*îvôpamardakârin.

[3] Karma is of two kinds, airyapathika, arising from 'walking,' i.e. from those actions which are indispensable to a virtuous life or the conduct of monks, and sâmparâyika, arising from the passions.

of misery, so his bad thoughts (or sinfulness) increase. (11)

Those who have good places (in heaven, &c.) must surely leave them (some time). We live together with relations and friends but a limited time. (12)

Considering this, a wise man should conquer his greed, and enter upon the noble (path), which contains all virtues and is not blamed[1]. (13)

Whether he know the pith of the Law by intuition or through instruction, a houseless (monk) should exert himself and abstain from sins. (14)

When a wise man, in whatever way, comes to know that the apportioned space of his life draws towards its end, he should in the meantime quickly learn the method (of dying a religious death)[2]. (15)

As a tortoise draws its limbs into its own body, so a wise man should cover, as it were, his sins with his own meditation. (16)

He should draw in, as it were, his hands and feet, his mind and five organs of sense, the effect of his bad Karman, and every bad use of language. (17)

The virtuous exert themselves with regard to the distant end (viz. Liberation[3]). One should live

---

[1] Savvadhammamagôviya*m*. According to the commentator the meaning of this phrase is: which is not blamed or shown to be wrong by all (heretical) Laws.

[2] See Uttarâdhyayana, Fifth Lecture.

[3] *S*îlâṅka quotes and comments upon four different readings of the first line of this verse, the last of which is rendered above as it is the textus receptus of the Dîpikâ. (1) Abstaining from even small pride and from deceit, one, &c. (2) 'Great' for 'even small.' (3) I have heard from some men: This is the valour of the virtuous man, that, &c. After this verse *S*îlâṅka quotes another which, he says, is not found in MSS. of the text, but

indifferent to one's own happiness, calm, and without any attachment. (18)

Do not kill living beings, do not take what is not freely given, do not talk false, treacherous speech! This is the Law of him who is rich in control. (19)

Do not desire by words or thoughts what is a transgression (of the Law); guarding yourself in all ways, and subduing (the senses), practise control. (20)

A man who guards his self and subdues his senses, abhors all sins, past, present, and future ones. (21)

Benighted men of wrong faith, (though) they be renowned as heroes, exert themselves in a bad way, which will have, in all respects, evil consequences for them. (22)

Wise men of right faith, who are renowned heroes, exert themselves in a good way which will have no (evil) consequences whatever for them. (23)

Penance is of no good if performed by noble men who have turned monks (for the sake of fame); but that penance of which nobody else knows anything (is meritorious). Do not spread your own fame[1]! (24)

A pious man should eat little, drink little, talk little; he should always exert himself, being calm, indifferent, a subduer (of his senses), and free from greed. (25)

Meditating and performing religious practices,

---

is found in the *T*îkâ. It is, however, the identical verse I, 3, 4, 20, see above, p. 271, which occurs again I, 11, 11.

[1] Compare Matthew vi. 1–6.

abandoning his body, regarding forbearance as the paramount duty, a monk should wander about till he obtains liberation. (26)

Thus I say.

NINTH LECTURE,

CALLED

THE LAW.

What is the Law that has been preached by the wise Brâhma*n*a [1] (i.e. Mahâvîra)? Learn from me the noble Law of the *G*inas as it is. (1)

Brâhma*n*as, Kshattriyas, Vai*s*yas, *K*â*nd*âlas, Vukkasas, hunters [2], merchants [3], *S*ûdras, and others who are accustomed to do acts; (2)

The iniquity [4] of all these men who cling to property goes on increasing; for those who procure themselves pleasures by sinful acts will not get rid of misery. (3)

After a man has done acts which cause the death of living beings, his pleasure-seeking relations take possession of his wealth, whilst the doer of the acts must suffer for them. (4)

'Mother, father, daughter-in-law, brother, wife, and sons will not be able to help me, when I suffer for my own deeds [5].' (5)

---

[1] The word brâhma*n*a (mâha*n*a) is here, as in many other passages, a mere honorific title which could be rendered by 'ascetic.'

[2] Êsiya. [3] Vêsiya. [4] Vêra = vaira.

[5] This verse recurs in Uttarâdhyayana VI, 3; above, p. 25.

Taking to heart this truth from which flow the most important truths, a monk, without property and without egoism, should follow the teaching of the *G*inas. (6)

Leaving his wealth, sons, relations, and property, leaving sorrow that never ceases, (a monk) should wander about without any worldly interests. (7)

Earth, water, fire, and wind; grass, trees, and corn; oviparous animals, the two kinds of viviparous[1] animals; beings engendered in fluids and in dirt, and plants; (8)

These six classes of living beings a wise man should know and treat tenderly, in thoughts, words, and acts; he should neither do actions nor desire property whereby he might do them any harm. (9)

Untrue speech, sexual intercourse, personal property, taking things that are not freely given: all these causes of injury to living beings a wise man should abstain from. (10)

Deceit[2], greed[3], anger[4], and pride[5]: combat these causes of sin; a wise man should abstain from them. (11)

Washing, dyeing, making urine, evacuation of the bowels, vomiting, anointing of the eyes, and whatever is contrary to the rules of conduct[6]: from all this a wise man should abstain. (12)

---

[1] Pôya*g*arâû = pôta*g*arâyu, i.e. born alive (as elephants, &c.) and born together with the chorion (as cows, &c.)

[2] Paliu*ñk*a*n*a = pariku*ñk*ana, i.e. mâyâ.

[3] Bhaya*n*a = bha*g*ana, i.e. lôbha.

[4] Tha*nd*illa, i.e. krôdha.

[5] Ussaya*n*a = u*kkh*raya, i.e. mâna. These four passions are named here from the way in which they are supposed to act upon the soul. Similar names occurred above, p. 248, notes 3–6.

[6] Palimantha.

Perfumes, wreaths, bathing, cleansing of the teeth, property, actions referring to women: from all this a wise man should abstain. (13)

Alms that have been prepared, or bought, or stolen, or brought for the sake of a monk, or alms that contain particles of the above mentioned, or such alms as are unacceptable (for one cause or other), from all these a wise man should abstain. (14)

Invigorating food, anointing of the eyes, greed, damaging others, washing (one's limbs), (rubbing them with) Lôdhra-powder, &c.: from all this a wise man should abstain. (15)

Deliberating with laymen, praising their work, answering their questions, eating the householder's meals: from all this a wise man should abstain. (16)

He should not learn to play chess[1], he should not speak anything forbidden by the Law; a wise man should abstain from fights and quarrels. (17)

Shoes, an umbrella, dice, chowries, working for another, helping each other: from all this a wise man should abstain. (18)

A monk should not void his excrements or urine among plants; he should never rinse his mouth (even) with distilled water after having removed (everything endowed with life). (19)

He should never eat or drink out of a householder's vessel; nor wear his clothes, especially if he

---

[1] Ash*t*âpada. This does not necessarily, in this place, mean chess-board, but any game played on a similar chequered board may be intended. The earliest unmistakable mention of chess, that I have met with, occurs in Ratnâkara's Haravi*g*aya XII, 9, a mahâkâvya written in the first half of the ninth century A.D. in Kashmir.—Another explanation of a*tth*âvaya*m* is arthapadam = artha*s*âstram 'means of acquiring property.'

is a naked monk: from all this a wise man should abstain. (20)

A stool or bed or a seat in a house, asking of news and recollection (of past sports): from all this a wise man should abstain. (21)

Fame, glory, and renown; honours and respectful treatment; all pleasures in the whole world: from all this a wise man should abstain. (22)

A monk (should be content) with such food and drink as will sustain his life; he should give a portion of it to others: [from all this a wise man should abstain[1].] (23)

Thus spoke the Nirgrantha, the great sage Mahâvîra; he who possesses infinite knowledge and faith has taught the Law and the sacred texts[2]. (24)

In speaking (a monk) should use as few words as possible; he should not delight in another's foibles; he should avoid deceiving speech[3], and should answer after ripe reflection. (25)

One will repent of having used the third kind of speech[4]; a secret should not be made known. This is the Nirgrantha's commandment. (26)

---

[1] The last part of this verse is here repeated from the preceding ones; but it is quite out of place here.

[2] Here apparently ended the original treatise; the following verses are not directly connected with it.

[3] Mâi*tth*â*n*a*m*, always rendered mâtr*i*sthânam. I think it is a regular corruption for mâyâsthânam. The second syllable of the word becomes short before two consonants, and then the ya was changed into i with which it is almost interchangeable.

[4] The four kinds of speech are (1) true speech, (2) untrue speech, (3) speech partly true and partly untrue, (4) speech which is neither true nor untrue, see part i, p. 150.—Inaccurate statements are intended here.

(A monk) should not call one names[1], nor 'friend,' nor by his Gôtra; 'thou, thou' is vulgar; never address one by 'thou!' (27)

A virtuous monk should never keep company (with the wicked); for thereby he incurs dangers (for his conduct) disguised as pleasures. A wise man should be aware of them. (28)

(A monk) should not stay in the house of a householder except by constraint; nor should he amuse himself too long (by looking) at the sports of the children of the village[2]. (29)

Not desirous of fine things, he should wander about, exerting himself; not careless in his conduct, he should bear whatever pains he has to suffer. (30)

If beaten, he should not be angry; if abused, he should not fly into a passion; with a placid mind he should bear everything and not make a great noise. (31)

He should not enjoy pleasures though they offer themselves; for thus he is said (to reach) discernment. He should always practise what is right to do in the presence of the enlightened ones. (32)

He should obey and serve a wise and pious teacher, (such teachers) as are heroes (of faith), who search for the benefit of their souls, are firm in control, and subdue their senses. (33)

These men, who do not see the light (as it were) in domestic life, are the beloved of the people; these heroes, free from bondage, do not desire life. (34)

---

[1] Hôlâ, which is said to be a Dê*s*î word of abuse. The same word occurs also in the Â*k*ârâṅga Sûtra, see part i, p. 151, where I translated it by 'loon.'

[2] According to *S*îlâṅka: (he should not join) the sports of the children of a village, nor amuse himself too long.

They do not long for sensual pleasures, they do not engage in works. All that (the heretics) always talk about, is opposed to the right faith. (35)

Excessive pride and deceit, all worldly vanities: all this a wise man knows and renounces, and thus brings about his final Liberation. (36)

Thus I say.

TENTH LECTURE,

CALLED

CAREFULNESS[1].

The wise (Arhat) having pondered on the Law proclaimed it; learn from me correctly what is carefulness. A monk who forms no resolutions and is possessed of carefulness, should wander about, giving no offence to any creature; (1)

To no living beings, whether they move or not, whether above or below or on earth, by putting a strain upon them by his hands or feet[2]. Nor should he take from householders anything that is not freely given. (2)

Having mastered the Law and got rid of carelessness, he should live on allowed food[3], and treat

---

[1] Samâhi = samâdhi. This word has not only the meaning 'meditation,' but also a much wider one. Here it is explained as 'the means of obtaining Môksha.' I have chosen 'carefulness,' because it is less technical than 'control,' which I have used in other places.

[2] The first part of verse 2 to be construed with the last part of the preceding verse.

[3] Lâdhe.

all beings as he himself would be treated; he should not expose himself to guilt by his desire for life; a monk who performs austerities should not keep any store. (3)

Restraining his senses from women, a sage should wander about free from all worldly ties. See, every creature and every being suffers pain and is afflicted. (4)

Doing harm to these beings, an ignorant man becomes involved in sins. Sin is committed by injuring (beings), and one sins also by employing others (in such acts). (5)

He too who leads a miserable life, commits sin. Therefore (the *G*inas) have enjoined thorough carefulness. One should know the truth, delight in control and sound judgment, cease from injuring beings, and be of a settled mind. (6)

Looking at all people with an impartial mind, one should not do anything to please or to harm them. After a virtuous beginning some become miserable and lose heart, (since) they desire honour and fame. (7)

Desiring unallowed[1] food and accepting such, the sinner, careless in his conduct, is attached to women, and tries to acquire property. (8)

Given to violent deeds he accumulates (Karman); on his decease he (meets with) really distressing misery. Therefore a wise man considers well the Law; a sage wanders about free from all worldly ties. (9)

He should not expose himself to guilt by his desire for life, but he should wander about without any attachment. Speaking after due consideration,

[1] Ahâga*d*a=yathâk*ri*ta; cf. p. 131, note 7, 1.

and combating his worldly desires, he should say nothing that involves slaughter of living beings. (10)

He should not desire unallowed food, and he should not mix with people who desire such; he should mortify his flesh, thinking (of his duty), and giving up his sorrows without regard (to worldly interests). (11)

Try to realise that you are single and alone; thereby you will obtain Liberation; mind, this is no false assertion! This Liberation is not anything unreal, but the best thing. An ascetic is free from anger, and delights in the truth. (12)

Abstain from sexual intercourse with women, do not acquire property; a man possessed of carefulness will, beyond doubt, be a saviour (to others) in all circumstances. (13)

A monk having conquered aversion to control and delight in sensual objects[1], should bear all troubles caused by (pricking) grass, cold, heat, and insects; he should endure pleasant and unpleasant smells. (14)

Guarding his speech and possessed of carefulness, acquiring (pure) Lêsyâ[2], he should wander about; he should not thatch a house for himself or for others, nor behave towards other people like a householder. (15)

Questioned by somebody who maintains the unchangeable character of the soul[3], he should expound the true (doctrine); those who engage in works and

---

[1] This is, according to Sîlâṅka, the meaning of the words araim raim vâ, see, however, above, p. 111, note 1.

[2] See Uttarâdhyayana, Lecture XXXIV.

[3] Akiriyaâyâ = akriyâtman.

are held in worldly bondage, do not know the Law which leads to Liberation. (16)

Men here have various opinions; (they adhere) to the doctrine of the Kriyâvâdins and Akriyâvâdins. The iniquity of an unrestrained sinner, who after having been born injures the body (of beings to procure his own happiness), goes on increasing. (17)

Forgetting that his life will have an end, a rash and foolish man is full of selfishness; he toils day and night, greedy of wealth, as if he never should grow old or die. (18)

Leave wealth and cattle, all relations and dear friends! (A man) always talks (about these things), and he is infatuated with them; but other people will take away his wealth. (19)

As smaller beasts keep at a distance from a lion, being afraid of him, so a wise man keeps aloof from sin, well considering the Law. (20)

A wise man who has become awakened should turn away from sin, when he considers the evils arising from slaughter and the great dangers entailed by his cruel disposition. (21)

A sage setting out for the real good[1] (viz. Liberation), should not speak untruth; this (rule, they say,) comprises Nirvâ*n*a and the whole of carefulness. He should not do works, nor cause others to do them, nor assent to others doing them. (22)

When he gets pure (food), he should not be affected (by love or hate), and he should not be too

---

[1] Attagâmî = âptagâmin. Âpta is either Môksha as assumed in my translation, or it denotes the 'highest authority;' in the latter case we can translate: who proceeds on the right path.

fond (of such food) nor long for it. A pious monk, free from bonds, should wander about desiring neither honours nor fame. (23)

A monk who has left the house and is free from desires should abandon his body, annihilating his sins; he should not desire life nor death, and walk about, having got beyond the Circle (of Births)[1]. (24)

Thus I say.

ELEVENTH LECTURE,

CALLED

THE PATH.

What is the Path that has been preached by the wise Brâhmana[2] (i.e. Mahâvîra), having correctly entered upon which path a man crosses the flood (of Samsâra) which is difficult to pass? (1)

O monk and great sage, tell us this best path which leads to liberation from all misery, as you know it! (2)

Tell us how we should describe that path, if somebody, a god or a man, should ask us about it! (3)

If somebody, a god or a man, ask you about it, tell them the truth about the path. Listen to me! (4)

The very difficult (path) explained by the Kâsyapa, following which some men from this earth

---

[1] Or, the fetter of sin.

[2] See note on IX, 1.

have formerly passed over (the Sa*m*sâra) like traders over the ocean [1], pass over it (even now), and will pass over it in future; (this path which) I have learned, I shall explain in due order: men, listen to me! (5, 6)

Earth-lives are individual beings, so are water-lives, fire-lives, and wind-lives; grass, trees, corn; (7)

And the remaining, (viz.) the movable beings; thus are enumerated the six classes of living beings; these are all the living beings, there are no more besides. (8)

A wise man should study them with all means of philosophical research. All beings hate pains; therefore one should not kill them. (9)

This is the quintessence of wisdom: not to kill anything. Know this to be the legitimate conclusion from the principle of the reciprocity with regard to non-killing [2]. (10)

He should cease to injure living beings whether they move or not, on high, below, and on earth. For this has been called the Nirvâ*n*a, which consists in peace [3]. (11)

Master (of his senses) and avoiding wrong, he should do no harm to anybody, neither by thoughts, nor words, nor acts. (12)

A wise man who restrains his senses and possesses great knowledge, should accept such things as are freely given him, being always circumspect with regard to the accepting of alms, and abstaining from what he is forbidden to accept. (13)

---

[1] The same simile occurs also in I, 3, 4, 18, above p. 271.

[2] The same verse occurred above, I, 1, 4, 10, p. 247.

[3] We have had the same verse above, I, 3, 4, 20, p. 271.

A true monk should not accept such food and drink as has been especially prepared for him along with slaughter of living beings. (14)

He should not partake of a meal which contains but a particle of forbidden food[1]: this is the Law of him who is rich in control. Whatever (food a monk) suspects (to be impure), he may not eat. (15)

A man who guards his soul and subdues his senses, should never assent to anybody killing beings.—In towns and villages cases (will occur, which place) the faithful (in a dilemma)[2]. (16)

Hearing the talk of people, one should not say, 'this is a good action,' nor 'this is a bad action.' For there is an objection (to either answer). (17)

He should not say that it is meritorious, because he ought to save those beings, whether they move or not, which are killed there for the sake of making a gift. (18)

Nor should he say that it is not meritorious, because he would then prevent those for whose sake the food and drink in question is prepared, to get their due. (19)

Those who praise the gift, are accessory[3] to the killing of beings; those who forbid it, deprive (others) of the means of subsistence. (20)

Those, however, who give neither answer, viz.

---

[1] This is the meaning of the phrase pûtikarma na sêvêta.

[2] When well-meaning people sink a well, offer a sacrifice, or feed persons, &c.

[3] Literally, wish.

that it is meritorious, or is not so, do not expose themselves to guilt, and will reach Beatitude[1]. (21)

Knowing that Beatitude is the best thing as the moon is among the stars, a sage always restrained and subduing his senses brings about Beatitude. (22)

A pious man[2] shows an island to the beings which are carried away (by the flood of the Sa*m*sâra) and suffer for their deeds. This place of safety has been proclaimed (by the Tîrthakaras). (23)

He who guards his soul, subdues his senses, puts a stop to the current (of the Sa*m*sâra), and is free from Âsravas[3], is (entitled to) expound the pure, complete, unparalleled Law. (24)

Those who do not know this (Law), are not awakened, though they fancy themselves awakened; believing themselves awakened, they are beyond the boundary of right faith[4]. (25)

Eating seeds and drinking cold water[5] and what

---

[1] *S*îlâṅka quotes the following Sanskrit verse to show the application of the maxim to the digging of a well: satya*m* vaprêshu *s*îta*m* *s*a*s*ikaradhavala*m* vâri pîtvâ prakâma*m* vyu*kkh*innâ*s*êshat*ri*sh*n*â*h* pramuditamanasa*h* prâ*n*isârthâ bhavanti | *s*ôsha*m* nîtê *g*alaughê dinakarakira*n*air yânty anantâ vinâ*s*a*m* tênô*s*dâsînabhâva*m* vra*g*ati muniga*n*a*h* kûpavaprâdikâryê || 'Forsooth, when living beings drink to their hearts' content the cool water of ditches, which is white like the moon, their thirst is completely allayed and their heart is gladdened; but when all the water is dried up by the rays of the sun, numberless creatures must die; therefore the sages decline every interest in the construction of wells and ditches.'

[2] The commentators connect sâhu as adjective with dîvam, and supply Tîrthakara, &c. as subject.

[3] See above, p. 55, note 1.

[4] Samâdhi.

[5] Vîôdaga = bî*g*ôdaka.

has been especially prepared for them, they enter upon meditation [1], but are ignorant of the truth, and do not possess carefulness. (26)

As *dh*aṅkas, herons, ospreys, cormorants, and pheasants meditate upon capturing fish, (which is) a sinful and very low meditation, so some heretical, unworthy *S*rama*n*as contemplate the pursuit of pleasures; (they are) sinful and very low like herons. (27, 28)

Here some weak-minded persons, abusing the pure path, enter upon a wrong path. They thereby will go to misery and destruction. (29)

As a blind-born man getting into a leaky boat wants to reach the shore, but is drowned during the passage [2]; so some unworthy, heretical *S*rama*n*as, having got into the full current (of the *S*a*m*sâra), will incur great danger. (30, 31)

But knowing this Law which has been proclaimed by the Kâ*s*yapa, (a monk) crosses the dreadful current (of the Sa*m*sâra), and wanders about intent on the benefit of his soul. (32)

Indifferent to worldly objects, a man should wander about treating all creatures in the world so as he himself would be treated. (33)

A wise man knowing (and renouncing) excessive pride and deceit, (in short) giving up all (causes of worldly existence), brings about his Liberation [3]. (34)

He acquires good qualities, and leaves off bad qualities; a monk, who vigorously practises austerities, avoids anger and pride. (35)

The Buddhas [4] that were, and the Buddhas that

[1] Comp. I, 3, 3, 12.

[2] Verses 30, 31 *a*=I, 1, 2, 31, 32 *a*.

[3] The first line of this verse occurred in I, 9, 36.

[4] Here Buddha is a synonym for Tîrthakara.

will be, they (as it were) have Peace as their foundation, even as all things have the earth for their foundation. (36)

And if any accidents whatever befall him who has gained that (foundation), he will not be overpowered by them as a mountain by the storm[1]. (37)

A restrained, very learned, and wise (monk) should accept such alms as are freely given him, being free from passions and waiting for his end. This is the doctrine of the Kêvalin. (38)

Thus I say.

TWELFTH LECTURE,

CALLED

THE CREED[2].

There are four (heretical) creeds[3] which the disputants severally uphold: 1. the Kriyâvâda, 2. the Akriyâvâda, 3. the Vinayavâda, and 4. the Agñânavâda. (1)

The agnostics[4], though they (pretend to) be

---

[1] *S*îlâṅka says that by exercise the power of resistance will be increased, and in confirmation of this he relates the well-known story of the herdsman who daily carried a calf from its birth till it was two years old.

[2] Samôsara*n*a = samavasara*n*a. This word and the verb samôsarai are commonly used when Mahâvîra preaches to a meeting (mêlâpaka) gathered round him.

[3] Compare Uttarâdhyayana XVIII, 23, above p. 83, note 2.

[4] Annâ*n*iyâ = a*gñ*ânikâs, the followers of the fourth sect.

clever, reason incoherently, and do not get beyond the confusion of their ideas. Ignorant (teachers) speak to ignorant (pupils), and without reflection they speak untruth. (2)

Believing truth to be untruth, and calling a bad man good, the various upholders of Vinaya, asked about it, explain their tenet[1]. (3)

Without perceiving the truth they speak thus: this object (viz. Môksha) is realised by us thus (viz. by Vinaya). The Akriyâvâdins who deny Karman[2], do not admit that the action (of the soul is transmitted to) the future moments[3]. (4)

They become involved in contradiction in their own assertions; they falter in their speech and are unable to repeat what is said to them[4]. This (their opinion) has a valiant counter-opinion, this (our opinion) has no valiant counter-opinion; and Karman has six sources[5]. (5)

The Akriyâvâdins who do not understand the truth, bring forward various opinions; many men

---

[1] Viz. that Môksha is arrived at through Vinaya, discipline.

[2] Lavâvasaṅkî. Lava is explained by karman, and avasaṅkî by apasartu*m* *s*îla*m* yêshâ*m* tê.

[3] The meaning is that as everything has but a momentary existence, there is no connection between the thing as it is now, and as it will be in the next moment. This is a doctrine of the Bauddhas. But the Sâṅkhyas are also reckoned among the Akriyâvâdins, because, according to them, the âtman does not act.

[4] *S*îlâṅka in commenting upon this passage has to say a good deal about the Bauddhas. It is perhaps of interest that he mentions their 500 *G*âtakas, and not thirty-four which is the recognised number of *G*âtakas according to the Northern Buddhist. How *S*îlâṅka came to a knowledge of the numbers of *G*âtakas accepted by the Southern Buddhists, I cannot tell.

[5] Viz. the six Âsravas.

believing in them will whirl round in the endless Circle of Births. (6)

'There rises no sun, nor does it set; there waxes no moon, nor does it wane; there are no rivers running, nor any winds blowing; the whole world is ascertained to be unreal[1].' (7)

As a blind man, though he have a light, does not see colours, &c., because he is deprived of his eye(sight), so the Akriyâvâdin, having a perverted intellect, does not recognise the action (of the soul) though it does exist. (8)

Many men in this world who have studied astrology, the art of interpreting dreams, divination from diagrams, augury, divination from bodily marks, and from portents, and the eight branches (of divination from omens), know the future[2]. (9)

(The opponents say that) some forecasts are true, and the prophecies of others prove wrong; therefore they do not study those sciences, but they profess to know the world, fools though they be[3]. (10)

The (Kriyâvâdins) *S*rama*n*as and Brâhma*n*as understanding the world (according to their lights), speak thus: misery is produced by one's own works, not by those of somebody else (viz. fate, creator, &c.)[4]. But right knowledge and conduct lead to liberation. (11)

---

[1] This is the opinion of the *S*ûnyavâdins, who are considered to belong to the Akrîyâvâdins, because they deny all actions, even such as are perceived by everybody (*S*îlâṅka).

[2] This would be impossible if the whole world was unreal.

[3] A various reading, commented upon by the scholiasts, runs thus: âha*m*su vi*gg*âpalimokkham êva, 'they say that one must give up science.'

[4] The Kriyâvâdins contend, according to *S*îlâṅka, that works alone, by themselves, without knowledge, lead to Môksha.

The (Tîrthakaras), being (as it were) the eyes of the world and its leaders, teach the path which is salutary to men; they have declared that the world is eternal inasmuch as creatures are (for ever) living in it, O ye men! (12)

The Râkshasas and the dwellers in Yama's world, the troops[1] of Asuras and Gandharvas, and the spirits that walk the air, and individual beings[2]: they will all be born again and again. (13)

(The Sa*m*sâra) which is compared to the boundless flood of water, know it to be impassable and of very long duration on account of repeated births[3]. Men therein, seduced by their senses and by women, are born again and again both (as movable and immovable beings). (14)

The sinners cannot annihilate their works by new works; the pious annihilate their works by abstention from works; the wise and happy men who got rid of the effects of greed, do not commit sins. (15)

They know the past, present, and future ways of the world; they are leaders of other men, but follow no leader; they are awakened, and put an end to mundane existence. (16)

Averse to injury of living beings, they do not act, nor cause others to act. Always restraining them-

---

[1] Kâya. The commentators explain this word as denoting the earth-bodies, &c., but from the context it will be seen that it refers to Asuras and Gandharvas, and must be translated by 'troops.'

[2] Pu*dh*ô siyâ = pr*i*thak *s*ritâ*h*; according to *S*îlâṅka, pr*i*thivyâ*s*ritâ*h*. This expression is generally used to denote the lower order of beings.

[3] To render bhavagahana.

selves, those pious men practise control, and some become heroes through their knowledge. (17)

He regards small beings and large beings, the whole world as equal to himself; he comprehends the immense world, and being awakened he controls himself among the careless. (18)

Those who have learned (the truth) by themselves or from others, are able (to save) themselves and others. One should always honour a man, who is like a light and makes manifest the Law after having well considered it. (19)

He who knows himself and the world; who knows where (the creatures) go, and whence they will not return; who knows what is eternal, and what is transient; birth and death, and the future existences of men; (20)

He who knows the tortures of beings below (i. e. in hell); who knows the influx of sin and its stoppage[1]; who knows misery and its annihilation,— he is entitled to expound the Kriyâvâda[2], (21)

Being not attached to sounds and colours, indifferent to tastes and smells, not desiring life nor death, guarded by control, and exempt from the Circle (of Births). (22)

Thus I say.

---

[1] Âsrava and sa*m*vara.

[2] It is evident that the *G*ainas considered themselves Kriyâvâdins. I had overlooked this passage when penning the note on p. 83.

THIRTEENTH LECTURE,

CALLED

THE REAL TRUTH.

I shall now expound, in accordance with truth, the various qualities of men; I shall explain the virtue and peace of the good, the vices and the unrest of the wicked. (1)

Having learned the Law from men who exert themselves day and night, from the Tathâgatas[1], they neglect the conduct in which they had been instructed, and speak rudely to their teacher. (2)

Those who explain the pure doctrine according to their individual opinion, falsify it in repeating (it after their teachers); those who speak untruth from pride of knowledge, are not capable of many virtues. (3)

Those who on being questioned conceal the truth, defraud themselves of the real good. These bad men who believe themselves good and are full of deceit, will go to endless punishment. (4)

He who is of a wrathful disposition and calls everything by its true name[2], who renews a composed quarrel, will, like a blind man groping his way with

---

[1] According to the commentators, *G*aina teachers, inclusive of the schismatical ones, are intended. Tathâgata is a synonym of Tîrthakara and Buddha; but it is less frequently used by the *G*ainas than by the Bauddhas with whom it is of very common occurrence.

[2] *G*aga*tth*abhâsî = *g*agadarthabhâshin. *S*îlâṅka proposes also *g*ayârthabhâshin, who speaks dogmatically.

a stick, do harm to himself, being still subject to passion and possessing evil Karman. (5)

He who is quarrelsome and talks improperly, is not impartial nor beyond the reach of deceit[1]; but he who executes the commands (of his teacher) and controls himself, sees nothing but the truth and is exempt from deceit. (6)

He who conforms to admonitions however many he receives, is kindly spoken, subtile, manly, noble, and a well-doer; (such a man) is impartial and beyond the reach of deceit. (7)

He who believes himself rich in control, or inconsiderately vaunts his knowledge, or fancies himself purified by austerities, will look upon other men as shadows. (8)

He is always turned round by delusion, and has no place in the Gôtra where the Vow of Silence is practised (viz. in the *G*aina church), who not being awakened puts himself forward in order to gain honours through something different from control. (9)

A Brâhma*n*a or Kshattriya by birth, a scion of the Ugra[2] race or a Li*kkh*avi[3], who enters the order eating alms given him by others, is not stuck up on account of his renowned Gôtra. (10)

His pedigree on his mother's and on his father's

---

[1] A*gh*a*ñgh*apatta. *Gh*a*ñgh*â (tempest) = mâyâ.

[2] Concerning the Ugras, see above, p. 71, note 2.

[3] Le*kkh*ai. According to the *G*ainas the Li*kkh*avi and Mallakis were the chiefs of Kâ*s*i and Kô*s*ala. They seem to have succeeded the Aikshvâkas, who ruled there in the times of the Râmâya*n*a. The Li*kkh*avis became a powerful race, who held the supreme power in Eastern India during many centuries after the beginning of our era.

side will be of no use to him, nothing will but right knowledge and conduct: when after becoming a monk he acts like a householder, he will not succeed in obtaining final Liberation. (11)

If a poor monk subsisting on the meanest food is attached to vanities, desires fame, and not being awakened, (makes his monkhood) a means of subsistence, he will suffer again and again (in the Circle of Births). (12)

A monk, who is eloquent, speaks very well, has bright ideas, is clever, possesses a fine intellect, and has purified his soul, may (perhaps) despise other men on account of his intellect. (13)

Thus an intelligent monk who puts himself forward, has not yet realised carefulness; or rather he is a weak-minded man who elated by his success blames other men. (14)

A monk should combat pride of genius, pride of sanctity, pride of birth, and (pride of good) living, which is enumerated as the fourth; such a man is wise and of the right stuff. (15)

The wise leave off these kinds of pride, the pious do not cultivate them; the great sages are above all such things as Gôtra (&c.), and they ascend to the place where there is no Gôtra at all (viz. to Môksha). (16)

A monk who looks upon his body as on a corpse and fully understands the Law, will on entering a village or a town distinguish between what may be accepted and what may not, and will not be greedy of food or drink. (17)

A monk having conquered aversion to control and delight in sensual objects, living in company with many brethren or leading a single life, should silently repeat to himself: 'A man must come and go (according to his Karman) alone' (i. e. without deriving any help from others). (18)

Knowing it by intuition or having learned it from others, one should teach the Law which is a benefit to men; the pious are not given to blameable sinful practices. (19)

If (a monk preaches the Law to some one) whose disposition he has not ascertained, that man, not believing (what he is taught), will become angry, and may wound him in a way that will shorten or end his life. When he knows their disposition, he (may teach) others the truth. (20)

A wise man by suppressing his Karman and his will should renounce his interest in everything else. (For) through the objects of sight (i.e. senses) which are causes of danger, men come to harm. Knowing the truth with regard to movable and immovable beings (a monk should exert himself)[1]. (21)

Not desiring honour or fame, he should say nothing to anybody either to please or to irritate him. Avoiding all evils, a monk should without embarrassment and passion (preach the Law). (22)

Well considering (his duties) in accordance with truth, abstaining from doing injury to living beings, not desiring life nor death, he should wander about released from the Circle (of Births). (23)

Thus I say.

[1] The commentators make out the following meaning: A wise (preacher) should ascertain (his hearers') occupations and inclinations, and then (try to) better their evil disposition. Through the objects of sight which are causes of danger, men are led astray. A wise man knowing (the disposition of his hearers should preach the Law which is wholesome) to all living beings whether they move or not.

FOURTEENTH LECTURE,

CALLED

THE NIRGRANTHA.

He who has given up all worldly ties and is instructed in our creed, should practise chastity, exerting himself; obeying the commands (of his teacher) he should make himself well acquainted with the conduct; a clever (monk) should avoid carelessness. (1)

As (birds of prey), e. g. *Dh*aṅkas, carry off a fluttering young bird whose wings are not yet grown, when it attempts to fly from the nest, but is not able to do so, because it is too young and its wings are not yet grown; (2)

Just as they carry off a young bird whose wings are not yet grown, so many unprincipled men will seduce a novice who has not yet mastered the Law, thinking that they can get him in their power, when they have made him leave (the Ga*kkh*a)[1]. (3)

A good man should long to live with his teacher in order to perform his duties[2], knowing that he who does not live with his teacher will not put an end to his mundane existence. Making manifest

---

[1] Nissâriya*m* = ni*h*sâritam. I follow in the text the interpretation of the commentators. But I think that instead of mannamâ*n*â we must read, as in the preceding verse, mannamâ*n*a*m*; and translate: believing himself rich in control (vâsima*m*) though he be still wanting in strength (nissâriya*m*).

[2] Samâhi*m*.

the conduct of the virtuous, an intelligent (monk) should not leave the (company of his teacher). (4)

(A monk) who complies with the rules for Yatis[1] as regards postures, lying down, sitting, and exertion, who is thoroughly acquainted with the Samitis and Guptis, should in teaching others explain each single (point of conduct). (5)

Whether he hears (pleasant) sounds or dreadful ones, he should not allow himself to be influenced by them, and persevere in control; nor should a monk be sleepy or careless, but by every means he should get rid of doubts. (6)

If admonished by a young or an old monk, by one above him or one of equal age, he should not retort against him[2], being perfectly free from passion; for one who is (as it were) carried away (by the stream of the Sa*m*sâra), will not get to its opposite shore. (7)

(He should not become angry) if (doing anything wrong) his own creed is quoted against him by a heretic, or if he is corrected by (somebody else) be he young or old, or by a female slave engaged in low work or carrying a jar, or by some householder. (8)

He should not be angry with them nor do them any harm, nor say a single hard word to them, but he should promise not to commit the same sin again; for this is better than to do wrong. (9)

As to one who has lost his way in the wood, others who have not, (show it, thus some) teach the

---

[1] Susâdhuyukta.

[2] Samma*m* taya*m* thiratô nâ-bhiga*kkh*ê. I translate according to the commentators, as I am unable to understand the words in the text.

path which is salutary to men. Therefore (he should think): this is for my good that those who know put me right. (10)

Now he who has lost his way should treat with all honour him who has not. This simile has been explained by the Prophet. Having learned what is right one should practise it. (11)

As a guide in a dark night does not find the way since he cannot see it, but recognises the way when it has become light by the rising of the sun; (12)

So a novice who has not mastered the Law, does not know the Law, not being awakened; but afterwards he knows it well through the words of the *G*inas, as with his eye (the wanderer sees the way) after sunrise. (13)

Always restrained with regard to movable and immovable beings which are on high, below, and on earth, (a monk) should wander about entertaining no hostile thoughts (towards them) and being steadfast (in control). (14)

At the right time he may put a question about living beings to a well-conducted (monk), who will explain the conduct of the virtuous; and what he hears he should follow and treasure up in his heart, thinking that it is the doctrine of the Kêvalins. (15)

Living in this (company of the teacher) and protecting (himself or other beings) in the three ways (viz. in thoughts, words, and acts), he (gets) peace and the annihilation (of sins) as they say. Thus speak those who know the three worlds, and they do not again commit faults! (16)

A monk by hearing the desired Truth gets bright ideas and becomes a clever (teacher); desiring the highest good and practising austerities and silence, he will obtain final Liberation (living on) pure (food). (17)

Those who having investigated the Law expound it, are awakened and put an end to mundane existence; able to liberate both (themselves and others), they answer the well-deliberated questions. (18)

He does not conceal (the truth) nor falsify it; he should not indulge his pride and (desire for) fame; being wise he should not joke, nor pronounce benedictions. (19)

Averse to injury of living beings, he does not disgrace his calling[1] by the use of spells; a good man does not desire anything from other people, and he does not give utterance to heretical doctrines. (20)

A monk living single should not ridicule heretical doctrines, and should avoid hard words though they be true; he should not be vain, nor brag, but he should without embarrassment and passion (preach the Law). (21)

A monk should be modest[2] though he be of a fearless mind; he should expound the Syâdvâda[3]; he should use the two (permitted) kinds of speech[4], living among virtuous men, impartial and wise. (22)

He who follows (the instruction) may believe something untrue; (one should) kindly (tell him) 'It is thus or thus.' One should never hurt him by

---

[1] Gôtra, explained by mauna.

[2] Saṅkiggiyâ = *s*aṅkyêta.

[3] Vibha*g*yavâda. The saptabhaṅgînaya or seven modes of assertion are intended by the expression in the text. See Bhandarkar, Report, 1883–84, p. 95.

[4] See above, p. 304, note 4. The first and fourth kinds of speech are here intended.

outrageous language, nor give long-winded explanations of difficult passages. (23)

(If the pupil does not understand his short explanation), he should explain at greater length. When the pupil has heard it, he will correctly understand the Truth. A monk should utter pure speech, which is in accordance with the creed (of the *G*inas), and should declare the distinction of sin. (24)

He should well learn the (sacred texts) as they have been revealed; he should endeavour (to teach the creed), but he should not speak unduly long. A faithful man who is able to explain the entire creed[1] will not corrupt the faith. (25)

He should not pervert nor render obscure (the truth); he should fabricate neither text nor meaning, being a saviour; being devoted to the Teacher and considering well his words, he delivers faithfully what he has learned. (26)

He who correctly knows the sacred texts, who practises austerities, who understands all details of the Law, who is an authentic interpreter, clever, and learned—such a man is competent to explain the entire creed. (27)

Thus I say.

---

[1] Samâhi = samâdhi.

FIFTEENTH LECTURE,

CALLED

THE YAMAKAS [1].

What is past, present, and to come, all this is known to the Leader, the Saviour, who annihilates the hindrances to right faith. (1)

The annihilator of doubt knows the incomparable (Law); he, the expounder of the incomparable (Law), is not inclined towards this or that (heretical doctrine). (2).

On this or that (article of the creed he has) the correct opinion; hence he is rightly called a true (man); he who always possesses the truth, is kind towards his fellow-creatures. (3)

Towards your fellow-creatures be not hostile: that is the Law of him who is rich in control; he who is rich in control renounces everything, and in this (world meditates on the) reflections on life [2]. (4)

---

[1] This lecture has been named from its opening words *g*amaîyam, which also means, consisting of yamakas (compare Journal of the German Oriental Society, vol. xl, p. 101). For in this lecture each verse or line opens with a word repeated from the end of the preceding one. This artifice is technically called *sri*ṅkhala-yamaka, or chain-yamaka, a term which seems to be contained in another name of our lecture, mentioned by the author of the Niryukti (verse 28), viz. âdâniya-saṅkaliyâ. For saṅkaliyâ is the Prâk*ri*t for *sri*ṅkhala (e.g. in our text I, 5, 2, 20), though *S*îlâṅka here renders it wrongly saṅkalita; and âdâniya by itself is used as a name of our lecture.

[2] These are the twelve bhâvanâs or meditations on the vanity of life and the world in general, and on the excellence of the Law, &c.

He whose soul is purified by meditating on those reflections is compared to a ship in water; like a ship reaching the shore he gets beyond misery. (5)

A wise man gets beyond it who knows the sins of this world; sinful acts are got rid of by him who does not undertake any new acts. (6)

He who does not undertake new acts does not acquire Karman, and he verily understands (Karman); understanding it he becomes a Great Hero [1], who is not born (again) and does not die. (7)

A Great Hero, who has no Karman, does not die.—As the wind extinguishes a light, (so he puts down) the lovely women in this world. (8)

Those men whom women do not seduce, value Môksha most; those men are free from bondage and do not desire life. (9)

Turning from worldly life, they reach the goal by pious acts; by their pious acts they are directed (towards Liberation), and they show the way to others. (10)

The preaching of the Law (has different effect) on different creatures; he who is rich in control, is treated with honour [2], but does not care for it; he exerts himself, subdues his senses, is firm, and abstains from sexual intercourse. (11)

(He should not yield to temptations as a pig which) is decoyed by wild rice, being proof against sins, and free from faults. Being free from faults he always

---

[1] Mahâvîra.

[2] Pûyanâsaê, explained by pûganâ-âsvâdaka. I should prefer pûgâ-nâsaka, who abolished the worship of gods, in which case the following word anâsaê = an-âsaya might be rendered: he makes no plans.

subdues his senses, and has reached the incomparable cession of Karman[1]. (12)

Knowing the incomparable (control), he should not be hostile towards anybody, in thoughts, words, or deeds, having eyes (to see everything). (13)

He truly is the eye of men who (dwells so to speak) on the end[2] of desire; on its end (i. e. edge) glides the razor, on its end (i. e. rim) rolls the wheel. (14)

Because the wise use the ends (of things, i. e. bad food, &c.), they are called 'makers of an end' here. Here in the world of men we are men to fulfil the Law. (15)

In this creed which surpasses the world, (men) become perfected saints or gods, as I have heard; and I have heard that outside the rank of men this is not so[3]. (16)

Some (heretics) have said that they (viz. the gods) put an end to misery[4]; but others (*G*ainas) have repeatedly said that this (human) body is not easily obtained. (17)

To one whose soul has left (human life), it is not easy again to obtain instruction (in the Law), nor is such a mental disposition which they declare appropriate for adopting the Law[5]. (18)

How can it even be imagined that he should

---

[1] Sandhipattê. Sandhi is explained Karmavivaralaksha*n*am bhâvasandhim.

[2] There is a play on the word 'end' in this and the next verse which to a modern mind savours more of the absurd than the profound.

[3] Perfection cannot be obtained by other creatures than men.

[4] I. e. reach final beatitude.

[5] The words as they are preserved do not construe; the meaning, however, must have been about what I have given in the translation.

be born again, who professes the pure, complete, unparalleled Law, and is a receptacle of the unparalleled Law? (19)

How could the wise Tathâgatas be born again, the Tathâgatas who engage in no undertakings, the supreme, the eyes of the world? (20)

And there has been declared by the Kâsyapa the supreme condition [1], by realising which some happy and wise men reach excellence. (21)

A wise man who has gained strength (in control) which leads to the expiation of sins, annihilates his former works, and does not do new ones. (22)

The Great Hero does no actions which are the effects of former sins. By his actions he is directed (towards Môksha), abstaining from works which are entailed by birth [2]. (23)

That which all saints value highly (viz. control), destroys the thorn (viz. Karman); practising it some have been liberated, and others have become gods. (24)

There have been wise men, and there will be pious men, who having come to the end and made manifest the end of the incomprehensible path, have been liberated. (25)

Thus I say.

---

[1] Viz. control.

[2] *Gammayam.* The commentators explain it yan matam; but I think it is = *g*anma*g*am.

SIXTEENTH LECTURE,

CALLED

THE SONG[1].

Now the Venerable One said: He who thus subdues his senses, who is well qualified (for his task)[2] and abandons his body, is to be called a Brâhma*n*a, a *S*rama*n*a, a Bhikshu, a Nirgrantha. (The pupil) replied: Why is he who thus subdues his senses, who is well qualified (for his task) and abandons his body, to be called a Brâhma*n*a, a *S*rama*n*a, a Bhikshu, a Nirgrantha? Tell this, O great sage! (1)

He is a Brâhma*n*a for this reason that he has ceased from all sinful actions, viz. love, hate, quarrel, calumny, backbiting, reviling of others, aversion to control, and love of pleasures, deceit, untruth, and the sin of wrong belief; that he possesses the Samitis, always exerts himself, is not angry, nor proud. (2)

He is a *S*rama*n*a for this reason that he is not hampered by any obstacles, that he is free from desires, (abstaining from) property, killing, telling lies, and sexual intercourse; (and from) wrath, pride, deceit, greed, love, and hate: thus giving up every passion that involves him in sin, (such as) killing of beings. (Such a man) deserves the name of a *S*rama*n*a, who subdues (moreover) his senses, is well qualified (for his task), and abandons his body. (3)

[1] Gâhâ = gâthâ. In this lecture, which is in prose as regards form and contents, there is nothing that could justify the title given it.

[2] Daviê = dravya.

He is a Bhikshu for this reason that he is not conceited, but modest, and obedient (to his Guru), that he subdues his senses, is well qualified (for his task), and abandons his body, that he sustains all troubles and calamities, that he practises with a pure mind the (prescribed) conduct, exerts himself well, is steadfast, and eats but a moderate quantity[1] of food which is given him by others. (Such a man) deserves the name of a Bhikshu. (4)

He is a Nirgrantha for this reason that he is single[2], knowing the absolute (âtman), awakened, proof against sins, well disciplined; that he possesses the Samitis and equanimity, knows the true nature of the Self, is wise, has renounced the causes of sin both (objectively and subjectively[3]), does not desire honour, respect, and hospitality, but searches and knows the Law, endeavours to gain Liberation, and lives restrained. (Such a man) deserves the name of a Nirgrantha, who subdues his senses, is well qualified (for his task), and abandons his body. (5)

Know this to be thus as I have told you, because I am the Saviour. (6)

Thus I say.

---

[1] Sa*m*khâya. The commentator takes this word as a gerund and explains it: knowing (the vanity of the world).

[2] Êka, i.e. free from love and hate.

[3] Dravyatô bhâvatas *k*a.

SECOND BOOK[1].

FIRST LECTURE[2],

CALLED

THE LOTUS.

O long-lived (*G*ambûsvâmin)! I (Sudharman) have heard the following Discourse from the Venerable (Mahâvîra). We now come to the Lecture called 'the Lotus.' The contents of it are as follows: (1)

There is a lotus-pool containing much water and mud, very full and complete, answering to the idea (one has of a lotus-pool), full of white lotuses, delightful, conspicuous, magnificent, and splendid. (2)

And everywhere all over the lotus-pool there grew many white lotuses, the best of Nymphaeas, as we are told, in beautiful array, tall, brilliant, of fine colour, smell, taste, and touch, (&c., all down to) splendid. (3)

And in the very middle of this lotus-pool there grew one big white lotus, the best of Nymphaeas,

---

[1] With the exception of the fifth and sixth lectures, the whole Book (*s*rutaskandha) is in prose. I have adhered to the subdivision of the lectures exhibited in the Bombay edition, which, on the whole, agrees with that of most MSS.

[2] The lectures of this Book are called, according to the Niryukti, Great (mahâ) Lectures.

as we are told, in an excellent position, tall, (&c., all down to) splendid. (4)

[§§ 3 and 4 are to be repeated with the word 'all' or 'whole' added to 'lotus-pool'[1].] (5)

Now there came a man from the Eastern quarter to the lotus-pool, and standing on the bank of it he saw that one big white lotus, (&c., as above). Now this man spoke thus: 'I am a knowing, clever, well-informed, discerning, wise, not foolish man, who keeps the way, knows the way, and is acquainted with the direction and bent of the way. I shall fetch that white lotus, the best of all Nymphaeas.' Having said this the man entered the lotus-pool. And the more he proceeded, the more the water and the mud (seemed to) extend. He had left the shore, and he did not come up to the white lotus, the best of Nymphaeas, he could not get back to this bank, nor to the opposite one, but in the middle of the lotus-pool he stuck in the mud. (6)

This was the first man. Now (we shall describe) the second man. There came a man from the Southern quarter to the lotus-pool, and standing on the bank of it he saw that one big white lotus (&c., all as above). There he saw one man who had left the shore, but had not come up to the white lotus, the best of Nymphaeas, who could not get back to his bank, nor to the opposite one, but stuck in the mud in the middle of the lotus-pool. Now the second man spoke of the first man thus: 'This man is not knowing, not clever, (&c., see above, all down to) not acquainted with the direction and bent

[1] In the text the words savvâvanti *k*a *n*am are prefixed to the text of §§ 3 and 4. I give the explanation of *S*îlâṅka.

of the way.' For that man said: 'I am a knowing, (&c., all down to) I shall fetch that white lotus, the best of Nymphaeas.' But this white lotus, the best of Nymphaeas, cannot be got in the way this man tried. (7)

'However, I am a knowing, clever, (&c., all down to the end of the paragraph) he stuck in the mud.' This was the second man. (The same thing happened to a third and a fourth man, who came from the Western and Northern quarters respectively, and saw two and three men respectively sticking in the mud. Some MSS. give the story at length, others abbreviate it.) (8, 9)

Now a monk living on low food and desiring to get to the shore (of the Sa*m*sâra), knowing, clever, (&c., all down to) acquainted with the direction and bent of the way, came to that lotus-pool from some one of the four quarters or from one of the intermediate points (of the compass). Standing on the bank of the lotus-pool he saw the one big white lotus, (&c., as above). And he saw there those four men who having left the shore, (&c., all as above) stuck in the mud. Then the monk said: 'These men are not knowing, (&c., all down to) not acquainted with the direction and bent of the way; for these men thought: We shall fetch that white lotus, the best of Nymphaeas. But this white lotus, the best of Nymphaeas, cannot be got in the way these men tried. I am a monk living on low food, (&c., all down to) acquainted with the direction and bent of the way. I shall fetch that white lotus, the best of Nymphaeas.' Having said this the monk did not enter the lotus-pool; but standing on the bank of it he raised his voice: 'Fly up,

O white lotus, best of Nymphaeas!' And the white lotus, the best of Nymphaeas, flew up. (10)

I have told you, O long-lived *S*rama*n*as, a simile[1]; you must comprehend the meaning of it[2]. The Nirgrantha monks and nuns worshipped and praised the Venerable Ascetic Mahâvîra, and then spoke thus: 'You have told, O long-lived *S*rama*n*a, the simile, but we do not comprehend its meaning, O long-lived *S*rama*n*a!' The Venerable Ascetic Mahâvîra addressed the crowd of Nirgrantha monks and nuns, and spoke thus: Ah, you long-lived *S*rama*n*as! I shall tell, declare, explain, expound, and demonstrate it with its meaning, reasons, and arguments. Thus I say: (11)

O long-lived *S*rama*n*as[3], meaning[4] the world I spoke of the lotus-pool. Meaning Karman I spoke of the water. Meaning pleasures and amusements I spoke of the mud. Meaning people in general I spoke of those many white lotuses, the best of Nymphaeas. Meaning the king I spoke of the one big white lotus, the best of Nymphaeas. Meaning heretical teachers I spoke of those four men. Meaning the Law I spoke of the monk. Meaning the church[5] I spoke of the bank. Meaning the preaching of the Law I spoke of (the monk's) voice. Meaning Nirvâ*n*a I spoke of (the lotus') flying up. Meaning these things, O long-lived *S*rama*n*as, I told this (simile). (12)

---

[1] Nâê=*gñ*âtam, literally, that which is known.

[2] In the text the sentence closes with bhante, a word frequently used in addressing members of the order.

[3] These words are in the original repeated in each of the following sentences. I drop them in the translation.

[4] Appâha*tt*u=âtmany âh*ri*tya, literally, having in my mind.

[5] Dharmatîrtha.

Here in the East, West, North, and South many men have been born according to their merit, as inhabitants of this our world, viz. some as Âryas, some as non-Âryas, some in noble families, some in low families, some as big men, some as small men, some of good complexion, some of bad complexion, some as handsome men, some as ugly men. And of these men one man is king, who is strong like the great Himavat, Malaya, Mandara, and Mahêndra mountains, (&c., all down to) who governs his kingdom in which all riots and mutinies have been suppressed[1].

And this king had an assembly of Ugras[2] and sons of Ugras, Bhôgas[2] and sons of Bhôgas, Aikshvâkas and sons of Aikshvâkas, *Gñ*â*tri*s and sons of *Gñ*â*tri*s, Kauravas and sons of Kauravas, warriors and sons of warriors, Brâhma*n*as and sons of Brâhma*n*as, Li*kkh*avis and sons of Li*kkh*avis, commanders and sons of commanders, generals and sons of generals. (13)

And of these men some one[3] is full of faith. Forsooth, the *S*rama*n*as or Brâhma*n*as made up their mind to go to him. Being professors of some religion (they thought) 'We shall teach him our religion.' (And they said): 'Know this, dear sir, that we explain and teach this religion well. (14)

'Upwards from the soles of the feet, downwards

---

[1] This is one of the var*n*aka or typical descriptions which are so frequent in the canonical books. The full text is given in the Aupapâtika Sûtra, ed. Leumann, § 11, p. 26 f. Of the many meanings the word var*n*aka may have, 'masterpiece' seems the one in which it must be taken here. Many var*n*akas are, partly at least, composed in a curious metre which I have named Hypermetron, see Indische Studien, vol. xvii, pp. 389 ff.

[2] Concerning the Ugras and Bhôgas compare note 2 on p. 71.

[3] Apparently the king is meant.

from the tips of the hair on the head, within the skin's surface is (what is called) Soul [1], or what is the same, the Âtman. The whole soul lives; when this (body) is dead, it does not live. It lasts as long as the body lasts, it does not outlast the destruction (of the body). With it (viz. the body) ends life. Other men carry it (viz. the corpse) away to burn it. When it has been consumed by fire, only dove-coloured bones remain, and the four bearers return with the hearse to their village. Therefore there is and exists no (soul different from the body). Those who believe that there is and exists no (such soul), speak the truth. Those who maintain that the soul is something different from the body, cannot tell whether the soul (as separated from the body) is long or small, whether globular or circular or triangular or square or sexagonal or octagonal or long, whether black or blue or red or yellow or white, whether of sweet smell or of bad smell, whether bitter or pungent or astringent or sour or sweet, whether hard or soft or heavy or light or cold or hot or smooth or rough. Those, therefore, who believe that there is and exists no soul, speak the truth. Those who maintain that the soul is something different from the body, do not see the following (objections): (15)

'As a man draws a sword from the scabbard and shows it (you, saying): "Friend, this is the sword, and that is the scabbard," so nobody can draw (the soul from the body) and show it (you, saying): "Friend, this is the soul, and that is the body." As a man draws a fibre from a stalk of Muñga grass and shows it (you, saying): "Friend, this is the stalk, and that is the fibre;" or takes a bone out of the flesh, or the

[1] *Gîva.*

seed of Âmalaka[1] from the palm of his hand, or a particle of fresh butter out of coagulated milk, and shows you both things separately[2]; or as he presses oil from the seed of Atasî[3], and shows the oil and oil-cake separately, or as he presses the juice from the sugar-cane, and shows the juice and the molasses[4] separately, so nobody can show you the soul and the body separately. The same applies also when fire is churned from Ara*n*i-wood. Those who believe that there is and exists no soul, speak the truth. Those who say that the soul is different from the body, are wrong.' (16)

This murderer says: 'Kill, dig, slay, burn, cook, cut or break to pieces, destroy! Life ends here; there is no world beyond.'

These (Nâstikas) cannot inform[5] you on the following points: whether an action is good or bad, meritorious or not, well done or not well done, whether one reaches perfection or not, whether one goes to hell or not. Thus undertaking various works they engage in various pleasures and amusements for their own enjoyment. (17)

Thus some shameless men becoming monks propagate a Law of their own. And others believe it, put their faith in it, adopt it, (saying:) 'Well, you speak the truth, O Brâhma*n*a, (or) O *S*rama*n*a! We shall present you with food, drink, spices, and sweetmeats, with a robe, a bowl, or a broom.'

---

[1] Emblica Myrobalanos.

[2] I have somewhat condensed this passage.

[3] Ayau*tt*asî in Prâk*ri*t; it is Linum Usitatissimum.

[4] *Kh*ôya. See Grierson, Peasant Life of Bihar, p. 236. The word is apparently derived from root kshud.

[5] Pa*d*ivêdenti = prativêdayanti. The commentators, however, explain it as 'understand.'

Some have been induced to honour them, some have made (their proselytes) to honour them. (18)

Before (entering an order) they were determined to become *S*rama*n*as, houseless, poor monks who would have neither sons nor cattle, to eat only what should be given them by others, and to commit no sins. After having entered their order they do not cease (from sins), they themselves commit sins, they cause others to commit sins, and they assent to another's committing sins. Thus they are given to pleasures, amusements, and sensual lust; they are greedy, fettered, passionate, covetous, the slaves of love and hate; therefore they cannot free themselves (from the Circle of Births), nor free anybody else from it, nor free any other of the four kinds of living beings from it. They have left their former occupations, but have not entered the noble path. They cannot return (to worldly life), nor get beyond it; they stick (as it were) in pleasures and amusements. Thus I have treated of the first man (as one who believes that) soul and body are one and the same thing. (19)

Now I shall treat of the second man[1] (as one who believes that) everything consists of the five elements.

Here in the East, (&c., see §§ 13, 14, all down to) teach this religion well. (20)

'There are five elements[2] through which we explain

---

[1] According to the commentators the Lôkâyatikas or the Sâṅkhyas are intended. The latter explain the whole world as developed from the Prâk*ri*ti or chaos, and contend that the âtman does not act. The Lôkâyatikas deny the separate existence of the âtman, and maintain that the elements are called âtman when they manifest intellect (*k*aitanya).

[2] Mahabbhûya=mahâbhûta.

whether an action is good or bad, (&c., see § 18, all down to) hell or not. Everything down to a blade of grass (consists of them). (21)

'And one should know the intermixture[1] of the elements by an enumeration of them. Earth is the first element, water the second, fire the third, wind the fourth, and air the fifth. These five elements are not created, directly or indirectly, nor made; they are not effects nor products; they are without beginning and end; they always produce effects, are independent of a directing cause or everything else; they are eternal. Some, however, say that there is a Self besides the five elements. What is, does not perish; from nothing nothing comes. (22)

'All living beings, all things, the whole world consists of nothing but these (five elements). They are the primary cause of the world, even down to a blade of grass. (23)

'A man buys and causes to buy, kills and causes to kill, cooks and causes to cook, he may even sell and kill a man. Know, that even in this case he does not do wrong.'

These (Nâstikas) cannot inform you, (&c., see §§ 15–18, all down to) they stick (as it were) in pleasures and amusements.

Thus I have treated of the second man (who believes that) everything consists of the five elements. (24)

Now I shall treat of the third man (who believes that) the Self[2] is the cause of everything.

---

[1] Samavâya.

[2] The word used in the text is îsara = îsvara, but afterwards purisa = purusha is used in its place. Both words are synonymous

Here in the East, (&c., see §§ 12, 13, all down to) teach this religion well. (25)

'Here all things have the Self for their cause and their object, they are produced by the Self, they are manifested by the Self, they are intimately connected with the Self, they are bound up in the Self.

'As, for instance, a tumour is generated in the body, grows with the body, is not separate from the body, but is bound up in the body: so all things have the Self for their cause, (&c., all as above).

'As, for instance, a feeling of indisposition is generated in the body, grows with the body, is never separate from the body, but is bound up in the body: so all things have the Self for their cause, (&c., all as above).

'As, for instance, an anthill is made of earth, grows through earth, is not separate from earth, but is bound up in earth: so all things, (&c., all as above).

'As, for instance, a tree springs up on earth, grows on earth, is not separate from earth, but is bound up in earth: so all things, (&c., all as above).

'As, for instance, a lotus springs up in earth, grows on earth, is not separate from earth, but is bound up in earth: so all things, (&c., all as above).

'As, for instance, a mass of water is produced by water, grows through water, is not separate from water, but is bound up in water: so all things, (&c., all as above).

'As, for instance, a water-bubble is produced in water, grows in water, is not separate from water,

with âtman, the first may denote the highest âtman as in the Yôga philosophy, or the paramâtman as in the Vêdânta.

but is bound up in water: so all things, (&c., all as above). (26)

'And the twelve Aṅgas, the Canon of the Gaṇins[1], which has been taught, produced, and declared by the Sramaṇas, the Nirgranthas, viz. the Âkârâṅga (all down to) the Drishṭivâda, is wrong, not true, not a representation of the truth; but this (our doctrine) is correct, is true, is a representation of the truth.'

The (heretics in question) make this assertion, they uphold this assertion, they (try to) establish this assertion.

Therefore they cannot get out of the misery produced by this (error), even as a bird cannot get out of its cage. (27)

These (heretics) cannot inform you, (&c., see §§ 16–19, all down to) they stick, as it were, in pleasures and amusements.

Thus I have treated of the third man (who believes that) the Self is the cause of everything. (28)

Now I shall treat of the fourth man who believes that Fate is the cause of everything.

Here in the East, (&c., see §§ 12, 13, all down to) teach this religion well. (29)

'There are two (kinds of) men. One man admits action, another man does not admit action. Both men, he who admits action, and he who does not admit action, are alike, their case is the same, because they are actuated by the same force[2]. (30)

---

[1] Gaṇipiḍaga.

[2] Viz. Fate. For it is their destiny to entertain one belief or the other, and they are not amenable to it. This is the interpretation of the commentators. But to the phrase kâraṇam âpanna they give here a meaning different from that in the following paragraphs. I therefore propose the following translation of the end of the

'An ignorant man thinks about the cause as follows: "When I suffer, grieve, blame myself, grow feeble[1], am afflicted, or undergo great pain, I have caused it; or when another man suffers, &c., he has caused it." Thus an ignorant man thinks himself or another man to be the cause of what he or the other man experiences. (31)

'A wise man thinks about the cause as follows: "When I suffer, &c., I did not cause it; and when another man suffers, &c., he did not cause it[2]."

'A wise man thinks thus[3] about the cause of what he himself or another man experiences. I say this: "Movable or immovable beings in all the four quarters thus (i.e. by the will of Fate) come to have a body, to undergo the vicissitudes of life, to lose their body, to arrive at some state of existence, to experience pleasure and pain[4]."'

Entertaining such opinions these (heretics) cannot inform you, (&c., as in § 17, down to the end). (32)

These worthless men entertain such opinions, and believe in them till they cannot return, (&c., as in § 19 down to) amusements.

---

paragraph: 'are equally (wrong), (err) alike as regards the cause (of actions).'

[1] Tippâmi, explained 'lose strength of body.' The word cannot be tripyâmi, because it means 'I am satisfied.' The word is probably derived from the root tik 'to kill.' Tippâmi would be an irregular passive, just as sippâmi from sik, see Zeitschrift für vergleichende Sprachforschung, vol. xxvii, p. 250. Leumann, Aupapâtika Sûtra, glossary s.v. tippanayâ, explains this word by 'crying' on the authority of Abhayadêva. Either meaning suits the passages where it occurs in our text.

[2] But Fate is the cause.

[3] That is to say, that Fate distributes pleasure and pain.

[4] I render the rather ambiguous expressions in the original according to the interpretation of the commentators.

I have treated of the fourth man who believes that Fate is the cause of everything. (33)

These four men, differing in intellect, will, character, opinions, taste, undertakings, and plans, have left their former occupations, but have not entered the noble path. They cannot return (to worldly life) nor get beyond it; they stick (as it were) in pleasures and amusements. (34)

I say: here in the East, West, North, and South there are some men, viz. Âryas, non-Âryas, (&c., as in § 13, all down to) ugly men. They own small or large houses and fields, they own few or many servants and peasants. Being born in such-like families, they renounce (their possessions) and lead a mendicant's life. Some leave their kinsmen and their property to lead a mendicant's life; others, who have no kinsmen nor property, lead a mendicant's life. Whether they have kinsmen and property or not, they renounce them and lead a mendicant's life. (35)

Previously, however, they thought thus: 'Here, indeed, a man, who is on the point of turning monk, makes the following reflections with regard to different things: I possess fields, houses, silver, gold, riches, corn, copper, clothes, real valuable property, as riches, gold, precious stones, jewels, pearls, conches, stones, corals, rubies[1]. I enjoy sounds, colours, smells, tastes, and feelings of touch. These pleasures and amusements belong to me, and I belong to them.' (36)

A wise man, previously, should thus think to

---

[1] The same enumeration of valuable things occurs elsewhere, e. g. Kalpa Sûtra, Lives of the *G*inas, § 90.

himself: 'Here, indeed, some painful illness or disease might befall me, unwished for, unpleasant, disagreeable, nasty[1], painful and not at all pleasant. O ye dear pleasures, take upon you this painful illness or disease, unwished for, unpleasant, disagreeable, nasty, painful and not at all pleasant, that I may not suffer, grieve, blame myself, grow feeble, be afflicted, and undergo great pain[2]. Deliver me from this painful illness or disease, (&c., all as above).' But this desire of his has never yet been fulfilled. (37)

Here, in this life, pleasures and amusements are not able to help or to save one. Sometimes a man first forsakes pleasures and amusements, sometimes they first forsake him. Pleasures and amusements are one thing, and I am another. Why then should we be infatuated with pleasures and amusements which are alien (to our being)? Taking this into consideration, we shall give up pleasures and amusements. A wise man thinks them alien to himself. (38)

There are things more intimately connected with me, viz. my mother, father, brother, sister, wife, children, grandchildren, daughters-in-law, servants, friends, kinsmen, companions, and acquaintances. These my relations belong to me, and I belong to them. A wise man, previously, should think thus to himself: 'Here, indeed, some painful illness or disease might befall me, (&c., all as in § 37 down to the end, but substitute "relations" for "pleasures"). (39)

---

[1] The original has six synonyms for disagreeable, which it is impossible to render adequately in English.

[2] The same words occurred in § 31.

'Or some painful illness or disease, unwished for, (&c., all down to) not at all pleasant might befall my dear relations. I will take upon me this painful illness or disease, &c., that they may not suffer, (all down to) undergo great pain. I will deliver them from this painful illness or disease.' But this desire of his has never yet been fulfilled. For one man cannot take upon himself the pains of another; one man cannot experience what another has done[1]. (40)

Individually a man is born, individually he dies, individually he falls (from this state of existence), individually he rises (to another)[2]. His passions[3], consciousness, intellect, perceptions, and impressions belong to the individual exclusively. Here, indeed, the bonds of relationship are not able to help nor save one. (All as in § 38 down to the end; substitute 'bonds of relationship' for 'pleasures and amusements.') (41)

There are things more intimately connected with me, viz. my hands, feet, arms, legs, head, belly, character, life, strength, colour, skin, complexion, ear, eye, nose, tongue, and touch; they are part and parcel of me. But I grow old with regard to life, strength, (all down to) touch. The strong joints become loose, the body is furrowed with wrinkles, the black hair turns white, even this dear body which has grown with food, must be relinquished in due time.

---

[1] I.e. his Karman.

[2] According to the commentators the last two passages should be translated: 'individually he leaves (his possessions, &c.), individually he is joined (to them).'

[3] *Ghañghâ* = kalaha.

Making such reflections, a monk should lead a mendicant's life and know that all things are divided into living beings and things without life, (and living beings again into) movable and immovable ones. (42)

Here, indeed, householders are killers (of beings) and acquirers of property, and so are even some *S*rama*n*as and Brâhma*n*as. They themselves kill movable and immovable living beings, have them killed by another person, or consent to another's killing them. (43)

Here, indeed, householders are killers (of beings) and acquirers of property, and so are even some *S*rama*n*as and Brâhma*n*as. They themselves acquire sentient or senseless objects of pleasure, have them acquired by another person, or consent to another's acquiring them. (44)

Here, indeed, householders are killers (of beings) and acquirers of property, and so are even some *S*rama*n*as and Brâhma*n*as. But I am no killer (of beings) nor an acquirer of property. Relying upon[1] householders and such *S*rama*n*as and Brâhma*n*as as are killers (of beings) and acquirers of property, we shall lead a life of chastity. (He should, however, part company with them.) (The pupil asks): What is the reason thereof? (The teacher answers): As before (their ordination they were killers of beings), so (they will be) afterwards, and vice versâ. It is evident that (householders) do not abstain (from sins) nor exert themselves (in control); and (as monks) they will relapse into the same (bad habits). (45)

---

[1] Nissâe=ni*s*rayâ, explained â*s*rayê*n*a.

The householders and those *S*rama*n*as and Brâhma*n*as, who are killers (of beings) and acquirers of property, commit sins both (from love and hatred). But a monk who takes this into consideration, should lead a life subject to neither (love nor hatred). (46)

I say: in the East, West, North, and South (a true monk) will have renounced works, be exempt from works, will have put an end to them. This has been taught (by the prophets, &c.). (47)

The Venerable One has declared that the cause (of sins) are the six classes of living beings, earth-lives, &c. As is my pain when I am knocked or struck with a stick, bone, fist, clod, or potsherd; or menaced, beaten, burned, tormented, or deprived of life; and as I feel every pain and agony from death down to the pulling out of a hair: in the same way, be sure of this, all kinds of living beings feel the same pain and agony, &c., as I, when they are ill-treated in the same way[1]. For this reason all sorts of living beings should not be beaten, nor treated with violence, nor abused, nor tormented, nor deprived of life[2]. (48)

I say: the Arhats and Bhagavats of the past, present, and future, all say thus, speak thus, declare thus, explain thus: all sorts of living beings should not be slain, nor treated with violence, nor abused, nor tormented, nor driven away. This constant, permanent, eternal, true Law has been taught by wise men who comprehend all things. Thus a monk abstains from (the five cardinal sins:) slaughter of living beings, &c. He does not clean his teeth with

---

[1] The text repeats the phrases just translated.

[2] The same words form the text of the homily in Â*k*ârâṅga I, 4.

a tooth-brush [1], he does not accept collyrium, emetics, and perfumes. (49)

A monk who does not act, nor kill, who is free from wrath, pride, deceit, and greed, who is calm and happy, should not entertain the following wish: May I, after my departure from this world, by dint of my intellect, knowledge, memory, learning, or of the performance of austerities, religious duties, chastity, or of this habit to eat no more than is necessary to sustain life, become a god at whose command are all objects of pleasure, or a perfected saint who is exempt from pain and misery. (Through his austerities) he may obtain his object, or he may not obtain it. (50)

A monk should not be infatuated with sounds, colours, smells, tastes, and feelings of touch; he should abstain from wrath, pride, deceit, and greed, from love, hate, quarrel, calumny, reviling of others, aversion to control and delight in sensual things, deceit and untruth, and the sin of wrong belief. In this way a monk ceases to acquire gross Karman, controls himself, and abstains from sins. (51)

He does not kill movable or immovable beings, nor has them killed by another person, nor does he consent to another's killing them. In this way a monk ceases to acquire gross Karman, controls himself, and abstains from sins. (52)

He does not acquire sentient or senseless objects of pleasure, nor has them acquired by another person, nor does he consent to another's acquiring them. In this way, (&c., all as above). (53)

---

[1] Or rather a piece of wood with which the Hindus rub their teeth.

He does no actions arising from sinful causes [1], nor has them done by another person, nor does he consent to another's doing them. In this way (&c., all as above). (54)

A monk should not take food, drink, dainties, and spices when he knows that (the householder) to satisfy him, or for the sake of a co-religionist, has bought or stolen or taken it, though it was not given nor to be taken, but was taken by force, by acting sinfully towards all sorts of living beings [2]; nor does he cause another person to eat it, nor does he consent to another's eating it. In this way (&c., all as above). (55)

A monk may think as follows: The (householders) have the means (to procure food for those) for whose sake it is prepared; viz. for himself [3], his sons, daughters, daughters-in-law, nurses, relations, chiefs, male and female slaves, male and female servants; for a treat of sweetmeats, for a supper, for a breakfast the collation has been prepared. This food is to be eaten by some people, it is prepared by some one else, it is destined for some one else, it is free from the faults occasioned either by the giver or by the receiver or by the act of receiving it [4], rendered pure [5], rendered free from living matter [6], wholly free from living things [7], it has been begged, has been given to the monk on account of his profession [8],

---

[1] Sâmparâyika. The commentators say: ta*k* *k*a pradvêsha-nihnavamâtsaryântarâyâ*s*âtanôpaghâtair badhyatê.

[2] Compare Â*k*ârânga Sûtra II, 1, 1, 11.

[3] Apparently the householder is intended.

[4] Udgama, utpâdanâ, êsha*n*â. See above, p. 131, note 7.

[5] *S*astrâtîtam.

[6] *S*astrapari*n*âmitam.

[7] Avihi*m*sitam.

[8] Vaishikam.

it has been collected in small bits[1], it is food fit for a learned monk, it is lawful to eat it at the present occasion, it is of the prescribed quantity, it greases, as it were, the axle of the carriage and anoints the sore, being just sufficient to enable one to practise control and to carry the burden of it; he should consume that food (without delay) even as the snake returning to its hole; that is to say: one should eat when it is time for eating, drink when it is time for drinking, dress when it is time for dressing, seek cover when it is time for seeking cover, and sleep when it is time for sleeping. (56)

A monk who knows the proper measure (in all things) travelling in one direction or other, should teach, explain, and praise (the Law), preach it unto those who exert themselves well, and to those who do not, to all who come to listen. (He should preach to them): indifference for the peace of mind, cessation of passion, Nirvâ*n*a, purity, simplicity, humility, freedom from bonds[2]. He should preach the Law which prohibits to kill any living being, after having well considered it. (57)

When a monk preaches the Law, he should preach it not for the sake of food, drink, clothes, resting-place, or lodging, nor for any objects of pleasure; but he should preach the Law indefatigably, for no other motive than the annihilation of Karman. (58)

Those heroes of faith who are instructed in the Law by such a monk and exert themselves well, are

---

[1] Samudânikam, i.e. as bees collect honey from many flowers. Cf. p. 80, note 1.

[2] Compare Â*k*ârâṅga Sûtra I, 7, 4, 1, part i, p. 68, note 3.

possessed of all (virtues), abstain from all (sins), cease from all (passions), conduct themselves well in every way, and reach final beatitude. (59)

Such a monk searches the Law, knows the Law, and endeavours to gain Liberation; as it has been said: 'He may get the white lotus, the best of Nymphaeus, or he may not get it.' Such a monk knows and renounces actions, worldly occupations, and the life of a householder; he is free from passions, possesses the Samitis, is wise, always exerts himself; he is to be called: a *S*rama*n*a, a Brâhma*n*a, calm, a subduer of his senses, guarding himself, liberated, a seer, a sage, virtuous, wise, a monk, living on low food, desiring to get to the shore (of the Sa*m*sâra), fulfilling the general and particular virtues [1]. (60)

Thus I say.

SECOND LECTURE,

CALLED

ON ACTIVITY [2].

O long-lived (*G*ambûsvâmin)! I (Sudharman) have heard the following Discourse from the Venerable (Mahâvîra). We now come to the Lecture called 'on Activity.' The contents of it are as follows:

---

[1] *K*ara*n*akara*n*apâravid. *K*ara*n*a is explained by mûlagu*n*a, kara*n*a by uttaragu*n*a. The mûlagu*n*as consist in the observance of the five vows, the uttaragu*n*as are the five Samitis, the three Guptis, &c., in short, the duties of a monk.

[2] Kiriyâ*th*â*n*ê = kriyâsthânam, literally, the subject of activity.

It treats, briefly, of two subjects: merit and demerit. (The former is when the Self is) at rest, (the latter, when it is) in disturbance[1]. (1)

Now the explanation[2] of the first subject, viz. demerit, is as follows. Here in the East, West, North, and South, (&c., all as in II, 1, 12, down to) ugly men. (2)

And as regards committing of sin[3], among denizens of hell, brute animals, gods, men, and whatever other suchlike beings there be, the sentient beings feel[4] the pain. (3)

And these beings practise the following thirteen kinds of activity—

1. sinning for one's interest;
2. sinning without a personal interest;
3. sinning by slaying;
4. sinning through accident;
5. sinning by an error of sight;
6. sinning by lying;
7. sinning by taking what is not freely given;
8. sinning by a mere conceit;
9. sinning through pride;
10. sinning through bad treatment of one's friends;
11. sinning through deceit;
12. sinning through greed;
13. actions referring to a religious life. (4)

---

[1] Upasânta and anupasânta.

[2] Vibhanga, more literally, case.

[3] Dandasamâdâna, explained pâpôpâdâna.

[4] A difference is made between feeling (anubhavanti) and knowing (vidanti): (1) the saññins or rational beings feel and know impressions; (2) the Siddhas only know them; (3) the reasonless beings only feel them; (4) things without life neither know nor feel them. Sentient beings are those in Nos. 1 and 3.

1. The first kind of committing sins is that prompted by a motive. This is the case when a man for his own sake, for the sake of his relations, his house, his family, his friends, for the sake of Nâgas, Bhûtas, or Yakshas does injury to movable or immovable beings, or has it done by another person, or consents to another's doing it. Thereby the bad Karman accrues to him. This is the first kind of committing sins, that prompted by a motive. (5)

2. We now treat of the second kind of committing sins, viz. that which is not prompted by personal interest. This is the case when a man slays, kills, cuts, pierces, hacks, mangles, or puts to death movable living beings, not because he wants their body, skin, flesh, blood, heart, bile, feathers of their tail, tail, big or small horns, teeth, tusks, nails, sinews, bones, or marrow; nor because he has been wounded by them, or is wounded, or will be wounded; nor in order to support his children, or to feed his cattle, or to enlarge his houses, nor for the maintenance of *S*rama*n*as and Brâhma*n*as, nor for the benefit of his body; setting aside reason a fool acquires the habit of cruelty, being a wanton killer. (6)

This is the case when a man slays, &c. (see above) immovable living beings as Ikka*t*a-reed, Ka*th*ina, *G*antuka-grass, Para-grass[1], Môksha-trees[2], grass, Ku*s*a-grass, Ku*kkh*aka[3], Pappaka[4], or straw, not

[1] Compare Â*k*ârâṅga Sûtra II, 2, 3, 18, note 1. One MS. reads êraga for paraga. Êraka is the name of a reed.

[2] Môksha is the name of a tree = mushkaka. The Â*k*ârâṅga and one of our MSS. have môraga, peacocks' feathers. But that is out of place here.

[3] Ku*kkh*a is a white water-lily. The Â*k*ârâṅga Sûtra has ku*kk*aka = kûr*k*aka, brush.

[4] Pa*kk*aka in the Â*k*ârâṅga Sûtra.

in order to support his children, (&c., all down to) wanton killer. (7)

Or when a man on a marsh, a lake, a sheet of water, a pasture-ground, a place surrounded by a ditch, a moat, a thicket, stronghold[1] in a thicket, forest, stronghold in a forest, [mountain, stronghold on a mountain[2]], piles up grass and lights a fire, or has it lighted by another person, or consents to another's lighting it. Thereby the bad Karman accrues to him. This is the second kind of committing sins, that prompted by no personal interest. (8)

3. We now treat of the third kind of committing sins, called slaying. This is the case when a man thinking that some one has hurt, hurts, or will hurt him, or one of his people, or somebody else, or one of that person's people, kills movable and immovable beings, has them killed by another person, or consents to another's killing them. Thereby the bad Karman accrues to him. This is the third kind of committing sins, called slaying. (9)

4. We now treat of the fourth kind of committing sins, called accidental[3]. This is the case when in marshes (&c., all as above, down to) strongholds in

---

[1] Or a group of trees.

[2] A nearly identical enumeration of places occurs in Âkârâṅga Sûtra II, 3, 3, 2. The words in brackets seem to be added later; for Sîlâṅka does not comment upon them, and expressly mentions ten places. They are generally omitted in the sequel when the same passage occurs again.

[3] Akasmâddaṇḍê. The commentators remark that the word akasmât is in Magadha pronounced by the people as in Sanskrit. The fact is that we meet here and in the end of the next paragraph with the spelling akasmât, while in the middle of the paragraphs it is spelled akamhâ, which is the true Prâkrit form.

a forest, a man who lives on deer, who likes deer, who dotes on deer, goes a hunting deer. Fancying to see deer, he takes aim with his arrow to kill the deer. Thinking that he will kill the deer, he kills a partridge, or a duck, or a quail, or a pigeon, or a monkey, or a francoline partridge. Here instead of one (being) he hurts another, (therefore he is called) an accidental killer. (10)

This is the case when a man weeding rice, Kôdrava[1], panic seed, Paraka, or Râlaka, uses his knife to cut some weeds. Fancying that he is cutting some weed-grasses[2], he cuts rice (&c., down to) Râlaka. Here instead of one (plant) he hurts another; (therefore he is called) an accidental killer. Thereby the bad Karman accrues to him. This is the fourth kind of committing sins, called accidental. (11)

5. We now treat of the fifth kind of committing sins, viz. by an error of sight. This is the case when a man living together with his mother, father, brothers, sisters, wives, sons, daughters, or daughters-in-law, and mistaking a friend for an enemy, kills the friend by mistake. (12)

This is the case when during a riot in a village[3],

[1] Paspalum Sobriculatum.

[2] They are specialised in the text as *S*yâmaka*m* tri*n*a*m*, mukundaka vrîhiûsita, and kâlêsuka. Only the two first are mentioned in our dictionaries.

[3] In the Dîpikâ the following versus memorialis is quoted, in which the names of places mentioned in the text are defined: grâmô v*ri*tyâ v*ri*ta*h* syân nagaram uru*k*aturgôpurôdbhâsi*s*ôbham khê*t*a*m* nadyadrivêsh*t*a*m* pariv*ri*tam abhita*h* kharva*t*am parvatêna | grâmair yuktam ma*t*ambam dalitada*s*a*s*atai*h* (?) pattana*m* ratnayônir drô*n*âkhya*m* sindhuvêlâvalayitam atha sambâdhana*m* vâ*s*dri*sri*ṅge || It will be seen that the meaning of these terms given in this verse differs from that given in notes 3–11, p. 176.

or a scot-free town, or a town with an earth wall, or a poor town, or an isolated town, or a large town, or a sea-town, or a mine, or a hermitage, or a halting-place of processions or caravans, or a capital, a man mistaking for a robber one who is not, kills him by mistake. Thereby the bad Karman accrues to him. This is the fifth kind of committing sins, viz. by an error of sight. (13)

6. We now treat of the sixth kind of committing sins, viz. by lying. This is the case when a man for his own sake, or for the sake of his relations, his house, or his servants tells lies, causes another person to tell lies, or consents to another's telling lies. Thereby the bad Karman accrues to him. This is the sixth kind of committing sins, viz. by lying. (14)

7. Now we treat of the seventh kind of committing sins, viz. by taking what is not freely given. This is the case when a man for his own sake (&c., as above) takes himself what is not freely given, has it taken by another person, or consents to another's taking it. Thereby the bad Karman accrues to him. This is the seventh kind of committing sins, viz. by taking what is not freely given. (15)

8. Now we treat of the eighth kind of committing sins, viz. by a mere conceit. This is the case when a man, without being disappointed by anybody in any way, meditates, melancholy, sorry, angry, downcast, anxious in thoughts and ideas, plunged in a sea of sorrow and misery, reposing his head on the palm of his hand, overcome by painful reflections, and casting his eyes on the ground[1]. There are four

[1] The same passage occurs Kalpa Sûtra, Lives of the *G*inas, § 92, part i, p. 249.

mental, but real, conditions (of this kind), viz. wrath, pride, deceit, and greed; for wrath, pride, deceit, and greed are mental conditions. Thereby the bad Karman accrues to him. This is the eighth kind of committing sins, viz. by a mere conceit. (16)

9. Now we treat of the ninth kind of committing sins, viz. through pride. This is the case when a man drunk (as it were) with pride of caste, family, beauty, piety, knowledge, success, power, intelligence[1], or any other kind of pride, slights, blames, abuses, reviles, despises somebody else and extols himself, (thinking:) 'he is my inferior, I am of better caste or family, and possess greater power and other advantages.' When he leaves this body and is only accompanied by his Karman, he, without a will of his own, goes forth from womb to womb, from birth to birth, from death to death, from hell to hell. He is cruel, stubborn, fickle, and proud. Thereby the bad Karman accrues to him. This is the ninth kind of committing sins, viz. through pride. (17)

10. We now treat of the tenth kind of committing sins, consisting in bad treatment of one's friends. This is the case when a man living together with his mother, father, brothers, sisters, wives, sons, daughters, or daughters-in-law, severely punishes even the smallest offence of theirs; e.g. he ducks the offender[2] in cold water, or pours hot water over him, or scalds him with fire, or lashes his sides sore with a halter, reed, rope[3], strap of leather, whip, or

[1] These are the eight kinds of pride, madasthânâni.

[2] The original has kâya*m*, the body.

[3] Nettê*n*a = nêtrê*n*a. The commentator says that it is a particular tree; but I think the usual meaning of nêtra, viz. rope, suits better.

thong of a whip, or he beats the offender with a stick, bone, fist, clod, or potsherd. When such a man is at home, (his people) are miserable; but when he is abroad, they rejoice. Such a man, who is for ever punishing, severely punishing, is hateful in this world and the next, irritable, passionate, an extortioner[1]. Thereby the bad Karman accrues to him. This is the tenth kind of committing sins, consisting in bad treatment of onc's friends. (18)

11. We now treat of the eleventh kind of committing sins, viz. through deceit. Those who conceal their thoughts, who are shrouded in darkness, who are light as the feather of an owl or heavy like a mountain, use unworthy[2] speech though they be Âryas. They believe themselves different from what they really are; asked one thing, they answer another, they speak different from what is to be spoken. (19)

As a man in whose body sticks an arrow[3], does not extricate it (fearing the pain), nor has it extricated by somebody else, nor destroys it, but hides it; and the arrow, being not removed, goes deeper and deeper (in the flesh); so a deceitful man, having practised deception, does not confess it, expiate it, blame the deed to himself or others, does not remove it, annihilate it, and endeavour not to do it again, does not practise the prescribed austerities and penance. A deceitful man is generally not trusted[4] in this world, a deceitful man is not trusted in the next world. He blames and reviles (the person

---

[1] Pi*tth*ima*m*sî, literally, who eats the flesh of the back.

[2] Anârya.

[3] *S*alya.

[4] Pa*kk*âyâti, pratyâyâti. Dîpikâ: avi*s*vâsyatayâ pratyâyâti prakhyâti*m* yâti.

whom he has deceived), he praises himself, and rejoices, and does not desist (from his vile practices); he conceals the wrong he has done to others, and does not acquire a pure Lêsyâ. Thereby the bad Karman accrues to him. This is the eleventh kind of committing sins, viz. through deceit. (20)

12. We now treat of the twelfth kind of committing sins, viz. through greed. Those (heretical monks) who live in woods, in huts, about villages, or practise some secret rites, are not well controlled, nor do they well abstain (from slaying) all sorts of living beings. They employ speech that is true and untrue at the same time[1]: 'do not beat me, beat others; do not abuse me, abuse others; do not capture me, capture others; do not torment me, torment others; do not deprive me of life, deprive others of life[2].' And thus they are given to sensual pleasures, desire them, are held captive by them, passionately love them for four or five years, for six or ten years—(the period) may be shorter or longer. After having enjoyed these pleasures, and having died at their allotted time, they will be born in some places inhabited by Asuras and evildoers. And when they are released therefrom, they will be born deaf and dumb, or blind[3], or dumb by birth. Thereby the bad Karman accrues to him. This is the twelfth kind of committing sins, viz. through greed. (21)

---

[1] Concerning the fourfold division of speech see above, p. 135, and part i, p. 150, note 2.

[2] The meaning is that Brahmans declare it a capital crime to kill a Brahman, but a venial one to kill a Sûdra.

[3] Tammûyattâe = tamômûkatvêna, explained either, blind by birth, or absolutely stupid or ignorant.

These twelve kinds of committing sins should be well understood by a pious *S*ramana or Brâhma*n*a[1]. (22)

13. We now treat of the thirteenth kind of acquiring Karman, that having reference to religious life[2]. A monk[3] who controls himself for the benefit of his soul, who in walking carefully avoids to cause the death of any living creature[4], who uses gentle and righteous speech[5], who receives alms in a manner to avoid the forty-two faults[6], who is careful in receiving and keeping of things necessary for religious exercises[7], who performs the operations of nature (excrements, urine, saliva, corporal impurities and mucus) in an unfrequented place[8], who is careful with regard to mind, speech, and body[9], who guards his mind, speech, and body so as to protect his soul from passions[10], who guards his senses, who leads a chaste life regulated by the three Guptis, who carefully walks, stands, sits down, lies down, and speaks, who carefully takes up and lays

---

[1] The Karman of the preceding twelve kinds of sins is called sâmparâyika (see p. 298, n. 3). It takes hold of the Âtman till it is annihilated; it is a lasting Karman, while that described in the next paragraph is of a momentary existence.

[2] Iriyâvahiya = îryapathika or airyapathika. The term îryapatha literally means, way of walking, but technically it denotes the actions of which the life of a correct ascetic consists, and airyapathika, therefore, is the Karman inseparable from it.

[3] The text consists of a string of technical terms, many of which have been explained already. I here incorporate the explanation in the translation. For more particulars see Bhandarkar's Report, p. 98.

[4] Îryâsamita. [5] Bhâshâsamita. [6] Êsha*n*âsamita.

[7] Bhâ*nd*amâtrâdânanikshêpâ*n*asamita.

[8] U*kk*âra-prasrava*n*a-*s*lêshma-*g*alla-*sri*ṅghâ*n*a-parish*th*âpanikâ-samita. [9] Ma*n*a*h*-, vâk-, kâya-samita.

[10] Mana*h*-, vâk-, kâya-gupta.

down his cloth, alms-bowl, blanket, broom,—(even) such a monk performs various subtile actions called îryapathika (if it did but consist in moving an eyelash). This Karman is acquired and comes in contact (with the soul) in the first moment, in the second moment it is experienced, in the third it is destroyed; thus it is acquired, comes in contact (with the soul), takes rise, and is destroyed. For all time to come (the person in question) is exempt from Karman[1]. Thereby the bad Karman accrues to him[2]. This is the thirteenth kind of acquiring Karman, that inseparable from a religious life. (23)

All the Arhats and Bhagavats of the past, present, and future have told, tell, and will tell, have declared, declare, and will declare the above thirteen kinds of acquiring Karman. They have practised, practise, and will practise the thirteenth kind of acquiring Karman. (24)

As a supplement[3] to the above (discussion) will

---

[1] An almost identical passage occurs in the Uttarâdhyayana XXIX, § 71, above p. 172.

[2] This typical passage is repeated here though it is apparently out of place.

[3] Not only this paragraph but also all that follows up to the last paragraph seems to be a later addition. For in the last paragraph the subject treated of in §§ 1–27 is taken up again and brought to its conclusion. After the supplement §§ 25–27 a separate treatise on the main subject is inserted §§ 28–60 (28–57 on demerit, 58–59 on merit, § 60 on a mixed state); after this follows a similar treatise in §§ 61–77 (61–68 on demerit, 69–74 on merit, 75–77 on a mixed state). In § 78 we have again a supplement, and §§ 79–82 contain another supplement (or perhaps two). §§ 83–85 give the conclusion of the first treatise (§§ 1–24) and must originally have followed immediately after § 24. So we have here, besides some appendices, three distinct original treatises on the same subject, very awkwardly pieced together to form one continuous lecture.

now be told the subject of men's success by occult sciences. Some men differing in intellect, will, character, opinions, taste, undertakings, and plans, study various evil sciences; (25) viz. (the divination) from terrestrial accidents, from strange phenomena[1], from dreams, from phenomena in the air, from changes in the body, from sounds, from mystical signs[2], from seeds[3]; (the interpretation of the) marks of women, men, elephants, cows, partridges, cocks, ducks, quails, of wheels, parasols, shields, sticks, swords, precious stones, jewels[4]; (26) the art to make one happy or miserable, to make a woman pregnant, to deprive one of his wits; incantations[5], conjuring[6]; oblations of substances; the martial arts; the course of the moon, sun, Venus, and Jupiter; the falling of meteors; great conflagration; divination from wild animals[7], the flight of crows, showers of dust, rain of blood, the Vaitâlî and Ardhavaitâlî arts[8], the art of casting people asleep, of opening doors, the art of *K*â*nd*âlas, of *S*abaras, of Dravi*d*as, of Kaliṅgas, of Gau*d*as, of Gândhâras; the spells for making somebody fall down, rise, yawn; for making him immovable, or cling to something; for making him sick, or sound;

---

[1] E. g. the laughing of monkeys.

[2] Laksha*n*a. The mystical signs meant are the svastika, &c.

[3] Vya*ñg*ana. The seeds are sesamum, beans, &c.

[4] Kâki*n*î, rendered ratna in the commentary.

[5] Âtharva*n*î.

[6] Pâka*s*âsanî = indra*g*âla.

[7] M*r*iga*k*akra.

[8] According to the commentary the Vaitâlî art teaches to raise a stick (? da*nd*am utthâpayati, perhaps to lay a punishment on somebody) by spells; and the Ardhavaitâlika, to remove it. In Pâli vêtala*m* means the magic art of bringing dead bodies to life by spells, see Childers' Dictionary of the Pâli Language, sub voce.

for making somebody go forth, disappear, (or come)[1]. These and similar sciences are practised (by some men) for the sake of food, drink, clothes, a lodging, a bed, and various objects of pleasure. They practise a wrong science, the unworthy, the mistaken[2] men. After having died at their allotted time, they will be born in some places inhabited by Asuras and evildoers. And when they are released therefrom, they will again be born deaf and dumb, or night-blind. (27)

Some man for his own sake or for the sake of his relations, family, or servants, or entering the service of an acquaintance or neighbour of his, becomes his companion or his helpmate, or he goes to meet him, or he becomes a burglar, or a cut-purse, or he tends sheep, or he becomes a hunter[3], or he catches birds, or he uses nets (for catching deer), or he becomes a fisherman or a cowherd or a slayer of cows or a dog-keeper or he hunts with dogs. (28)

A man, becoming the companion of another man, will follow him everywhere, (and having inspired him with confidence) beats, cuts, pierces, tears, thrashes, or puts him to death, and thereby gets his food. By these very evil deeds he degrades himself[4]. (29)

A man, becoming the helpmate of another man, always attends on him, (and having inspired him with confidence) beats, &c. (all down to) degrades himself. (30)

---

[1] Âyamaṇim, it is omitted in some MSS. and in the commentaries.

[2] Vipratipanna.

[3] Sôvariya, translated saukarika.

[4] I. e. he will be born in one of the low courses of existence.

A man, going to meet somebody, on the road, beats, &c. (all down to) degrades himself. (31)

A man, becoming a burglar, breaks into a house and beats, &c. (all down to) degrades himself. (32)

A man, becoming a cut-purse, cuts the purse and beats, &c. (all down to) degrades himself. (33)

A man, becoming a tender of sheep, beats, cuts, pierces, tears, thrashes, or puts to death a ram or some other animal. (The rest as above.) (34)

A man, becoming a hunter, beats, &c. (all down to) puts to death a buffalo or some other animal. (The rest as above.) (35)

A man, using nets (for catching deer), beats, &c., an antelope or some other animal. (The rest as above.) (36)

A man, catching birds, beats, &c., a bird or some other animal. (The rest as above.) (37)

A man, becoming a fisherman, beats, &c., a fish or some other animal. (The rest as above.) (38)

A man, becoming a cowherd, beats, &c., a cow or some other animal. (The rest as above.) (39)

A man, slaying cows, beats, &c., a cow or some other animal. (The rest as above.) (40)

A man, becoming a dog-keeper, beats, &c., a dog or some other animal. (The rest as above.) (41)

A man, becoming the helpmate of a dog-keeper, beats, &c., a dog or some other animal. (The rest as above.) (42)

A man, rising in an assembly, may promise to kill some (animal) and he will beat, &c., a partridge, duck, quail, pigeon, monkey, a francoline partridge, or some other animal. (The rest as above.) (43)

A man, being angry for some reason, e.g. because

his granary or his liquor-cask runs short[1], sets fire to the cornfields of the householders or their sons, has the fire set by another person, or consents to another's setting fire to them. (The rest as above.) (44)

A man, being angry for some reason, e.g. because his granary or liquor-cask runs short, makes a deep cut in the strong limbs of the camels, cows, horses, or donkeys of the householders or their sons, has it made by another person, or consents to another's making the cut. (The rest as above.) (45)

A man, being angry for some reason, e.g. because his granary or his liquor-cask runs short, covers with brambles or twigs the householders', or their sons', stable for the camels, cows, horses, or donkeys, and burns them, or has them burnt by another person, or consents to another's burning them. (The rest as above.) (46)

A man, being angry for some reason, &c. (as above), steals a householder's or his sons' earrings (or girdle)[2], or jewels, or pearls, has them stolen by another person, or consents to another's stealing them. (The rest as above.) (47)

A man, being angry, &c. (as before), robs *S*ramanas or Brâhmanas of their umbrella, stick, staff, small property, pot, chair, clothes, blanket, leather boots, knife, or scabbard, has it done by another person, or consents to another's robbing them. (The rest as above.) (48)

A man, without consideration (and without any

[1] Khaladâ*n*êna vâ surâthâlaê*n*a vâ. My translation is conjectural.

[2] Gu*n*a; omitted in the printed text.

provocation), sets fire to the cornfields of the householders, &c. (All as in § 44.) (49)

A man, without consideration, makes a deep cut in the strong limbs of the camels, &c. (All as in § 45.) (50)

A man, without consideration, covers with brambles and twigs the stables for the camels, &c., and burns them, &c. (All as in § 46.) (51)

A man, without consideration, steals the earrings, &c. (All as in § 47.) (52)

A man, without consideration, robs *S*rama*n*as or Brâhma*n*as of their umbrella, &c. (All as in § 48.) (53)

A man, on seeing *S*rama*n*as or Brâhma*n*as (whom he detests), degrades himself by various evil deeds. Either he gives them a slap with the open hand to turn them away [1], or he abuses them. And when the monk at the proper time calls (at his house on the begging-tour), he does not give him alms (but says): those who become *S*rama*n*as are the meanest workmen, men unable to support (their family), low-caste men, wretches, idlers! (54)

Such men praise this life, this miserable life; they do nothing on behalf of the next world; they suffer, grieve, blame themselves, grow feeble, are afflicted, and undergo great pain; they do not cease to cause others to suffer, grieve, &c., to slay and to put men in fetters; and while they make suffer or kill, or make suffer and kill (beings), and do various evil

---

[1] A*kkh*arâê apphâlettâ bhavai = apsarâyâ*s* *k*apu*t*ikâyâs âsphâlayitâ bhavati. I am not sure that I have hit the meaning; apsarâ is perhaps derived from apasârayati, the word is wanting in our dictionaries.

deeds, they enjoy the excellent pleasures of human life; viz. such a man eats at dinner-time, he drinks at drinking-time, he dresses himself at dressing-time, he goes to bed at the proper time, and sleeps at sleeping-time. Doing everything in its turn, he bathes, makes the offering (to the house-gods)[1], performs auspicious rites and expiatory acts, washes his head, hangs a wreath round his neck, adorns himself with precious stones and golden (trinkets), puts on (his head) a chaplet of flowers; with his body strengthened, with a wreath hanging down to the girdle of his loins, dressed in new clothes, his limbs and body anointed with sandal, (sitting) on a large throne in a lofty upper room (of his house), surrounded by women and a troop of followers, in the light (of torches) burning the whole night, under the great din of uninterrupted story-telling, dramatical plays, singing, and music, as beating of time, performing on the Vî*n*â, Tûryâ, the great drum, and Pa*t*upa*t*aha[2], he enjoys the excellent pleasures of human life. (55)

When he gives an order to one man, even four or five men will, without being asked, go up to him (and say): 'Speak, beloved of the gods, what shall we do? what shall we fetch? what shall we give you? what (trinket) shall we put on you? what is your heart's desire? what relishes your mouth?'

Unworthy men who see him will say: 'Forsooth, this man is a god; this man is the anointed of the gods, this man will support (us), as he supports

[1] Compare Kalpa Sûtra. Lives of the *G*inas, § 66, notes. Our commentator explains the prâyas*k*itta (expiatory acts) as ceremonies counteracting bad dreams.

[2] Compare Kalpa Sûtra, Lives of the *G*inas, § 14, part i, p. 223.

others.' But noble men who see him will say: 'This man does cruel actions, and maintains himself by them. His is the southern region, the hell, the dark fortnight[1]. In the future he will not easily obtain enlightenment.' (56)

(The conduct described in the preceding) part[2] is agreeable to some (heretical) monks, to some householders, to men governed by love of life. This conduct is unworthy, impure, void (of virtues), not holy, not right, not eradicating sins; it is not the road to perfection, liberation, Nirvâna, final delivery, not the road of those who are freed from all misery; it is thoroughly untrue, and bad.

This is the explanation of the first subject, viz. demerit. (57)

Now the explanation of the second subject, viz. merit, is as follows:

Here in the East, West, North, and South there are some men, viz. Âryas, non-Âryas, (all down to) ugly men. They own fields and houses, (&c., all as in II, 1, §§ 34-59, down to) reach final beatitude. (58)

(The conduct described in this) part is holy, right, (all just the reverse of what was said in § 58, down to) thoroughly true, and good. This is the explanation of the second subject, viz. merit. (59)

Now the explanation of the third subject, viz. the mixed state, is as follows:

Those who live in woods, in huts, near villages, (&c., all as above, § 21, down to) or blind. (The

---

[1] For according to the commentaries the worst of all regions is the south, the worst state of being that of denizens of hell, and the dark fortnight is the worse half of the month.

[2] *Thânê* = sthânam.

conduct described in this) part is not holy, (&c., all as in § 57, down to) thoroughly untrue, and bad.

This is the explanation of the third subject, viz. the mixed state. (60)

Now the explanation of the first subject, viz. demerit, is as follows:

Here in the East, West, North, and South live some men; they are householders, men of great desires, great undertakings, great possessions, unrighteous men, men practising unrighteousness, very unrighteous men, men speaking unrighteously, living unrighteously, thinking unrighteously, given to unrighteousness, men of unrighteous character and conduct, men gaining an unrighteous livelihood. (61)

They beat, cut[1], pierce, skin, are bloody-handed, violent, cruel, wicked, rash; they habitually practise bribery[2], fraud, deceit, imposture, dishonesty, and trickery; they are of bad character and morals, they are difficult to please, they do not abstain from killing living beings; as long as they live they do not abstain from wrath, (&c., all as in II, 1, 51, down to) the sin of wrong belief; nor from bathing, rubbing, painting, anointing themselves; from sounds, touches, tastes, colours, smells; from wreaths and ornaments; from cars, carriages, vehicles, litters, swings[3], coach and pair[4], palankins[5], beds, seats;

---

[1] These words are in the 2nd person sing. of the imperative, which, according to Pâ*n*ini III, 4, 2, may be used to express a repeated or habitual action.

[2] Utku*ñk*ana.

[3] Gilli, purushadvayôtkshiptâ *gh*ôllikâ.

[4] Thilli, explained: a vehicle drawn by a pair of mules; but, according to Leumann s.v., saddle.

[5] Sîyasandimâ*n*iyâ, explained *s*ibikâvi*s*êsha.

from enjoying a ride or drive; from having many followers; from buying, selling, doing business with Mâshas[1], half Mâshas, and Rupees; from silver, gold, riches, corn, precious stones, pearls, conches, stones, and corals; from using wrong weights and measures; from undertakings and slaughter; from working and making others work; from cooking and making others cook; from cutting, pounding, threatening, beating, binding, killing, and causing pain; and whatever other suchlike wicked and sinful actions of worthless men there be, that cause pains to other beings: these men do not abstain from them as long as they live. (62)

As some idle, cruel men wantonly injure Kalama[2], Masûra[3], sesamum, Mudga[4], beans, Nishpâva[5], Kulattha[6], Âlisanda[7], Êlami*kkh*a[8], so an idle, cruel man wantonly hurts partridges, ducks, quails, pigeons, francoline partridges, deer, buffaloes, boars, iguanas, tortoises, and snakes.

A man will (occasionally) severely punish even the smallest offence of his domestics, viz. a slave or messenger or hired servant or vassal[9] or parasite; e.g. punish him, pull out his hair, beat him, put him in irons, in fetters, in stocks, into prison, screw up in a pair of shackles (his hands and feet)

---

[1] Mâsha is a weight of gold.

[2] A sort of rice.

[3] A sort of pulse or lentil.

[4] A sort of kidney-bean.

[5] Probably Dolichos Sinensis.

[6] A sort of pulse, Dolichos Uniflorus.

[7] I cannot identify this plant, our dictionaries do not contain this or a similar word.

[8] This word ought perhaps to be divided in two; êlâ are cardamoms, but what mi*kkh*a is I cannot say.

[9] Bhâgilla = bhâgika, one who gets the sixth part of the products (e.g. of agriculture) of the work for which he is hired.

and break them, cut off his hands or feet or ears or nose or lips or head or face (?)[1], pierce his feet, tear out his eyes, teeth, tongue, hang him, brush him, whirl him round, impale him, lacerate him, pour acids (in his wounds), belabour him with cutting-grass, bind him to a lion's tail (!), or a bull's tail, burn him in a wood on fire, let him be devoured by crows and vultures, stop his food and drink, keep him a prisoner for life, let him die any of these horrid deaths. (63)

A man will (occasionally) severely punish even the smallest offence of his next of kin, viz. his mother or father or brother or sister or wife or sons or daughters or daughters-in-law; e.g. he ducks the offender in cold water, (&c., all as in § 18, down to) hateful in this world and the next. They suffer, grieve, blame themselves, grow feeble, are afflicted, and undergo great pain; they do not cease to cause others to suffer, grieve, &c., to slay and to put men in fetters[2]. (64)

And thus they are given to sensual pleasures, desire them, are held captive by them, passionately love them for four or five years, for six or ten years —the period may be shorter or longer[3]. Having enjoyed pleasures, having produced the effects of iniquity, having acquired the Karman of many sinful actions which generally bear him downwards, (he goes to the bottom of the hell)[4]. As a ball of

---

[1] The following two words, vêga*kkh*ahiya and aṅga*kkh*ahiya, I cannot translate.

[2] Compare § 55. [3] Compare § 21.

[4] These words from the end of the paragraph are to be supplied here, or rather the following passage has been inserted in the

iron or stone, when thrown in the water, sinks below the surface of the water till it stops at the bottom, so a man of the sort we are treating of, who is full of Karman, full of sin, full of demerit, full of disgrace[1], full of iniquity, full of wicked thoughts, deceit, imposture, and fraud, and, as a rule, kills animals, having died at the allotted time, will sink below this earth, and go to the bottom of the hell. (65)

These hells are round inside, square outside, on their floor razorlike arrows are thick-set (and covered with flowers), they are filled with perpetual darkness, never lighted up by the planets, moon, sun, Nakshatras, and stars; their floor is slippery with a coating of marrow, fat, flesh, blood, and matter, and besmeared with grease; these hells are impure, smelling detestably, black, of the colour of fire, very rugged, difficult to pass, horrid. And horrid are the pains in these hells. (66)

And those who are condemned to live in these hells, do not sleep nor slumber, nor do they get any consolation[2] or comfort or recreation or encouragement; but the denizens of hell there suffer exquisite, great, deep, hard, rough, violent, painful, sharp, intolerable agonies. (67)

As a tree growing on a hill falls by its weight when its roots are cut, on a low, rugged, inaccessible place, so a man of the sort we are treating of

---

middle of the sentence so that it is apparently cut in two, of which the first lacks the verb.

[1] There is, apparently, a pun in the three words vagga, paṅka, ayasa, for they mean also steel, mud, iron.

[2] Muim or sâyam or suim. The Dîpikâ has sruti. The following words are rati, dhriti, mati.

wanders from womb to womb, from birth to birth, from death to death, from hell to hell, from pain to pain. His is the southern region, the hell, the dark fortnight[1]. In the future he will not easily obtain enlightenment. (The conduct described in the preceding) part is unworthy, impure, (&c., see § 57, all down to) it is thoroughly untrue, and bad. This is the explanation of the first subject, viz. demerit. (68)

Now the explanation of the second subject, viz. merit, is as follows:

Here in the East, West, North, and South there are some such men as abstain from undertakings and possessions, righteous men, men practising righteousness, (&c., all as in § 58, but substitute 'righteous' for 'unrighteous,' down to) men gaining a righteous livelihood. They are of good character and morals, they are easy to please and good. They abstain from killing living beings as long as they live, (&c., all just the reverse of what was said in § 62, down to) whatever other suchlike wicked actions there be, that cause pains to other beings: these men abstain from them as long as they live. (69)

There are such monks as in walking carefully avoid to occasion the death of any living creature, (&c., all as in § 23, down to) as lead chaste lives regulated by the three Guptis, as are free from anger, pride, deceit, and greed, as are calm, tranquil, passionless, happy, free from the Âsravas, and bondage, without sorrow; as water does not adhere to a copper vessel, or collyrium to mother-of-pearl

[1] Compare § 56 and note 1 on p. 372.

(so sins find no place in them); their course is unobstructed like that of Life; like the firmament they want nothing to support them; like the wind they know no obstacles; their heart is pure like the water (of rivers or tanks) in autumn; like the leaves of a lotus they cannot be soiled by anything; their senses are well protected like the limbs of a tortoise; they are single and alone like the horn of a rhinoceros; they are free like birds; they are always waking like the fabulous bird Bhâru*nd*a; they are valorous like elephants, strong like bulls, difficult to attack like lions, steady and firm like Mount Mandara, deep like the ocean, mild like the moon, refulgent like the sun, pure like excellent gold; like the earth they patiently bear everything; like a well-kindled fire they shine in their splendour[1]. (70)

There are no obstacles anywhere for these reverend men. The obstacles have been declared to be of four kinds, viz. animals born from eggs, viviparous animals, things belonging to somebody, articles necessary for religious exercises[2]. In whichever direction they want to go, there they meet with no obstacle; but being pure and free, full of learning, control, and austerities, they purify themselves. (71)

These reverend men practise the following mode

---

[1] The same passage occurs, mutatis mutandis, in the Kalpa Sûtra, Lives of the *G*inas, § 118; see part i, p. 261, and notes 1 and 2.

[2] The author of the Dîpikâ offers diverse interpretations of this division of obstacles, which are apparently guesses and not based on a solid tradition. In the parallel passage of the Kalpa Sûtra, § 119, the division is according to: matter, space, time, and affects.

of living which just suffices for carrying on existence; they eat but one meal in two, three, four, five, six, seven days, in half a month, in one, two, three, four, five, six months; they (have vowed to) live on such food only as has been taken out of the cooking-vessel, or as is still in it, or the first kind of food in one place and the second in another, or on low food, or bad food, or food collected in small bits, or food given with a dirty hand, or the reverse, or food given with a hand, &c. soiled by it; they (have vowed to) accept such alms only as are within sight (when they beg), or are out of sight, as they are asked whether they would accept, or as they are not asked about, as are given with contempt, or the reverse; they beg (in houses where they are) unknown, or when food is scarce[1]; they accept only such things as are at hand, or only a limited number of gifts, or only a fixed quantity of food; they beg according to the rules (laid down for begging); they eat low food or bad food or tasteless food or badly tasting food or rough food or disagreeable food; they lead a low or mean life; they drink sour gruel, they eat nothing seasoned with ghee or similar materials; they do not drink liquors or eat meat, they do not eat highly-flavoured food; they eat standing, or supported by something, or sitting on a stool or an armchair; they lie down stretched out like a stick, or curved like a bent piece of wood[2]; they sit in the sun,

[1] The author of the Dîpikâ states that such monks beg in the morning.

[2] Laga*nd*asâi*n*ô. They lie in such a position that only their heels and head, or the back touch the ground.

they go naked[1]; they do not scratch themselves; they do not spit; they do not cut their beard, hair, and nails, they do not take any care of their person. (72)

Living in this way they practise many years *S*rama*n*ahood, and if then they fall sick, or even if they do not, they refuse food and omit many meals by abstaining from food. When they have attained that for whose sake they went about naked and bald-headed, did not bathe, nor clean their teeth, nor protect their head from the sun, nor wear shoes; they slept on the bare ground or a plank or a piece of wood, plucked out their hair, led a life of chastity, entered the houses of strangers, and bore, with indifference, success, failure, honour, disgrace, slights, blame, reviling, threatening, beating, all sorts of hardships[2], and the twenty-two calamities and troubles; (when they have attained their end), they reach, while they are breathing their last, the highest knowledge and faith, called Kêvala, which is infinite, supreme, unobstructed, unimpeded, complete and full; and then they obtain absolute perfection, enlightenment, deliverance, final beatitude, and put an end to all misery. (73)

Some become liberated[3] without assuming another body (after quitting the last). But others, having died at the allotted time, are, on account of a residue

---

[1] I leave out agattayâ or agamayâ, which is not explained in the Dîpikâ.

[2] Grâmaka*n*/aka, either the abuse met with in villages, or the objects of the senses (indriyagrâma).

[3] Bhayantârô bhavanti. Bhayantârô is explained: who go (gantâra*h*) from bhava to Môksha.

of (good) Karman, born in one of the regions of the gods. Among very beautiful, very splendid, very excellent, very glorious, very strong, very powerful, very happy (gods), they become very beautiful, very splendid, &c., gods[1]; their breasts shining with necklaces; their arms encumbered with bracelets and armrings; wearing ear-ornaments[2] which play on their cheeks, and earrings which hang down to the bracelets on their upper arms; wearing various ornaments on their hands; their crowns adorned with gay wreaths; putting on highly perfumed, excellent clothes; using beautiful, excellent garlands and ointments; their splendid body ornamented with a long down-reaching garland; having divine colours, touches, constitution (of the body), and rank; lighting up and illumining all ten quarters (of the universe) with their divine beauty, splendour, lustre, brightness, brilliancy, and light; beautiful when they go, beautiful when they rest, and happy also in the time to come.

(The conduct described in the preceding) part is worthy, pure, (&c., see § 57, all down to) it is thoroughly true, and good.

This is the explanation of the second subject, viz. merit. (74)

Now the explanation of the third subject, viz. the mixed state, is as follows:

Here in the East, West, North, and South there are some such men as have few desires, few undertakings, few possessions, righteous men, men

---

[1] The following description contains passages recurring in the Kalpa Sûtra, §§ 14, 15.

[2] Kar*n*apî*th*a.

practising righteousness, (&c., all as in § 69, down to) men gaining a righteous livelihood. They are of good character and morals, easy to please, and good. They abstain, as long as they live, from one kind of killing living beings, but they do not abstain from another, (&c., similar as in § 62, all down to) whatever suchlike wicked actions there be, that cause pains to other beings, from some of them these men abstain as long as they live, from others they do not abstain. (75)

There[1] are, for instance, followers of the *S*rama*n*as, who comprehend (the doctrine about) living beings and things without life, who understand (the difference between) virtues and sins, who are well grounded in (the knowledge of) the Âsravas, Sa*m*vara, the realisation and annihilation (of Karman), the subject of actions[2], bondage, and final liberation; who, without anybody to back them[3], cannot be seduced from the creed of the Nirgranthas by hosts of gods, Asuras, Nâgas, Suvar*n*as, Yakshas, Râkshasas, Kinnaras, Kimpurushas, Garu*d*as, and snake-gods; who have no doubts, scruples, or misgivings about this creed of the Nirgranthas, but have grasped its meaning, got hold of its meaning, got information about its meaning, ascertained its

[1] *S*îlânka says with regard to § 76: 'The MSS. of the text generally differ from one another in this passage; the text commented upon in the *T*îkâ does not agree with that of any MS. I therefore comment upon the text exhibited in one MS. If, therefore, my text does not agree with that (of the reader) he should not be alarmed.' All the MSS. I use have the same text, that of the commentator. It is characteristic of the way in which Harshakula, the author of the Dîpikâ, worked, that he copies *S*îlânka's above remark with some verbal alterations.

[2] Kriyâdhikara*n*a.

[3] Asahâyâ.

meaning, and understood its meaning; whose very marrow[1] of the bones has been penetrated by their love (for the Nirgrantha creed), avowing that it alone is true, and all others futile. They keep the bar[2] (of their gates) raised and their door open, having no desire to enter a stranger's house or his seraglio. They strictly keep the Pôsaha-fast on the fourteenth and eighth days of the month, on certain festivals[3], and on full-moon days. They provide the Nirgrantha *S*rama*n*as with pure acceptable food, drink, dainties and spices, with clothes, alms-bowls, blankets and brooms, with drugs and medicines, with stools, planks, beds, and couches. They purify themselves by practising the *S*îlavratas and Gu*n*avratas[4], the Virama*n*a, the Pratyâkhyâna,

---

[1] Here the commentator inserts the following story: In Râ*g*agr*i*ha lived a friar versed in magic arts; he carried off every woman he saw. On the citizens complaining about the rape, the king resolved to find out and punish the man. Catching sight of him at last on the fifth day, the king went after him till the friar disappeared in a hollow tree of the park, which led to an underground room. There the king followed and killed him. He released all the women whom the friar had captured. But one of them would not return to her husband, being desperately smitten with love for her seducer. On the advice of some wise men she was made to drink the friar's (pounded) bones mixed up with milk. This took the spell off her and cured her of her strange passion.

[2] Ûsiyaphaliha=u*kkh*ritaparigha. The commentator mistakes phaliha for spa*t*ika, and vainly labours to make out a sound meaning.

[3] Uddish*t*a.

[4] Concerning the Gu*n*avratas see Bhandarkar's Report, 1883, 1884, p. 114. The *S*îlavratas are apparently identical with the A*n*uvratas, ibidem. Hoernle translates this passage: by exercises in the moral restraints (imposed) by the religious vows as well as in the (general) renunciations and (special) Pôsaha-abstinences. Uvâsaga Dasâo, translation, p. 41.

the Pôsaha-fasts, and austerities which they have vowed to perform[1]. (76)

Living in this way they are for many years followers of the *S*rama*n*as, and if then they fall sick, or even if they do not, they refuse food and omit many meals by abstaining from food. Having confessed their sins and expiated them, and having attained perfection[2], they die at their allotted time, to be born again as gods in one of the regions of the gods, (&c., all as in § 74, down to) it is thoroughly true, and good.

This is the explanation of the third subject, viz. the mixed state. (77)

He who does not practise cessation[3] (from sin), is called a foolish man; he who practises cessation (from sin), is called a wise man; he who in one regard practises cessation (from sin) and in another does not, is said to be in a state partaking of that of a wise man and that of a foolish man.

The conduct of him who does not practise cessation from all (sins), is that of a man who kills living creatures; it is unworthy, (&c., all down to) thoroughly untrue, and bad.

The conduct of him who practises cessation from all (sins), is that of a man who does not kill living creatures; it is worthy, pure, (&c., all down to) thoroughly true, and good.

The conduct of a man who in one regard practises cessation from all (sins) and in another does not, is

---

[1] The same passage occurs below, 7, 4, and Aupapâtika Sûtra, § 124. Upâsakadasâ, § 66.

[2] Samâdhi, which is elsewhere explained by môksha, but in our case it cannot be final liberation, but a state of purity of the soul.

[3] Virati.

that of a man who kills some living creatures and does not kill others; it is worthy, pure, (&c., all down to) thoroughly true, and good. (78)

Those whom we have been treating of, fall under the two heads: merit and demerit; (the former is when the Self is) at rest, (the latter, when it is) in disturbance.

Now the explanation of the first subject is as follows:

There are enumerated three hundred and sixty-three philosophical schools[1]: those of the Kriyâvâda, those of the Akriyâvâda, those of the A*gñ*ânikavâda, and those of the Vainayikavâda. These (philosophers) teach final beatitude, they teach final deliverance, they speak as *S*râvakas, they speak as teachers of *S*râvakas[2]. (79)

All these philosophers, founders of systems of their own, differing in intellect, will, character, opinions, taste, undertakings, and plans, formed one large circle, and every one of them stood in his place.

One man took hold of a vessel quite full of

---

[1] According to the commentators there are 180 schools of Kriyâvâdins, 84 of Akriyâvâdins, 67 of A*gñ*ânikavâdins, and 32 of Vainayikavâdins. These numbers are arrived at by calculation, not by actual observation. E.g. the 180 possible schools of the Kriyâvâdins are calculated in the following way. The nine categories of the *G*ainas are: *g*îva, a*g*îva, âsrava, sa*m*vara, nir*g*arâ, pu*n*ya, pâpa, bandha, and môksha. Each of them may be regarded as svata*h* and parata*h*, as nitya and anitya with regard to kâla, î*s*vara, âtma, niyati, and svabhâva. By multiplying 9 successively in 2, 2, 5, we find 180 to be the number of possible schools of Kriyâvâdins.

[2] I.e. they learn these heresies from their teachers, and teach them to their pupils.

burning coals by an iron pair of tongs, and addressed those philosophers, founders of systems of their own, differing in intellect, (&c., all down to) undertakings and plans, in the following way: 'Heighho! ye philosophers, (&c., all down to) undertakings and plans! take this vessel full of burning coals and hold it for a minute in your hands! But do not take hold of it by a pair of tongs, nor put out the fire, nor come to the help of one of your own creed or of an alien creed (by putting out the fire, &c.); but fair and honest[1], without using any trick, stretch out your hands.' Having thus spoken, the man took hold of the vessel quite full of burning coals by an iron pair of tongs, and (offered to) put it in the hands of those philosophers. But the philosophers, (&c., all down to) undertakings and plans, held back their hands. On this the man addressed all the philosophers, (&c., all down to) undertakings and plans, in the following way: 'Heighho, ye philosophers, (&c., all down to) undertakings and plans! why do you hold back your hands?' 'Our hand will be burned.' 'What then, if it is burned?' '(We shall suffer) pain.' 'Because you are afraid of pain, you hold back your hands!' (So are all creatures averse to pain). This is a maxim of general application[2], it is a true principle, a religious reflection[3]; this maxim, this principle, this religious reflection holds good with regard to every (living being). Therefore those *S*rama*n*as and Brâhma*n*as who say that all sorts of living beings may be beaten or treated with violence or abused or tor-

---

[1] Niyâgapa*d*ivanna. [2] Tulâ.

[3] Samôsara*n*a = samavasara*n*a, explained: dharmavi*k*âra, viz. of the true adage: âtmavat sarvabhûtâni ya*h* pa*s*yati sa pa*s*yati.

mented or deprived of life, will in the time to come[1] suffer cutting or piercing, will experience birth, old age, death, conception in the womb, the Circle of Births, regeneration, existence as a foetus, the whole scale of mundane existences, and suffer a variety of pains[2]. (80)

They will many times undergo punishment, pulling out of the hair, threatening, putting in irons, (&c., similar as in § 63, all down to) whirling round; (they will witness) the death of their mothers, fathers, brothers, sisters, sons, daughters, and daughters-in-law; (they will experience) poverty, bad luck, company of hated people, separation from those whom they love, misery, and despair; they will again and again wander about in the beginningless and endless, immense wilderness of the fourfold Sa*m*sâra. They will not reach perfection, (&c., all down to) not put an end to all misery.—This is a maxim of general application, (&c., all down to) holds good with regard to every (living being). (81)

But those *S*rama*n*as and Brâhma*n*as who say that all sorts of living beings should not be beaten, &c., will in the time to come not suffer cutting, &c. They will not undergo many punishments, (&c., all just the reverse of what has been said in §§ 80, 81, down to) put an end to all misery. (82)

Thus those beings who practise the first twelve kinds of actions[3], have not attained perfection, (&c., all down to) have not, nor do, nor will put an end to all misery. (83)

---

[1] Âgantu. [2] Kalaṅkalîbhâva.

[3] Described in §§ 5–21. See p. 365, note 3.

But those beings who practise the thirteenth kind of action, have attained perfection, (&c., all down to) have put, or put, or will put an end to all misery. (84)

Thus a monk who obtains his soul's good and benefit, who guards himself, who (well directs the functions) of his soul, who well exerts himself, who protects himself (from evil), who is careful of himself, who saves himself (from the Samsâra), should withhold his soul (from the twelve kinds of committing sins). (85)

Thus I say.

THIRD LECTURE,

CALLED

KNOWLEDGE OF FOOD.

O long-lived (*G*ambûsvâmin)! I (Sudharman) have heard the following discourse from the Venerable (Mahâvîra). We now come to the Lecture called 'Knowledge of Food.' The contents of it are as follows:

Here in the East, West, North, and South there are, all in all, in the world four kinds of seed: seeds generated at the top (of the plant), at its root, at its knots, at its stem[1]. According to the seed and place

[1] The commentators here give the reading of the Nâgâr*g*unîyas: 'the growth of seeds of the plants is fivefold, viz. they grow from the top (of the plant), its root, its knots, its stem, and its beads;

(of growth) of these plants some beings—born in earth, originated in earth, and grown in earth, having in it their birth, origin, and growth, being impelled by their Karman, and coming forth in it on account of their Karman, growing there in particles of earth, the origin of various things—come forth as trees[1]. (1)

These living beings feed on the liquid substance[2] of these particles of earth, the origin of various things; these beings consume earth bodies, water-bodies, fire-bodies, wind-bodies, bodies of plants; they deprive of life the bodies of manifold movable and immovable beings; the destroyed bodies which have been consumed before, or absorbed by the rind, (are) digested and assimilated (by them). And the bodies of these (trees) which bring forth their different parts, are of manifold colours, smells, tastes, touches, forms, and arrangement of corporeal particles[3].

---

and some are of a sixth kind called sammûr*kh*ima' (i.e. those plants which are believed to be originated by the coalescing particles of the substance in which they grow, e.g. grass springing up on ground lately cleared by fire).—The various readings of the Nâgâr*g*unîyas are occasionally quoted in commentaries (see e.g. part i, p. 32, note 2). But I do not think that it has been satisfactorily made out who these Nâgâr*g*unîyas were.

[1] The meaning is, that souls who on account of their Karman are to be born as trees, previously are embodied in earth, and thence they are transferred by their Karman to the seed which brings forth the tree.

[2] Si*n*êha, explained: snigdhabhâva. In the sequel where plants are spoken of, I shall render this word by 'sap' or 'humours,' as the context may require.

[3] I.e. the food assimilated by the tree is the material of which its different parts, as root, stem, leaves, &c., are formed, and these parts are of manifold form, colours, &c.

These beings (animating trees) come into existence because of their Karman; so we are taught (by the Tîrthakaras, &c.) (2)

And again it has been said of old: some beings born in trees, originated by trees, sprung from trees, (&c., as in § 1, down to) springing from trees that originated in earth, come forth as trees originated by trees[1]. These beings feed on the sap of the trees originated in earth, (&c., all as in § 2, down to the end). (3)

(In the same way, and in nearly the same words, the offshoots of the trees mentioned in the preceding paragraph are treated of.) (4)

And again it has been said of old: some beings born in trees, (&c., all as above, down to) growing in trees, that are originated by trees, come forth as their roots, bulb, stem, branches, twigs, leaves, flowers, fruits, and seeds[2]. These beings feed on the sap of those trees originated by trees, (&c., all as in § 2, down to) and the bodies of the roots, bulb, stem, &c. are of manifold colours, (&c., all as in § 2, down to the end). (5)

(The four paragraphs that come next, 6–9, are identical with the preceding ones, except that 'creeper[3]' is substituted for 'tree.') (6–9)

(In the same way 'grass[4]' is treated in four paragraphs, but the whole is much abridged; then

---

[1] Apparently trees sprung from shoots, sprouts, aerial-roots, &c. are meant. They are considered as a class different from those whose offshoots they are.

[2] One soul, *gîva*, pervades the whole tree; it is the soul of the tree. Separate *gîvas*, however, reside in the roots, &c.

[3] A*ggh*ôruha = adhyârôha, explained in the Dîpikâ: vallîv*ri*ksha.

[4] T*ri*na.

it is said that 'herbs[1]' and 'plants[2]' are to be treated in four paragraphs each.) (10–15)

And again it has been said of old: some beings born in earth, (&c., all as in § 1, down to) growing there in particles of earth that are the origin of various things, come forth as Âya, Kâya, Kuha*n*a, Kandu, Uvvêhaliya, Nivvêhaliya, Êsava, Sa*kkh*a, *Kh*attaga, Vâsâ*n*iya[3]. (The rest as in § 2, but substitute the words Âya, &c. for 'trees.') Here there is only one paragraph, the remaining three do not apply here[4]. (16)

And again it has been said of old: some beings born in water, (&c., all as in §§ 1–11, substitute only 'water' for 'earth.' Thus we have four paragraphs for trees, four for creepers, four for grass, four for herbs, four for plants). (17)

Now it has been said of old: some beings born in water, (&c., all as above, down to) growing in particles of water that are the origin of various things, come forth as Udaga, Avaga[5], Pa*n*aga, Sêvâla[6], Kalambuya[7], Kasêruya[8], Ka*kkh*abhâ*n*iya, Uppala,

---

[1] Ôsahi = Ôshadhi. [2] Hariya = harita.

[3] All the commentators say about the words Âya, &c. (which offer some various readings in the MSS.), is that they denote particular plants (vanaspativi*s*êsha) which must be learned from people (who know them). I give the words in their Prâk*ri*t form, and do not attempt to transpose them into Sanskrit.

[4] For there are no Âyas originated by Âyas except through their seed.

[5] Avakâ, a grassy plant growing in marshy land, Blyxa Octandra.

[6] *S*aivâla, the aquatic plant Vallisneria.

[7] Kadamba, Nauclea Kadamba.

[8] Ka*s*êru, Scirpus Kysoor.

Pauma, Kumuya, Nal*in*a [1], Subhagasô*n*iya, Po*nd*ariya, Mahâpo*nd*ariya, Sayavatta, Sahassavatta, Kalhâra, Kôka*n*ada, Tâmarasa [2], as stalks and fibres of lotus, as Pukkhala [3], and Pukkhalatthibhaga. (The rest similar as in § 2.) (18)

And again it has been said of old : some beings come forth as movable beings from trees born in earth, from trees originated by trees, from the roots, (&c., down to) seeds produced by trees, originated by creepers born on trees, from creepers born on creepers, from the roots, &c. of creepers born on creepers, from grass [4], from herbs [4], from plants [4], from Âya, (&c., all down to) Kûra born in earth ; from trees born in water (the rest similar as with trees born in earth), from Udaga, (&c., all down to) Pukkhalatthibhaga born in water. (19)

These creatures feed on the sap of the trees, creepers, grass, herbs, plants, be they born in earth or water, on trees or creepers or grass or herbs or plants ; (the sap) of their roots, (&c., all down to) seeds, of Âyas, &c., of Udakas, &c. And these creatures consume earth-bodies, (&c., all as in § 2, down to) assimilated by them. And the bodies of these beings born of trees, creepers, grass, herbs, plants, their roots, &c., of Âyas, &c., of Udagas, &c., are of manifold colours, (&c., the rest as in § 2, down to the end). (20)

---

[1] The last four are well-known varieties of lotus, called in Sanskrit: utpala, padma, kumuda, nalina.

[2] The Sanskrit of the last seven items is: pu*nd*arîka, mahâpu*nd*arîka, *s*atapattra, sahasrapattra, kahlâra, kôkanada, and tâmarasa ; they are all varieties of lotus.

[3] Pushkara.

[4] This is to be detailed in the same way as with trees and creepers.

And again it has been said of old: a man and a woman combine in cohabitation in a cunnus, which was produced by their Karman, and there they deposit their humours. Therein are born the souls of different men, viz. of those born in Karmabhûmi [1], or in Akarmabhûmi, or in the minor continents, of Âryas and barbarians, as women or men or eunuchs, according to the semen and blood of the mother [2] and the other circumstances [3] (contingent on their coming into existence). These beings at first feed on the menses of the mother and the semen of the father, or both combined into an unclean, foul (substance). And afterwards they absorb with a part (of their bodies) the essence [4] of whatever food the mothers take. Gradually increasing and attaining to the proper dimensions of a foetus [5] they come forth from the womb, some as males, some as females, some as neuters. As long as they are babies, they suck the mother's milk; but when they grow older, they eat boiled rice, or gruel, or both movable and immovable beings. These beings consume earth-bodies, (&c., all as before, down to) assimilated by them. And the bodies of these men, viz. those born in Karmabhûmi, or Akarmabhûmi, or in the minor continents, of Âryas and barbarians, are of mani-

---

[1] Compare note 1, p. 225.

[2] Both are indicated in the text by bîga. According to Sîlâṅka, a male will be produced if the semen is in excess; a female, if the blood; a neuter, if they are equally balanced.

[3] Avakâsa. According to Sîlâṅka, a male is produced from the right side of the womb, a female from the left, a neuter from both together.

[4] Ôyam = ôgas.

[5] Paliyâgam, explained garbhaparipâka.

fold colours, (&c., all as in § 2, down to the end). (21)

(This paragraph is nearly identical with the preceding one, but substitute 'aquatic animals of five organs of sense, viz. fishes, (all down to)[1] porpoises,' for 'different men' in the beginning and the end. The following sentence in the middle is slightly different; it runs thus: 'as long as they are young, they feed on the mothers' humours, but when they grow older they eat plants, or both movable and immovable beings.') (22)

(This paragraph treats of) quadrupeds[2], terrestrial animals with five organs of sense, viz. solidungular animals, biungular animals, multiungular animals, and animals having toes with nails. (All as in the last paragraph, only 'as long as they are young, they feed on their mothers' milk.') (23)

(This paragraph treats of) reptiles moving on the breast, (being) terrestrial animals with five organs of sense, viz. snakes, huge snakes[3], Âsâlika, and dragons[4]. (All as before, but the following passage is different.) Some bring forth eggs, some bring forth living young ones; some come out of the egg as males, some as females, some as neuters. As long as they are young, they live on wind. (The rest as above.) (24)

(This paragraph treats of) terrestrial animals with five organs of sense, walking on their arms, viz. iguanas, ichneumons, porcupines, frogs, chameleons,

---

[1] See Uttarâdhyayana XXXVI, 173; above, p. 223.

[2] Compare Uttarâdhyayana XXXVI, 180, ibidem.

[3] Agagara, literally serpents which devour goats.

[4] Mahôraga. According to the Guzeratî gloss these snakes are a thousand yôganas long.

Khôras, Gharakôillas [1], Vissa*m*bharas [2], rats, mangooses, Païlâiyas, cats, *G*ôhas, *K*âuppâiyas [3]. (The rest as in the last paragraph.) (25)

(This paragraph treats of) aerial animals with five organs of sense: birds with membranous wings, birds with feathered wings, birds with wings in the shape of a box, and birds (which sit on) outspread wings [4]. (All as before; only the following passage is different): 'As long as they are young, they are hatched by their mothers' warmth.' (The rest as above.) (26)

And again it has been said of old: there are beings of manifold birth and origin, (&c., all as in § 1, down to) growing there on the animate or inanimate bodies of manifold movable or immovable creatures, come forth as parasites [5]. These beings feed on the humours of various movable and immovable creatures, &c. And the bodies of these movable and immovable parasites are of manifold colours, (&c., as above). (27)

In the same way vermin generated in filthy substances [6] and in the skin of living animals [7] are to be treated of. (28, 29)

And again it has been said of old: there are some beings of manifold birth and origin, (&c., all as in § 1,

---

[1] G*ri*hakôkila, probably identical with g*ri*hagôlika, a lizard.

[2] Visva*m*bhara is given in the smaller Petersburg Dictionary as the name of a scorpion or some similar animal. However, it must denote here some other animal.

[3] This may be *k*atushpâdika, quadruped; but then the word must be taken in a restricted sense, perhaps, small quadrupeds.

[4] See Uttarâdhyayana XXXVI, 187; above, p. 224. Perhaps beetles and butterflies are intended by the two last kinds of pakshins?

[5] A*n*usûya = anusûta or anusyûta.

[6] Durûvasa*m*bhava. [7] Khuruduga.

down to) growing thereon (or in) the animate or inanimate bodies of manifold movable or immovable creatures as that (water)-body[1], which is produced by wind, condensed by wind, and carried along by wind; it goes upwards, when there is an upward wind; it goes downwards, when there is a downward wind; it goes in a horizontal direction, when there is a horizontal wind; (its varieties are) hoar-frost, snow, mist, hailstones, dew, and rain. These beings feed on the humours of these manifold movable and immovable creatures, &c. And the bodies of these (water-lives, viz.) hoar-frost, &c., produced by manifold movable or immovable creatures, are of manifold colours, (&c., as above)[2]. (30)

And again it has been said of old: some beings, born in water, (&c., all similar as in § 1, down to) come forth in water(-bodies) in the water produced by manifold movable or immovable beings. These beings feed on the humours of the water(-bodies) produced by manifold movable and immovable creatures. (The rest similar as above.) (31)

And again it has been said of old: some beings, born in water, (&c., all similar as in § 1, down to) come forth in water-bodies produced by other water-bodies. These beings feed on the humours of those other water-bodies produced by water-bodies. (The rest similar as above.) (32)

And again it has been said of old: some beings, born in water, (&c., all similar as in § 1, down to) come forth as movable creatures in the water

[1] There is apparently no predicat in this sentence.

[2] This paragraph gives the 'scientific' explanation of the way by which water-bodies or the bodies of water-lives are produced by wind.

produced by water-bodies. These beings feed on the humours of the water(-bodies) produced by water. (The rest similar as before.) (33)

And again it has been said of old: some beings, of various birth and origin, (&c., all as in § 1, down to) come forth as fire-bodies in the manifold animate or inanimate bodies of movable or immovable creatures[1]. These beings feed on the manifold movable or immovable creatures. (The rest similar as before.)

The remaining three paragraphs are similar (to those treating of) water-bodies. (34)

(This paragraph treats of wind-bodies in the same way as the preceding ones treated of fire-bodies; like it, it consists of four paragraphs). (35)

And again it has been said of old: some beings, of various birth and origin, (&c., all as in § 1, down to) come forth, in the manifold animate and inanimate bodies of movable and immovable creatures[2], as earth, gravel, &c. Here the following verses (from the Uttarâdhyayana XXXVI, 74-77) are to be made use of:

1. Earth, gravel, sand, stones, rocks, rock-salt, iron, copper, tin, lead, silver, gold, and diamond;

2. Orpiment, vermilion, realgar, Sâsaka, antimony, coral, Abhrapa*t*ala, Abhravâluka; these are varieties of gross (earth-)bodies, and precious stones.

---

[1] E.g. when two bulls or elephants rush upon one another, sparks of fire are seen issuing from their horns or teeth. Fire is produced when two pieces of wood or stone are rubbed one against the other.

[2] According to the commentators, earth-bodies are produced in the shape of precious stones, in the head of snakes, of pearls in the teeth (sic) of elephants, and so in reeds, &c.

3. Hyacinth, natron, Aṅka, crystal, Lôhitâksha, emerald, Masâragalla, Bhu*g*amô*k*aka, and sapphire;

4. *K*andana, red chalk, Ha*m*sagarbha, Pulaka, and sulphur; *K*andraprabha, lapis lazuli, *G*alakânta, and Sûryakânta.

These beings feed on the humours of these manifold movable and immovable beings. (The rest as above.)

The remaining three paragraphs are similar (to those treating of) water-bodies. (36)

And again it has been said of old: all sorts of living beings, of manifold birth, origin, and growth, born in bodies, originated in bodies, grown in bodies, feeding on bodies, experience their Karman, are actuated by it, have their form and duration of life determined by Karman, and undergo changes through the influence of Karman. This you should know, and knowing it you will be careful and circumspect with regard to your food, and always exert yourself. (37)

Thus I say.

FOURTH LECTURE,

CALLED

RENUNCIATION OF ACTIVITY.

O long-lived (*G*ambûsvâmin)! I (Sudharman) have heard the following Discourse from the Venerable (Mahâvîra). We now come to the Lecture called 'Renunciation of Activity.' The contents of it are as follows:

It is the Self that may[1] not renounce (activity), that may be accustomed to act, that may adhere to errors, that may be prone to sin, that may be thoroughly ignorant, that may be thoroughly stolid[2], that may not consider the operations[3] of mind, speech, and body, that may not avoid and renounce sins.

The Venerable One has said, 'He (i. e. the Self) is uncontrolled, unresigned, does not avoid and renounce sins, is active, careless, prone to sin, thoroughly ignorant, thoroughly stolid. Though a fool does not consider[4] the operations of his mind, speech, and body, nor does see even a dream[5]; still he commits sins[6]. (1)

The opponent says to the teacher: 'There can be no sin, if (the perpetrator of an action) does not possess sinful thoughts, speech, and functions of the body, if he does not kill, if he has no internal organ, if he does not consider the operations of mind, speech, and body, if he does not see even a dream.'

---

1 'May' is to render yâvi = *k*âpi. This word is used here to indicate that the reverse is true in other cases. This paragraph emphasises the *G*aina doctrine that the Self or âtman is the direct cause of all actions of an individual being, in opposition to the Sâṅkhya philosophers who maintain the absolute inactivity of the purusha, and to the Bauddhas who deny the existence of a separate âtman altogether.

2 Literally, sleeping (sutta = supta).

3 Literally, speeches (vakka = vâkya).

4 We ought, perhaps, to translate: if he is not conscious of, &c.

5 I.e. when consciousness is fainter than in a dream.

6 The doctrine of the *G*ainas is that Karman is the result of the action of every being, even of those whose intellect or consciousness is not developed, as with the êkêndriyas or beings who possess but one organ of sense. The opponent, however, maintains that only conscious actions of intelligent beings bring about Karman. This question is discussed in the following paragraphs.

What is the meaning of the opponent in making this statement? 'When there is a sinful mind, there is sin of the mind; when there is sinful speech, there is sin of the speech; when there is a sinful body, there is sin of the body. When one kills, possesses an internal organ, and considers the operations of mind, speech, and body, when one sees even a dream, then there is sin. Only he who has these qualities can commit sin.' The opponent goes on to say, 'Those who say: There is sin, though (the perpetrator of an action) does not possess sinful thoughts, speeches, and functions of the body, though he does not kill, though he does not possess an internal organ, though he does not consider the operations of mind, speech, and body, and though he does not see even a dream,—those who say this, are wrong.' (2)

Here the teacher says to the opponent: 'It is true what I have just said: there is sin, though (the perpetrator of the action) do not possess sinful thoughts, (&c., all as above, down to) though he do not see even a dream.' 'What is the reason thereof?' (The Âkârya says)[1]: 'The Venerable One has assigned the six classes of living beings as the reason: the earth-lives, (&c., all down to) movable beings. With regard to these six classes of living beings, the Self does not avoid and renounce sins, he is wicked and does harm through cruelty: (this holds good with regard to the five cardinal sins:) killing of living beings, &c. (and the passions): anger, &c. (down to) the sin of wrong belief.' (3)

(The Âkârya says): 'The Venerable One has illustrated this by the example of a murderer:

[1] These words here and in the sequel are in Sanskrit; they probably are a gloss.

a murderer (who hates) a householder or his son or the king or his servant, resolves, on an occasion offering, to enter (the victim's house) and to kill him when he finds an opportunity[1]. Is not this murderer who has formed this resolution[2], (a man) who, day and night, whether sleeping or waking, is full of hostility and wrong; who is wicked and does harm through cruelty? An unbiassed opponent before whom this is laid, will answer: Indeed, he is!' (4)

(The Â*k*ârya says): 'As this murderer who has formed the above resolution is a man who (&c., all as in § 4, down to) does harm through cruelty—(and this holds good with regard to the five cardinal sins:) killing of living beings, &c. (and the passions:) anger, &c., (down to) the sin of wrong belief—so it has been said of him by the Venerable One: he[3] is uncontrolled, unresigned, he does not avoid and renounce sins, he is active, careless, prone to sin, thoroughly ignorant, thoroughly stolid. Though a fool does not consider the operations of his mind, speech, and body, nor does see even a dream, still he commits sins. (5)

As a murderer who entertains (murderous) intentions towards a householder, &c., is a man who (&c., all as in § 4, down to) does harm through cruelty; so an ignorant man who entertains (cruel) intentions towards all sorts of living beings, is a man

[1] The Nâgâr*g*unîyas have another reading (where, is not stated by *S*îlâṅka): If he sees no opportunity, or his proposed victim is always on his guard, he does not kill him, but he resolves in his mind: If I get an opportunity, or I find that man off his guard, I shall certainly kill him.

[2] The original repeats the preceding passage in full. I abridge it here and in the sequel.

[3] I.e. every soul, even that of a being with but one organ of sense.

who (&c., all as in § 4, down to) does harm through cruelty. (6)

(An opponent might object): This is no good reasoning. (For) there are many living beings which one, during one's whole life, never saw, nor heard of, nor cared for, nor took notice of. Towards these beings, therefore, one cannot (be said to) entertain (murderous) intentions, nor to be one who, day and night, whether sleeping or waking, is full of hostility and wrong, (&c., the rest as in § 4). (7)[1]

(The Â*k*ârya says): The Venerable One has refuted this by two illustrations, one of a sentient being, the other of a senseless being. The first is as follows: A sentient being, possessing five organs of sense and a developed internal organ, may with regard to the six classes of living beings, viz. earth-bodies, (all down to) movable beings, impose some restriction upon himself; (e.g.) that he will meet his wants, or have them met by others, by means of earth-bodies only. His intention is: I shall meet my wants, or have them met by others, by means of earth-bodies only. His intention is not (to make use of) this or that (particular earth-body): he meets his wants, or has them met by others, by means of earth-bodies in general. With regard to them,

[1] *S*îlâṅka here makes it clear that the discussion, in the preceding paragraphs, is carried on in the form of a syllogism of five parts established in Hindu logics. § 1 contains the proposition, pratig*ñ*â, § 3 the cause, hêtu, § 4 the exemplification, udâhara*n*a or d*ri*sh*t*ânta, § 5 the upanaya or that part which shows that the hêtu is in the subject of the syllogism, and § 6 the conclusion, nigamana. We thus see how deeply rooted in, and how genial to, the mind of the Hindus was the pa*ñk*âvayavam anumânam or syllogism of five parts; for the author conforms to it, I dare say, unintentionally.

therefore, he is uncontrolled, unrestrained, does not avoid and renounce sins. The same applies to the remaining five classes of living beings.—Some one may meet his wants, or have them met by others, by means of the six classes of living beings. His intention is: I shall meet my wants, or have them met by others, by means of the six classes of living beings; it is not: by means of some particular beings. He meets his wants, (&c.) by means of living beings in general. With regard to them, therefore, he is uncontrolled, &c. (This holds good with the five cardinal sins): killing of living beings, &c., (and with the passions): anger, (&c., all down to) the sin of wrong belief. The Venerable One has said that such a creature, (&c., all as in § 1, down to) commits sins. (8)

The illustration of senseless beings is as follows: Senseless beings, viz. earth-bodies, (&c., all down to) plants, to which must be added, as a sixth item, some movable beings, which have no reason nor consciousness, nor intellect, nor mind, nor speech, in order to do something, or to have it done by others, or to consent to others' doing it; these benighted creatures (are to be considered as murderers), are full of hostility and wrong (all as in § 4)[1] against all

[1] If the passage were printed in full, the most glaring contradictions would stare the reader in the face. The cause hereof is not that the passage cannot correctly be rendered, but that the authors of the Sûtras always make use of set phrases whether all parts of them suit the case in hand or not. Sometimes we can avoid downright nonsense by selecting a somewhat different rendering from what was given in another part of the book; and so I do in the last sentence of this paragraph. But this is only a makeshift.

sorts of living beings. (This holds good with the five cardinal sins :) killing of living beings, &c., (and with the passions, all down to) the sin of wrong belief. Know this: though these beings have neither mind nor speech, yet as they cause pain, grief, damages, harm, and injury, they must be regarded as not abstaining from causing pain, &c. (9)

Thus even senseless beings are reckoned instrumental in bringing about slaughter of living beings, (&c., all down to) the sin of wrong belief. Beings, whatever their origin, who were sentient (in one existence) will become senseless ones (in another) and vice versâ. Not getting rid of, nor shaking off, nor annihilating, nor destroying their Karman, the thoroughly wicked and ignorant wander from the body of a senseless being into that of sentient ones, or from the body of a sentient being into that of senseless ones, or from the body of a sentient being into that of another, or from the body of a senseless being into that of another. The sentient beings and the senseless ones, both are wrong in their conduct and commit sins through cruelty. The Venerable One has said that such a (creature) is uncontrolled, (&c., all as in § 1, down to) commits sins. (10)

(The opponent asks): 'What must one do or cause to be done, in order to become controlled and restrained, to avoid and renounce sins?' (The Â*k*ârya answers): The Venerable One has declared that the cause (of sins) are the six classes of living beings, earth-lives, &c. As I feel pain, so they do. Therefore they should not be injured or killed[1].

[1] I here abridge the text which is identical with II, 1, 48 ff., p. 351.

This constant, permanent, eternal, true Law has been taught by wise men who comprehend all things. Thus a monk abstains from (the five cardinal sins): slaughter of living beings, &c., (and of vices, all down to) the sin of wrong belief. He does not clean his teeth with a tooth-brush, he does not accept collyrium, emetics, and perfumes. Such a monk does not act nor kill, he is free from wrath, pride, deceit, and greed, he is calm and happy. The Venerable One says that such a (monk) is well controlled and restrained, does avoid and renounce sins, is not active, but careful and thoroughly wise. (11)

Thus I say.

FIFTH LECTURE,

CALLED

FREEDOM FROM ERROR.

A very clever (monk) who practises the vow of chastity, should not adopt the following (heretical) doctrines, nor behave badly in this religion. (1)

He should not believe that (this world) is without beginning or without end, eternal or not eternal, according to the argumentation (of heretics)[1]. (2)

From these alternatives you cannot arrive at

---

[1] The *G*ainas decide all such questions with the help of the syâdvâda, which in an admirable way removes all difficulties; e.g. the world is eternal as far as that part is concerned which is

truth; from these alternatives you are, certainly, led to error. (3)

One should not say: that there will be an end of beings who (know and) teach the truth[1]; nor that all beings are not alike, nor that they shall be in (perpetual) bondage, or (that the prophets are) eternal. (4)

From these alternatives you cannot arrive at the truth, &c. (see verse 3). (5)

One should not say: the guilt of killing small and great animals is the same, or not the same. (6)

From these alternatives, &c. (7)

One should know that those who accept things especially prepared for them[2], will be affected by demerit (in some cases), or will not be affected (where it is allowed by scripture). (8)

From these alternatives, &c. (9)

One should not maintain the identity of the audârika[3], âhârika, and kârmana bodies, nor

---

the substratum of the idea (sâmânya) 'world'; it is not eternal as far as its ever-changing state is meant.

[1] *Sâstârah*, teachers, here those who reach perfection. The meaning is that the world would become empty if all beings should reach perfection. This should not be maintained, nor the opposite opinion, that some beings are qualified for Nirvâna and others not.

[2] Ahâkammâni, see p. 131, note 7.

[3] The Gainas assume that each individual possesses five bodies: (1) audârika, or the body that is seen; (2) kârmana, receptacle of Karman, it is composed of Karman particles; (3) taigasa, a body composed of particles of fire, it causes digestion; (4) âhâraka, a subtile body of the soul, with which he goes to distant places (e.g. when a katurdasapûrvin goes to the Kêvalin to clear up some doubt); (5) vaikriya, a subtile body which can be changed at will. All these 'bodies,' except the first, are what in common language are called spirits or souls. We have here a Hindu counterpart of the belief in the plurality of souls shared

that everything cannot everywhere come into existence[1], nor that it can. (10)

From these alternatives, &c. (11)

Do not maintain that the world does not exist, maintain that it exists. (12)

Do not maintain that *G*îva and A*g*îva do not exist, but that they exist. (13)

Do not maintain that Dharma and Adharma do not exist, but that they exist. (14)

Do not maintain that bondage and liberation do not exist, but that they exist. (15)

Do not maintain that virtue and vice[2] do not exist, but that they exist. (16)

Do not maintain that Âsrava and the stoppage of Âsrava do not exist, but that they exist. (17)

Do not maintain that the experiencing of the effect, and the annihilation of Karman do not exist, but that they exist. (18)

Do not maintain that activity and non-activity do not exist, but that they exist. (19)

---

by many ancient and modern nations. Compare the following verses quoted in Tylor, Origin of Culture, Chapter XI:

'Bis duo sunt homini, manes, caro, spiritus, umbra:
Quattuor haec loci bis duo suscipiunt.
Terra tegit carnem, tumulum circumvolat umbra
Manes Orcus habet, spiritus astra petit.'

I am inclined to believe that the idea of the âhâraka and vaikriya *s*arîras is developed from the popular belief that the soul in sleep leaves the body and travels far away. Compare also the Sâṅkhya terms vaik*ri*ta and tai*g*asa, Garbe, Die Sâ*m*khya-Philosophie, pp. 236, 249.

[1] According to the commentator this is said against the Sâṅkhya philosophy, for as everything is an effect of Prak*ri*ti, and Prak*ri*ti is present everywhere, everything may come into existence everywhere.

[2] Pu*n*yam and pâpam. The one is the good Karman (*s*ubham karmapudgalam); the other, the bad.

Do not maintain that anger and pride do not exist, but that they exist (20)

Do not maintain that deceit and greed do not exist, but that they exist. (21)

Do not maintain that love and hate do not exist, but that they exist. (22)

Do not maintain that the fourfold Circle of Births does not exist, but that it exists. (23)

Do not maintain that there are no gods and goddesses, but that there are. (24)

Do not maintain that there is no such thing as perfection and non-perfection, but that there is such a thing. (25)

Do not maintain that there is no place exclusively reserved for those who attain to perfection, but that there is such[1]. (26)

Do not maintain that there are no pious and wicked men, but that there are. (27)

Do not maintain that there is no such thing as good and bad, but that there is good and bad. (28)

The theory will not work that (a man is always) good, or (always) bad. The wrongly instructed *S*rama*n*as do not comprehend the (soul's) bondage[2] (through Karman). (29)

(Do not assert) that everything is imperishable, or full of pains, nor that criminals should be put to death or not be put to death; one should not speak in this way. (30)

Do not assert that those men are well-behaved monks who lead a pure life, and that those others lead an impure life. (31)

---

[1] See Uttarâdhyayana XXXVI, 62, 63, p. 212.

[2] Vêra = vaira, explained karmabandha.

A wise monk should not say: we get alms (from this householder) or we do not; but he should improve his chances for final liberation[1]. (32)

A monk should conform himself to these opinions taught by the *G*inas, and wander about till he reaches final liberation. (33)

Thus I say.

SIXTH LECTURE,

CALLED

ÂRDRAKA[2].

Gô*s*âla.

'Listen, Ârdraka[3], to what (Mahâvîra) has done. At first he wandered about as a single monk: but now he has surrounded himself by many monks, and teaches every one of them the Law at length. (1)

---

[1] Santimaggam *k*a vûhaê = *s*ântimârga*m* *k*a v*rim*hayêt.

[2] The commentators relate a romantic story about prince Ârdraka, which need not be repeated here. Suffice it to say that he became monk, and after many adventures held the disputation which forms the subject of our lecture. After having vanquished his opponents, he was about to join Mahâvîra, when a newly-tamed elephant broke his chain, rushed on him, but just in front of him went down on his knees and paid him reverence. King *S*rê*n*ika witnessed this scene, and wondered how the elephant could have broken his chains. Ârdraka replied that it was still more strange that a man could break the fetters which worldliness had fastened upon him. The whole story must be very old, for it is epitomised in ten gâthâs by the author of the Niryukti.—The names of the opponents not stated in the text of the verses are supplied from the commentaries.

[3] This name is spelt either Ârdra or Ârdraka, Adda in Prâk*ri*t.

'The inconstant man has decided upon this mode of life[1]: to stand up in a crowd of men, surrounded by monks, and to teach his doctrines for the benefit of many people. Therefore his former and his present life are not of a piece. (2)

'Either to live as a single mendicant (was right conduct) or his present life; therefore both do not agree with each other.'

Ârdraka.

"His past, present, and future lives agree with each other; for he is really always single and alone (though he be now surrounded by many followers). (3)

"For if a *S*rama*n*a or Brâhma*n*a who causes peace and security, comprehends the nature of movable and immovable living beings and explains it in a crowd numbering thousands, he realises singleness, remaining in the same mental condition as before[2]. (4)

"It is no sin to teach the Law, if (he who teaches it) is patient and resigned, subdues his senses, avoids bad speech, and uses virtuous speech. (5)

"He who (teaches) the great vows (of monks) and the five small vows (of the laity[3]), the five Âsravas and the stoppage of the Âsravas, and control, who avoids Karman in this blessed life of *S*rama*n*as, him I call a *S*rama*n*a." (6)

---

[1] According to the commentators, Gô*s*âla intimates that Mahâvîra had found it very inconvenient to live alone, because he was then exposed to many injuries; so he set up as a Tîrthakara.

[2] Taha*kk*e = tathâr*k*a. Âr*k*â is here explained as equal to lê*s*yâ.

[3] A*n*uvrata. They are a modification of the great vows, intended for the laity. See Bhandarkar's Report, p. 114.

Gôsâla.

('As your Law makes it no sin for Mahâvîra to surround himself by a crowd of disciples), so according to our Law an ascetic, who lives alone and single, commits no sin if he uses cold water, eats seeds, accepts things prepared for him, and has intercourse with women.' (7)

Ârdraka.

"Know this: those who use cold water, eat seeds, accept things especially prepared for them, and have intercourse with women, are (no better than) householders, but they are no *S*rama*n*as. (8)

"If those who eat seeds, use (cold) water, and have intercourse with women, are admitted to be *S*rama*n*as, then householders too are *S*rama*n*as; for they do the same things[1]. (9)

"Monks who eat seeds and use cold water, who beg alms as a means of living, will, though they leave their relations, be born again and again, and will not put an end to mundane existence." (10)

Gôsâla.

'In making this statement you blame all philosophers alike!'

Ârdraka.

"Every philosopher praises his own doctrines and makes them known. (11)

"*S*rama*n*as and Brâhma*n*as blame one another when they teach (their doctrines). (The truth, they

---

[1] I.e. if the characteristic mark of a *S*rama*n*a is to wander about without a companion, and to bear all sorts of hardship, then householders are included in this definition; for some of them also wander about without a companion and bear the same hardships.

say,) is all on their side; there is none on that of the opponents. But we blame only the (wrong) doctrines and not at all (those who entertain them). (12)

"We do not detract from anybody because of his personal qualities; but we make known the path pointed out in our creed. I have been taught the supreme, right path by worthy, good men. (13)

"If a well-controlled man, afraid of injuring any movable or immovable living beings, above, below, or on earth, condemns (evil deeds), he does not at all blame (anybody) in this world." (14)

Gôsâla.

'Out of fear your *S*rama*n*a will not stay in houses for travellers or in public garden-houses; for in such places he would meet with many clever people, with lower or nobler men, with talkative or silent ones. (15)

'He will not stay there because he fears lest some monks, wise, well instructed, learned men, who are well versed in the sacred texts and their meaning, should put questions to him.' (16)

Ârdraka.

"Doing nothing without a purpose, nor without consideration, neither on the behest of the king nor from fear of anybody, he answers questions or not (according to the circumstances); but he (answers) worthy people with a definite purpose (in his mind)[1]. (17)

---

[1] As the commentators explain: he is actuated by the Karman, by virtue of which he has become a prophet (tîrthakaranâma-karman); and this Karman must take effect and so be annihilated.

"He, the wise man, impartially teaches (the Law) whether he goes (to his pupils) or not; because unworthy men have fallen from the true faith, he does not go to places (frequented by them)." (18)

Gôsâla.

'As a merchant desirous of gain (shows) his wares and attracts a crowd to do business, in a similar way (acts) the *S*rama*n*a *G*ñâtr*i*putra. This is what I think and calculate about it.' (19)

Ârdraka.

"(Mahâvîra) acquires no new (Karman), he annihilates the old, avoiding wrong opinions; and thus the saviour said to others: Herein is contained the vow (leading to) Brahman (i. e. Môksha); this is the gain which a *S*rama*n*a is desirous of. Thus I say. (20)

"A merchant kills living beings and desires property; not leaving his kinsmen, he attracts a crowd in order to do business. (21)

"Desiring riches and addicted to sensuality, merchants wander about to earn their living. But we (say) that they are passionately fond of pleasures, unworthy, and desiring the enjoyment of love. (22)

"They do not abstain from slaughter and the acquirement of property, they are in bondage and full of wickedness; and their gain of which you spoke, will be the endless Circle of Births and pains manifold[1]. (23)

"They do not always make profit, nor does it last

---

[1] *N*êhâ or *n*êdhâ. According to *S*îlâṅka it is = na iha: 'not even here (do they find the profit they seek).' I think it may be the Prâkr*i*t of anêkadhâ. It may, however, stand for snêhâ*h*, in which case the meaning would be: love's (reward will be) pain.

for ever; they meet with both results (success and failure) in their quest of gain[1]. The profit (of the teacher), however, has a beginning, but no end; the saviour and sage shares his profit (with others). (24)

"Him who kills no (living beings), who has compassion on all creatures, who is well grounded in the Law, and causes the truth of the Law to be known, him you would equal to those wicked men! This is the outcome of your folly." (25)

A Buddhist[2].

'If (a savage) thrusts a spit through the side of a granary[3], mistaking it for a man; or through a gourd, mistaking it for a baby, and roasts it, he will be guilty of murder according to our views. (26)

'If a savage[4] puts a man on a spit and roasts him, mistaking him for a fragment of the granary; or a

---

[1] Vayanti te dô vi gu*n*ê*x*dayammi = vra*g*anti tê dvâv api gu*n*âv udayê. The usual reading adopted by the commentators is gu*n*ô for gu*n*ê. They translate: vadanti tê dvau vigatagu*n*ôdayau bhavata iti: (the experts) say that both (kinds of profit) are without value and duration. It is obvious that this interpretation is wrong.

[2] Ârdraka after having put down Gô*s*âla is met, on his way to Mahâvîra, by Buddhists who engage him in the following discussion.

[3] Pi*nn*âgapi*nd*i. The commentators explain pi*nn*âga (= pi*n*yâka) by khala, and pi*nd*i by bhinnaka (?) or *s*akala. *S*îlâṅka gives the following explanation. During a struggle with savage men (mlê*kkh*a) some one runs away and throws his cloak off on a granary. An enemy in pursuit of that man mistakes it for him and takes hold of it, together with the part of the granary.—This interpretation looks absurd; but it will appear not so if we remember that granaries are beehive-shaped reservoirs made of sun-baked mud or wattle and mud; compare Grierson, Bihâr Peasant Life, p. 17.

[4] Milakkhu = mlê*kkh*a.

baby, mistaking him for a gourd, he will not be guilty of murder according to our views. (27)

'If anybody thrusts a spit through a man or a baby, mistaking him for a fragment of the granary, puts him on the fire, and roasts him, that will be a meal fit for Buddhas to break fast upon. (28)

'Those who always feed two thousand worthy monks, acquire great merit[1] and become powerful gods in Arûpa (dhâtu)[2].' (29)

Ârdraka.

"Well-controlled men cannot accept (your denial of) guilt incurred by (unintentionally) doing harm to living beings. It will cause error and no good to both who teach such doctrines and who believe them. (30)

"A man who knows the nature of movable and immovable living beings, above, below, and on earth, who is afraid of injuring them and abstains from wicked deeds, may speak and act (in accordance with our Law); he will not be guilty of any (sin). (31)

"It is impossible to mistake (a fragment of the granary) for a man; only an unworthy man can say it. How can (the idea of a man) be produced by a fragment of the granary? Even to utter this is an untruth. (32)

"Do not use such speech by means of which you do evil; for such speech is incompatible with virtues. No ordained (monk) should speak empty words[3]. (33)

---

[1] Pu*nn*akhandha = pu*n*yaskandha.

[2] Âroppa. This is apparently derived from Arûpa as rendered in the text. Arûpadhâtu is the highest heaven of the Buddhists; compare Burnouf, Le Lotus de la Bonne Loi, p. 807.

[3] Urâla = udâra, here explained nissâra, void of sense.

"Oh! you have explored this subject; you have thoroughly examined the consequences of acts[1] of living beings; your (fame) reaches the Eastern and Western oceans; you view (the universe as if) it stood on the palm of your hands! (34)

"Thoroughly examining the consequences of acts of living beings, (our monks) have found out a pure way of sustaining life. It is a maxim[2] of the monks of our creed[3], that nobody who lives by secret sins[4], should lay down the Law. (35)

"A man who always feeds two thousand worthy monks, does not control himself, and will be blamed in this world like a man with bloody hands. (36)

"They kill a fattened sheep, and prepare food for the sake of a particular person; they season the meat with salt and oil, and dress it with pepper. (37)

"You are irreligious, unworthy men, devoted to foolish pleasures, who say that partaking heartily of this meat you are not soiled by sin. (38)

"All who partake of such food, commit sins in their ignorance; but the wise do nothing of the kind. Even to utter it is an untruth. (39)

"In compassion to all beings, the seers, the *Gñâtri*putras[5], avoid what is sinful; afraid of it, they abstain from food especially prepared for them. (40)

"They abstain from wicked deeds, afraid of injuring living beings, and do no harm to any creature; therefore they do not partake of such food. This is a maxim of the monks of our creed. (41)

---

[1] A*n*ubhâe = anubhâga*h*, explained karmavipâka.

[2] Anudharma.

[3] Iha sa*m*yatânâm, who control themselves in this (creed of the *G*ainas).

[4] *Kh*annapadôpa*g*îvin.

[5] I.e. the *G*ainas.

"(Having reached) this perfection[1] in the Law of the Nirgranthas and standing firm in it, one should live without deceit[2]. The awakened sage who is endowed with all virtues thereby obtained very great fame." (42)

A Vêdic Priest.

'Those who always feed two thousand holy[3] mendicants, acquire great merit and become gods. This is the teaching of the Vêda.' (43)

Ârdraka.

"He who always feeds two thousand holy cats[4] (i.e. Brâhma*n*as), will have to endure great pains in hell, being surrounded by hungry (beasts). (44)

"He who despises the Law that enjoins compassion, and praises the Law that permits slaughter, and who feeds but a single unprincipled man, even if he be a king, will go to darkness[5], and not to the gods." (45)

A Vêdântin[6].

'Both of us follow (very much the same) Law; we stood firm in it, and shall do so in the time to come; (we believe that) virtue consists in good conduct, and that knowledge (is necessary for liberation); and with regard to the Circle of Births there is no difference between us. (46)

---

[1] Samâdhi. [2] A*n*ihê. [3] Snâtaka, cf. Manu XI, 1.

[4] Kulâlaya = kulâ*t*a, explained mâr*g*âra. Another explanation is: who live (âlaya) in houses.

[5] Nisa*m*, literally, night.

[6] *S*îlâṅka calls this opponent an Êkada*nd*in, and ascribes to him the views of the Sâṅkhya philosophy. But it is evident from the sequel that he is a Vêdântin, as the commentators admit in their comment on the next verse.

'(But we assume) an invisible, great, eternal, imperishable, and indestructible Soul, who excels all other beings in every respect, as the moon excels the stars.' (47)

Ârdraka.

"(If there were but one Soul common to all beings) they could not be known (from one another), nor could they experience different lots; there would not be Brâhma*n*as, Kshattriyas, Vai*s*yas, and *S*ûdras[1], insects, birds, and snakes; all would be men and gods. (48)

"Those who do not know all things by Kêvala (knowledge), but who being ignorant teach a Law (of their own), are lost themselves, and work the ruin of others in this dreadful, boundless Circle of Births. (49)

"Those who know all things by the full Kêvala knowledge, and who practising meditation teach the whole Law, are themselves saved and save others. (50)

"You have, in your mind, made equal both those who lead a blameable life, and those who in this world practise right conduct. Friend, you are deluded." (51)

A Hastitâpasa[2].

'Every year we kill one big elephant with an arrow, and live upon it in order to spare the life of other animals.' (52)

---

[1] Pessâ = prêshya, literally, servants or slaves.

[2] The Hastitâpasas are thus named from the fact that they kill an elephant and live upon its flesh for a whole year or for six months, as *S*îlâṅka adds, explaining thus the words avi ya (api *k*a) after sa*m*va*kkh*arê*n*a. The Hastitâpasas are mentioned in a list of the different Tâpasas in the Aupapâtika Sûtra, ed. Leumann, § 74.

Ârdraka.

"If every year you kill but one animal without abstaining from sin, though you are not guilty of the slaughter of other creatures, there is little difference between you and a householder. (53)

"If a man kills every year but one animal, and lives (in other respects) as a *S*rama*n*a, he is unworthy, and works his perdition. Such men will not become Kêvalins." (54)

A (monk) who has achieved his religious perfection through the instruction of the Awakened One[1], and stands firm in it, who guards himself in the threefold way (i. e. with regard to thoughts, words, and acts), and who possesses the things requisite for crossing the immense ocean of existence, may preach the Law. (55)

Thus I say.

SEVENTH LECTURE,

CALLED

NÂLANDÂ.

At that time, at that period, there was a town of the name Râ*g*agr*i*ha: it was rich, happy, thriving, &c.[2] Outside of Râ*g*agr*i*ha, in a north-eastern

---

[1] Buddhassa â*n*âi.

[2] This '&c.' refers to the typical description of towns. Our text contains only the first words of the description, but the Aupapâtika Sûtra, § 1, gives it at length.

direction, there was the suburb Nâlandâ; it contained many hundreds of buildings, &c.[1] (1)

In that suburb Nâlandâ there was a householder called Lêpa; he was prosperous, famous; rich in high and large houses, beds, seats, vehicles, and chariots; abounding in riches, gold, and silver; possessed of useful and necessary things; wasting plenty of food and drink; owning many male and female slaves, cows, buffaloes, and sheep; and inferior to nobody. (2)

This householder Lêpa, a follower of the *S*rama*n*as, comprehended (the doctrine of) living beings and things without life, (&c., all as in II, 2, 76, p. 382, down to the end of the paragraph). (3)

This householder Lêpa possessed, in a north-eastern direction from the suburb Nâlandâ, a bathing-hall, called *S*êshadravyâ[2]; it contained many hundreds of pillars, was beautiful, &c. In a north-eastern direction from this bathing-hall *S*êshadravyâ, there was a park called Hastiyâma. (Description of the park[3].) (4)

And there in some house the Venerable Gautama was staying. The venerable (man) was in the garden, and so was Udaka, the son of Pê*dh*âla, a Nirgrantha and follower of Pâr*s*va[4], of the Mêdârya Gôtra. He went there where the Venerable Gautama was, and said: 'O long-lived Gautama, I want to ask you about a point (of faith); O long-lived one,

[1] I cannot tell where the full description occurs.

[2] The name denotes: the rest of materials, i.e. the hall which was built with the materials not used (in building the house), the well-known 'few remaining bricks.'

[3] The text is given in the Aupapâtika Sûtra, § 3.

[4] Compare the Twenty-second Lecture of the Uttarâdhyayana.

please explain it to me so as it has been taught (by the Tîrthakara).' And the Venerable Gautama spoke thus to Udaka, the son of Pê*dh*âla: "Well, long-lived one, I shall see about it, when I have heard and understood (your question)." And Udaka, the son of Pê*dh*âla, spoke thus to the Venerable Gautama: (5)

'O long-lived Gautama, there are Nirgrantha *S*rama*n*as, called Kumâraputras, who profess your creed; they make a zealous [1] householder, a follower of the *S*rama*n*as, renounce injury to movable beings except on the order (from an established authority), as the householder caused one of the captured thieves to be set free [2]. Those who make this renunciation, make a bad renunciation; those who cause this renunciation to be made, cause a bad renunciation to be made; in causing another to make this renunciation, they annul their own allegation [3]. Why do I say this? Beings belong to the Circle of Births; though they be (now) immovable beings, they will (some time) become movable ones, or though they be (now) movable beings, they will become immovable ones; when they leave the bodies

---

[1] Uvasampanna.

[2] These words seem to refer to an apologue told by the commentator: King Ratna*s*êkhara of Ratnapura, once making a pleasure trip, issued an order that nobody should remain in the town. Six brothers disobeyed, were brought before the king, and sentenced to death. Their father in vain implored the king to spare them, or to spare five, four, three, two of his sons. At last the king consented to pardon the eldest son, at which the old father rejoiced.—The six sons are likened to the six classes of living beings. As a householder cannot altogether abstain from injuring them, as monks do, he is content to abstain from injuring movable beings or animals.

[3] Viz. that by abstaining from slaughter of living beings they kill no living beings.

of immovable beings, they will be born in bodies of movable ones, and when they leave the bodies of movable beings, they will be born in bodies of immovable ones. When they are born in bodies of immovable beings, it is no sin to kill them. (6)

'(But if they make him renounce) injury to creatures which are, for the time being, movable beings, except on the order (from an established authority)—as the householder caused one of the captured thieves to be set free—(if they take this vow), those who make this renunciation, make a good renunciation; those who cause this renunciation to be made, cause a good renunciation to be made; in causing another to make this renunciation, they do not annul their own allegation. Though in this way[1] a correct expression is found, some (monks) from anger or greed cause the householder to make the renunciation (without the necessary restriction). Is not this our interpretation right? O long-lived Gautama, do you approve of it?' (7)

And Gautama spoke thus to Udaka, the son of Pê*dh*âla: "O long-lived Udaka, we certainly do not approve of it. The *S*rama*n*as or Brâhma*n*as who say thus, speak thus, declare thus, and explain thus, do not speak as *S*rama*n*as or Nirgranthas, they speak noxious speech. They mislead laymen. They make void all vows undertaken for sparing particular living beings[2]. Why do I say this? Beings belong

[1] I.e. by specifying the movable beings as beings which are movable ones for the time being.

[2] E.g. if a man vows to kill no Brâhma*n*a (and does not add the restriction 'for the time being'), he may kill no man or animal whatever; for the soul of that man or animal may, in the past, have been embodied in a Brâhma*n*a.

to the Circle of Births; though they be (now) immovable beings, they will (some time) become movable ones, (&c., all as in § 6, down to) when they leave the bodies of movable beings, they will be born in the bodies of immovable ones. When they are born in the bodies of movable beings, it is a sin to kill them." (8)

And Udaka, the son of Pê*dh*âla, spoke thus: 'Which beings do you call movable beings? movable ones or others?'

And Gautama spoke thus to Udaka, the son of Pê*dh*âla: "O long-lived Udaka, what you call beings which are, for the time being, movable ones, we call movable beings; and what we call movable beings, you call beings which are, for the time being, movable ones. Both expressions are equal, and mean the same thing. O long-lived one, why do you think it more correct to say: beings which are, for the time being, movable ones; and why do you think it incorrect to say: movable beings, that you censure the one expression, and applaud the other? This your interpretation is not right. (9)

"And the Venerable One has spoken thus: Some men there are who say: we cannot, submitting to the tonsure, renounce the life of a householder and enter the monastic state, but we shall gradually conform to the Gôtra (i. e. community of the monks). Accordingly they make known the limits[1], fix the limits, determine the limits (beyond which they will not go in the enjoyment of worldly goods); and

[1] Literally, the number. A sample of such vows is given in the beginning of the Uvâsaga Dasâo, see Hoernle's edition, § 16 ff.

renounce injury to movable beings, except on the order[1] (of an established authority)—as the householder caused one of the captured thieves to be set free. And this turns out to their benefit. (10)

"Movable beings are called so, when they get this character[2] through the taking effect of the Karman relating to movable beings. But when their duration of life as movable beings comes to its close, the (soul), embodied in a movable being, leaves its life as such and becomes embodied in an immovable being. Immovable beings are called so, when they get this character through the taking effect of the Karman relating to immovable beings. But when their duration of life as an immovable being comes to its close, the (soul), embodied in an immovable being, leaves its life as such and takes again a new form of existence; they are (then) called[3] animated beings, (animals) of large bodies, or of long life." (11)

And Udaka, the son of Pê*dh*âla, spoke thus to the Venerable Gautama: 'Is there not a chance, that a follower of the *S*rama*n*as, though he has renounced slaughter of but one class of living beings, ceases altogether to injure any[4]? Why do

[1] Abhiyôga. *S*îlânka enumerates four kinds of abhiyôga: ga*n*a-, bala-, devatâ-abhiyôga, and gurunigraha.

[2] Nâma, literally, name.

[3] They are called (vu*kk*anti = u*k*yantê) is apparently equivalent with: they get the name (nâma); 'name,' however, means in *G*aina and Bauddha terminology as much as 'the nature of the thing.' The words of the text, therefore, come to mean: 'they become or are animated beings,' &c.

[4] The question discussed in the following paragraphs is whether, at some future time, all movable beings in the Sa*m*sâra might not die out, and none but immovable beings be left. This idea is combated at great length by Gautama.

I say this? Beings belong to the Circle of Births, though they be (now) immovable beings, they will (some time) become movable ones, and though they be movable beings, they will become immovable ones. When they leave the bodies of immovable beings, all are born in bodies of movable ones, and when they leave the bodies of movable beings, all will be born in bodies of immovable ones. When they are born in bodies of immovable beings, they may be killed[1].' (12)

And the Venerable Gautama spoke thus to Udaka, the son of Pê*dh*âla: "O long-lived one, we[2] do not admit what you say; viz. that there is a chance that a follower of the *S*rama*n*as should cease to do injury to any kind of living beings. Why do we say this? Beings belong to the Circle of Births, (&c., all as above, down to) when they are born in bodies of movable beings, it is a sin to kill them. They are called animated beings, (animals) of large bodies, or of long life. There are always a great many animate beings, (the slaughter of) which a follower of the *S*rama*n*as must renounce, there are none, (the slaughter of) which he need not renounce. If he ceases, or has done with, or has given up (injuring) the large class of movable beings, his renunciation is

---

[1] The meaning is, that at some future time movable beings may have ceased to exist, since they are all born as immovable beings, and vice versâ. If the latter is the case, a layman, who abstains from killing animals, practically does injury to no being whatever; if the former is the case, he cannot transgress his vow even if he would.

[2] The text has the Sanskrit word asmâkam, of which the commentator alleges that it was thus pronounced by all people in Magadha, compare note 2, p. 358.

good. What you or somebody else says, that there is a chance of a layman's ceasing to do an injury altogether, by renouncing slaughter of one kind of beings; this interpretation of yours is not right." (13)

The Venerable One[1] gave an illustration: "I put a question to the Nirgranthas: O long-lived ones, (suppose) there be some men who have made the following declaration: 'I shall not inflict punishment on those who, submitting to the tonsure, renounce the life of a householder and enter the monastic state; but I shall inflict punishment on those who lead a domestic life.' Some *S*rama*n*a, who for four or five years, or for six or ten years—the period may be shorter or longer—has wandered about in the land, returns to domestic life. Now answer me: does the man break his word when he puts to death this (renegade) householder?" 'Certainly not!' "It is just the same with a follower of the *S*rama*n*as, who has renounced injury to movable beings, but not to immovable ones. If he kills immovable beings, he does not transgress his vow. This you acknowledge, O Nirgranthas, this you must acknowledge!" (14)

The Venerable One gave another illustration: "I put a question to the Nirgranthas. O long-lived Nirgranthas, (suppose) there be householders or sons of householders, born in respectable families, who come to you for instruction in the Law. Ought they to be instructed in the Law?" 'Yes, they should.' "When they have learned and understood this Law, will they say: this creed of the

[1] Gautama.

Nirgranthas is true, supreme, excellent, full of virtues, right, pure, it removes doubts, it is the road to perfection, liberation, Nirvâ*n*a; it is free from error and doubts, it is the road of those who are free from all misery; those who adopt it will reach perfection, (&c., all down to) put an end to all misery; exerting ourselves we shall control ourselves with regard to all kinds of living beings.—Will they speak thus?" 'Yes.' "Should such men be admitted to the order?" 'Yes, they should.' "Should such men be instructed in the discipline and kept to attend to religious instruction?" 'Yes, they should.' "Do they renounce injury to every living being?" 'Yes, they do.' "Now (suppose) one of these men who lead such a life, after wandering about in the land for four or five years, or for six or ten years—the period may be shorter or longer—returns to domestic life. Will this man (still) abstain from doing injury to every living being?" 'No.' "The same man[1] who at first (as a householder) had not renounced injury to every living being, who afterwards has renounced, and who now does not renounce injury to every living being, did at first not control himself, did so afterwards, and does not so now. As long as he does not control himself, he does not renounce injury to every living being[2]. This you acknowledge, O Nirgranthas, this you must acknowledge!" (15)

The Venerable One gave (another) illustration: "I put a question to the Nirgranthas. O long-lived

[1] Sê *g*ê sê *g*îvê, literally, his soul.

[2] Here the last sentence but one of the preceding paragraph ought to be repeated. But there is no trace of it in my MSS. or the commentary.

Nirgranthas, (suppose) there be monks or nuns of other sects, who come to you for instruction in the Law, (all as before, down to) attend to religious instruction." 'Yes, they should.' "Is it lawful to eat with such men?" 'Yes, it is.' "Now (suppose) some of these people who lead such a life, (&c., all as before, down to) return to domestic life. Is it lawful to eat with them then?" 'No, it is not[1].' "The same man with whom to eat was not lawful at first, was lawful afterwards, and is not lawful now, was no *S*rama*n*a at first, was a *S*rama*n*a afterwards, and is no *S*rama*n*a now. It is not lawful for Nirgrantha *S*rama*n*as to eat together with him. This you acknowledge, O Nirgranthas; this you must acknowledge!" (16)

And the Venerable One spoke thus: "There are some followers of the *S*rama*n*as, who have made this declaration: we cannot, submitting to the tonsure, renounce the life of a householder and enter the monastic state, but we shall strictly observe the Pôsaha on the fourteenth and the eighth days of each fortnight, (on the new-moon, and) full-moon days, we renounce gross ill-usage of living beings, grossly lying speech, gross taking of things not given, (unlawful) sexual intercourse, (unlimited) appropriation of property; we shall set limits to our desires in the two forms and in the three ways[2]. They will also make the following renunciation: 'neither do nor cause anything (sinful) to be done for my sake.'

---

[1] Nô i*n*-a*tth*ê sama*tth*ê; I think the Sanskrit of this phrase, which is not explained by the commentator, is nô ayam artha*h* samartha*h*.

[2] Viz. 'I will not do it, nor cause it to be done, either in thought or in word or in deed.' Compare Uvâsaga Dasâo, Hoernle's edition, § 13 ff.

Having (on Pôsaha-days) abstained from eating, drinking, bathing, and using beds or chairs, may they, on their decease, be said to make a (righteous) end of their life?" 'Certainly, they do make such an end of their life.' "They are called animated beings, (&c., all as in § 13, down to) this interpretation of yours is not right." (17)

The Venerable One spoke thus: "There are some followers of the *S*rama*n*as, who have made this declaration: we cannot, submitting to the tonsure, renounce the life of a householder and enter the monastic state; we also cannot strictly observe the Pôsaha on the fourteenth and the eighth days of each fortnight, (on the days of new-moon) and full-moon; but while we are preparing ourselves for death by fasting[1], we shall abstain from food and drink without longing for the end; we shall renounce all ill-usage of living beings, all lying speech, all taking of things not given, all sexual intercourse, all property, (saying): 'neither do nor cause anything (sinful) to be done for my sake.' (All the rest as in the preceding paragraph.)" (18)

And the Venerable One spoke thus: "There are some men of great desires, great undertakings, &c.[2], who do not abstain from all ill-usage of living beings, (&c., down to) from all property. During the whole time, from their taking the vows of a follower of the *S*rama*n*as till their death, they abstain from injury to living beings. Then they die; in their next existence they experience their Karman, and receive an evil lot. (The rest as before.)" (19)

And the Venerable One spoke thus: "There are

[1] Sa*m*lêha*n*a*gh*ûsa*n*â*gh*ûsiyâ. [2] See II, 2, 61.

some men of no desires, no undertakings, who abstain from all ill-usage of living beings, (&c., down to) from all property. During the whole time, from their taking the vows of a follower of the *S*rama*n*as till their death, they abstain from injury to living beings. Then they die; in their next existence they experience their Karman, and receive a happy lot. (The rest as before.)" (20)

And the Venerable One spoke thus: "There are some men of few desires, few undertakings, who abstain from ill-usage of one sort of living beings, (&c., down to) from one sort of property. During the whole time, (&c., the rest as in the last paragraph)." (21)

And the Venerable One spoke thus: "There are some men who live in woods, in huts, near villages, or practise some secret rites, who are not well controlled, do not well abstain (from slaying) all sorts of living beings. They employ speech that is true and untrue at the same time: do not beat me, beat others, (&c., all as in II, 2, 21, down to) having died at their allotted time, they are born in some places inhabited by Asuras[1] and evil-doers. And when they are released therefrom, they will be born deaf and dumb or blind. They are called animated beings, (&c., the rest as in § 13)." (22)

And the Venerable One spoke thus: "There are some beings of a long life, which a follower of the *S*rama*n*as abstains from injuring through life. They die after him. They are called animated beings, (&c., the rest as in § 13)." (23)

[1] Âsuriya. *S*îlâṅka here offers a second explanation of this word, viz. asûrya, where no sun ever shines.

(The two next paragraphs treat in exactly the same way of beings of an equally long life, which die simultaneously with him, and of beings of a short life, which die before him.) (24, 25)

And the Venerable One spoke thus: "There are some followers of the *S*rama*n*as, who have made this declaration: we are not able to strictly observe the Pôsaha-days, but we are able, when preparing ourselves for death by fasting, to abstain from food and drink without longing for the end. The vow of such a man is the Sâmâyika Dê*s*âvakâ*s*ika[1]: (he declares) in the morning: (I shall travel) only thus or thus far in an eastern, western, southern, northern direction. He renounces injury to all beings: I shall cause peace and security to all sorts of living beings.

"Within those (limits) the movable living beings, which the follower of the *S*rama*n*as abstains from injuring till his death, will leave their life, and will then be born, within the same limits, as movable living beings, which the follower of the *S*rama*n*as abstains from injuring till his death. With regard to them the follower of the *S*rama*n*as has made a good renunciation. They are called animated beings, (&c., the rest as before). (26)

"The movable beings within those limits, &c.[2], will,

---

[1] The Dê*s*âvakâ*s*ika 'consists in drawing closer or contracting every day the limits already laid down (in accordance with the Gu*n*avratas) to the range of one's travels,' &c. The Gu*n*avrata referred to is the Digvirati, i.e. 'to lay down a limit beyond which one shall not travel in the different directions, or a limit as to the countries one shall visit for the acquisition of wealth.' From Bhandarkar Report, p. 114 f. The explanation in the commentary materially agrees with the above.

[2] The original repeats the phrases of the preceding paragraph.

after their death, be born within the same limits as immovable beings, from injuring which without a purpose the follower of the *S*rama*n*as abstains till death, but not with a purpose[1], (&c., the rest as before). (27)

"The movable beings within those limits, &c., will, after their death, be born, beyond those limits, as movable or immovable beings, (&c., the rest as before). (28)

"The immovable beings within those limits, &c., will, after their death, be born, within the same limits, as movable beings, (&c., the rest as before). (29)

"The immovable beings within those limits, &c., will, after their death, be born, within the same limits, as immovable beings, (&c., the rest as before). (30)

"The immovable beings within those limits, &c., will, after their death, be born, beyond those limits, as immovable beings, (&c., the rest as before). (31)

"The movable and immovable beings beyond those limits, &c., will, after their death, be born, within those limits, as movable beings, (&c., the rest as before). (32)

"The movable and immovable beings beyond those limits, &c., will, after their death, be born, within those limits, as immovable beings, (&c., the rest as before). (33)

"The movable and immovable beings beyond those limits, &c., will, after their death, be born, beyond

I abridge them as far as possible, and give the full text only where it differs from that of § 26.

[1] This clause comes always after the words 'immovable beings' down to § 34.

those limits, as movable and immovable beings, (&c. the rest as before)." (34)

The Venerable One spoke thus: "It has never happened, it does not happen, nor will it ever happen, that all movable beings will die out and become immovable ones, nor that all immovable beings die out and become movable ones. Since movable and immovable beings never die out, there is no chance, as you or somebody else say, that a layman ceases to do injury altogether by renouncing slaughter of one kind of beings; this interpretation of yours is not right." (35)

And the Venerable One spoke thus: "If (a man) who has been instructed in right knowledge, faith, and conduct for the avoidance of sins, blames a (righteous) *S*rama*n*a or Brâhma*n*a though he is well disposed towards them, he effects the loss of his merit for another world; but if he does not blame them, he heightens the purity of his merit for another world."

On this Udaka, the son of Pê*dh*âla, took no further notice of the Venerable Gautama and was about to return in the direction in which he had come. (36)

And the Venerable One spoke thus: "O long-lived Udaka, he who has learned from a *S*rama*n*a or Brâhma*n*a whomsoever even one noble religious truth, and considers himself thereby furthered with regard to his peace and happiness, will respect, acknowledge, praise, salute, honour, reverence, and worship him even as a blessed and holy deity or sacred shrine." (37)

Then Udaka, the son of Pê*dh*âla, spoke thus to the Venerable Gautama: 'As I had not before known, heard, understood, and comprehended these words, I did not believe in the meaning (of your words), which I had never perceived nor heard nor understood nor appreciated, and which were never explained nor defined nor delivered nor made clear to me, nor pondered over by me. But now, Reverend Sir, as I do know, &c., these words which I have perceived, heard, &c., I believe, accept, and approve of their meaning. It is just as you say!' (38)

Then the Venerable Gautama spoke thus to Udaka, the son of Pê*dh*âla: "Believe it, sir; accept it, sir; approve of it, sir; it is just as we have said." Then Udaka, the son of Pê*dh*âla, spoke thus to the Venerable Gautama: 'I desire, Reverend Sir, in your presence to pass from the creed which enjoins four vows[1], to the creed which enjoins the five great vows and the Pratikrama*n*a[2].' (39)

Then the Venerable Gautama went with Udaka, the son of Pê*dh*âla, to the Venerable Ascetic Mahâvîra. Then Udaka, the son of Pê*dh*âla, solemnly circumambulated the Venerable Ascetic Mahâvîra three times from the left to the right, and having done so he praised and worshipped him, and then he spoke thus: 'I desire, Reverend Sir, in your presence to pass from the creed which enjoins four vows, to the creed which enjoins the five great vows and the Pratikrama*n*a. May it so please you, beloved of the

[1] See above, p. 121, note 2. In this way the creed of Pâr*s*va is characterised in contradistinction to that of Mahâvîra.

[2] 'Pratikrama*n*a is the expiation of sins . . . by means of Nindana Garha*n*a, Âlô*k*anâ, and other processes. Nindana is condemning the sinful act or repenting of it to oneself; Garha*n*a is doing the same before a Guru; and Âlô*k*anâ is making a confession of it to the Guru.' Bhandarkar, Report, p. 9, note ‡.

gods, do not deny me!' Then, in the presence of the Venerable Asketic Mahâvîra, Udaka, the son of Pê*dh*âla, passed from the creed which enjoins four vows, to the creed which enjoins the five great vows and the Pratikrama*n*a. (40)

Thus I say.

INDEX OF NAMES AND SUBJECTS.

INDEX OF

SANSKRIT AND PRÂK*RI*T WORDS

OCCURRING IN THE TEXT AND THE NOTES.

CORRECTION.

Page 102, verse 18, the phrase purâna purabhêdanî has been wrongly translated: 'which is among towns what Indra is (among the gods);' it simply means: 'an old town.' For purabhêdanî is the Prâkrit equivalent of the Sanskrit and Pâli word putabhêdanam, town. Cancel note 2.

Transliteration of Oriental Alphabets adopted for the Translations of the Sacred Books of the East.

Consonants.	Missionary Alphabet. I Class.	II Class.	III Class.	Sanskrit.	Zend.	Pehlevi.	Persian.	Arabic.	Hebrew.	Chinese.
Gutturales.										
1 Tenuis	k	...	...	क	𐬐	[illegible]	ک	ک	כּ	k
2 „ aspirata	kh	...	...	ख	𐬑	[illegible]	...	...	כ	kh
3 Media	g	...	...	ग	𐬔	[illegible]	گ	...	גּ	...
4 „ aspirata	gh	...	...	घ	𐬖	[illegible]	...	...	ג	...
5 Gutturo-labialis	q	...	...	...	...	...	ق	ق	ק	...
6 Nasalis	ṅ (ng)	...	...	ङ	{ 𐬢 (ng) / 𐬣 (N) }	...	...	...	...	...
7 Spiritus asper	h	...	...	ह	𐬵 (𐬷 *hv*)	[illegible]	ه	ه	ה	h, hs
8 „ lenis	’	...	...	...	...	...	ا	ا	א	...
9 „ asper faucalis	‘h	...	...	...	...	...	ح	ح	ח	...
10 „ lenis faucalis	’h	...	...	...	...	...	ع	ع	ע	...
11 „ asper fricatus	...	*‘h*	...	...	...	...	خ	خ	ח	...
12 „ lenis fricatus	...	*’h*	...	...	...	...	...	...	...	...
Gutturales modificatae (palatales, &c.)										
13 Tenuis	...	*k*	...	च	𐬗	[illegible]	چ	...	...	*k*
14 „ aspirata	...	*kh*	...	छ	...	...	...	...	...	*kh*
15 Media	...	*g*	...	ज	𐬘	[illegible]	ج	ج	...	...
16 „ aspirata	...	*gh*	...	झ	...	...	ژ	ژ	...	...
17 „ Nasalis	...	*ñ*	...	ञ	...	...	...	...	...	...

CONSONANTS (*continued*).	MISSIONARY ALPHABET. I Class.	II Class.	III Class.	Sanskrit.	Zend.	Pehlevi.	Persian.	Arabic.	Hebrew.	Chinese.
18 Semivocalis	y	. . .	. . . .	य	[illegible]; [illegible] [illegible] init.	[illegible]	ي	ي	י	y
19 Spiritus asper	. . .	(ẏ)	. . . .	. . .	. . . .	. . .	. . .	. . .	. . .	. . .
20 ,, lenis	. . .	(ẏ)	. . . .	. . .	. . . .	. . .	. . .	. . .	. . .	. . .
21 ,, asper assibilatus . .	. . .	*s*	. . . .	श	[illegible]	[illegible]	ش	ش	. . .	. . .
22 ,, lenis assibilatus . .	. . .	*z*	. . . .	. . .	[illegible]	[illegible]	ژ	. . .	. . .	*z*
Dentales.										
23 Tenuis	t	. . .	. . . .	त	[illegible]	[illegible]	ت	ت	תּ	t
24 ,, aspirata	th	. . .	. . . .	थ	[illegible]	. . .	. . .	. . .	ת	th
25 ,, assibilata	. . .	. . .	TH	. . .	. . . .	. . .	ث	ث	. . .	. . .
26 Media	d	. . .	. . . .	द	[illegible]	[illegible]	د	د	דּ	. . .
27 ,, aspirata	dh	. . .	. . . .	ध	[illegible]	. . .	. . .	. . .	ד	. . .
28 ,, assibilata	. . .	. . .	DH	. . .	. . . .	. . .	ذ	ذ	. . .	. . .
29 Nasalis	n	. . .	. . . .	न	[illegible]	[illegible]	ن	ن	נ	n
30 Semivocalis	l	. . .	. . . .	ल	. . . .	[illegible]	ل	ل	ל	l
31 ,, mollis 1	. . .	*l*	. . . .	ळ	. . . .	. . .	. . .	. . .	. . .	. . .
32 ,, mollis 2	. . .	. . .	L	. . .	. . . .	. . .	. . .	. . .	. . .	. . .
33 Spiritus asper 1	s	. . .	. . . .	स	[illegible]	[illegible]	س (ث)	س	שׁ	s
34 ,, asper 2	. . .	. . .	s (ʃ)	. . .	. . . .	. . .	. . .	. . .	ס	. . .
35 ,, lenis	z	. . .	. . . .	. . .	[illegible]	[illegible]	ز (ذ)	ز	ז	z
36 ,, asperrimus 1	. . .	. . .	z (ȥ)	. . .	. . . .	. . .	ص	ص	צ	ȥ, ȥh'
37 ,, asperrimus 2	. . .	. . .	z (ȥ)	. . .	. . . .	. . .	ض	. . .	. . .	. . .

Dentales modificatae (linguales, &c.)										
38 Tenuis	...	*t*	...	ट	...	...	ط	ط	ט	...
39 ,, aspirata	...	*th*	...	ठ	...	...	ظ	ظ	...	...
40 Media	...	*d*	...	ड	[illegible]	[illegible]	...	...	...	...
41 ,, aspirata	...	*dh*	...	ढ	...	...	...	ض	...	...
42 Nasalis	...	*n*	...	ण	[illegible]	...	...	...	...	...
43 Semivocalis	r	...	...	र	[illegible]	[illegible]	ر	ر	ר	...
44 ,, fricata	...	*r*	...	...	...	...	...	...	...	*r*
45 ,, diacritica	...	...	R	...	...	...	...	...	...	...
46 Spiritus asper	sh	...	...	ष	[illegible]	[illegible]	...	...	...	sh
47 ,, lenis	zh	...	...	...	...	...	...	...	...	...
Labiales.										
48 Tenuis	p	...	...	प	[illegible]	[illegible]	پ	...	פּ	p
49 ,, aspirata	ph	...	...	फ	...	...	...	...	פ	ph
50 Media	b	...	...	ब	[illegible]	[illegible]	ب	ب	בּ	...
51 ,, aspirata	bh	...	...	भ	...	...	...	...	ב	...
52 Tenuissima	...	*p*	...	...	...	...	...	...	...	...
53 Nasalis	m	...	...	म	[illegible]	[illegible]	م	م	מ	m
54 Semivocalis	w	...	...	...	[illegible]	...	...	...	...	w
55 ,, aspirata	hw	...	...	...	...	...	...	...	...	...
56 Spiritus asper	f	...	...	...	[illegible]	[illegible]	ف	ف	...	f
57 ,, lenis	v	...	...	व	»	[illegible]	و	و	ו	...
58 Anusvâra	...	*m*	...	अं	[illegible] ã	...	...	...	...	...
59 Visarga	...	*h*	...	अः	...	...	...	...	...	...

VOWELS.	MISSIONARY ALPHABET. I Class.	II Class.	III Class.	Sanskrit.	Zend.	Pehlevi.	Persian.	Arabic.	Hebrew.	Chinese.
1 Neutralis	0	. . .	. . . .	. . .	. . . .	. . .	. . .	. . .	ְ	ă
2 Laryngo-palatalis	ĕ	. . .	. . . .	. . .	. . . .	. . .	. . .	. . .	. . .	. . .
3 „ labialis	ŏ	. . .	. . . .	. . .	. . . .	𐭠 fin.	. . .	. . .	. . .	. . .
4 Gutturalis brevis	a	. . .	. . . .	अ	𐬀	𐭠 init.	ـَ	ـَ	ַ	a
5 „ longa	â	(*a*)	. . . .	आ	𐬁	𐭠	ـَا	ـَا	ָ	â
6 Palatalis brevis	i	. . .	. . . .	इ	𐬌	. . .	ـِ	ـِ	ִ	i
7 „ longa	î	(*i*)	. . . .	ई	𐬍	𐭉	ـِي	ـِي	ִי	î
8 Dentalis brevis	*li*	. . .	. . . .	ऌ	. . . .	. . .	. . .	. . .	. . .	. . .
9 „ longa	*lî*	. . .	. . . .	ॡ	. . . .	. . .	. . .	. . .	. . .	. . .
10 Lingualis brevis	*ri*	. . .	. . . .	ऋ	. . . .	. . .	. . .	. . .	. . .	. . .
11 „ longa	*rî*	. . .	. . . .	ॠ	. . . .	. . .	. . .	. . .	. . .	. . .
12 Labialis brevis	u	. . .	. . . .	उ	𐬎	. . .	ـُ	ـُ	ֻ	u
13 „ longa	û	(*u*)	. . . .	ऊ	𐬏	𐭅	ـُو	ـُو	וּ	û
14 Gutturo-palatalis brevis	e	. . .	. . . .	. . .	𐬈(e) 𐬉(*e*)	. . .	. . .	. . .	ֶ	e
15 „ longa	ê (ai)	(*e*)	. . . .	ए	𐬊, 𐬋	𐭉	. . .	. . .	ֵ	ê
16 Diphthongus gutturo-palatalis	âi	(*ai*)	. . . .	ऐ	. . . .	. . .	ـَيْ	ـَيْ	. . .	âi
17 „ „	ei (ĕi)	. . .	. . . .	. . .	. . . .	. . .	. . .	. . .	. . .	ei, êi
18 „ „	oi (ŏu)	. . .	. . . .	. . .	. . . .	. . .	. . .	. . .	. . .	. . .
19 Gutturo-labialis brevis	o	. . .	. . . .	. . .	𐬊	. . .	. . .	. . .	ָ	o
20 „ longa	ô (au)	(*o*)	. . . .	ओ	𐬋	𐭅	. . .	. . .	וֹ	. . .
21 Diphthongus gutturo-labialis	âu	(*au*)	. . . .	औ	𐬁𐬎 (*au*)	. . .	ـَوْ	ـَوْ	. . .	âu
22 „ „	eu (ĕu)	. . .	. . . .	. . .	. . . .	. . .	. . .	. . .	. . .	. . .
23 „ „	ou (ŏu)	. . .	. . . .	. . .	. . . .	. . .	. . .	. . .	. . .	. . .
24 Gutturalis fracta	ä	. . .	. . . .	. . .	. . . .	. . .	. . .	. . .	. . .	. . .
25 Palatalis fracta	ï	. . .	. . . .	. . .	. . . .	. . .	. . .	. . .	. . .	. . .
26 Labialis fracta	ü	. . .	. . . .	. . .	. . . .	. . .	. . .	. . .	. . .	ü
27 Gutturo-labialis fracta	ö	. . .	. . . .	. . .	. . . .	. . .	. . .	. . .	. . .	. . .